D0786994

—Laura—
Z

BY LAURA Z. HOBSON
Novels

The Trespassers

Gentleman's Agreement

The Other Father

The Celebrity

First Papers

The Tenth Month

Consenting Adult

Over and Above

Untold Millions

Autobiography

Laura Z

Books for Children

A Dog of His Own

"I'm Going To Have A Baby"

Laura Z

A LIFE

BY **LAURA Z. HOBSON**

ARBOR HOUSE · NEW YORK

Copyright © 1983 by Laura Z. Hobson

All rights reserved, including the right of reproduction in whole or in part in any form. Published in the United States of America by Arbor House Publishing Company and in Canada by Fitzhenry & Whiteside, Ltd.

Library of Congress Catalogue Card Number: 83-45342

ISBN: 0-87795-469-0

Manufactured in the United States of America
10 9 8 7 6 5 4 3 2 1

This book is printed on acid free paper. The paper in this book meets the guidelines for permanence and durability of the Committee on Production Guidelines for Book Longevity of the Council on Library Resources.

"The Perfect Man" by Laura Z. Hobson, first published by the author under the name Laura Mount, is reprinted by permission; © 1932, 1960 The New Yorker Magazine, Inc.

Photograph of Eric Hodgins is by Joe Steinmetz, Sarasota, Florida.

This Book Is For
My Sons
Michael Z.
And
Christopher Z.

A note of thanks

My own materials for this book I could research right in my own house, in my scrapbooks, datebooks, work logs, manuscripts, letters, pressbooks and all the paraphernalia of a writing life.

But when it came to external materials, the stuff that gets into the newspapers or encyclopedias, I needed help, and here I was fortunate, in having as my researcher a young journalist, Billy Holliday, whose ability to dig it out of old microfilmed newspapers or libraried record books gave me the secure sense of accuracy I so much wanted.

He is a woeful speller, but a wonderful uprooter and locater of many matters that might have been lost to me without him. I have often thanked him in private, but now I want to make my gratitude public.

ONE

THE Z IS FOR ZAMETKIN, my maiden name, and I have clung to it through all my years because it held my identity intact before that Anglo-Saxon married name of Hobson.

I was born Laura Zametkin in New York City when the new century was five months and nineteen days old, and now as I begin to write my autobiography in the summer of 1981, I can truly say that the century was young when I was young, was in its middle years when I was middle-aged and now is in its late years during my own late years.

I've been asked ten thousand times what the *Z* stood for, at least one thousand with the suggestion, "Zuleika," supplied before I could reply, making me sure that my questioner had once read Max Beerbohm's novel, *Zuleika Dobson.*

Zelda? Zoe? Zillah? Zilpah? Each time a name was proffered along with the question, I would draw some conclusion of my own. Ah, a Fitzgerald reader. A theatergoer who saw Zoe Akins's *The Old Maid* or *The Greeks Had a Name for It.* And finally, a close reader of the Bible, especially Genesis. Who else would think of Zillah or Zilpah? (I had to go look them up for myself.)

On the telephone, in a passport office, in hospitals, in banks, whenever I had to spell out my full name, complete with initial,

7

I always said, "Z as in zero," and still do. Why this self-depre-cation I will never know, but it must be there, tucked away somewhere in all the countless times I've said it, rather than the usual "Z as in zebra" of Western Union and the telephone com-pany, or "Z as in zed" of the British.

When it was a friend or new acquaintance asking, when it was a reporter or researcher, who gave me time to answer, I always said, "It's for Zametkin, my maiden name. My father was Russian and Jewish, and it's easy to pronounce: "Zam-ET-kin."

To certain people it was not easy to pronounce, and I must have learned that over and over again in my childhood. We had a neighbor, across from our house in Jamaica, Long Island, then a small town, who got into a back-fence rage over something or other, and yelled at my mother, "Jews, what's more, *Russian* Jews, ZamETSKI!" I was about seven then, and that must have been my first taste not only of antisemitism but also of xeno-phobia.

And perhaps my very first experiment at fighting back came from that name of mine as well, came twelve years later in Ithaca, New York, where I was at Cornell taking a course in "Baby Greek" from a certain Professor Horace L. Jones. It was a special course in beginning Greek, a six-times-a-week, 8 A.M. course for bright students, and for weeks or months, when I was called upon to recite, the Professor addressed me as Miss Zamooski, or Miss Zimenky, or Miss Zamky, and once even Miss Dji-morskey.

Even today, writing about it, I get a small heave in the stomach as I relive the moment of decision that led me at last to say, "Professor Jones, might I say something?"

"Of course."

"Sir, if we're supposed to pronounce names like Clytemnestra correctly, and Iphigenia, and Agamemnon, and Aeschylus, don't you think you could say Zametkin? It's really quite easy."

I no longer remember what he answered. I do know that I was never addressed as Zamooski or Djimorskey again.

And I knew too, vaguely, thinly, I think, that there was some-thing awfully good in making a stand. I'm not sure, I can't be sure, that I felt it then and there in that classroom in beautiful

Goldwyn Smith Hall up on the hill; it might be an illusion that I felt it there, an afterthought transposed backward in time for emotional effect. Now as I write, despite the heave in my stomach, I find myself smiling and wishing only that I'd finished it all off by saying, "Z as in xenophobia."

So my parents were Russian, and Jewish, and old-fashioned socialist, and agnostic, and internationalists, and nonsectarians, and pro-labor and antimilitarist, and hotly opposed to every form of oppression, injustice, exploitation, infringement of freedom to speak out, to write, to vote, to oppose. They were marvels, both of them—though to small children, to my twin sister Alice and me as little girls, my father could also seem a monster when he was "in a mood."

I wrote about my parents and my "radical childhood" in my longest novel, *First Papers*, begun in my fifties, blocked up and abondoned for years, then finished in my sixties and published in 1964. In it, as is true in many of my novels, there was that mysterious amalgam of what really happened and what I made up for the purpose of telling a story—an amalgam, in other words, of fact and invention.

When people used to ask, "Was your father like Stefan Ivarin in your book?" I always replied, "Ivarin is just the way my father was, and just the way I always wished he would be."

That is true of many of the characters and many of the scenes in many of my books—but I'll come to that as I come to the books themselves. With one exception, I never gave any frivolous answers to the question, because it seemed totally natural to me that a reader of any book—including perhaps this one—will wonder how much of it is true and how much of it is made up.

In this one nothing will be made up, nothing invented, nothing knowingly shaded to put a better light on some crisis, no special pleading to exonerate me in some quarrel or misfortune. I don't mean that I will permit myself no reticences, nor that I will feel obliged to weep in public over whatever griefs and disappointments and sorrows there have been along with the delights and joys. I simply promise that there will be no invention. If it is written here, it will be true.

Having stated that so confidently, I am instantly faced with a dilemma, for I know full well how sly and cunning the unconscious can be in repressing memory, how artistically it can rearrange facts to polish and preen the ego. Perhaps I had better content myself with saying if it is written in this book, it will be as true as if I were in some courtroom, murmuring, "So help me God."

A bad analogy, for I am an agnostic, as were my parents before ever I was born. They were unlike the usual immigrants dwelling in novels, for they were both teachers and writers, my father the first editor of the *Jewish Daily Forward*, one of its founders before the celebrated Abraham Cahan took over, one of Cahan's major colleagues for years—and major critic too, and my mother for twelve of her middle years a regular columnist on a lesser Jewish newspaper, *The Day*.

I have a heavy book I can't read a word of, and the handwritten inscription in it, opposite its title page, reads, "To Laura, from her mother, Adella Kean Zametkin, June 18, 1930. A birthday present."

My birthday on June 18? Didn't I just write that the century was five months and nineteen days old when I was born? Didn't my mother know my real birthday? Don't *I* know?

Actually, unlike most mortals, I have *two* birthdays, because my twin was born before midnight on June 18th and I about an hour later on the 19th. This seemed too complex for the people who issued birth certificates, so Alice and I shared ours, which gives June 18 for both of us.

While we were kids, it was her fancy to announce grandly on June 18th, "I'm a year older than you are—you have to do what I say." And later, in our thirties, when we began to worry about advancing age, I got it all back. "I'm a year younger than you!"

For years, if the 18th fell on an inconvenient day, we would have our party on the 19th, and for further years, even on passports or driver's licenses, I'd write either the 18th or 19th, until I finally decided that, mnemonically, 19 went with 1900 and stuck to 19 ever since.

In any case, that heavy book my mother inscribed to me on my birthday, and which I could never read, was a collection of her own pieces for the newspaper, *The Day*, printed in Yiddish, which is why I can't read it. But I can read its page numbers, ordinary English numbers, and, leafing backwards from that title page to its last page, I come at last to 648.

Some of these pages have the familiar itemized format found in any cookbook, so I can tell they were her pieces about proper nutrition and pure foods, complete with recipes, urging her uneducated readers to regard with horror all "denatured" foods like white flour, white sugar and pale raisins, and extolling the virtues of "unrefined" foods like brown sugar, brown rice and whole wheat bread.

But most of the 648 pages are free of the itemized lines, which tells me they were the articles she was happiest writing, articles to educate her readers about how to bring up their children in modern ways, how Madame Montessori's methods of teaching were fast becoming the accepted standards of leading educators, and more than anything else, how to make "real Americans" of their young sons and daughters.

There is a formal printed dedication, too, four brief lines, and these I must have asked her about, for underneath them, in my own handwriting, in pencil, is the translation she gave me:

Dedicated
to those women
who are never
too old to learn

The book was published one year before her death. I have always meant to get parts of it translated, but I never have. I have kept it, though, for fifty years, and her printed picture, which makes its frontispiece, is one of the two that are all I have. All the pictures she saved were of us children.

I also have another book, this one written and printed in English, only 135 pages long, bound in dark green paper, and fairly crumbling to bits despite my careful outer binding in heavy cellophane wrappers. In silver letters on the dark green cover it says "*A Russian Shylock: A Play in Four Acts* by M. Zametkin," and down below, still on the cover is the legend, "Printed by the Author. 239 Sackman Street, Brooklyn, New York. Price

25 Cents." It was never produced, and to me, all these years later—it was copyrighted in 1906—that legend has a wistful sound, an admission that nobody else would publish it. It too has a formal printed dedication.

Dedicated to
Adella Kean,
My dearest friend and comrade.
The Author

I finally read the play when I was in college—I sort of had to by then, and knew I was expected to write him what I thought of it. I bore that knowledge as a burden for endless time, or so it seemed before I finally got to it. I may have that letter, but I will search for it later . . . putting it off once more. But it reminds me that I also had the burden of presenting some of his work in original mathematics to another professor at Cornell, and that too I put off as long as possible. What other co-ed had a father whose hobby was original mathematics?

No, they were nothing like the usual immigrant parents dwelling in novels. And yet, as a child I was ashamed of them, and squirmed when I brought schoolmates home. They were different from everybody else's mothers and fathers. They were *foreigners*, they had an accent, they did outlandish things, especially my mother, who would talk socialism to the milkman and the iceman, would talk votes for women to one and all, and who would hold forth on the dire consequences of pouring ketchup on a frankfurter because the heartless manufacturers used preservatives like benzoate of soda in it—and in the hot dog too.

One of her heroes, quoted endlessly, was Dr. Harvey Wiley, a chemist and pure-food expert who fought to get Congress to enact the first Food and Drug Act in 1906, and I seem to have equated the name of Dr. Wiley through all my childhood with the name of a saint, and benzoate of soda with Beelzebub. The organic-food enthusiasts of the 1980s would regard her as a pioneer, but back there in 1910, all the friends I had—and their mothers—regarded her as a freak.

Even our house at 400 Flushing Avenue—now Parsons Boulevard—was fairly freaky. It was tall and thin and elongated on its 40-by-100-foot plot of ground, raised about three feet above the sidewalk on an embankment. "Normal people" would have had the property leveled off, so the house wouldn't be perched up there like some huge wild tubular bird, but we perched.

It was a shingled house, the shingles brand new, not the good gray color of Cape Cod cottages, but new raw wood, a faint pinkish yellow hue that made me hate the look of it for its first years.

The porches were different too. Instead of the regulation front and back porch of other kids' nice little stucco or brick houses, ours had a proliferation of porches, a total of four, the two extra ones being a square block of a sleeping porch set midway atop the front porch, and a tiny four-foot-square side stoop, complete with its own slanted roof.

Worst of all, though, was our staircase inside. All staircases in the world, straight, curving, circular—all of them might arise from the front hall near the front door, but not our staircase. Oh no, not our staircase. Ours began at the back of the house, by that tiny side porch at the side entrance, next to the kitchen and near the pantry, and then shot straight upward toward the front of the house on the floor above.

My father had selected himself as the architect of the house to save fees, disdaining the fact that he had no whit of training in the field of architecture. He could calculate, couldn't he? He knew figures and numbers, was absorbed by mathematical theory, was the easy master of square feet and such miniscule matters. In those days you could buy two lots for $400 and build your own house—nine rooms, cellar, attic, bathroom, lavatory and four porches—for $5,000, first mortgage all arranged for. But that took every dime of their savings, so why waste any of those precious dollars for architects and their blueprints, except for such intricacies as plumbing and wiring?

My first memory of the "monster" in my father surely came from the shouting quarrels about that staircase—I seem to hear my own small voice crying out, "But Pa, *nobody* has a staircase going backwards—everybody will laugh at me!" And my mother's voice, protesting the lack of a needed cupboard here, the misplacing of the laundry tubs, the insufficiency of lighting over the kitchen range and sink.

He would shout her down, she would dissolve in tears, he would finally rush out of the house and go to the *Forward* on East Broadway in the city, or go to one of the cafés near the paper and sit there for hours, playing chess, and then remain in a bad mood for days, depressed, irascible. He knew that "irritability," as he preferred to call it, was his major flaw, but he seemed unable to conquer or control it until his old age, when my mother was gone and it was too late.

Though the two of them knew in their adult wisdom that their hot flaring quarrels were "nothing," two little girls not yet ten must have seen them only as horrible fights that threatened them.

The staircase and the freaky house and pure foods and socialism and suffrage weren't the only things that made me wish fervently from time to time that I could have been blessed with parents who were like everybody else's parents.

There was the terrible time in the spring of 1911 when they decided "to do something" as a protest about the Triangle fire in New York, on Washington Square, where 154 young workers had either burned to death over the close-packed sewing machines, or had leaped ten floors to their death on the sidewalks below. Most of them were from the ghetto, most of them only girls; name after name in the hideous lists of the dead in the newspapers was followed by the phrase, *age 16, age 17.*

All of New York was rocked by the horror of the "skyscraper fire"; there were public outcries everywhere about the locked doors to the single exit, the lack of fire escapes; churches and synagogues were organizing special services, the Red Cross and other organizations were raising relief funds for the stricken families, a funeral procession of three hundred thousand garment workers was being arranged by the Women's Trade Union League, giant mass meetings were held at Grand Central Palace and even at the Metropolitan Opera House.

But that wasn't enough for my parents. Once again, especially for my mother. "Everybody out here is already forgetting those dead burned children," she said a day or two later. "We ought to do something to make them remember, something public, to remind them of all the other deathtraps in the sweatshops everywhere."

A dire premonition filled my heart. It wouldn't be just a conventional black rosette and streamers hanging from our front door—of that I was sure. *Anybody* could do that.

But little did I expect that that "something" would turn out to be a wholesale draping of the white pillars of our front porch in black bunting, all six of them, the two flanking the front door and then the others from right to left, top to bottom. My mother had bought several bolts of the bunting, hundreds of yards of that insufferable stuff, obviously with the approval of my father.

For there he was the next day, a man who never willingly drove in a thumbtack inside the house, up on a ladder on the porch, with a huge hammer, a mouthful of nails, attaching the top end of the bolt held below by my mother, he starting the winding process and my mother circling the pillar with the bolt like a rotund little shuttle, hardly able to pass it around the pillar and catch it with her other hand. When the six pillars were finished, they began on the picket-fence railing that ran the length and sides of the porch, and went right on draping, now in vertical strokes instead of circular, but blacker than ever.

It was public all right. Even during the winding and draping, the neighborhood kids gathered to gawk and giggle and ask why? And then next day, my adored teacher, a Miss Hyatt, walked slowly by, looked up at me on the porch, then at the pillars, then back at me. I hadn't missed a day at school, so "death in the family" was clearly out.

"Did Shag die, Laura?" Shag was our huge English sheepdog, known to the entire neighborhood.

"Oh, no, Miss Hyatt." I can hear again the tight anguish of shame in my voice. "It's to protest the Triangle fire."

I hated Miss Hyatt then, but I hated my mother more.

And then the following year, in 1912, there was the winter-long strike of the textile workers in Lawrence, Massachusetts. My father had gone up there several times to lecture, as other union speakers had done, to assure continuing support of New

York's unions to the two hundred thousand workers striking the American Woolen Mills, the Pacific Cotton Mills, the Everett and Arlington mills and the rest, striking to raise their wages from nine cents an hour to eleven cents, from $4.86 for a fifty-four-hour week to a munificent $5.94! Bread lines and soup kitchens were inadequate; union strike funds were running out; in the New England blasts and blizzards of winter, people were starving, falling sick, dying, especially young children.

When he came back from one of his trips he told my mother that a new committee was being formed to search out families that could take in a striker's child as long as the strike continued.

"If only we lived right there!" she cried.

"They may also try to find families out of state who'd be willing to—"

"Oh my goodness!" It was one of her expressions, variously meaning joy, sadness, despair, hope, apology. This time it meant hope. She must have turned pink with eagerness, as she sometimes did, or with pleading to the Fates that they should let it happen.

Two weeks later two little girls arrived by train, escorted by a union official from Lawrence, Massachusetts on the long trip. They were Phronsie, eight, and Damsie, seven, both blond, thin, in ragged coats, no rubbers, torn shoes soaked with snow, hands blue with cold, hair oily and dirty with lack of washing and care.

From the moment they came through the front door, my mother treated them like two new daughters, and Alice and I somehow took to them too. They were so scared, so scrawny and big-eyed, staring uncertainly at us—it was a new experience for us, feeling like benefactors, and we liked it.

But then came the news: we would have to take them to school with us, though they'd be in lower classes. Truancy was not permitted by the laws of New York State, not even for displaced refugee children, and as soon as the official business of transfers could be arranged, to school they would have to go.

They were too young to go by themselves; we'd have to lug those two skinny little things along with us every morning and take them home every afternoon. The old refrain came slamming at me: everybody would laugh at me.

And yet, there was excitement in the whole thing too. There was the hubbub of the transfers to P.S. 6, there were shopping trips to get them shoes and rubbers, there was my mother at her sewing machine half the night to make them warm woolen dresses and there was, too, the repeated washing of their hair at bedtime with tincture of larkspur, to guarantee total extermination of the probable nits and lice imported from Lawrence, Massachusetts.

I can't remember how many weeks they lived with us, but I do know that when the interminable strike finally ended and the news came that Phronsie and Damsie could go home again, I felt not only a relief that there'd be no more snide remarks at school about "your Polack cousins," but also a sort of sadness at not having a couple of little sisters around to play with and feel superior to. When their official escort came for them, they both cried over saying good-bye. But so did I.

The draping of the house, the refugee children, the backward staircase, the house itself may have struck even the most hostile neighborhood critic as merely eccentric, but to me as a child, it all seemed to mark us off from everybody normal and "regular." Taken together with my father's bursts of temper, my mother's fits of misery and crying because of them, the following days when there was a hushed world for all of us—this was not any formula for a child's happiness.

But I never did think I had an unhappy childhood, though it was no sunny family life with a storybook father, either. He was never a father who took us to the park, never a father who played games or told us stories, never a father to have fun with. He worked all night at the paper, slept part of the day when he was home and then disappeared to his own room whenever he could to get at his hobbies of original mathematics or championship-level chess. When he played with world champions like Emanuel Lasker and José Raúl Capablanca, they would give him a handicap of a pawn and a move, no more. And then he was forever going off on his lecture tours, away from us completely for days at a time, because a lecture brought in ten dollars of extra money.

Many years had to pass before I could begin to see around my father's domineering flares of rage and see clearly the man

17

within those brackets of pain-giving. My sister, unhappily enough, never did get to that point for the rest of her life—she died in 1980 at the age of seventy-nine. With her, though, that anger at him that continued unabated so long, was rooted not so much in childhood, but in something not even suspected until much later on—a political chasm that was to develop between him and her, the same unbridgeable chasm that was to cause so much estrangement and suffering between her and me.

I see that I've given the impression that we were the only children. In effect it was true, though we did have a half-brother, Joel, and a full brother, Fred. But Joel was seventeen years older and Fred ten years older than we were, both married, with homes of their own and children of their own, so in our minds, they belonged to the world of grown-ups, uncles instead of brothers. Uncles, what's more, who were none too eager to come out from Brooklyn to Jamaica for visits with the family.

What childhood miseries we had to bear, Alice and I, we bore alone.

Everybody will laugh at me. I don't know how far into my life that longing for conformity pursued me, but I would guess that its insidious little clutch tugged at me for a good long while, though it's likely that at last I learned how to counterbalance it with slightly loftier values.

And of course there were plenty of aspects of life even in childhood that were loaded with conformity—we had roller skates and sleds and bicycles like everybody else, and although we never had a Christmas tree or Chanukah candelabra, we were saved from feeling like total agnostic outcasts by being told that ancient pagan holidays at the end of each year meant we could have little gifts, games, books, dolls.

And there was even one nonconformist thing that I, for one, actually seemed to understand and approve of. It had to do with money, the wrong kind of money, money you didn't earn by writing or teaching or lecturing, but money that money earned, what bankers called interest. "Unearned increment" was a capitalist evil in the eyes of any good socialist, and if you had a few hundred dollars saved in a bank, the one thing you could never touch was the new money it sat there earning for you while you weren't looking.

So four times a year, my father would withdraw the tiny but indecent interest on the family savings, march off to the post office and send a money order to some Committee for the Defense of Political Prisoners in Russia.

Refusing to take money that other people thought was yours— *that* I thought one of the most exciting things I'd ever heard of. It's possible that the words *political prisoners* are what touched off my understanding and approval. For my father had been in prison.

A political prisoner, of course, and in Russia, of course. He was born in Odessa in 1859, son of a mother, Malka, whom he remembered as "kind but with a terrible temper," and of a father, Chaim Yoel, who was a small contractor, employing fifteen to eighteen workers, all at work right there in the house. They manufactured *papakhi*, the high fur caps, usually black karakul, that were worn by men richer than they were.

His father frequently boasted of an ancestor who had borne the impressive title of Rabbi of All the Southern Russias. Despite this awesome heritage, my father wanted nothing of the religious schooling expected of him and, once he was beyond the lower grades, held out for a regular Russian education. His parents were afraid he would lose his religion and become too Russified, but he had already lost his religion and in the end he won out.

The 1860s and 1870s in Czarist Russia was a period of liberalism, when a few Jews were permitted to enter the gymnasia and universities. At the University of Odessa he was soon known as a brilliant mathematician, but his greatest interest was in politics. He joined a group of young anti-Czarist rebels, Jews and Christians alike, about two dozen in all, socialists who dreamed of ridding Mother Russia of palaces and nobles, of making the emancipation of the serfs a reality instead of just a proclamation.

In parentheses here, let me say that when this book says socialist or socialism, it is not using today's synonyms or code words for communist or communism, but using the words in the pristine nineteenth-century concept of a system that would own the means of production, but exclude tyranny, guarantee free speech, the freedom to write, to organize, to protest.

My father's group had a printing press, a small handpress bought from a junk dealer and set up in the cellar; they were all engaged in writing leaflets and pamphlets for their great cause, and they soon discovered that Zametkin could write the perfect inflammatory sentence.

Discovery was always possible; arrest and imprisonment were a constant danger to them all. One night it happened—and my father was the only one in the cellar when the uniformed police arrived.

Name? Address? Occupation? Religion?

"I have no religion," he said. "My father is a Jew."

Again in parentheses, I want to say that when I put something down in dialogue in this book, particularly in the parts dealing with things that happened decades ago, it is not that I am sidestepping my resolve to invent nothing, to make up nothing. If the words in direct quotes are brief, that will mean that some memorable phrase or sentence took hold of me and remained fixed in my memory.

And if I put a longer bit of dialogue into quotes, it will be because, being a novelist, dialogue comes more readily to me when I am trying to recreate a scene than the use of summary or the narrative past tense. In this particular instance, those nine words of my father are the very words I heard many times as a child, usually in conjunction with some newspaper report of an arrest and the "third degree" in the world of labor.

For he went to prison indeed, and was tortured in all the classic ways, to make him tell the names of the others involved with him in the nefarious group. He refused and was beaten with the knout, and still he refused. He went on a hunger strike, and what for him was worse, on a tobacco strike, but he refused.

Sometimes in recent years when I have seen how certain people have made what I can only call a whole career of their nobility, because they refused to name names for McCarthy in the House Un-American Activities Committee, where there were no armed guards with whips, where they could and did take the Fifth Amendment to stay out of jail, while still thinking of themselves as heroic—sometimes I think back to my father's day, and the beating and wrecked nervous systems and possible deaths in those Russian prisons, and I find myself contemplating the extent of self-adulation the world seems now to accept.

My father never said much about his imprisonment. He was finally rescued by his comrades, concealed in a large crate marked "Red Roosters," and then shipped off to America, with holes punched in the wood so he could breathe, even in the awful steerage section of the ship. Or so I firmly believed through all my earliest years.

When skepticism began to dawn, at about age twelve, and made me realize that no crate of red roosters would be shipped across land and sea to America where the streets were paved with gold, I refrained from checking it out with my mother and father. Maybe the stupid crate was used only to get him beyond the prison gates, but I preferred to keep the high drama of my own version intact.

Whenever my mother said, "When papa was in prison..." a ring of pride sounded, as if she were saying, "when papa was elected to Congress..." and that at least was something I would boast about to my best friends. What I never told anybody was that he had recurrent nightmares about prison all his life, screaming nightmares, and they had a direct effect on me, for it was always I who had to go and wake him out of them. My mother had taken to sleeping downstairs in a small room off the dining room, called the "sewing room," and with her door closed she didn't hear a thing. My sister and I had separate cots in our room upstairs, but somehow Alice never seemed to stir when the terrible sound began to tear the night open.

His nightmares would begin with a wailing moaning cry, like an animal's grinding roar, and rise in pitch and volume and intensity as it went on.

I would lie there and wait and hope somebody else would wake him this time. Then I would go into the dark where he lay, calling, "Papa, Papa, wake up." My voice would only turn into the shouting of the prison guards, he once explained, and his cries became even wilder.

There was nothing for it but to shake him by the shoulder.

But that touch would turn into the slash of the knout, and with one final shout he would leap up and it would be over.

"I had a bad dream," he would always say. "What time is it?"

I can't remember feeling any sympathy for him for those nightmares of his, only resentment at my being the one who had to go in and wake him. I would hear him leave his room after I went back to my own, and go to the bathroom; sometimes he would leave the door open and I could hear him urinate, and my only emotion was how disgusting and awful he was.

For the rest of his life, my father's nightmares were in Russian, even after he began to have ordinary dreams in English. The first time he did dream in English, he woke up exulting, "At last I'm an American—you dream in your native tongue."

His mother tongue was Russian, far more so than the Yiddish or Hebrew of his childhood. He was not sure why this was so. At the university where everybody spoke Russian, he had begun to feel, with the other intellectual Jews, that Yiddish was a ghetto language, the language of the oppressed in the shtetls of Russia and Poland.

In *World of Our Fathers*, Irving Howe wrote at one point that "Michael Zametkin . . . a veteran of the eighties . . . bemoaned the fact that immigrant workers, not knowing English, had to use the mishmash of the Russian-Hebrew-German jargon that went under the name of Yiddish."

When I read that word jargon, it sounded too snobbish for my father, but later I came across an explanation for it. In an interview in Paris, Leon Trotsky was once asked why he had used the term jargon for Yiddish in his autobiography. "It is because," he had replied, "in the years of my youth in Odessa, the Jewish language was not called Yiddish, as today, but 'jargon.' Such was the expression of the Jews themselves, who did not consider it a sign of superciliousness."

When my father began to lecture on New York's Lower East Side, he spoke in Russian, as did many of his contemporaries, but soon he had to give that up, and turn to the language of his audiences, Yiddish. There is, however, very little memory for me of Yiddish spoken at our house, except when my mother was giving English lessons to one of her immigrant pupils. The language for secrets between my parents was Russian.

I've occasionally been asked how it is that I don't understand Yiddish, nor speak it, nor read it, and there is the answer right there. But none of us ever learned Russian either, or the fair amount of French and Polish and German my parents had.

To think that I might have been a linguist! But the whole purpose of their moving away from New York in my earliest childhood, first to Brooklyn, and then to a small town on Long Island, away from their colleagues and friends, away from their co-workers on newspapers and in labor unions—the whole point was to bring up their children as total Americans, with no trace of foreign accent, no smallest inflection or gesture that was not native to this their beloved country.

Mostly, of course, I applaud their decision, but perhaps if I had been linguist enough to know the Russian words my father was shouting out in those prison nightmares of his, I might have felt something a little more human than resentment.

Prisons played a part in the life of my mother's family too, in a less harrowing way. Years later, her own mother, then age ninety-four, was still making regular weekly visits to prisons in Southern Russia, carrying in an innocent-looking basket of fruit right past the prison guards. Each pear or apple or peach in the basket had tucked into it a secret message to the political prisoner she was visiting, written in indelible ink on a snippet of cloth.

My mother was born Adella Emanuelovna Khean in Mohilev, in the Ukraine, one of fourteen children. Her parents were saloon-keepers, and thus rather looked down on by some, but financially they were far better off than my father's family, with servants and a pleasant place to live.

Her father was looked up to in the region for his learning; he had read the first Hebrew novel, *The Love of Zion*, had many books in Hebrew, Russian and French, and was an amateur astronomer who could astound his family by shouting one night, "I have just weighed the world."

When she was little, Adella was bored with school, learning to read and write with no sign of enthusiasm, but in adolescence she found an old grammar in the attic and asked if she could quit school and have private lessons instead. For six years a Mme. Steinberg tutored her in Russian, Hebrew, French, English, German, mythology, and she was at last called "the most educated girl in the Ukraine."

She was always too plump, but she must have been attractive and pretty, for she was engaged twice, once to a young manufacturer and once to an insurance salesman. Each time she stayed engaged for about six months and then found herself so restless and disillusioned that she broke it off. Once she fainted as she informed her fiancé that it was no go, and he shouted at her, "Socialist! Go to Siberia!"

Though she too lived during the "rationalist" period, there were plenty of irrational pogroms, more at Easter than at Christmas, because the weather was milder, more conducive to boisterous outdoor activity. Once when she was nearly sixteen, she had to hide under the rafters in the attic, and then hung on to her father's neck afterwards, pleading, "Father, darling, let's go to America."

When she did, she went without her parents and with only one of her brothers and sisters. He was to become a physician and spend his life on the staff of Barnes Hospital in St. Louis, and I don't remember his first name. Some busy little fellow at Ellis Island had transliterated both their names to a simple Kean, and he was known to all of us always as "Uncle Kean."

So my mother did not arrive in America as a poor immigrant, looking for a job. Her trunk was full of good clothes, and some furs, and silver candlesticks and other pieces of silver.

My sister and I particularly liked the candlesticks and a certain shallow bowl of sterling silver, and were going to take turn and turn about with them when we had homes of our own.

But the exchanging was never to take place. To this day, I have, as the centerpiece on my dining table, that silver bowl, about nine by six inches, with a delicate hinged and movable handle, and in it a hand-wrought etching of a large manor house set within a filigreed border. Four small round silver balls serve as its legs, and among the minute marks of the silversmith on the back of it is the date, 1883. She was twenty then.

The way she met my father and fell in love with him might

24

drive some latter-day feminists into a disapproving snit, for it was in its way the prototypical scene of the superior man and the adoring inferior woman—at least in the physical sense.

For he was up on a platform lecturing, and she was down in the front row of the audience, gazing raptly up at him. He was a fiery public speaker, according to various comments about him in books about the early labor-union movement in this country, and that night, she said, he was at his best.

The meeting was in a big hall on the Lower East Side in New York City, where he was one of the principal speakers addressing workers in what was then called the "needle trades," and later became the formidable International Ladies Garment Workers Union. To this day I can never hear the television jingle they sing in commercials, "So look for the union label," without feeling my throat go tight in some deep recognition that to help make a union and keep it strong was one of the most noble things a human being could do.

She met him that night after the lecture. He was married to a woman named Fanny Lint, and they had a baby son, Joel. They fell in love, and soon enough she was taking care of the baby Joel while he was off at work or on a lecture tour. I never did know why Fanny Lint relinquished her child, but there he was, from their first hours together.

In 1889 there was a legal divorce from Fanny, and my father "married" my mother. I put the quotes around the word married, for it was without recourse to rabbi, minister, marriage bureau at City Hall or anything as conventional as that. Common-law marriage was quite the usual thing among the young socialists of the East Side back there in the eighties and nineties, "perfectly legal after five years," as my mother would sometimes interpolate when she spoke of it.

On their fortieth anniversary in 1929, with all the family gathered together for once, my brother Joel and his wife Rebecca, my brother Fred and his wife Bertha, four nephews and nieces, my sister and I, all together in our house in Jamaica to celebrate, my father suddenly said to all of us at large, but turning to her as he was speaking, "Well, this trial marriage has lasted long enough. I think we should go ahead and make it official."

She was seriously ill by then, but she seemed as active and energetic as ever. For over twenty-five years she had had diabetes, discovering it only when she had to go to the hospital after a fall down the cellar steps in our house in Brooklyn. The world had not yet discovered insulin back in 1906, and I can see again the tiny metal scale in the kitchen which she used three times a day to measure off the grams of those foods she was permitted to take.

There is only one episode of my early childhood I wish I could forget to include, so ugly was it, and yet so moving in the end. Much later on, in my middle thirties, when I was in a period of despair deep enough to send me into a lengthy psychoanalysis, it emerged from a thousand other child-momentous events as a major trauma, what some people today would call of "primal scream" importance.

It happened when I was six and a half, still living on Sackman Street, before we moved to Jamaica, and I was in the first grade at school.

At recess one day, my teacher told me to stay in because I had the sniffles, and I remained alone in the classroom, watching the kids playing outside in the schoolyard below me. I was kneeling, I remember, over the warm radiator, looking out the window, when suddenly I felt someone kneeling just behind me.

I looked around and grinned at our janitor, who was always nice to all of us. He was crouching down as if he wanted to watch the children too, but he began to move from side to side against my back and say, half under his breath but loudly enough so I could hear that awful word, "Fuck, fuck, fuck, fuck." It was over before I knew what to do, and he was gone, and all I can actually recall of the way I felt then was surprise and interest.

But if that was all, I do not know why I didn't tell a single soul about it. But I did not. Not my best friend, not my sister, not my teacher and certainly not my mother. I think I must have set it aside as part of the mystery surrounding grown-ups and what they did, or perhaps even of men and what they could do, but be that as it may, I know I had no fear of the janitor, and when he next stopped to speak to me, friendly as ever, I must have been friendly too.

For he told me he had a present for me, a wonderful toy, down in the basement, nodding to the heavy steel door that led to the stairs going down from the main floor.

"What kind of toy?" I went right along, dying to see what it would be, obviously not reluctant, for he had no need of any sort of persuasion, not even a hand on my shoulder.

There was a little footstool not far from the furnace, about ten or twelve inches high. Before I could have my present, he said, I was to stand up on the footstool—it was like a little game we'd play. I got up with alacrity, and a moment later my underpants were around my ankles and he was putting his "thing," as little girls called it then, between my thighs, about halfway up between my knees and "there," that other word that nice little girls used then.

Again he whispered that word, and again it was all over in a moment. He said something about keeping a secret, and gave me a box with a toy in it. Even in a classic three-year Freudian analysis, I could never remember what kind of toy.

This time I didn't tell anybody either, but this time I knew something bad and terrible had happened, and decided that I must have been bad and terrible or it couldn't have happened. I remember running up the stairs with my toy, and running along the slate floor of the school corridor and out the front door, but memory of that day stops there.

It was three full years before I told a soul about that janitor and that footstool and that cellar, and then it was, of all people, my mother to whom I blurted it all out. I was a little past nine by then, and was in tears about something else, and my mother was comforting me, and before I knew it, with no transition, with no preamble, I was at last sobbing out the whole story of that janitor in the public school in Brooklyn.

She was holding me in her arms before I was halfway through, rocking me as if I were still little instead of a big girl of nine. "Oh my goodness," she would say every once in a while, and she kept telling me I was not bad or terrible, not in any way, not to blame at all.

"Was there any blood anywhere?" she asked when I came to the end. "Did anything hurt?"

"Blood, mama? Of course not. *Blood?*"

"No bleeding, Laura? No sign of bleeding?"

I kept saying no, asking why she'd even think of bleeding, and all she did was to keep murmuring over me, and holding me in that gentle rocking motion, and saying that being filled with curiosity was natural in bright children, and how they wanted to see everything and find out about everything and go everywhere, and that nobody in the world could think I had been a bad girl.

I have never been able to write about a cruel mother, a mother who was a villain—not in my short stories, novelettes or novels. I have never been able to do a scene where the mother was petty or cold or mean-spirited or indifferent—and if ever I tried to, that scene never rang true.

She had many faults, my mother; she wept too easily, she was sure you'd been in an accident if you were half an hour late, she could proselytize you to death about pure foods and a better world, but that was about the depth of her iniquity.

She was pure mother, not only to us her children, but to her immigrant pupils who came to her for lessons in English, to others who read her columns, to still others who sought out her support in starting new organizations for women who worked to earn a living.

When she lay dying, in long hours of deep coma, at Columbia-Presbyterian Hospital in New York, on a May day in 1931, and I leaned down over her, trying to reach her through that coma, "Mama, it's Laura, Mama, it's Laura," she finally stirred, and without opening her eyes, said, "Yes, darling, yes," with a reassuring inflection in her voice, as if she were telling a hurt child, "I'll be there in a minute."

TWO

THE FIRST TIME I wrote anything that I thought might be published, I was fifteen and a pupil at Jamaica High School. It wasn't signed, and it wasn't long, but it did see the bright black sheen of printer's ink. For I was assistant editor of *The Oracle*, the school's monthly magazine.

My name was right up there on the masthead, side by side on the top line with the editor in chief, Helen Alida Bassett, whom I no longer remember. Ranked below us were the seven subeditors whose sections were called Alumni, Art, Assemblies, Boys' Athletics, Gossip, Societies and something called Exchange.

It was the first public acknowledgment that I had some affinity for the written word, albeit a subordinate affinity. But to be any kind of editor of anything that went regularly to press and sold for ten cents a copy was glory enough in the world as I knew it then.

I was fifteen, too, when I first earned actual money by writing something for it. Writing for a real honest-to-goodness New York newspaper, what was more. How I got the idea that I might try for any such grandiose role I do not know, but one day I set forth for the city by streetcar, and then by elevated train and subway, with an appointment to see one of the editors of the *Evening Mail*, Rheta Childe Dorr, who, in the parlance of the day, "conducted" the School page in the afternoon and home editions.

I must have written for an appointment, must have been astonished to receive an answer and more astonished that the well-known editor would actually interview me when I appeared.

What I was after was permission to send in school news from Jamaica High. She said I could try. If she printed anything, it would be paid for at five dollars a column or twenty-five cents a stick. A stick, she told me, was one inch of type, seven printed lines. If I sent in any items about school elections or dramatics or sports, she would read them herself and decide whether they belonged in a big city newspaper or not.

Even that much commitment aroused in me the first dazzling thrill of professionalism. Three months before, I had begun a diary—also a first—and part of the entry for May 7, 1916 reads, "I am writing for a newspaper and getting paid for it! . . . I can't tell yet what the average of pay is, because although it is about a month since it started, I have only gotten two checks—one for 50¢—that was for one day's work—& one for $5.50."

Little did I dream then that sixty-five years later a visit to the newspaper annex of New York's great public library on Fifth Avenue would still yield the actual items that had earned me that first literary income of six dollars. This was the first one:

JAMAICA HIGH BUYS NEW BANNER

The students of Jamaica High School own their new beaver banner, not only theoretically but practically, because in answer to a recent appeal from the financial managers of the G.O. each student chipped in one cent for it, covering the cost nicely.

The banner is thirty feet long and twenty-four feet broad. On a blue background is a monstrous red beaver—Jamaica High insignia and colors. The banner is striking and artistic.

There was another printed on the same day, April 4, 1916. It was about a prize essay contest by the Nature Club, on "The

Housefly and How to Control It." In rapid succession, there came news of an art contest for a new cover design for *The Oracle*, news about the Glee Club, the Tramp Club, a story contest, the *Beaver Handbook* and like matters, a total of eight that first month.

And there was one piece of news I must have been positively eager to send in, for I was not only reporting it, I was *part* of it. Jamaica High was giving a parody of four Shakespeare plays— 1916 was the three-hundredth anniversary of Shakespeare's death, and every school and college in the nation was doing something especially Shakespearean. The parody was called *The Ladies Speak At Last*. Sad to say, I neglected to mention the author's name, an omission I have often excoriated in all the years since, but I did list the names of the four principal members of the cast, which included Juliet, Lady Macbeth, Ophelia and Portia.

"Lady Macbeth . . . Laura K. Zametkin." My name was in the paper!

No wonder my excitement about those first sticks of type spilled into my diary! But the diary is not, alas, all on so lofty a plane. On page two there appears the name Kenneth—it was to reappear fifty times through the rest of the ten entries in the book, each one running on for about ten penciled pages at a clip. They were not very big pages, only five-by-three, ruled, in a little red book with a flip-top, like a salesclerk's pad of sales slips. I wrote in a large hurried hand, apparently always in such a fever of writing that I had no time to spell out *and*—the pages are freckled with &'s and gashed with dashes.

Why I saved it, and its older sister that was to follow in a year or so, I do not know. I must have started out as a magpie, saving not only those diaries, but a scrapbook of my years at Cornell, letters to and from my parents while I was away at school, college receipts, ("Sage Hall, 1 bed . . . 30¢") and for a year or so in my early twenties, an adult Journal, capital J and all.

Later on, for a couple of decades, the magpie gene must have gone through a mutation, for I threw away hundreds of letters I now wish I had saved, personal letters, love letters, "big name" letters from people I met mainly through being married to a publisher. Only when I started to write did I begin again to save everything connected with a manuscript.

But on and off through my whole writing life, that early need to "write it down" that impelled me to that little red book remained as some subterranean force in me. Whenever I began thinking out an idea for a story, or, later on, for a novel, I would turn to the typewriter, roll in a sheet of blank paper and head it, "Possible Plot for Story?" or "Possible Novel?" and then frequently, "Notes on Novel?" and subsequently, "More Notes on Novel?"

The question mark was an integral part of the phrase until the manuscript, short or long, for magazines or for the publisher of books, frivolous or serious—until that manuscript really got under way. Then, if I needed to "write it down" the question mark disappeared and the phrase itself changed. It became, quite firmly, "The Rest of the Story."

But there was very little firmness in the opening entry in that red flip-top diary, dated February 12, 1916. I was fifteen and a half.

> I went to class-day & had a fine time, mostly. The exercises were good, especially a play in which Kenneth had a part. He was splendid & looked awfully handsome in a false moustache. But he didn't dance with me once. I danced mostly with Eber Kessler & he's a fine dancer. I danced with Marcus but oh he's abominable. Wherever I go he goes too. Towards the end, K. asked Anna Mathes to dance & she did. That spoiled the evening for me. I tried not to mind but I did. Coming home Bertha told me I had a weak chin. I felt pretty sad about everything, tried to be philosphical & ended in something akin to jealousy.

(Note to printer: Please stet all puncuation & spelling.) Exactly one week later comes the second entry:

> I am so happy. Yesterday I went to a dance & Kenneth danced an awful lot with me. I get a queer feeling whenever I think of him. I was standing & talking to Hazel Beirman while waiting for the grand right & left of a nantucket. All

of a sudden someone comes up & says, 'come & dance with me.' I looked at him & it was Kenneth. I did & danced fine for a minute & then the instructor told us we had to go back to our old partners. I was awfully sorry. I didn't dance with him for quite a long time & when I was sitting over by the window with Martin Gillan & he came over to talk to Martin & I never even said hello even. Then he asked me if I wanted to dance with him & I said yes.

Then I danced about 5 or 6 dances with him, one after another. I was so happy I didn't dance very well. I tried to teach him the waltz in a secluded corner of the room & when the music stopped he kept his arm around me for an instant. I was so happy. Maybe I was silly but I felt so badly that he had stopped looking at me even, & then to have him dance with me so much. I think the reason that he asked me was that when he came in, I never looked at him at all. I absolutely *snubbed* him. I never looked at him. We went out to get some lemonade & he talked to me about things. (I had the impulse to write, 'I love him,' but that's so foolish. I don't really. I'm awfully romantic that's all. The thot came into my head the same way a person says of a teacher, 'I love her.')

Kenneth, false moustache and all, was also fifteen when I was so smitten. His last name was McLaughlin (I'm not sure of the spelling), and I think his father had once been the principal of Jamaica High. If Kenneth should, by happy chance, read this book, I want to thank him now for asking me to dance when he did ask me, and tell him I forgive him for those terrible times when he did not.

There were dozens of other boys in that diary, also dozens of girls: Anna Mathes, blond and pretty, about whom I was forever telling myself I was not jealous, Carmelita Doane, brunette and well-developed, ("Carmelita came to the house & stayed overnight & Fred was there & she flirted with him. Imagine!") and fair-haired twins named Alva and Jean Ritter, who had invited us, at the age of eleven or so, to go to church with them, giving me my first experience of organized religion, indeed of any religion.

That was at the Grace Episcopal Church of Jamaica, and because they were twins who were good Christians and we were twins who were nothing, not even properly religious little Jewish girls, their parents apparently gave this whole missionary zeal their blessing.

And my parents gave their full permission for this inquiry into the devout life; my mother bought brown tweed and made new dresses for Alice and me, with stiff white Buster Brown collars for the grand occasion. I immediately loved church, but Sunday school proved to be an entirely different matter. All the kids knew we had never been baptized, and they had very little Christian charity in letting us know they knew it.

My sister, who was later to become a scientist, very quickly decided on the data available that there was nothing in the whole thing for her, but to me church was lovely. I kept going every Sunday for over a year, and at last the tall handsome minister climbed the hill to our house to call on my parents and propound the idea that I be confirmed and officially received into the arms of Christianity.

It was one of the times when even I knew that my parents behaved beautifully, though I'm certain that my father's extended conversation with the minister of Grace Episcopal Church of Jamaica must have included references aplenty to Charles Darwin, Karl Marx's opium of the people, and to the then-famous Bob Ingersoll, "the great agnostic."

My father said yes, I assuredly could be officially confirmed, and my mother agreed with him. It was a free country; freedom of opinion should be guaranteed to everybody, as well as one's right to worship as one saw fit.

There was only one proviso: I would have to wait for this great step until I reached the age of sixteen.

Long before I was sixteen, of course, I was to find doubt gnawing at the thin edge of my heart and at my mind; I began to wonder whether what I loved so much wasn't perhaps Grace Church itself, its stained glass windows, its arches, its music and maybe most of all, the sense of belonging to all those attractive, nicely dressed people in all the pews, who weren't socialist or foreign or Jewish or *anything*.

There is not one solitary word about church in that diary of mine, but not all of it concerned boys, clothes or dancing either.

34

One entry deals with "some resolutions I really have tried to live up to . . . the day Fred brought home his powdered malted milk (in that giant jar) I took a resolution *never* to touch any myself. So far I've succeeded. It was hard, during the time I lost my diary, but I did live up to my resolution. One reason I want a diary so much is that it will keep tabs on me. I'll feel awful to write down that I've not had strength to resist a temptation & so my will power will be made stronger. I also took a resolution not to cry so much because Bertha said my crying goes hand in hand with my weak chin."

Bertha was Fred's wife. They had married when they were both nineteen, they were both teachers with limited salaries, and by now had two small sons, Walter and Teddy. They were moving from Brooklyn to a house in Baldwin, Long Island, and at the time of Bertha's interest in my chin, they were living with us.

In that entire little red diary there is only one entry that is brief, indeed abrupt. Here it is, all of it:

> I measured myself & I'm not so awfully gawky & broad—
> Height 55.5
> Shoulders 17.0
> Hips 31.0
> Bust 31.0

> I won't have to wear a 42 size waist as Mrs. Hoffman so cheerfully predicted!

I had just turned sixteen, and it was a time of fearful anxiety about my looks and my figure. My sister already had what everybody called the figure of a Dresden doll: tiny waist, curving hips, small pretty breasts, and I was still flat as a board, straight as an arrow, strong as an ox with no sign of any feminine curve anywhere.

One Saturday when we were expecting visitors, my mother told me to scrub the floor of the side entrance, scrub the flight of stairs, (they were bare wood, uncarpeted) and then clean the bathroom thoroughly. I did it all in record time and then burst into tears.

"I'm not even tired—I'm going to be an Amazon."

The basic cause of this dread was that Alice had "begun" when she was twelve, and every other girl we knew had begun at twelve or thirteen. But not me. My Montessori-minded mother had told us all about menstruation and the variations there could be in the schedule for the start of it, and for a year or so I was unconcerned at being late.

But at thirteen and still not? At fourteen? At fifteen? And what about sixteen? No wonder I kept on taking measurements of my shoulders.

The usual sibling rivalries and jealousies were multiplied a thousand times by my own perception of myself as a scrawny boyish lunk compared to my graceful feminine sister. Whatever reverse rivalry and jealousy she had of me must have been deliciously disposed of during this era of her supremacy.

But there was plenty of cause for her to feel me as a threat. For all their intelligence and modernity, both my parents had made all sorts of mistakes with us in our early childhood, mistakes any psychoanalyst today could recognize as potentials for dire future results.

A hundred times while we were small children, my mother would tell us how tiny and weak Alice was when she was born, weighing about four pounds to my husky six. "For the first six months," she would say, "I could lay Alice down at the edge of the kitchen table and leave the room—she was too weak to roll off."

My father too was guilty. I was the first one to walk, and he would hand me two lumps of sugar, saying, "Here, Laurabus, one is for you, and then take the other one to Elsiebus." (He had some fondness for Latin endings.)

Alice would be sitting across the room on the carpet, not yet able to negotiate a step. She would watch me pop the sugar into my mouth and then start toward her. How she must have detested me, down deep in her baby unconscious, for my sturdy little strut across the distance between us.

And all through our childhood it was I who was sent out on errands, I who was given the harder chores, I who was treated as what today we would call the "can-do kid."

But by our adolescence, with me loathing my unique tardiness about "beginning," and she a willowy young lady, attractive and knowing with boys—then it was I who went through the agonies of inferiority.

(I was in my first semester at college when my laggard body finally caught up to all those fortunate girls. Furthermore, since I've always been a tall woman, 5-feet, 6½-inches, I feel sure that my anguished pencil must have knocked off a good eleven inches to record me as a dwarfish 4-feet, 7½-inches at sixteen. Still, as I just noted to the printer, anything from that diary is stet.)

Two days after those fretful statistics, all mundane matters were forgotten. The July 30, 1916 entry starts:

> We're going to college! Hunter of course but still college. For so long a time I was fearing that we'd have to go to training...But now college. It's going to be hard—awfully. But then everything worth while is hard...
>
> I have *got* to win a scholarship...it'll be awful if I don't....I'm going to take a bold step...and take all my Regents over for better grades....German II & III, French II, English Grammar & English III & Eng. IV. Then Intermediate Algebra, Am History, French III & German IV. So really I will take 10 Regents, but since the three English ones are in one day, it's only eight. *Only!*
>
> Well, it's nice to have ambitions. I feel strong. I'm not afraid of going to college. I know I can do things. That's not conceit. I know I can. I feel awfully nice of late. Everybody thinks well of me—the same thing—they think I can do things. It helps to have people have faith in you. And it makes me feel less conceited to know that when I say I can do things that it is probably true.

By September this high mood had several sharp dents in it.

> I'm afraid Alva & Jean Ritter are lost to us. I don't care. I'm beginning to realize that only among our own kind will we find friends that will last. Anna M. went to camp with them & and is probably going to Cornell with Alva, so it's natural they should be drawn to each other. I don't care a bit & I'm really not jealous of Anna at all.
>
> I wonder if I want to be a teacher; I don't, I want to work on a paper.

Kenneth McLaughlin was also planning to go to Cornell. I didn't care a bit about that either.

It seems likely that my own passion to go to Cornell had its roots in all this talk of the others who wanted to go there. Why none of the girls even mentioned Vassar or Radcliffe or Barnard, why Kenneth never considered Harvard or Yale or Columbia, why they never considered anything as lowly as city colleges, I certainly do not know.

My own parents took it for granted that Alice and I would go to Jamaica Training School for Teachers; it was a two-year course, and that struck my father as all any reasonable child could demand in the way of higher education. It was also free. It had been good enough for Fred, and Joel had also earned his D.D.S. at a free city college.

Even though Hunter was tuition-free also, it would take four long years before you were earning your own living—to him that was an absurdity. As for one of the private colleges, away from home—that was only for the "children of the rich."

So even getting permission to go to Hunter was a triumph. My fierce need for a scholarship had nothing to do with tuition, but I knew there'd be lab fees and books and clothes and other little pleasures that went with being a college girl—these I knew I could never have unless I somehow earned them for myself. And how better than by the munificence of a $100 a year in a scholarship?

That final semester at Jamaica High must have been my first perfect experience of continuing, concentrated hard work. I gave up school sports, movies, reading, just about everything that meant fun. Day after day, night after night, week after week, from September until February, I studied, getting up at six, often working until 1 A.M. During the five days of Regents Week I did take all ten of those exams, once taking three consecutively in a single day, in an unbroken nine-hour stretch, with a teacher staying on as proctor when I was the only pupil left in the school building.

And seven months of suspense lay ahead. I wouldn't know until the end of next summer whether I had won a scholarship or not.

The final entry in my "dear little book" is dated January 7, 1917. I had even given up writing in *it* for most of that semester. I did keep on sending in my stick or two of type to the *Evening Mail*, and earning my fifty or eighty cents or an occasional couple of dollars a week. But the school items and the cramming were still not the only things that occupied me.

Four months since I've written! That's awful & so many things have happened too—I've met Bernie, I got a new coat, my first taffeta afternoon dress, my first corset, my first real strong ambitions, also my first big trouble—

Mama's been quite sick. Pa thinks it's nothing though, even when the doctor thought there was danger of her falling into coma. That was two months ago—but she isn't so very well now. She's on a starvation diet to get pus out of her kidney...I'm so worried. Seems to me I'm the only one at home who is worrying.

I wonder whether I ought to go to Hunter. Sometimes...I think I might give it up and take stenography. I'm sure I'd make good, & mama would have eight dollars at least every week. She could go to the mountains...

I didn't say half enough about mama & I'm glad. There's no use trying to make sure I'll remember the terror. Bertha & Fred had to live with us a whole week. It was awful. And pa *showed* no sympathy or worry or anything...

I'm writing large and leaving big margins for a reason. In twenty-two days I begin college. I was going to write "maybe" but even the thought hurts. I want to begin a new [diary]. A new period of my life will begin. I hope it's a happy one. I used to think I could never be happy among Jewish people but now, since I met Bernie, and some of Eleanor's friends, I know that they can be just as American and nice as I am...

I just wrote, "Good night, little red book"—but I erased it in disgust. It does sound gushy—but what should I write? I feel like saying goodnight & I can't just say goodnight. I have to address something...if I were a fool I'd let myself kiss it—but I hope I'm not. Maybe when I write that I got a letter from B. I will!!! I *am* a fool.

39

Hunter College was, and is, situated at the very center of New York's fashionable and attractive Upper East Side, on Park Avenue in the Sixties, but that was about the only attractive thing about it. It took me only a few weeks to discover that going to Hunter was nothing like the dreams I'd had of college life. It seemed like another high school with longer assignments, with hours of travel instead of just a quick run down the hill from our house, first by Long Island Railroad to Penn Station, then by subway to Forty-second Street, then by shuttle across to the East Side, then again by subway up to Sixty-eighth Street—and the reverse every afternoon. There was no campus with leafy trees, no lovely buildings, no football games, no boys.

I began to skip classes, I did badly in exams, I dropped Latin entirely because I'd taken so many cuts in it, and I ended my first term, in June, with exactly half the credits I should have had.

I got a job as soon as vacation started, a real nine-to-five job, another first, to save money for—for what I didn't know. It was at the office of the Aeolian Piano Company in Long Island City. I was a file clerk, but at lunchtime I stayed in with my sandwich lunch from home, and took over the telephone switchboard, thinking it might be a skill I could use in a pinch in later life. I also set out to learn to type on the office typewriter, thinking that too might be a skill I could gainfully use some rainy day.

I earned nine dollars a week, having achieved this princely sum by machinations undreamed of by me before I hit the world of commerce. A coup to write about in my diary—but there was none.

For six months I had had no little red book to turn to. But these momentous events virtually demanded that I begin a new one, and in July I did, this one more normal in size, 7½ by 4½ inches, and opening sideways like a real book. I wrote in it not in the old childishly large penciled scrawl, but with ink and a fountain pen, in a more adult calligraphy. Boys and clothes still appear incessantly, plus a steady note of revulsion at my sister Alice and some of our friends for going out with soldiers—we had entered the Great War that spring—and letting the soldiers kiss them and neck with them. "Ugh! disgusting! I'd die before I'd let anybody..."

But my new job and my Machiavellian skill in negotiating for it received a big play in the new diary.

> I'm Miss Laura Z. Keane in the office. Joel said he admired my courage in doing it. It wasn't that at all. It was cowardice. The office manager is so very nice. I couldn't tell him Zametkin. He said, "Would you be willing to start at $8 or $9 a week?" I brightly answered, "When you say $8 or $9, do you mean $8—or $9?"
>
> I'm glad I did. It was businesslike, cute, clever. A nice combination....
>
> I just read my diary through. Am I honest or just conceited?

My sister also used my mother's name for the job she took that summer, though she did not add the letter *e*, which to me somehow seemed an essential act of balance and design, since there were five letters in my first name. Laura Z. Kean, I felt, looked lopsided, out of true, like the Leaning Tower of Pisa.

But Alice didn't take an office job, despite the munificent weekly pay every Saturday noon. She and two other girls, our new best friends whom we had met at Hunter, were waitresses at a seaside resort in Oceangrove, New Jersey, at four dollars per week plus board, so they could have afternoons off every day for swimming and sunbathing, and evenings off for dancing with the soliders from Fort Dix and all the army camps springing up everywhere.

My diary helped me here too.

> When I think of Rose & El & Al in Oceangrove—I pity myself, feel sorry, yet glad. I must admit a good deal of the gladness lies in the anticipation of ma & Mrs. Ford & Joel & Fred & Bertha & everybody admiring my courage & pluck & resolve. Plugging away in a hot city office. But also the rest of the gladness lies in my knowledge that I am accomplishing it, I'm reaching out for Cornell.

41

Off and on during the dismal months of Hunter, I'd wondered about other free colleges, like Ohio State or Michigan, and had even confided in my mother about it. But I never would have been able to afford holiday trips home, not even for summer vacations, and the very idea of losing me for an unbroken stretch of four years would bring tears to her eyes.

"I want to go to college," I wrote on July 4, 1917, as if I had not gone to Hunter at all.

> I want to go—to Cornell maybe. If ma & pa would go to Russia, my conscience would be eased. They won't tho. Will I ever go away to college, knowing that it would hurt ma so infinitely much? I hope so!! I can't live for ma. And yet I guess I will.

This daydream that shipped my parents so conveniently off to Russia, arose from all their joyous talk about the Russian Revolution, the first one, the moderate one in February, with Kerensky becoming Premier in early summer. Just as my penciled high school diary had never once mentioned church, so this collegiate one never found time for even a sentence about minor matters like America's entry into the Great War in Europe, or that first "good revolution" or the Bolshevik one that followed in October. All I could think of when I faced my diary was college and important things, and I kept on writing about that trip to Russia that would set me free.

> It's ugly, the way I feel. I honestly wish—honestly, coldly wish, that mama and papa would go to Russia—even tho— oh, I can't write it. Once I said to Rose that I would scarcely be grief-stricken if my mother and father were killed in a railroad accident. It's positively true. I'd say, I suppose and feel really, truly, pain, but oh, then I could live my life. I'm so selfish. And I can't help being. It's so unfair for me to give up all the wondrous plans for everything because it would hurt mama so.
>
> And yet I don't see why I feel that way either. I may go. I have her permission. It isn't her fault I won't go. It isn't her fault I won't be able to hurt her so . . . Heavens, it's hard.

And here began what was to be my first experience of betrayal by somebody I loved and trusted. (I almost wrote "loved & trusted" in true adolescent diary style.) It was my older brother Joel. I had been seeing him regularly for several weeks because he was a dentist, the family dentist when necessary, and in the late spring, playing tennis on a grass court that was newly rained upon, I had made a fancy swooping lunge for a low backhand, had fallen flat on my face and loosened my two front teeth. I had been trying to impress another boy, no doubt, named Bill Berke, changed from William Morris Berkowitz—we were all doing that that summer, getting our first jobs.

Inevitably I began to tell Joel what I felt about Hunter, how I longed for college that was *real*. He had gone to dental college himself, and he knew from the start how I felt. Of course it was Cornell I was saving for, of course that was why I had done all that crazy cramming to win a scholarship—not just for pin money and clothes, but Cornell.

One day he said he would see to it that I got there. My diary exulted.

> Joel seems positive that if I had my tuition paid, board for 5 weeks ahead, I absolutely could do it! I think so too. Joel admires 'push.' At first he said that he would pay half the difference between my $100 scholarship and the tuition fee. But we talked and then he said, 'You get your scholarship and you'll go to college.' Heavens, it would be wonderful.

And so the summer passed. One day I met a man on a train, Mr. Ferber, and he seemed to have some sort of literary influence on my life for rather a spell. "No relation to Edna," I told my diary, "and yet an acquaintance. What might that mean? He's so intelligent and courteous and everything that a man who speaks to a girl on a train merely because she's reading Ibsen's *Doll's House* should be."

He wasn't a boy, this Mr. Ferber, not related to Edna; he was a grown-up man. He told me I ought to try to get other school news assignments from other papers, and at once I set about the attempt. I went to the office of the *Tribune*, the *World*, the *Journal*, seeking further assignment. I began to read novels by Edna Ferber and Fannie Hurst.

My diary underwent a sea-change.

> I hardly know whether I like the office. I do yearn for the open...I like the work, but I do get so very tired. The 8-hr. day is so very endless. And then coming home. Jammed in among men and women, sweaty, smelly, hot. Women and men who jeer and joke in coarse language. And girls and men who are so tired. Like me. Only much more help-lessly worse. The pity of it all is that they don't pity them-selves. They accept it so very much for granted. It is as it should be, has been, and will be. Lord, *I'm* going to college. I have that.

The & was disappearing. I was taking the time to spell out *and*, and using a slew of new phrases. *So very much*, indeed.

> I told Joel about Mr. Ferber. He wasn't shocked...Joel is so very nice, so very interested in me, work, college plans, future, me, everything. I told him what I thought about me writing. It seems so remote, so rather improbable, that I, of all the girls I know who write good essays, peachy letters, get good marks, and whom I can't imagine are going to be writers—ever should succeed.
>
> I don't think I have more ability—truly, tho, I do—and so at times, at most times, perhaps, I was a wee bit dis-heartened. But I have a new axiom for myself. I think that a good many people—most people, who are clever at all, can write and talk, but that being a writer does not depend so much on inherent talent or genius but just on push...
>
> I've noticed how much I've improved with only Miss Parks' training. And so practise and determination and push is going to make me write. If I try hard enough, I'll write.
>
> I like Edna Ferber's writings. This is going to strike me queerly in time, but as I read her 'Fanny Herself,' I often feel that I'm reading my own stuff. I do write in her style. Short sentences. Queer little phrases.
>
> Oh, Lord, why can't I write a story? Is it that I haven't the 'push'? I wonder. No, I don't either. I know.

I was also reading a bit beyond Mr. Ferber's acquaintance.

> I dipped into Elizabeth Barrett Browning again. I do love the beginning of Aurora Leigh. I'm going to know that...going to study it. It is beautiful.... And a wee bit of G.B.S. His preface to the *Unpleasant Plays*. He is very wonderful, I *feel* that. I take Ibsen for granted.

And on summer Sundays there were still boys and romance — or the lack of same. Bernie still appears in the diary, and Bill Berke, who had given me my first nickname, Zowie, and another boy named Walter Conable, nephew of family friends, Giles and Winonah Ford, with a place at the beach.

> I paddled all the time practically. And swam a lot too. And enjoyed everything but Walter. He's such a fierce nut. He's tall—too tall. He looks like a beast. Not that he isn't handsome. I like tall, good-looking ugliness. But not his kind. His feet are so heavy and big. And he eats so much...I know I'm being snobbish but I can't help it. The way he takes one home! Grabs your elbow and hustles. Bill wouldn't [do any of that]. Bill wouldn't make me refuse 2 chocolate ice cream fraps.

It must have been a summer of mounting tension. At the end of July, with a whole month to go before I could hear from the Board of Regents at Albany, I wrote,

> I absolutely cannot imagine how I will react to the news that I did not get my scholarship. It's scarcely probable, but possible of course. I don't know. I'll be so shattered. It will be very, very hard.
> But somehow I don't imagine I won't get it. I tried so hard. And I have pretty nearly always succeeded at things. I think of nothing big that I attempted & failed. Things *are* easy.

And then at the end of August came the great news.

> I got a letter from Albany. I have my scholarship!!! Oh those crazy months of paralyzing doubt, and fears, and hopes,

and everything. And now this. I'm rather breathless. How in the world could they write such a sedate business-like letter? How could they keep from shouting it at me the way I feel like shouting it at everybody I meet in the street? Oh, oh, oh, at last Cornell is practically a certainty.

I'm still a bit worried about the fact that they haven't given me definite work, but I'm sure I'll get it. I wrote to Dr. Matske again tonight & begged her to hurry. Oh, I'll get there now. Four years of hard work, hard study, hard play. How I'm going to love them...

Oh, I'm a lucky girl—except for the impossibility of getting on with mama at home, and that's a lot—I'm afraid of marriage *just* because of that. One's character towards one's friends is not much—but towards one's mother—and I *can't* get on with ma. I get so irritated.

Bertha suggested that it's because ma's so terribly nervous and a wee bit cranky from living with a crank for years and years. That's a straw. But when Al, in a fight, says, "I pity your husband," I catch my breath. "So do I," I could almost say. And yet it hurts too much.

Is it just adolescence and youth's natural impatience with halfway querulous age?

I wonder.

I can't worry now. College is too near too dear a possibility. And I'm to be Laura Z. Keane, I believe I've decided. It's taken several months. First it was a joke. And then there was the office. And then everybody I know seriously advised my doing it—except pa and ma. I suppose it hurts them.

I really feel that mustn't stand in my way. And I'm not going to let it. It's a selfish viewpoint, but not a thoroughly selfish one. I've decided to the best of my ability that in every possible way—sheer vanity, convenience, *not* cowardice, I honestly believe, and horse sense—it is a wise thing to do.

I say the sheer vanity because a well-dressed college girl known in college as Zowie Keane is a pleasant picture. The rest is purer.

But Zowie Keane was not to go to Cornell that fall. The blow hit like the strike of a hammer, after I had begun to pack, after

I had told all my friends, after I had told all the people at the office during my last week there.

We all bear sudden blows as we go through life, learn to absorb the shock of smashed hope, but the news that Joel had changed his mind was my initial discovery of that special anguish that comes from a shattered trust.

Even turning to my little red book could not help me much.

Sept. 15, 1917. Back at Hunter. Last Sunday night I found out. Joel went back on me. All summer long he said, "Laura you get you're scholarship and you're going, and if you're in trouble write to me." More definitely, "Laura make a list of what you're going to need and what you've got and I'll see about the rest."

When I was filling out the blanks for application for work up there, he wouldn't here of my wanting domestic work of any kind, (like waiting tables.) When I said I could manage on one regular meal and the rest in my room, he fell on me for a fool. I found that I would have to spend the fifty dollars I'd saved for clothes, and that therefore after I paid tuition for the first semester, and fare and matriculation and books, I would be about $15 in debt—and not a day's board. I thought and worried all week and went to Joel last Saturday and told him and was confident.

First he suggested that I buy *no* clothes but go up just as I was dressed. I explained that if I had what a normal girl had, I would. But I had no underwear, or nighties, or stockings, or even hairpins. No hairbrush and comb, no gloves, no anything.

He saw I needed pretty nearly all the fifty. Then he suggested waiting table. I was staggered. Then he suggested eating one meal a day and getting the rest in my room. And then—"Why don't you go back to Hunter?"

And back to Hunter is where I went.

When I did finally get to Cornell two long years later, I went as Laura K. Zametkin. Neither Anna Mathes nor Alva Ritter nor Kenneth were there; years later I heard that Anna had become head file clerk at a branch of the New York Telephone Company, and that Alva and Jean had married. I never did hear what Kenneth went on to do or be.

47

But my forced return to Hunter didn't say to me, Well, you can quit your part-time jobs, now you don't have to save for anything beyond pin money and clothes. Cornell stayed in my bloodstream. I kept right on with the items for the school page, but I began a determined search for after-school work with some real money attached to it.

I tried being what was then called a governess, not a baby sitter, to two small children in a wealthy family in Westchester, commuting there by train after classes each afternoon, and then, once the kids were in bed, commuting back to New York, only to go on to my regular commute home to Jamaica the same evening. Fortunately I was fired after one week, so any collapse from overwork was mercifully averted.

And at last my search for a great big high-salaried after-school job produced a glorious result. I saw an ad in the *Times* for a night clerk to take classified ads over the phone; I went after it, landed it, and went to work from 5 to 9:30 P.M. every day. My pay was a dollar less than my high-priced summer job, but $8 a week seemed huge for only a half-time job. And the paper was nothing less than the New York *Times* itself.

Never mind that all I did was take Help Wanted ads over the telephone, never mind that I never saw a reporter or editor or city room; what counted then was that day after day I went to Times Square and entered that citadel of the press, not as a sightseer but by right, and that my memo pads and blank forms where I took down those condensed words about rooms for rent or situations wanted—that these all bore across their tops the legend of the world's greatest newspaper.

So much did I love being right on the staff of a paper that my heart's desire changed from wanting to write for a paper to a simpler one. "I want to work on the business end of a newspaper," I told the final pages of my teenage diary. Perhaps I doubted that I could ever get a full-time job as a writer or reporter, but knew I had already proved myself up to the demands of the business side.

After exactly eight weeks, the assistant manager, a Mr. Kenney, fell ill and I was promoted to assistant manager. Still at the same eight dollars, but a title!

The heady excitement assuaged some of my grief about Cornell, but did not, could not eradicate it for good. I stopped thinking about what my brother Joel had done, but could never quite forget it enough to feel close to him again. When I began to write this book, I asked my nephew, Robert Zametkin, Joel's only son (Joel stayed a Zametkin all his life, though Alice and Fred, both being teachers, had had their surname legally changed to Kean, without the balancing *e*) when I asked Bob whether he knew about this Cornell episode, he said, "I did know there was some sort of fracas between the two of you," but he was none too clear about specifics.

He is a man of seventy now, nephew though he be. He and his wife Olga have recently had their own fortieth anniversary, and their three grown children are all Zametkins. When I became Aunt Laura at the age of eleven, and my sister Aunt Alice, it seemed a family joke, always good for a laugh. Joel had married the daughter of another of the pioneers in the Jewish-socialist-labor movement, a writer and editor too, Benjamin Feigenbaum, also mentioned by Irving Howe as "a veteran of the eighties . . . an uncompromising assimilationist," totally opposed, as my father was, to the concept of nationalism, of Jewish nationalism, bemoaning that "mishmash of the Russian-Hebrew-German jargon" as he did.

Bob is retired now, but unhesitatingly described himself as a capitalist all his life, perhaps with a fling of defiance at both his socialist grandfathers. He is a wealthy man, possibly a millionaire, a graduate chemist who made his fortune in the manufacture of chemicals, doing well from the start but becoming wealthy when he opened a plant in Morganton, North Carolina, where labor was then dirt cheap and unions unheard of. Lucky for him his grandparents were long since silent!

He did remember certain other matters more distinctly. The story went that I had once saved his life when he was caught in the sharp undertow of the Atlantic Ocean at Long Beach, when he was a boy of nine. I was twenty then, a college girl in my own eyes at last, and visiting them at their cottage one Sunday afternoon.

I was a strong swimmer. For several summers my mother

had taken Alice and me to live in a "tent city" on the beaches of Edgemere, Long Island, and then at Cornell there were the wonderful swimming holes down at the bottom of Ithaca's deep beautiful gorges.

Bob knew that "saving-his-life" story, but when I said, "I bet you'd have made it out all by yourself," he rather seemed to agree that he would have, if only everybody would have waited long enough to give him a chance. The only primary memory I have of the whole affair was of a little blond-haired boy who looked about six inches tall under a crashing wave that seemed to tower a good forty feet above him.

One thing I asked Bob about. This was not back to childhood but after my marriage, during the Depression, in 1933, and once again it dealt with Joel. I was writing advertising copy for B. Altman & Company in New York, and one morning Joel telephoned me there to ask if I could see him right away. It was urgent. He would leave his office at Borough Hall in Brooklyn and come to New York; he would be at the corner of Madison Avenue and Thirty-fourth Street in half an hour and wait there for me. His voice seemed strange.

I met him. I had begun to go to a dentist in the city after college, and had seen Joel only a few times in the last ten or twelve years, and then only in family situations. I don't think we ever once mentioned the Cornell debacle.

That day we walked up and down Madison Avenue. He looked stricken, miserable, old. "Marion has polio," he blurted out after a moment. Marion was his younger child, Bob's sister, her name spelled with an *o* instead of the usual *a*. She was my niece, my only niece, then just starting out at college. At Cornell—where else?

Joel's voice broke as he said *polio*; nobody knew yet how serious it might be, whether she would come through it. He had spent everything he had on hospitals and doctors. Could I lend him some money?

My nephew Bob had never known about that trip of his father's to see me in New York. I told him of my surprise that Joel could ever be needing money, for I had always thought of him with a big, successful and prosperous practice.

"Not by that time," Bob said. "My mother had to go back to teaching, and it wasn't easy to get back into the school system at her age."

Bob remembered the family anguish of waiting during Marion's siege of polio. She did at last recover after about a year, with only a slight limp as her permanent badge of tribulation.

He asked me what I had said to Joel and how much I had lent him, and I said I didn't remember. I really don't. It couldn't have been much—I was earning seventy-five dollars a week. But I do remember that we stopped finally at the corner of Madison and Thirty-fifth Street, that I opened my purse, drew out my checkbook and wrote a check then and there.

I saw very little of Joel for the rest of his life. Ten years after that trip of his to ask for help, he died of a heart attack. He was sixty, and if he had ever once felt any remorse over that "fracas" between us, he kept it to himself to the very end.

What finally had made me a co-ed on the campus at Ithaca was in its way a fluke, earning me the only big money I ever saw during my school years. It happened in the summer of 1919, the first summer after the war, when everything seemed to be booming and the want ads were teeming with jobs at fancy pay.

My sister and I spotted a dozen that offered an unheard-of $30 a week, which would mean a haul of $240 each by the end of summer. The trouble was that the ads were for "slender young ladies to model clothes" for dress manufacturers in the garment district of New York.

Alice and I instantly decided to go after one. But we were both wary about the perils that might beset us, lounging around half-dressed behind the scenes, between the official "showings" to the out-of-town buyers.

We didn't tell our parents what we were contemplating because we well knew the fierce opposition we would meet, papa talking about showing off your body for money, virtual prostitution, and mama reminding us of the statistics of the White Slave Traffic, still flourishing according to Hearst.

So we went to no interview except together, in pairs, like nuns. We were both hired by a leading cloak and suit house,

Fishman and Nathanson, on Union Square, ending our nine-teenth summer not only with a private hoard but with marked-down tweed suits, the first high-fashion each of us had ever been able to call our own.

To this day I can imitate that strange "model walk," pelvis thrust slightly forward, a few short steps forward, a turn, a swift glance right and left at an imaginary audience of buyers. And to this day I know what they mean when they talk of "important clothes."

It was that blessed $240 that suddenly made Cornell mine. Never before had such a sum materialized before me in the space of eight weeks; eight hundred sticks of school news wouldn't have equaled such wealth; countless hours at want ad phones of the *Times* couldn't yield it in the one neat instant package.

Of course that $240 didn't do it all alone; I knew I'd have to keep on earning money, and I began to see that I would also have to borrow some as well. But now I had a solid base to stand on. Now I could do it. At last I was going to be a Cornellian.

I'VE OFTEN HEARD it said that to a novelist, nothing is ever lost, that every scrap of his of her past life somehow finds its way to a future use, large or small, in some piece or work, perhaps half a century in the future.

Tonight I think it must be so. In my ninth novel, there is an imaginary title of an imaginary short story. It's part of a minor subthread in the book, when its young heroine, Jossie, to comfort herself in an unhappy period, tries to write her first story. A title comes to her—from where she does not know—and she sets it down on a sheet of paper, printing it in block letters, and centering it on the page, as though it were already in type in some magazine with her own name beneath it.

THE FLAME-COLORED EVENING DRESS

As I was writing about troubled Jossie and her sudden acquisition of a title for a story, I was nearing eighty, and like Jossie, I had no idea where her title had come from. I liked it, and let Jossie use it for her story, and there it stands, now on page 99 of a published book, *Untold Millions.*

And tonight, slightly troubled myself, in a writer's familiar dilemma about how best to proceed from one point in a man-uscript to the next—tonight I suddenly discover where that flame-colored evening dress came from.

I was going through the last three entries of that girlhood diary, trying to decide whether to skip over the rest of my college days, and I came on the hidden clue. This was before Cornell, still during my miserable days at Hunter, and for a class assign-ment I had written *my* first short story.

"My story is the reason why all the moping pain I might have had about my terribly discouraging year is not," the third entry from the last says.

> I worked hard on the story and I enjoyed the working. I loved the old story. Dr. Williams sent it to me today. She called several parts of it, "Good Work" and of the end said, "This is a particularly capital conclusion. You do econom-ically all you meant to accomplish by way of thematic value," or something like that.
>
> She said the story was excellently written. . . . quite as well done as many from her short story class (at Columbia School of Journalism, where she had night courses.) And I'm will-ing to wager that I'm anywhere from four to 12 years younger than most of her pupils. They are mostly mature men and women who are studying the short story with the idea of becoming writers themselves. And I'm only a kid really and I haven't had any training or any experience either. Oh I'm glad.
>
> She pointed out a flaw in the technique—that I'd prom-ised the reader the treat of the dancing spectacle and then didn't give it, and also things about suspense and all. But that's technique. And technique is easy to acquire.

How I wish that I'd saved that first short story. All my diary gives me is its title. If I were to center it on a sheet of paper as Jossie did with her story it would read:

CHEEKS AND FROCKS, FLAME-COLORED

Nothing ever came of Jossie's story in my novel; nor did anything come of "Cheeks and Frocks, Flame-Colored." But when I finally got to Cornell on an early September day in 1919 and had my first meeting that week with my faculty adviser, I happily told him that I had no problems about what courses I wanted to take—they would all deal with writing: the short story, the novel, journalism, everything that bore directly or indirectly on the field of writing.

"*Cacoethes scribendi*," he said in a chiding voice, and then seeing my lack of comprehension, he gently translated, "The itch to scribble."

He was Lane Cooper, one of several professors then famous in the English department. "*Cacoethes scribendi*," he repeated, this time less gently. "If you wish to write, study Greek. Study the Greek classics. Educate yourself. If the writing is there, it will follow."

And study Greek I did. Not one of the credits I earned toward my degree at Cornell was in a course that might be called a course in writing. After a year of that Baby Greek course, meaning beginner's Greek, that met six mornings a week at 8 A.M., I was permitted to skip the second year and go straight on to third-year Greek, studying some of the plays of Aeschylus, Euripides, Sophocles in their original. And the New Testament in Greek.

I loved Greek. I loved to write its letters; they looked more beautiful than English letters, more ornamental, indeed even architectural. And how could the soft sounds of *alpha*, *beta*, *gamma*, *delta*, *epsilon* compare to the hard, curt sounds of *a*, *b*, *g*, *d*, *e*?

I also enrolled in another stiff course, not for "average students," Professor Cooper's own course, Translations of the Greek Classics. We were a selected handful of eight or nine, meeting only once a week in a kind of seminar, given assignments the likes of which I'd never heard in all my years of schooling.

"For next week, read the first sixteen pages of Aristotle's *De Poetica*," Professor Cooper said as the first session drew to a close. Only sixteen pages for a whole week? We students looked at each other. Was this going to turn out to be a cinch course after all?

At the end of the second week's class, the professor said,

55

"Your assignment for next week is to read the first sixteen pages of Aristotle's *De Poetica*."

And at the end of the third week—yes, the same sixteen pages. If any of us had started out thinking him peculiar or crotchety or mad, we soon grew out of the notion, for of course, we discovered soon enough what *study* meant in this professor's mind. On page four of the *Poetica*, for example, there were references to Empedocles, to the *Iliad* of Homer, and the *Centaur* of Chaeremon, all of which we had glided over the first time round and even the second.

By the third week, we were going to the Libe, and looking them all up in the *Brittanica*, or even reading some parts of the works themselves, and certainly getting some notion about what the works were and who their authors, and perhaps some glimmer of what Aristotle was driving at when he compared them. And seeing the justice of Lane Cooper's analogy, in brackets on that same page, "A similar distinction might be drawn between the poetry of Wordsworth and the versified botany of Erasmus Darwin."

How many times in my working life, when I have gone back at some balky paragraph again and again, gone back at some unsatisfying scene over and over, rewriting and rewriting, shifting emphasis here, subtracting verbiage there, clarifying, striking out what I always called "pear-shaped prose" in so-called beautiful writing by various contemporary authors—how often have I acknowledged my debt to those impossible Lane Cooper assignments that trained me to reject surfaces and dig below, to keep at it and at it and at it.

I was an honor student at Cornell, with an official notification on white vellum to that effect from the dean of the College of Arts and Sciences. But I never made Phi Beta Kappa, and the private story I was told about why not when my grades were so high, was another facet of my "education." In that uncatalogued, unnamed course, Antisemitism I.

Before the Phi Beta Kappa story, I'd had some preliminary coaching on the subject. One of my new friends at Cornell, Janet Gregg MacAdam, had the difficult task of telling me she would be putting me up for membership in Kappa Kappa Gamma, the most elite of sororities on campus, except that I wasn't "uh-uh-eligible."

At Hunter I had belonged to a nonsectarian sorority, Sigma Alpha Gamma, and at Cornell I was invited to be "rushed" by Sigma Delta Phi, originally Sigma Delta Gamma, then not very large, having only seven members, and nicknamed by a few campus bigots as Seven Doity Gews because of its original initials.

Apparently I knew even then that I didn't want to belong to anything that was all-Jewish, any more than I did to anything that was all Christian. I had never heard the word *restricted* as yet, but I sure knew what it meant. I wrote a formal letter of regret.

But the great wound of my youth was connected with Phi Beta. The story was told to me, in confidence, by a young assistant professor in the English department, Harry Caplan, then young enough to be friends with some of the seniors, later on to become famous himself to decades and decades of Cornellians.

He seemed bitter as he told me, almost driven to tell me, as if he had to defy the general rule that nobody on the faculty was ever to reveal anything that might be construed as nasty about the internal workings of things at Cornell.

There was a "personality movement" afoot, he said, in all the honor societies at the university that year, including Phi Beta Kappa itself. The feeling had been growing among the trustees and among some of the faculty as well that the general character of the honor societies had been changing in certain unacceptable ways in recent years.

"Too many greasy little grinds from New York," he said, "not enough people from other parts of the country." Not enough campus men, not enough athletes, not enough people who were more representative of America as a whole.

"It's a Jew clean-up," he ended. "They don't call it that, but that's just what it is. You look over the lists when they come out in the *Sun*." The *Sun* was the campus newspaper.

I did look. And not a name looked anything like Zamooski or Cohen or Epstein or Fineberg.

The only decent part of what Harry Caplan told me, the only part that made it bearable was about Lane Cooper. "At the meeting, Lane Cooper put his key down on the table and said he would resign if that sort of thing could happen in Phi Beta Kappa."

I loved Professor Cooper for putting his key on the table, though it could not remove the wound. But all wounds heal and this one lost its lurid vividness in due time. Though it must have become once again visible enough a quarter-century later when I began to write my second novel, *Gentleman's Agreement*.

And yet it was that very novel that was to cancel out that image of Professor Cooper taking off his beloved key and laying it upon the table. To my profound astonishment it was Lane Cooper himself who did the canceling. That was in 1947, and I was being interviewed about *Gentleman's Agreement* for Cosmopolitan magazine by Robert Van Gelder. It made a stunning anecdote for the interview, and of course Mr. Van Gelder printed every word of it.

Soon after there came a letter from Professor Cooper himself, addressed to me, sternly stating that the tale of the key was preposterous and totally untrue. He had never put his Phi Beta Kappa key down on any table in any offer to resign; he would never, not for any reason whatsoever, and whoever had told me such a taradiddle was inventing it.

Well, maybe. I saw Professor Caplan only once after that interview and that letter of denial, but I never told him of it. Long before then I had decided whom to believe and what to credit, and I have kept on believing Professor Caplan's tale, intact, alpha to omega.

But I still am grateful for that admonition to study Greek, educate yourself. *Cacoethes scribendi* must be a semaphore forever shining somewhere in my mind.

There were plenty of nonwounding things at Cornell though; the physical beauty of the place seems to have struck some latent nerve of response that had never really been touched before. The hills, the 250-foot gorges and ravines, the eternal shimmer of Lake Cayuga far down below the hill—all of it became a daily awareness somewhere inside me.

And despite all the study, I had fun: I made the Girls' Crew and won my numerals; I won them again on the Girls' Field Hockey Team; I played the romantic male lead in the annual play of the Women's Dramatic Club, and was elected to full membership. The play was Percy MacKaye's *A Thousand Years Ago*, and my scrapbook has not only the program and large pictures of the large cast, but also snapshots of the flowers I got and a letter to my parents: "Everybody is saying I should go on the stage."

There were boys too—college men as they were known by then, a Bill MacMillen who took me to my first college prom, me in largely borrowed evening finery, and then a track star, a student of the College of Agriculture, thus a Cornell Aggie. He was Simon Abrahams, nicknamed Jim by me, because I didn't like Si.

I thought I was in love, and he thought he was, and gave me a watch as an unofficial engagement present because I wouldn't take a ring, and because he, not being a fraternity man, couldn't "pin" me. Jim was a year ahead of me, and going to South Africa for three years, as soon as he had his degree, to enter his family's business, something to do with sheep, either breeding them or selling their wool and skins. I was to follow a year later and be married in Cape Town. When he sailed on the old *Imperator*, I was, in classic fashion, at the dock waving, weeping as the water widened between ship and pier.

But before many months of absence had gone by, as his letters had begun to arrive, as I began to wonder why they seemed so ordinary, even so boring, I began to have doubts about how much in love I really was. I began to wonder what life with a track star in the sheep business in South Africa would be like, and what Jim, bereft of cinder track and running shorts, would be like.

I never thought then of living among political horrors like apartheid; I was, as yet, totally unpolitical, and was to remain so through most of my twenties, except for voting for Alfred E. Smith because the anti-Catholic screaming in the presidential campaign of 1928 struck me as disgusting, and except for bouts of periodic rage about Sacco and Vanzetti or the Ku Klux Klan. I think now that my political passivity during the first years of my adult life must have risen from some interior protest against the endless political energy of my mother and father, but quite possibly that's merely me forgiving me.

In any case, long before my own graduation approached, and many months before I would have to arrange my own passage on the *Imperator*, I had to write Jim and tell him. It hurt; it must have hurt him too.

But that was my senior year at Cornell, and it teemed with matters more immediate than life after college, in Cape Town or anywhere else. There was an annual contest every year for the Barnes Shakespeare Prize; I had tried for it in my junior year, working fiendishly hard on it, and somebody else won it with an essay I never read but whose title I envied: "Shakespeare the Singer."

Stubbornly I tried all over again in my senior year, with no such poetic title to help my cause. I'm supposed to be good at titles, but if I am, it's a trait that developed much later. Today I might call that essay "Shakespeare and Guilt," but back then I burdened it with the ponderous phrase, "The Mental Response to Shakespeare."

And this time, heavyweight title and all, I did win the prize and the noble sum of fifty dollars that went with it. Students had to use pseudonyms on the papers they submitted, and the first time I had used "Simpson Brahms," for Si Abrahams, for Jim was still on campus. A year later, I signed myself Michael Keane, perhaps thinking that parents were luckier than track stars.

The small task I set myself in the essay was to compare the tragedies of "thundering Aeschylus" with those of "King Shakespeare." Nothing less.

Greek tragedy, I wrote, is "analogous to a sudden . . . clash of battle, a flash of a martial picture, impressive and terrible." A tragedy by Shakespeare "contains that but is more. It is more than photography, it is history. . . . there are vast differences between the two, vast enough to span two thousand years of dramatic development."

Aeschylus, for instance, has Agamemnon make his entrance when everything is set for his murder "except for his presence on the stage." The Greek chorus has already told the audience of his dark deeds in the ten preceding years—but that is narration, not drama. Agamemnon himsclf—the tragic hero—speaks only eight-two lines of the entire play!

The audience responds with pity and fear—catharsis—but that is a response of emotion, not of intellect.

Shakespeare, I contended, could never be satisfied with third-person summary or narrative. In all his great tragedies he makes us see the plotting, the conspiring, the evil deeds from the moment they begin. We watch Macbeth and his lady not only through the first murder to make him king of Scotland, but then through all his fears, his hallucinations, his necessities for new assassinations because of his inner torment—"He shall sleep no more, Macbeth shall sleep no more."

It is that relentless struggle to vanquish his guilt that "one watches . . . not only with emotions aroused, but with his intellectual faculties as well."

Thus, in briefest terms, the mental response of my title. "With the march of centuries," I wrote, "with the change from the simplicity of the Doric portico to the infinite variety of Westminster Abbey, came dramatic evolution, and in Shakespeare there is wealth."

The essay was five thousand words long, larded with quotation from the text of plays, every other page paved with footnotes in true college-thesis fashion. Recently I got a copy of it from the archives at the Cornell library and was duly impressed—I couldn't write that essay now!

The first telegram I cver received in my life is pasted into my scrapbook.

CONGRATULATIONS WE ARE PROUD OF YOU MOTHER AND FATHER.

They had never once signed themselves mother and father, but they must have felt the need for formal language to conceal their springing pride in their daughter.

I don't know how proud of myself I was, way back there in May of 1921, but I must have recognized the distance my writing had come from the "monstrous beaver" of my high school days.

* * *

61

My letters home, I think, tell more about me during those years at Ithaca than any scholarly essay ever could. I was apparently on good terms with both my parents then; they saved several of my letters, which I came upon when they were both gone, and the house in Jamaica was being emptied and sold.

"Dear Family" or "Dear ma and pa" was the salutation in all of them, except for the twelve-pager I finally got around to sending my father on his play, *A Russian Shylock*.

It wasn't an easy assignment. Not that it was such a bad play—to this day copies are in Harvard's Widener Library and at Brown University, as well as in the main branch of the New York Public Library.

The basic plot deals with the revenge a rich Jewish merchant plans on the Russian government when it rules that only Christians, no Jews, may be employed in his district. The letter I finally managed to write about it was as stiff as if I were doing a critique for a class paper, filled with references to Sophocles, Shakespeare, Bernard Shaw—twelve pages of evasiveness and uncomfortable praise.

Not once did I come right out and say, "It's a good idea but it's too talky—not enough action—too many speeches and soliloquies." The only time I did let myself go was over one phrase of his: "It's too good to be—false."

Here I perked up a little courage. "It's the sort of paradox Oscar Wilde, the lord of language, would write and I don't like it."

But in general I was either so tactful or so erudite that he must have known I was in deep hot water under all the thin ice. I ended the letter, "I was proud to do it, pa."

Other letters were full of clothes I did or didn't have, about my joy when pa got a raise and they sent me some money so I could buy a spring coat I was dying for, and even about the joy of thinking.

> I have just finished a 30-page paper on Kant. It was work incarnate but I loved it. Kant the Obscure is now partly mine...Certain things in the Kantian doctrine alleviate, others contribute to my own little religious turmoil that

began again several months ago and which has raged right through the little systems of the philosophers.

But certain things are beginning to congeal with certainty—I think. Most important, perhaps a mistrust of the materialistic arrogant attitude I used to accept, that what *man* cannot *prove*, simply cannot exist. Of course man is the measure of the universe, and there just cannot be any reality if man cannot see it!!!!!

Well, I'm shaken out of that, for one thing. And I'm almost ready to accept the fact that there may be a reality which by its nature cannot be *known*, which cannot be demonstrated but which we must accept with assurance.

But it's just a something with a small *s* still for me; I can't worship it or pray to it, any more than I do to the principle of gravity.

Also I can't see immortality—how can Tennyson write "In Memoriam," part of which is so *radiant* with light and tolerance, and still have faith that he'll meet A.H.H. in a life to come? Oh well, I'm still struggling.

I can see why my parents saved those letters from their student-daughter, I suppose, but there is one other letter saved all these years by *me*. I had sent my mother for her birthday a small bit of sentimentality as a present, a framed picture of a young mother rocking a cradle, looking off into the distance, her face speculative, and I hate to admit that it bore the mawkish title of "Dreams" or "Dreaming." I also wrote something equally mawkish on the back of it, about the two kinds of dreams she must have had all along, one for us and one for her newspaper work.

> My dear Laura,
>
> Your dear little present stirred up the foolish sentimental heart of mine. I had a good cry over it, but soon became calm and happy at the thought of how much deep feeling towards me you expressed by this little gift of yours.
>
> You're doubly dear to me, child...I have no words to express my bliss when I think of the warmth you show with your solicitude for my welfare and your unmistaken interest in my work...

It's by deep intuition that you gave the picture...the double interpretation which both fit my case exactly. I was the mother who dreamed dreams, and the cradle by my side pulled me away, and I had to give up, until the dreams for my own rosy future turned into dreams...for my little ones. At present both kinds of dreams are realized, thank goodness, but much hard struggle had to be put up until it became so.

With Joel at my side from the first day of my honeymoon, more than usual good spirit was needed to keep the honey from turning sour, and when Freddie came, the dreams which I dreamed had to be put aside for another while.

When I decided to become an independent woman and shake off the yoke of housewifery, Fred was 2½ and Joel 8½. I entered dental college in Philadelphia, leaving them at home with a nice old friend, the landlady of the house. For six weeks my heart was torn between the glorious pleasure of the college lectures and the different tales at home about Joel's naughtiness and Freddie's cuttings-up.

I took Fred to day nurseries... but the poor children there were all so underfed, so listless, so unhappy... that my heart would revolt at the idea of entrusting my beautiful healthy boy to the tender mercies of the caretakers of those institutions.

I tried everything but finally had to give up the dreaming. I dropped college and became the housewife, but not the typical one. I could not shake off the habit of dreaming, if not for myself, then there were others to dream for. I infused the dreaming element in all my pupils, and did the best I knew how to help make the world a fitter place to live in. . . .

But my dreams [were not] a fabric of ungrounded illusions, for at this moment, at the decline of my life, I find myself still spinning out dreams...with such satisfaction to my heart, so much appreciation of all my beloveds and such substantial regard from my readers.

Dearest Lol, may your little gift's meaning react upon the giver and may you dream first for yourself, in order that you may later dream for others, which is really the only thing to make us happy.

Your Ma

As I copy out this letter, though I wince at times, my mind seems to hold it up in a sort of challenge to all the angry young wives and mothers of so many recent novels, raging against the sandboxes and diapers and string beans and pacifiers in their drab lives. Try it yourself, I want to say to them. You can do what she did; just try! She fulfilled both sides of her nature sixty years ago, seventy years ago, and other women have done it too. Try! If you want to enough and are loving enough and strong enough, perhaps you will find your own ways to do it too.

She was fifty-seven when she wrote that letter, and often ill because of her chronic diabetes. But a year later, when Commencement Day at last rolled around, nothing could have kept her from coming up to Ithaca, to be right there with all the other proud mothers and fathers.

It never even occurred to my father that he might also go, but just as he had never been the kind of father who took us to the park or the movies or played games with us, so he had never gone to any of the other things fathers went to, class days, school plays, high school graduation. I was used to that feeling: your father was off on a lecture tour or tied to the paper or just swamped with work; only your mother came to your days of glory.

And when Commencement Day did arrive at Cornell, there she was on campus, ready for it. But once again she did it differently from everybody else's mother. Ordinary parents came by train or automobile, but my mother came in the sidecar of my brother Fred's adored Harley-Davidson motorcycle, squeezed into the little contraption at its side.

And so she saw me in my cap and gown, and her eyes filled, as I knew they would. She told me once that as she watched me go by in the procession, she kept thinking, Well, Laura did it; she hated Hunter and wanted to go to Cornell and all by herself she did it.

That wasn't quite true; she had sent me a few dollars every once in a while to help me manage. In any case it had come true, I had my B.A. and now dear college days were over. Yea Cornell!

FOUR

MY FIRST REAL JOB and my first real love were inter-twined experiences, and they both began about two years after I was out of college.

Not that I was for two whole years jobless—or for that matter loveless—but the romantic episodes were still very girlish and chaste ("I never have!"), and the jobs were all stopgaps, better than nothing while I kept hunting for work I could be happy doing.

That should have meant a job on a newspaper. But I had indeed borrowed money, a good deal more than I had at first thought would be necessary. At the beginning they were small sums, twenty dollars from my mother, twenty from some of her friends, even tens and twenties from some of her pupils, with no collateral anywhere except my promise to pay it back the minute I was out of college. And up at Ithaca I borrowed several times from the Student Loan Fund as well.

And so, once I was out, when job-seeking became the central concern of life, the idea of newspaper work had to be put aside for something where raises were said to come more rapidly. I was in $1,200 worth of debt, a sum that loomed as large then as a $10,000 debt would seem to a college graduate today. The largest amounts were to the university, at five percent interest, repayable in ten years, so they could be put out of mind, but the private debts, with no mention of interest, and often made by people with scarcely any extra money for their own needs—these stood there like dark boulders in the path ahead of me.

I felt I had no choice but to turn my back on Park Row and Times Square, where all the main newspapers were, and look instead to what we today would call Madison Avenue.

Except that my first full-time copywriting job was nowhere near Madison Avenue, and it was nepotism that landed it for me. Bertha's sister was married to an adman, Gabriel Heatter, who was later to become famous as the radio broadcaster who greeted his adoring public each evening with the phrase, "There's good news tonight."

He had a small agency, three or four small rooms, down on Lafayette Street, south of Wanamaker's. My first assignment was to extol Midol, a medication for the relief of menstrual cramps, a matter one couldn't even hint at in those respectable bowdlerized days. I do not know what I did manage to say about Midol; thanks be, I had not yet begun to keep a proofbook of my advertising copy.

But then in 1923 came the real thing, a job as cub copywriter with George Batten Company at $25 a week, $108 a month. Batten was no little pipsqueak place downtown; it was on Fourth Avenue at about Twenty-eighth Street, in a real office building a few blocks north of the old Madison Square Garden, with big offices and carpeted floors and a reception room and a president and many vice-presidents and copy chiefs and many copywriters, of which I fast became the fair-haired girl. To be writing copy for Batten, even then, before it united with another agency to become Batten, Barton, Durstine and Osborne, the prestigious B.B.D. & O., was to have started at the top of the heap. I just knew I was going to make good.

There was also at Batten a copywriter who was twenty-eight, a Princeton man, handsome, witty, attractive and married, a man named Thomas Ernest Mount. He had already written a short story that Mencken had printed in Smart Set, and meant to write others, perhaps even a book, for which he was already

67

keeping a notebook of ideas, phrases, bits of scenes. I was sure he would. He *sounded* like a writer.

He was unlike any man I had ever known; he made people like Jim Abrahams and Bill MacMillen at Cornell seem like college adolescents who were still proud of having to shave every day, and compared to him, my different bosses in the *Times* Classified Ad department seemed like humdrum office workers. Tom's only liability, as I first met him, was not so much his being married but his being not very tall—I never wore high-heeled pumps when we went out dancing. But he had thick brown hair, brown eyes, features so regular that he looked like a darker version of Scott Fitzgerald, whom he had known at Princeton, then the most famous young author in the world because of *This Side of Paradise*, published three years before, and *The Beautiful and the Damned*, two years later.

That first story Tom Mount had sold to Mencken was, in its way, a writing link to Scott Fitzgerald, and years later, in Fitzgerald's famous series of articles about himself, "The Crack-Up," Scott remembers back to his own first story and to Tom's.

They were both working at the Street Railway Advertising Company; Tom had his degree from Princeton, but Scott had left college early, without getting his. Scott had just "retired from business," as he put it, "not on my profits, but on my liabilities, which included debts, despair, and a broken engagement, and crept home to St. Paul to finish a novel." That was in 1920.

> Even having a first story accepted, had not proved very exciting. Dutch Mount and I sat across from each other in a car-card slogan advertising office, and the same mail brought each of us an acceptance check from the same magazine—the old Smart Set.
> My check was thirty—how much was yours?
> Thirty-five.
> The real blight, however, was that my story had been written in college two years before, and a dozen new ones hadn't even received a personal letter.

Tom had not written a dozen new ones by the time we met in the fall of 1923; I can't remember whether he had submitted any at all. But when he gave me that first triumph of his to read, and then read me bits from his notebook for the book he was planning, I knew that he was going to deal with loftier themes than the jazz age and its frivolities, like Scott's first two and the formula stories he was turning out for The Saturday Evening Post.

From the moment Tom and I met, I knew at last what people meant when they said, "When the real thing happens, you just know it." I knew it, and apparently Tom knew it too.

I was twenty-three, I had never been seriously in love and I was beginning to be vaguely distressed about my continuing state of "not knowing." I may have begun to wonder about my unchanging status as virginal girl, just as I had years before become so anxious about my not having "begun" at thirteen, fourteen, fifteen.

One evening, at home in Jamaica and in some mood of high spirits, I suddenly announced to both my mother and father, "If I've never been in love by the time I'm twenty-five, I'm going to have about twenty keys made to my front door and hand them out to everybody I know." I was living in a furnished room in the city by then, the first place of my own, going home for weekends. My mother looked shocked but laughed; my father remained composed but did not speak. His face, however, went red.

Tom was punctilious about telling me he was married. Having been that forthright, he proceeded as if he were not married at all, and in exactly the same way, I proceeded as if he were not married at all.

His wife Olive had been a nightclub singer when they met, a bit older than he, with two small sons by a previous marriage. When she and Tom married, he had legally adopted the two boys, so he was already a father as well as a husband. It was an open marriage, a modern marriage, with both of them "free to live their own lives." Now she was in Paris, studying opera, planning to stay abroad for a year or two, perhaps longer.

Possibly the sheer fact of her physical absence made me more able and willing to overlook her existence. Possibly that ocean of separation made it easier for Tom to overlook it too.

I do not know. I do not like people who always blame the other person when a love affair or marriage fails, and though it took me years to see it, I finally did realize that this first tremendous mistake in my life was as much my fault as it was his, for I chose to go ahead despite circumstances that were bound to hurt me.

Chose? That is a word of wisdom, of afterthought and analysis years later. There was no choosing at the time. I was impelled, driven on as only the infatuated can be, obsessed with discovery, not only of joy and happiness, but of concerts and art galleries and the opera and poetry, all of which Tom brought me to know.

There had been music at home, of course, a victrola you wound up, and endless records of Caruso singing arias from *Aïda* and *La Traviata* and the rest. We had an upright piano and I took piano lessons and could play *Für Elise* by Beethoven very well. We had books of all kinds—but now music and books became a newly enchanted part of life.

I still have *Chamber Music*, a slim book of poems by James Joyce, and a copy of *Ulysses* in an early edition, then still outlawed as obscene in the United States. I have Aldous Huxley's *Antic Hay* and *Chrome Yellow* and *The Dance of Life* by Havelock Ellis and all the plays and prefaces by Bernard Shaw. In many, the inside cover says, in my writing, *Laura Mount* or *Tommy and Laura Mount*.

We had taken a small apartment on Minetta Lane down in Greenwich Village, as man and wife, Mr. and Mrs. T. E. Mount. Nobody knew our secret at first, except for William Benton, also at Batten, who was to start his own agency, Benton and Bowles, and then go on into politics, as under-secretary of state for Roosevelt. He knew and never said a word at the office or anywhere else.

One night I did confide in my mother about Tom and me. She responded without wrath or rebuke; she was sad that Tom was already married, but happy that I was so happy. She didn't even comment about the fact that Tom wasn't Jewish—assimilation and intermarriage were part of my parents' creed. She seemed to believe what I so ardently assured her, that it "would all work out in a couple of years," though she must have kept her skepticism to herself rather than "interfere" or preach mo-

70

rality at me. She said not one word against Tom, nor against my living with him.

Now in the nineteen-eighties, none of that secrecy and pretense of marriage would even occur to people like Tom and me. But sixty years ago, jazz age though it was, with all the talk of Flaming Youth, such openness about "living in sin" was unheard of, except among outright bohemian types, and in the straitjacket world of business, would have been masochism personified. I would have been summarily fired, though presumably Tom would not have been.

And to get pregnant and be open about it? Even today I do not believe that, except for a liberated minority, an unmarried pregnancy strikes most girls and women as anything but a catastrophe.

And back then? I did get pregnant, after three months of our new life. I told Tom with none of the old storybook phrases or coy hints. Nor did he respond with any romantic gleam of joy in his eyes. We both knew it for catastrophe. But at least it was catastrophe stripped of dilemma. I would be lying if I pretended there was reluctance or sorrow in my heart then because I could not go ahead and remain pregnant.

It was Bertha to whom I went for help in finding a doctor; for once there was no talk of my weak chin or my crying, only sympathy and love. From her own gynecologist she got the name of a physician who did abortions, not in his office, but at his own apartment in a secret operating room. He was well-trained, safe, reliable, kept no records and charged fifty dollars in cash, payable before the door to the secret operating room was opened to any patient.

He was a cautious man, it turned out, going against the law to do abortions but not going a jot further. To give anaesthetic in a private office was illegal, so there would be none.

I didn't know that until I was on the operating table, with the first thrust of pain. I knew only that I lay there like an animal being slaughtered, and when my screams became too loud, the doctor would shout, "One more yell out of you and you can go have that baby."

I can't remember why Tom couldn't go with me that night,

71

but something interfered, probably at the office, and he wasn't free. So I went alone. And after it was over, I went home alone.

The doctor wouldn't permit me to leave at once, though; I had to remain there for an hour, lying on a cot in a curtained-off anteroom, until he could be sure there would be no hemorrhaging that might require a rush to a hospital emergency room, and thus put him in danger of discovery and disgrace.

I do remember lying there on that cot, hearing the screaming of the next patient, knowing suddenly—I had never thought of it before—that there would be somebody else after her, and then somebody else and somebody else forever. I tried not to think of that endless retinue of screaming girls and women, and I tried not to think of the particular one who was right there then, just beyond that muslin curtain.

But I kept on hearing, pierced by her screams as if they too were steel scraping away deep inside my own body.

At the office all went well. I seemed to have a flair for writing copy, and they kept giving me new assignments, one after another, Cliquot Club Ginger Ale, Dairymen's League, a collective farm group, Lustrite nail polish, half a dozen others whose names I can't recall. I got my first raise in six months, a jump from twenty-five dollars a week to forty, and I was supposed to be thrilled, for the usual raise for beginners was five a week.

But instead of being thrilled and silent, I went to the vice-president in charge of most of the accounts I was working on, William J. Boardman, and despite the racing sense of risk, I thanked him for the forty but asked if it "couldn't possibly be fifty?"

He was astounded. I explained about my debts, not the long-term Cornell ones, but private ones of ten or twenty or thirty dollars to family friends and even to my mother's pupils, working people all, who had helped me because of their feelings for her. I was fast becoming tense and even guilty about those private debts, I told him, not sleeping well, wondering if I might do a little free-lancing to earn more and get free again.

I got the fifty. But I earned it, and I earned every other raise I was to get at Batten during the three years I stayed there. My sad story to Mr. Boardman, true though it was, was only part of a larger truth, a newly developing condition in my life, whose inherent threat I had not yet begun to see: living with Tom meant I had to earn more money.

Tom and I were, of course, on a fifty-fifty basis about our living expenses, but living expenses were by no means the whole of it. His salary was large compared to mine, but his expenditures were always larger than his salary. It was one of his faults—but who didn't have faults, including me? He drank a lot, but who didn't, in that era of Prohibition and speakeasies and pocket flasks? (I didn't—even today I'm known as "the cheapest lush in town"—one drink and I've had it.)

But Tom had an insouciance about unpaid bills that I soon found I could not share. At his tailors, Wetzel, at Sulka and Knox and Dobbs and Brooks Brothers and other shops for men with expensive tastes, his accounts were all in his name and went to him at the office, where I never saw them, but at department stores, where you bought lamps and linens and blankets and furniture and pots and pans, the name on all the accounts was Mr. and Mrs. T. E. Mount.

Soon that began to mean me. As the monthly bills came in from Macy's and Gimbels and Altman and Saks and McCreery, from the grocer and the butcher and the telephone company and the rest, they seemed to pile up into a palpable tower of worry, just for me. Tom could ignore them; I could not. It was not yet a cause for quarrels between us; I seem to have been still so much in love that I willingly took on anything that struck me as "a chance to help."

I began to look for, and get, some free-lance copy to do in my spare time. It was not forbidden at the office; I felt no need to get specific permission, beyond Mr. Boardman's noncommittal look when I had said I might try it.

Again it was easy. I was paid what would seem like subhuman sums now, usually $10 for a piece of copy, but I was soon adding $100 a month to our income. And enjoying it. And paying off some of those offensive older bills.

By now we had begun to need other friends beyond Bill Benton, in the main other copywriters and their wives. We let it be known to a few of them that Tom and Olive had decided on a divorce, and that he and I had been quietly married. I should have known I would fall down some time or other if I engaged in this kind of duplicity—I was never much good at telling outright lies.

One day at the office I finally trapped myself, not by stumbling over a sudden question about us, but by answering too easily and too much. Years were to pass before I so much as heard the arrogant and slightly obnoxious axiom, "Never complain, never explain."

So I explained. One of the copy supervisors, a middle-aged woman named Alma Pinckney—how do I remember these names after all these years?—showed a sweet pleasure at the news that we were married, and was nice enough to tell me so, showing her interest, wanting to know the wheres and the whens.

I was ready with proper answers about City Hall and a specific date, but then she murmured something about the divorce itself. Where had it happened? Was it Tom who had brought the action or his ex-wife?

"Oh, it was by mutal consent," I assured her. "You know, for incompatibility, and living separately—I think the official term is desertion."

"Did she get it over there in Paris?"

"Oh no, right here in New York. They both wanted it and it seemed simpler to have Tom arrange it right here."

She gave me a look of delight and pure malice. I was nipped by unease but only later, when I told Tom about it, did I understand what I'd done. There was one ground only in New York State for divorce; incompatibility wasn't its name, nor desertion, just plain adultery. I was lying my head off and thinking I could get away with it. We weren't married at all.

The episode haunted me for days, despite Tom's comforting reassurances. How could I have been so naive, so unworldly? Tom and his friends in advertising had introduced me to a new smart life, where people were forever saying clever things, going to the right shows, reading the latest books, dancing the newest dances at nightclubs where the big bands played.

And I had opened my big mouth and acted like an unsophisticated country bumpkin. But I learned one very large lesson from my little performance with Alma Pinckney. You could get yourself gossiped about, snickered over, even laughed at, but after a few hot days, you would cool out and go right on living your own life, and the devil with what *they* thought.

As I began to grow restless about the unpaid bills, Tom began to grow restless about his job. He hated advertising. It was cheap and dishonest, touting merchandise to people who were uncertain of their lives, unsure of their worth, dissatisfied with their looks, their health, their children, their houses, even their own breath. *Halitosis* was the ad word for bad breath; it most assuredly was a household word.

He could never be happy writing this, the rankest kind of charlatanism and vulgarity. What he wanted to do was to write that book he had in mind. He read me further paragraphs he had been writing in his notebook; they too seemed wonderful. I was sure he could write the book he so longed to do; if only he were free of that enslaving job. If only I could help him— how marvelous to extend help to the human being you loved, how marvelous to be loved for doing it, to be told you were generous, a true helpmate. It would only mean that I'd have to get a few more free-lance accounts.

Eight months after we began to live together, I finally persuaded Tom to take a year off and write. We took a small cottage in the country, at Peekskill, on the shore of a small lake, and a new phase of our life began. For a few weeks it was idyllic; then Tom began to be restless all over again, and bored. His writing didn't go well, but more than that, he began to find other things boring, even irritating. Since I was commuting to New York every day, getting home no earlier than seven, he had undertaken to do all the shopping and marketing for food and all our other neccessities. For a few weeks he did, but then he began to put it off later and later each day, and meet me at the station, after my long ride in the steamy, smoky, dusty locomotive-drawn train, with all his chores undone.

I don't remember any quarrels over this failure of his to carry out even that much fair division of labor, but I'm sure there must have been tears. I always cried too easily when I was hurt, as my mother had done. I always blamed myself for this, as a fault—perhaps Bertha had sown the seeds of that self-doubt too deeply for me to have the good sense to ask, But why do I feel like crying? Is it possible, after all, that there's good reason to weep?

I do not remember that there were as yet any tears or any quarrels between us about our new arrangement, for Tom to be free and me to earn enough for all our needs. My free-lancing was going along better than ever; I had had another big raise at the office; I had paid off most of the worrying private debts to my mother's pupils and to family friends, and didn't any longer even think of the student loan at Cornell except as something off in the far distance.

The way was clear, then, for me to undertake this great experiment of freeing Tom. I knew it would mean hard work, and even knew there would be periods when his writing left him discouraged and moody. What I had not expected was that even while he was not working at a paying job, his attitude about unpaid bills would remain as insouciant as ever.

Periodically he would abandon the idea of the book and get a copy job again. But the sudden rush of his own money never struck him as a way to get squared away on old debts, simply as as a way to treat himself—and us—to new pleasures.

When we started our experiment, in May of 1924, I kept no records, but by August I saw that I had to, and began monthly accounts of income, expenses, old debts and bills, and payments on old debts and bills. Again some instinct made me save them, first from month to month, but in the end save them for good. I still have them.

The first sheet is dated August 1924 and there was $1,996 in debts. Five months later that sum was down to $578; that was January 1925. But by December 1925, the end of that same year, we were back to $3,507.

So it went for the next two years. I was earning about $800 a month at my endless free-lancing, and my salary had zoomed to $138 a week, over $7,000 a year. But no matter how much income there was—even when Tom was having one of his bouts of contributing—the expenditures always outran that income.

We were back to $3,507. Here I am being a little gallant, for though I was involved in part of the money rolling out, for my full share of rent, food, electricity, telephone and the rest, I did not let myself get rash about pretty clothes; I had no fur coat, no jewelry, no anything special.

But Tom had a sweeping grandeur about things he bought, good wines, new books, theater tickets, once a gorgeous present for us to share equally, an Electrola, one of the first of the new breed of "orthophonic" victrolas, that yielded an amazing sonority and beauty for us both to enjoy. It cost $500, I think, in so-called easy installments.

Another time, a year later, he bought—yes, truly—an airplane. It wasn't anything like the chic, costly, gleaming private planes of today; it was a lowly thing, second-hand, a leftover from the great war, a Canadian plane known as the *Canuck*, a biplane, with linen wings sized with aluminum paint, with a single engine, an OX–5, and an open cockpit.

It cost $1,200, also to be paid in installments. I helped him get it into shape, repainting the aluminized wings, planing off rust from the struts, and went flying with him, loving it. Tom had not been a pilot in any war; he had won his pilot's license after taking the prescribed number of lessons and the proper number of solo flying hours in the air at Roosevelt Field on Long Island.

He was a good pilot; I never had a moment of anxiety in that narrow cockpit, strapped in behind him, open to the skies, with no ceiling over my head, my hair flying in the wind, relying on his skill even when he did loop-the-loops to show me he could.

And yet, there had begun to be quarrels, and more times of tears and injured feelings. I had begun again to keep a Journal, this time with a capital J, to denote that it was no mere adolescent diary—it proved to be the last time in my life that I attempted anything as organized as a diary or journal. But during that first year together, I either did not recognize the growing total of these unhappy moments, or else needed to deny them by keeping no record of them.

I still believed—as did Tom—that "things would work out in a couple of years," as I had so earnestly assured my mother.

By now, he had written Olive several times, telling her about us, in the total honesty they practiced, and she had raised no great hullaballoo about it. She was not living the life of a nun in Paris, and he had accepted that too.

When the time came for her return to New York, he was positive we would all manage to find some civilized way of living, no *ménage à trois*, but some acceptable acknowledgment of all our needs and rights. It was what Tom's great hero, Havelock Ellis, had done with his wife Edith throughout their illustrious lives; it could be done by others, and we would do it.

Perhaps I should be too embarrassed to include this part of my story of first love; perhaps I should omit or try to rationalize this, that must strike any hostile observer as my total gullibility. But gullibility would mean that I had been taken in by a "deceiver," and I still feel that for all his faults, Tom Mount was no deceiver, that he deeply believed that we would rise above all the usual proscriptions of timid people and find the equitable solutions we hoped for. And I believed it too.

One particular entry in that new Journal of mine, dated April 1, 1924, shows me in that young willingness to believe. Tom was thinking of getting Olive to come home, to face our problems, and I wrote that this worried me, that "I had hoped for at least two years of just our life together, uninterrupted."

> I am truly accepting the situation in all peace and ease. I hope so that Olive will too—that we really will be three beautiful people who meet a strange problem with strength and capability—not morose and bitter and always reckoning dangers. It's a fine thing to look ahead to. I want to attempt worth-attempting problems, to be free of all absorption in stupidly little ones.
>
> Somehow I got thinking that yesterday, looking out the window at the snow in the distance, (toward the river). It was such a sunny haze that particular objects didn't detach themselves, but I knew it meant shipping, and freight, and flat-bellied barges, and, by extension, ocean liners and distant ports and countries—some notion of the huge scale of life staggered me for an instant.
>
> I want to live in accord—not the tight, furious little life that most people squirm around in, but a great, breathing

God-like hugeness. Oh, I mean this so truly—each time I conquer a stab of jealousy, or yearning for security and "normalcy," I conquer by just so much this possibility of being hemmed in by the tiny, cruel network of this Lilliputian scheme of things.

Yet, for all this high resolve, our times of tension and tears continued. *When the real thing happens, you'll know it.* That may be true about falling in love, but when that love begins to diminish, you do not know it at all. You have a quarrel and you patch it up; you weep, but you are comforted. For a long while no problem seems insoluble, nothing seems like an injustice, it never occurs to you to measure the shares each of you is putting into the common life you are leading. At least it never occured then to me.

By the summer of 1926, our third together, there was an acceleration of strain and a greater frequency of the bad moments. We had taken a small cottage on somebody's estate at Cold Spring Harbor, on Long Island, and I think this was again a period where Tom was trying to write. I alone commuted to New York every morning, not by train now, but in our expensive new car, a Willys-Knight roadster, with fat new balloon tires, and a million unpaid installments. Sometimes I had six or ten free-lance appointments in the steaming city and arrived home frazzled and weepy. I was probably hard to live with—I must have been.

I do not think I ever put it the other way around: "Tom is hard to live with." I was not yet capable of seeing the tapestry of error we were weaving out of our lives—only this or that detail. I had begun to spring awake at night when Tom began to snore; probably he had always snored, but now I began to toss and turn, hating the sound, finally going to the living room to sleep on the sofa. The odor of gin and juniper berry had begun to offend me on Tom's breath; he had become a heavier and heavier drinker.

He began to have an occasional brief affair—and told me about it, for like Olive and Tom, we also had made a pact to conceal nothing, lie about nothing, share everything. I hated hearing what he told me; I would suffer all the twisting knots of jeal-

79

ousy—and then feel that I wasn't holding up my half of our agreement to live as free people.

But one night, I told him of a dream I'd had about a man we knew, red-headed, tall, attractive, a dream of his kissing me, nothing more, and my returning that kiss. Tom flew into the rage of a madman, storming at me hour after hour.

Of course we made peace, but the tapestry kept growing on that loom of disaster, and I still did not see it whole. I still could not imagine life without Tom.

Then I got pregnant once more. Once again I realized that there was nothing for it but an abortion. Tom had once gone to Europe to see Olive and had come back with no sign of any permanent solution to their personal problems or ours. This time, the abortion was done with the beneficent aid of anaesthesia—I do not remember a single thing about the doctor nor where it happened nor whether I again went alone or not.

This total suppression of so large an event astonishes me whenever I think of it. I can only guess that it was first cousin to the impulse that had made me omit anything painful in that journal I kept during the first year of our complete happiness, never writing in it anything that revealed bad times, like a hypochondriac-in-reverse, who ignores the most flagrant symptoms of an approaching disease.

And then in that same summer, we had a quarrel unlike any other. It came close to outright violence; it started late one humid evening, when I had arrived home from a dreary day in the city. I remember Tom's face suddenly in a rage, remember him coming at me in the kitchen, his right hand holding aloft a long sharp kitchen knife. I knew even then that he would never use it, but the sight of him coming at me, the long gleam of that upraised steel—that stayed with me a long time.

And somewhere in that same summer, my mind seems to have reached a basic decision. I do not remember making it; I do not remember struggling toward it, nor discussing it, nor weighing it, pro and con, plus and minus, even with myself. Somehow it was there. I couldn't take it any more, the debts and bills and money and columns of figures; I couldn't drive that car to New York morning after morning and see my freelance clients, I couldn't write copy every night, long after Tom was asleep, I couldn't, I couldn't, not any more.

One day I went down to the offices of the New York *Evening Post*, then a sound liberal newspaper, and saw the book editor, Bill Soskin, whom we had met through friends. I asked for a job on the staff, not on that "business end" I had once thought to settle for, but a real job, right up there with the rest of the reporters.

I told him I was making about $14,000 a year. I had left Batten by then and was free-lancing full time; my fee was no longer the picayune $10 per piece of copy; I had no trouble getting or holding clients through small agencies; I had begun to carry around a professional proofbook of printed ads I had written. I showed them to him.

"A cub reporter," he said, "starts at twenty-five dollars a week. Even a man."

I said I knew it. I knew also that the *Post* had no women reporters at all. He introduced me to the city editor, a Mr. Byers, and I went through the whole story with him.

"It's always the other way round," he said. "Every man on this staff would give his eyeteeth to be making big money in advertising." He looked at me as if I were mad. "Including me," he added. Then he took me on.

Tom was delighted with my news—and immediately got himself a job at the New York *World*, assigned to the Police Court, also at $25 a week. I can't remember what he planned to do about the monthly checks to Olive and the boys in Paris, the monthly check to his ailing father, or the remaining installments on the roadster, the Electrola or the airplane. But we were both happy as larks again.

For the first time I was known professionally as Laura Mount. At Batten I had started as Laura Z. Keane, and even after we announced to the world that we had been married, I remained Miss Keane there.

When I was interviewed for the job, first by the personnel manager and then by Mr. Boardman, it was under the name of Keane, as at all interviews since the days of college, but before I was hired, I gave Mr. Boardman what had already become my standard little speech with possible employers.

"Keane is my mother's name," I would say. "My father's name, my last name, is Zametkin, but in business, people find it so hard to get over a telephone, that I use my mother's name."

I also took it upon myself to say, "That's a Russian name, and Jewish," and somewhere in the shakiness of a job interview I always felt easier once the words had been said.

But three years later I was Laura Mount to all our friends, and it was Laura Mount who reported for work at the *Post*. Again I was lucky, though there was one disaster I thought I would never live down. That was the first time I was ever sent on an out-of-town assignment, down to Washington, with all the city's top reporters, Nunnally Johnson, Oliver H. P. Garrett and twenty more. I had been on the paper only a few weeks by then, I had even had my first by-line, and another on this very story about the much publicized visit of Queen Marie of Rumania to the United States.

A GRACIOUS MARIE—BUT DIPLOMATIC

Loves America Already
by Laura Mount

The gracious, the beautiful, the diplomatic Marie, Queen of Rumania, had her first American interview before she had set foot on her first bit of American soil today.

And in it she showed herself gracious and beautiful—and very diplomatic indeed.

To the poised pencils and open notebooks of the 250 reporters who went down the bay to board the *Leviathan* at Quarantine, she offered only pleasantries. She parried every question that might be awkward. She laughed away others which might be audacious. She said only the delightful nothings which a clever and skilled diplomat might be expected to say in such an unguarded and informal moment.

It went on to the end, pleasing Mr. Byers because it stayed clear of the rather awed politeness of most of the other stories on Her Majesty's arrival.

Late that afternoon I was sent down to Washington by train,

for she was to be entertained at the White House in the usual stately fashion. I had had no particular instructions about how you covered a running out-of-town story, and I had never been sent out on one, except on a scientific symposium with no deadline imperatives attached to it.

So next morning in Washington, I did the intelligent and humble thing; I watched what the newspaper greats were doing, Nunnally Johnson and Oliver H. P. Garrett especially, went everywhere they went, kept adding new detail to my story for hours, and then went to Western Union myself, to put my copy on the fast wire as late as possible, to leave nothing out, just as they did.

The trouble was that they were both on morning papers, one on the *Times*, the other on the *World*, I think. The *Post* was an afternoon paper and expected dispatches from me right through the day, as press time came for each new edition.

The morning edition, which was on the streets before noon, came and went, but not one wire on Marie from Mount. The early afternoon edition—nothing. The final, and the late final, still nothing. Byers phoned every conceivable contact in the nation's capital. "She's with the story" was the only reply he got. That whole first day he was forced to go with whatever came in on the AP wire.

Late that evening, exhausted but happy with the stuff I had sent in, I went for a well-deserved rest at my hotel. There my city editor reached me. His final final had been out for hours; he set me straight, but none too gently. He did not yank me off the story, and the rest was all right, but there was nothing gentle about the ribbing I took from the rest of the reporters when I reached the city room once more.

And when, a month later, I was again sent out on a major story, the Hall-Mills murder trial in Somerville, New Jersey, that had the entire nation in an uproar for weeks on end—on that day, as I reached the far end of the city room, Mr. Byers's voice rang out, for the whole room to relish.

"Hey, Laura, send a postcard now and then, okay?"

It wasn't postcards I sent, but brand new leads for each edition, plus extra feature stuff, interviews, exclusives. By now I had learned the tricks that seasoned reporters were so good at, even to paying some neighborhood kid a few cents an hour to occupy a telephone booth in a drugstore across the way from the courtroom, in case all the lines in the press room were already taken. I was not the main reporter on the story—one of the men was always that, Ray Daniels, I think it was—but my assignment was to cover all the "sidebar" material, and there was plenty of that.

By-line after by-line came my way, and frequent small raises, even a few five-dollar prizes for the "best written story of the week." For the rest of the year I spent on the *Post*, I was sent out on most of the major stories, to do the "human interest" side of the news. By the end of the year my pay was fifty dollars.

Unhappily, Tom did not fare so well at the *World*. He found himself stuck tight in the lowly beat of the police blotter, with no chance of a by-line, nor of a raise, and after a few weeks of it, he suddenly quit cold. Again he went back to a well-paid job in advertising, this time at N. W. Ayer in Philadelphia. That meant that we began, for the first time, to live apart except for weekends.

I didn't enjoy spending my evenings alone. I never went out with men; I saw Alice and other friends, but often I behaved as if I were again at college, attending lectures, reading books that might have been assigned to me at Cornell, and writing little pieces of criticism about them in my Journal. Remy de Gourmont is there, and biographies, one about Shelley and another about George Sand; I even bought Nietzsche's *Thus Spake Zarathustra*, and apparently found it hard going, writing in my Journal, "But I will go on with Zar."

One entry shows that I went, by myself, to hear Julian Huxley lecture on evolutionary biology, and must have come out none too happy with the life I was leading.

> He's a quiet young man, poor speaker, yet with that peculiar dignity that surrounds the man who's doing honorable work. The hugeness of his interests makes me feel inferior...I feel cheap and banal, considering *my* interests, advertising, cheap newspaper articles, larger income, good clothes, attractive apartment, etc.
>
> And yet, I don't despair. Not only geniuses are privileged

to do worthy work—I will, one day, even though it be not very important.

But weekends brought Tom and me together without fail. Somerville and the Hall-Mills murder case were near Tom's old haunts at Princeton; each Saturday afternoon he would drive over from his new job at Philadelphia, and we would meet for a half-weekend at the Princeton Inn. We both tried to believe that all was well.

By the next summer, in 1927, soon after I had won some more by-lines covering the return of Lindbergh from his solo flight to Paris, I began to face up to the fact that the fourth estate was not quite the seventh heaven I had dreamed it would be. I still liked my work, and I had made good friends on the paper. Jim Thurber is the one I remember best, undoubtedly because it was while he was right there on the *Post* that he began to send in the pieces that turned him into James Thurber of the New Yorker.

Many mornings, waiting for our assignments from the desk, we would go downstairs to the cafeteria for coffee and large discussions of life and other matters. He was several years older than I and had worked for several newspapers since his college years at Ohio State, so I looked up to him as to an expert on the press. He rarely talked about his troubled vision, though he did tell me once about the shooting accident that had cost him the sight of one eye when he was a little boy.

He didn't behave like the humorist he was to become, was never one for the jokes and wisecracks of the day; my impression of him is that he always seemed a little remote, even when we were out somewhere with an after-hours newspaper crowd. He drank what seemed to me then to be an awful lot.

My one year of newspaper work turned out to be his last, for in the following year he left the *Post* to join the staff of the New Yorker, for a stay of about seven years. We remained friends after he left the paper, and when his first collection of drawings came out, *The Owl in the Attic*, I bought one of the first copies. He presented me with a copy of his next collection, *The Seal in the Bedroom*, and I still have it. It is inscribed, "To Laura, with love and kisses, Jim Thurber," and below that he drew me a four-inch rendition of one of his floppy, rueful dogs. Jim was the first person I ever knew who not only wanted to write something good, but who went ahead and wrote it.

I began to wonder, in those final months at the paper, what it would be like if I were to try it myself, a short story, a magazine article, a play. I never once thought, a book.

The next two years are a blur. I did leave the paper and again wrote advertising, this time for Young & Rubicam, on a six-month trial at high pay. I rather expected to be assigned to Steinway or another major account, but I started out with small interim stuff for Dental Digest, where flair and originality were as rare as hen's teeth, and somehow kept on writing only for the "trades."

As the trial period came to its worried end, I went to Raymond Rubicam myself, to resign and preempt the pink slip. He accepted with such alacrity, that I always said afterward, "I was canned by Young & Rubicam."

And further along in that blur, at the beginning of 1929, Tom and I knew we had reached the end. There had been increasing quarrels and tears, breaking-aparts and coming-togethers, each time vowing to change. If there was a last meeting I do not remember it; if a final quarrel I have long since suppressed it.

Before too long Tom chucked job, responsibilities, everything, and went off to Tahiti to write. Now a different ocean separated him from me, a wider ocean than the one Olive had crossed so long ago. Our life together was ended. But not our story.

Perhaps I should have sensed even then that somewhere on that dark page of parting, there was written, *To Be Continued.* But I was as blind to that as I had been to so much else.

FIVE

IF ANYBODY HAD SAID to me during that time of sadness and depression, "Never mind, soon you'll know people like Sinclair Lewis and Dorothy Thompson, Harry Luce, Clare Boothe Brokaw, Carl Van Doren and lots more," I might have answered, "By interviewing them? As a reporter again?"

Another chapter of my life was opening. In July 1930, I was married, legally, conventionally married, to a young publisher, Francis Thayer Hobson, a vice president at William Morrow & Company, then a small publishing house.

Perhaps it wasn't all that conventional, for though Thayer was only thirty-three, this was to be his third marriage. It may be that the thirdness of it made him reluctant to invite his older brother, the youngest bishop in the Episcopal church, or his two sisters and their many children, to our wedding. His family was somewhat distraught at the growing total of his trips to the altar or to a justice of the peace.

I was rather relieved myself at the idea of our going off alone to the Fairfield County courthouse in Connecticut; in truth I didn't want to ask my mother or father or any of my family either. Alice was in love with a lawyer, Milton Milvy, but they were not yet married and had no plans for any formalities about their own wedding-to-be, so my sister seemed only too pleased to be let off from any fuss. She had always been rather shy, and even uncomfortable, about seeing Tom, and I was later to find that she felt that same way about Thayer.

Both my parents had met Thayer and liked him, but they too were worried by that *third* marriage. It must have hurt my mother not to be asked to my wedding; it was to be at nine in the morning and she would have had to leave Jamaica at about seven to get to Fairfield. But she who had gone three hundred miles in a motorcycle sidecar to see me in cap and gown, would surely have managed the two-hour trip to Connecticut even if it were planned for five in the morning instead of nine.

But she said she understood why we were not asking our families to be there, and said she was not hurt. I wanted to believe her, so I did.

I also had been a bit setback when Thayer told me he had been divorced not once, but twice. This was soon after we met, and he was then thirty-one and I twenty-eight. But he was so reasonable in his attempts to reassure me, that I found myself quickly reassured.

"Most people who marry early make one mistake," he said. "Well, I made two mistakes—is that so terrible?"

I had already told him, fully, minutely about *my* mistakes with Tom, had told him we had never actually been married, and in time had also told him of the two abortions. He said that would never have to happen again, that we would have *children*, not abortions, and some knot of longing tightened in me, to be not just in love but to be part of a family, to have not a make-believe marriage but a real one.

We had met at a dance at the Cosmopolitan Club of New York, a black-tie affair to which Tom and I had been invited, possibly our last public appearance together anywhere.

It was at the beginning of the year that was to include the great Wall Street Crash of 1929, and already it had become harder to find good jobs. After I beat the pink slip by resigning from Young & Rubicam, I had found another job at another agency, Erwin Wasey, and here I did get big accounts to work on. But a few months later, calamity hit the agency itself—two of its major clients, almost simultaneously, took their accounts elsewhere; at once massive retrenchment was in order. About forty account executives and copywriters were fired in the span of five days. I was one of them.

It was not an easy time. Tom had sailed for the idyllic island of Tahiti, with its gorgeous color and girls; I would wake at night stabbed through with jealousy at Gauguinesque images of lush physical beauty and luscious love-making. I was living alone, I had no job. Thayer was a blessing. He was nothing like Tom—there would never be anybody like Tom—but that very attribute of being nothing like Tom was part of the blessing.

He was a good-looking man, fair, already beginning to show pink scalp under his thinning hair, and he had none of Tom's almost theatrical handsomeness, but he was half a head taller, and that freed me of my old "Amazon" fear that if I wore high heels with Tom, I would look too tall, and thus not feminine.

But the silly comfort that came from this physical difference was nothing to the solid inner comfort that arose from the disparity in basic character. There was nothing dissatisfied in Thayer's view of his working life; he was free of yearnings to be something other than he was, free of self-deprecation, not ridden with hungers to paint, compose, write a book.

He was a book publisher and wanted to be exactly that. He didn't even read much, except for the eternal manuscripts he brought home from the office, which the firm was considering or publishing. He didn't care much for music or poetry, and I worried at times that for all his education, he seemed a little ordinary. After Yale, he'd gone to the Sorbonne for a year, and then put in a further year teaching English at Westminster School, but he was no intellectual. He had a sneaky belief in astrology, which he half-belittled, but which he brought into consideration of any major step.

I could just hear Tom guffaw at the idea of any grown man harboring a belief in astrology, and that worried me too, try as I would to remember that anybody alive, including me, had little quirks that other people might find peculiar.

But an evening with Thayer was an evening without tension, without worry about money matters, bills, debts, any of the responsibilities that had lain on my shoulders for so long. It never occurred to him that we might go fifty-fifty when we went out; he took it for granted that he was the one to take care of everything. It was a new sensation for me, amazingly pleasant; he was thoughtful, kind, interested in helping me find a new job, and when I tried to write something, he was all for me on that.

And yet when he spoke of marriage I drew back. Years before, when I met Tom, I was ready to fall in love, but when I met Thayer, I was nowhere near ready to fall in love again. I was still in mourning for Tom, and, alas, compulsive about talking about him and what had gone so wrong. With sublime patience, Thayer put up with it, waiting for me to get over it at last.

In between sessions of job-hunting, I began to write articles for magazines, still under the name magazine editors might find familiar, Laura Mount. I was lucky; I sold the first four pieces I submitted, to Collier's and other Crowell publications. Not one could be called a think-piece or anything else intellectual, but I was paid the astonishing sum of $300 for each. In those days you could live for two or three months on $300.

The first of the four articles was on the Japanese art of flower-arrangement, the second a profile of the actress, Katherine Cornell, the third something called, "Coming Tennis Champs," and the fourth, "Talkies That Whisper Paris." This last must have been a winner; the check jumped to $400.

But apart from the magazine articles, I was also launched on something that I thought might be "real writing," not just earn-a-living writing. Almost at once I discovered that there was an excitement in trying to set down on paper not an interview, not a report of a fire or a murder trial, not an article about flowers or tennis champs, but something that wasn't anywhere except in my own head, something I had to spin out of the elusive threads of my own imagination.

It was a full-length three-act play, *The Muttering Wind*. The title came from Shelley:

> Our church shall be the starry night,
> Our altar the grassy earth outspread,
> And our priest the muttering wind.

The core of the plot was the challenge faced by its heroine Paula, and her second husband, a famous young scientist, rising star at New York's most prestigious Institute of Medical-Research, when they are told by a noted physician of an experiment he wants to undertake.

He is in charge of Paula's first husband Fred, brain-damaged in a car accident years before, successfully operated on and yet never fully restored mentally. He believes that Fred might now be on the verge of complete recovery, if only he could live a normal life again for a year, perhaps two years—the life he was living before the accident, when Paula was his wife and living with him. Could Paula consider giving him that final chance? Could her husband allow her to? What would the Institute do if a scandal arose as a result?

It was a play about courage, the ability to live free of constraint from the "moralists" of the world, and, as I said about my father's play, it couldn't have been all bad.

I quickly found an agent for it, and though the play came back from leading producers like Herman Shumlin and Jed Harris, and also from Katherine Cornell, it did, later on, receive an offer of production from the Arts Theatre Club of London, what we would call an off-Broadway group. They could offer no more than ten pounds for a three-month option, and half the usual ten percent royalty, but if the play should succeed and reach the West End, those terms would be renegotiated.

I should have cabled SURE. But just then I heard from James Light, of the Jed Harris office, who was impressed by the play and wanted to discuss it with me directly. He told me, most persuasively, that I hadn't faced all the implications in my last act, that if I did face them, did rewrite Act Three the way he was sure it ought to be, I would have a much stronger play, a truer play, a more daring play, a more successful play.

I agreed. I had fudged the ending; I would try again. So instead of that simple SURE, my agent cabled London asking for a brief delay for revisions.

What happened is what usually happens—in the end nobody took it. Years later a cynical Hollywood character told me, "If it pends, it peters," and I remembered how much pending I had permitted before my play petered out for good.

All this time I was seeing Thayer—I had become dependent on seeing him, on his presence, his devotion. He read my play and said I could be a playwright; he read my magazine pieces and said I could be a staff writer; he showed limitless concern for *my* work, *my* possible talent. Again and again he talked of marriage and the life we would have: we would have a long honeymoon abroad, and then come home and have a baby, and enjoy the stimulation of a publisher's life, and I could stop job-hunting for as long as I wanted to try to write.

At last, a year and a half after we met, we went up to that courthouse and were married, setting sail the next morning for nearly two months in Europe, in London, Paris, Deauville, Rome, Venice, the Riviera, the Lido.

I had been abroad only once, the year before, traveling alone, to try to get over the last of my grief about Tom, and Thayer had known that that was why I had gone. I was living like a student, on a franc-tight budget, mainly in Paris, with a brief stay at La Baule, on the coast of Brittany. I remember that I could still walk along that beautiful shore at sunset, and find my eyes suddenly full, thinking only of what it had been to be happy with Tom at the beginning, but Thayer's daily letters, which would pile up at American Express offices wherever I went, kept me more than ever aware of him, his goodness, his kindness, the old-fashioned stable marriage he was promising.

There was no student-budgeting on our honeymoon. At Deauville, we went to the casino to play chemin de fer—I had never heard of it—with Thayer staking me to a lot of francs, while I thought of how many theater tickets or concert seats that large sum would buy. In Paris, he took me to Lanvin for my first experience with haute couture, two evening dresses made to order just for me, one a web of black lace, the other a dark red flowered velvet. He rented a car and we drove south through the chateau country and the French Alps to the Riviera, staying at all the places I had read about, Cannes, Juan les Pins, Nice, Cap d'Antibes, Monte Carlo, and on to all the glories of the Italian Riviera.

Everything was new to me; in ten years as an adult, nobody had ever taken care of *me*. Those two Lanvin dresses were the first clothes since my childhood that I had not paid for myself.

The hotel bills were none of my affair; the car rental, the petrol, *essence, benzina,* all our meals—my husband took care of it all.

Before we left New York we had searched for an apartment to come home to, and leased a big terrace apartment on the seventeenth floor of a new building at Madison and Ninety-sixth Street, with wondrous views of the entire city, and Thayer had signed the leases and put down the advance rent; it was Thayer who bought our passage on the ship, Thayer who had set up a $5,000 letter of credit at Barclay's in London, so that if we felt like buying Venetian glass in Italy or English bone china or anything else for our apartment, we could easily and quickly manage it.

I had told Thayer of my childhood anguish about our funny house and backward staircase, and he promised me a place to live in that would be as attractive and inviting and pleasing as our own good taste could make it. He had some antique furniture, a great mahogany breakfront, a family heirloom, the most striking of all—and even I had some American antiques, collected by Tom and me on trips to New England in those days when we always spent more than we should—but beyond these pieces from our past lives, we were going to create a place to live in and entertain in that would be a private delight to us both.

A man was taking care of *me*, planning for the future we would share. A new kind of certainty arose in me, a new kind of self-worth, a new kind of being happy. Thayer wanted me to be happy and I loved him for that wanting. If I had counted the ways then, they would have been different, nearly every one, from my first understanding of love. But they were there.

"And then we'll have a baby." We had agreed to wait until we were at home again, after our long honeymoon, but we were both eager to have a child of our own.

Thayer knew what it was to be a parent, but he seemed as eager as I. His second marriage had produced a son, Timothy, a beautiful little boy whom I first saw when he was only four, on a visit to his father. That was before our wedding, and Thayer was living in a remodeled building on upper Madison Avenue, on the second floor, above a smart restaurant on the ground floor. When Timothy came for his visits, his mother left him just inside the door at street level, and he had to climb the long flight of stairs all alone to get up to Thayer's open door. I never got a glimpse of Priscilla, his mother, but I did watch that little child climbing all those stairs by himself and thought, That's never going to happen to any of our children.

I expected to get pregnant at once. After two unwanted pregnancies, a kind of free eagerness entered my intimate life, and we both began planning nine months ahead. But a month went by, and then another, and another. . . .

Any woman who has ever dreaded getting pregnant knows how blessed the relief is when she sees the first menstrual stain, but any woman who has longed to be pregnant knows just the opposite. By the sixth or seventh disappointment, there arose in me a fear that something was terribly wrong, that I was no longer the way I was, that I had been injured by those two abortions and would now have to pay for them in some fearful coin.

I was already thirty; a sudden sense of lost time invaded me, a sudden insistence that it happen. Thayer would reassure me; it would happen soon; we would have a baby, everything would be all right. But at last he conceded that perhaps I'd feel better if I went to one of the doctors who were specializing in these matters. It was the first time I had ever heard that there were gynecologists who were specializing in fertility problems.

The very phrase hurt. Was I now a fertility problem? I was sent to a man who was widely regarded as a leader in this newly developing field, Dr. Virgil Green Damon of Park Avenue and the Columbia-Presbyterian Hospital.

The tests began. A dozen tests, a hundred tests, tests to determine my ovulation dates, painful insufflation tests to see whether the fallopian tubes were obstructed, tests of ovarian function, basal metabolisms to check on thyroid, other tests on the pituitary gland—everything.

The basal metabolism test revealed I was abnormally low on thyroid, so low that I should have been lethargic, overweight, with little energy. All of which was so directly the opposite of the fact that I was tireless, full of energy, almost too slender, that they repeated the test twice before prescribing a grain of thyroid a day.

I never missed a visit; I obeyed every instruction, took every vitamin, every hormone prescribed for me. After a year of regular visits, Dr. Damon confirmed his first diagnosis: I had been badly injured in the brutal first abortion; because of the absence of anaesthesia, that doctor had operated with the greatest haste possible and had scraped the uterine lining so grossly that it was a wonder a second pregnancy had occurred at all.

"Perhaps a fertilized ovum made a lucky discovery," said Dr. Damon. "Hitting on one healthy area to embed itself in." But the uterus had self-healing properties, he went on to assure me. With enough time and proper treatment, I ought to be able to maintain a pregnancy once more.

"Maintain?"

"You may be getting pregnant every month," he said. "But the ovum can't hang on to anything."

It was layman's talk, but it gave me fantasies of an infinitesimal shipwrecked vessel searching for safe harbor.

"Try to forget all about your periods and getting pregnant," Dr. Damon ended. "If you become too tense, obsessed with the idea—we don't completely understand the interaction between the emotions and the body."

"I'll try not to think about it."

But it was not an easy assignment. Part of the treatment was a scheduling and calendarizing of our sex life; we were both all too aware of ovulation dates. We joked about it, sometimes bawdily, but we both knew a secret regret that something mechanical and unspontaneous was "just what the doctor ordered."

Everything else in our life was tranquil and gratifying. Thayer, as a publisher, needed an active social life, with authors and agents and editors and other publishers, cocktail parties, lunches, dinners. It seems that I quickly became an easy hostess. We had a maid who was a good cook—I never became a good cook— but I was gregarious, enjoyed meeting people and talking to "real live authors." After some evening affair at our house, Thayer would tell me I was meant to be a publisher's wife, and his approval gave me a social confidence more solid than any I had ever known.

Knowing real live authors was not only exciting, but also stimulating to me in other ways. I began for the first time to try my hand at short stories, not of a lofty literary type, I'm afraid, but aimed at popular magazines like the Saturday Evening Post and women's magazines. That slight note of apology as I tried "formula stuff" was to lead to one of my most memorable moments with no less a real live author than Sinclair Lewis.

The Nobel Prize for Literature had been bestowed upon him in 1930, the year Thayer and I were married, the first time it had been awarded to an American author. He had accepted it, although he had previously refused to accept the Pulitzer Prize for *Arrowsmith*. He was in young middle age then, just forty-five, and had been married for a couple of years to the famous foreign correspondent, Dorothy Thompson, his second wife.

Thayer had been in touch with her about a book she was writing that he wanted to publish, and we were invited up for a weekend at their summer place, Twin Farms, in Barnard, Vermont, a huge spread of hills and valleys. Despite my new confidence, I was a little nervous about meeting the brilliant political expert, Dorothy Thompson, and really intimidated as to the world-famous Sinclair Lewis.

He was on the hard-liquor wagon then, drinking only wine, though he drank a great deal of that, certainly a couple of bottles a day, at luncheon, dinner and much of the rest of the time as well. "Red" Lewis was a great talker, but so was Dorothy, and sometimes, even as early as that in their marriage, a rivalry would show openly about who was to have the floor. At times I, the youngest one there, would feel discomfort and even acute embarrassment.

Dorothy, one of the most eminent and widely known members of the European press corps, talked mainly of politics, of the state of affairs in Austria and Germany, of the upsurge of the Nazi party, of Hitler and his storm troopers, of his cohort in Rome, Mussolini. I had begun to be interested in foreign affairs and politics in general by then, and whenever she held forth, I was totally absorbed, like an eager student in a small special seminar.

Red, on the other hand, talked mainly of people, either real people or the characters in books, of publishers and agents, of movie stars and matinee idols, of pretentious characters in American public life. He was a wonderful mimic who could reel off yards of imaginary dialogue as if he were reading aloud from one of his manuscripts; he had an uncanny ability to improvise plots on the spot, for stories, plays, novels, as if he were snatching them out live from behind a magician's chiffon handkerchief, ears wiggling or wings fluttering.

Between Dorothy and Red, you became largely a listener—at least I did. I can't recall any verbal contribution of my own during that whole first weekend, except once, and that turned into the memorable occasion I can never forget.

One afternoon I happened to be alone with Red. Thayer and Dorothy were closeted together to talk about her manuscript and Red suggested that we go for a short walk. There was a meadow below their houses—they had two houses, the large main house and a small house set apart, where he went to be alone and do his writing. As we started off, I felt tongue-tied, searching for something to say. I don't remember what led to my telling him that I was trying to write short stories, but I do remember that the note of apology quickly sounded.

"Not anything very good," I said. "Just formula stuff."

He shook his head at me, as if he were showing mild displeasure at some child's folly. "Don't ever let yourself think that way," he said. "Whatever you write, it's as good as you can make it at the time you're writing it. You can't merely *decide*, 'I'll write something less good than the best I can write.'"

I knew he was telling me not to indulge in alibis for any bad writing I ever did, and I was slightly abashed. "It's kind of ridiculous," I said then, "for me to be talking to the winner of the Nobel Prize about what *I'm* trying to write."

He stopped walking, and I stopped too. We were at the edge of the meadow now; it was a large circular glen, bordered with all sorts of field flowers and planted flowers, nasturtiums, daisies, purple spikes of spirea, scarlet clumps of salvia. He seemed to be gazing at the flowers and the trees beyond them, as if he were alone, vaguely contemplating the delightful summer scene spread before him.

"Do you see those flowers?" he said at last, waving his hand in a broad circular sweep. "There's a secret about them, did you know that?"

"A secret?"

"They really make a secret code—they spell out something important."

My heart began to race. I had never seen him in this light mood; he was smiling in an odd way. I had seen him openly amused, uproariously laughing at some joke, his own as often as somebody else's. But this was different. He was quiet, his voice was quizzical.

"The flowers make a secret code?" I prompted. "Can you break it and know what they say?"

He nodded. He pointed to the daisies, and began to speak in widely separated syllables and words and phrases. "The daisies say, 'The—'"

He pointed next to the nasturtiums. "They say, 'No—'" He pointed to the salvia. "That says, '—bel'" He pointed to the spirea. "That says, 'Prize—'"

He waited a moment before continuing. Then very slowly, going around the circumference of the glen with his pointing finger, he finished. "Is—all—but—for—got—ten."

My breath caught before he was halfway through his slow deliberate counting off. *The Nobel Prize is all but forgotten.* Something caught in my throat. "Oh no, it isn't," I said, too passionately because I was young. "It never will be."

He simply nodded. His faint smile signaled, Oh-yes-it-is, and we continued our walk.

My mother died that year, a few weeks before this visit of ours to Twin Farms in Vermont. For two years she had put in endless hours of work, going through her printed articles for *The Day*, reading them all, selecting the ones she liked best, editing and cutting, writing in new transitions, getting them ready to be published in book form, in that 648-page book I have never been able to read. Once that huge job was done, she seemed unable to shake off her exhaustion.

And then, on a lovely May day, two months before our first

wedding anniversary, she phoned me to say her doctor was sending her to the hospital, where Dr. Dana W. Atchley would take charge of her case. The long years of diabetes had at last brought on kidney trouble, then called Bright's disease. But the hospital was Columbia-Presbyterian, way uptown in New York, at 168th Street, and papa and she both thought she was too sick to travel by Long Island Railroad and then by subway.

I went out for her in our car, an Oldsmobile roadster, to get her settled in. During the long ride from Queens, she twice told me she had to go the bathroom, and to my eternal shame, I was irritated at her for making me go through the embarrassment of stopping at a drugstore and saying to an indifferent clerk, "My mother is ill—please, could she use your bathroom?"

She had no idea she was near death; during the next few days she kept asking me to get Dr. Atchley to arrange permission for me to move her own bed from Jamaica, because she was unable to get any sound sleep in that hard hospital bed.

During the next days I was with her a great deal. I don't know about Joel or Fred—I never saw them there—but Alice did say she could not go to the hospital at all. She was pregnant then and gave that as her reason, though her son was not born until October.

I was angry and we quarreled about it, but later on, when our quarrels grew out of far weightier matters than family kindness, I was to wonder whether I shouldn't have seen long ago that in certain unhappy situations, something in my sister's nature would make her handle it by remaining absent.

Dr. Atchley decided that a blood transfusion was necessary. In those days there were no blood banks, no plasma, no way of storing blood, so a transfusion was done directly from one arm to the other. I was right there when the decision was made; my blood matched, and I was the donor. The procedure was carried out in a small treatment room, with mama lying on one narrow bed, and I beside her on another.

It was to be a double transfusion, done by a young resident doctor, and as I looked over at my mother lying there a foot away from me, I could actually see a pinkish hue coming back into her wax-white cheeks.

Just at that moment, Dr. Atchley opened the door and called out, "How are you feeling, Mrs. Zametkin?"

She lifted her head and in a bright, almost sassy voice, she answered, "Oh, mother and daughter doing nicely, thank you." I could never get that sentence out of my head.

For a day or two she seemed stronger. Then she slipped into coma, and one night Thayer brought some work with him and came to stay the night with me right there in her room. We took snatches of sleep in chairs, or out in the corridor, on those high, narrow rolling tables hospitals use for surgery patients. At dawn we were told the coma might go on for days, that we should go home for a few hours of rest. Thayer went to his office and I went home. My father was staying with us in those final days; he hadn't had much sleep either.

An hour later, the hospital called. It had happened. Papa asked me to make the phone calls and sign the papers that gave them permission to do what she had long ago said she wanted to do. "Leave my body to science."

Our family didn't believe in funerals, called them barbaric rites, so there was none. There were long obituaries about her in the Jewish press, and in the socialist magazine, the New Leader, and a shorter one in the *New York Times*. Even that shorter one said a lot about the kind of woman she was, way back there, long before the phrase, women's liberation, had ever been heard.

MRS. ZAMETKIN DEAD;

A SOCIALIST LEADER
Writer and Welfare Worker was
Wife of Editor of The Jewish
Daily Forward

Mrs. Adella Kean Zametkin, a prominent Jewish writer and leader of the Socialist party, died yesterday morning at Presbyterian Hospital after a long illness which was aggravated by work attending her last published volume, *A Woman's Handbook*, which includes articles contributed for thirteen years to *The Day*, Jewish daily newspaper. Mrs. Zametkin was 68 years old and came here from Russia in 1888.

Born in Mogilef-Podolsk, Russia, Mrs. Zametkin came to the United States to continue her humanitarian work among the underprivileged Jewish people of New York City. She devoted her whole life to this work and was a widely known figure on the east side, where her projects in Americanization were centered. The organization of several women's organizations was attributed to her zeal.

In 1889 she met and married Michael Zametkin, who was then a lecturer and teacher. Mr. Zametkin later became the first editor of the *Jewish Daily Forward* and Mrs. Zametkin served as its first cashier. It was during this period that Mrs. Zametkin assisted in the organization of the Socialist party. She was a forceful speaker and cultivated a large following within the party. At the last election, Mrs. Zametkin temporarily put aside her literary work and ran for the Assembly from the Jamaica (Queens) district. She was defeated, but polled more votes than had any previous Socialist candidate in the district.

Until two weeks ago, when Mrs. Zametkin went to the hospital suffering with diabetes, she lived at 84–55 Parsons Boulevard. She underwent a blood transfusion last Thursday but failed to rally.

Besides her husband, she is survived by twin daughters and a son.

My father stayed on with us for a while. Apartments like ours came equipped with at least one maid's room in those days, and ours was sparsely furnished because we were waiting for the time when we would turn it into a nursery. It had a small bathroom of its own, and though I offered him my own large bedroom, papa said he could be very comfortable in the other room, where he wouldn't be in my way when I was dressing.

But having him in our daily life soon proved to be very nearly a disaster. He still treated me as a child, ordering me about without knowing he was doing it. "A glass of tea," he would say, not even looking at me as he spoke, expecting me to jump up and get it for him. Which of course is just what I did.

But that was the least of it. All his life he had been the authority wherever he was; he could out-argue anybody in the family by raising his voice and having his face go red. Now he was doing it at our house, especially if the day's news contained anything about the Soviet Union and Stalin. Then there was no stopping him.

Back when I was seventeen, I had seen his joy at the Russian revolution, the first one, in February, when the moderate Mensheviks under Kerensky took power. But six months later, I had seen his rage and sorrow when the Bolsheviks threw the moderates out and set up their dictatorship of the proletariat.

"Now you will see such a reign of terror," he had said, "as the czars never dreamed of."

And now in 1931, with Stalin ruling Russia, with the first Five Year Plan, with news of purges and the liquidation of millions of kulaks, my father could scarcely talk about anything in the headlines without veering immediately to Stalin and the communists.

It wasn't that I disagreed with him, far from it. As yet I didn't know that Alice did, that she had already—perhaps because of Milton, perhaps on her own—had already turned in the direction so many decent young people were to adopt in the early thirties, as they viewed the human wreckage rooted in the Depression and unemployment and poverty.

But though I felt deeply that my father was right, as did Thayer, we soon also felt that our evenings were becoming political forums where we were slated to be the audience a good part of the time.

We both tried to be understanding and graceful; he was old himself, he had lost his life's companion—"Dedicated to Adella Kean, my dearest friend and comrade," his play had said—but it grew more difficult for us with every passing night. Even if we had guests, sooner or later he held the floor.

And still Thayer and I tried to help, to make allowances. I had always resisted chess, had never learned it, but now I let my father teach it to me, as if I were doing him a favor, this chessmaster who played with world champions, with no greater handicap than a move and a pawn.

One night he moved his queen under my pawn, where I could capture it. Instantly he saw his mistake, his breath audibly drawn in.

"There it is," he said. "The first break." He touched his forehead.

"Oh, pa, it's just thinking about mama—"

"That too," he said slowly. "But it's the first sign just the same."

I don't remember seeing him in tears about my mother's death, but I do remember one thing he said one evening while he was living with us. I had been talking about mama the last time I saw her in Jamaica, before the hospital, and he nodded to show that he remembered too. He looked thoughtful, and fell silent, and I waited.

"Life reserves its hardest lessons," he said then, slowly as if he were thinking it out for the first time, "for when we are too old to learn them."

My eyes filled, but his did not. He simply seemed to go on with his private thinking, until I said, "I'll go get us some tea."

He stayed with us only for ten days or so, and then went off to Alice and Milton, in their house in Croton-on-Hudson. He remained with them for about a month. The same irritations and conflicts went on up there, only more so, for Milton and Alice were opponents of everything he said about Russia. They tried too, but by then Alice was far into her pregnancy, and it became an impossible situation.

And so he went back to Jamaica to the empty house, saying he would be all right. He was a man who could barely boil an egg, but he was adamant. He would be better off alone.

During the summer he sent me a mahogany box, lined in felt, containing a set of large Staunton chessmen, made in France, widely considered the best chess pieces in the world. He had gone to Abercrombie & Fitch himself to select them, and he had bought an inlaid wooden chessboard, 25 × 25 inches in size and an inch thick, to go with them. On the back of the board he wrote, "July 23, 1931, from your pa."

July 23, 1931 was my first wedding anniversary. It is the only gift that I remember getting from him and the only one I still have.

In that same summer, I suddenly heard from Tom. He was still in Tahiti, and he sent an overnight cable to me "in care of Zametkin," out in Jamaica. He had no address for me; I don't know if he knew I was married. He did know some Americans out there, Charles Nordhoff and James Hall, who were finishing *Mutiny on the Bounty*, but they were not Morrow authors and would have no reason to know anything about it either.

I can't quote the cable; I had abandoned my magpie need to save everything, and in my impulse to wipe out the past, I had destroyed every letter of Tom's, had thrown away every snapshot of the two of us together, or of him alone. There was one exception, and I have no idea why it survived, but that snapshot did turn up years later in a yellowing envelope marked *Miscellaneous Pix.*

But I know the cable said something like,

BROKE COMMA DESPERATE COMMA NOBODY TO TURN TO BUT YOU STOP COULD YOU CABLE TWO HUNDRED LOAN TO PAY OFF PRESSING OBLIGATIONS HERE AND PERMIT RETURN TO CIVILIZATION AND JOB STOP THANKS IN ADVANCE ALWAYS TOM

Perhaps I should have stonily ignored that cable, and perhaps when I showed it to Thayer, he should have advised me to tear it up and do nothing whatever. But neither of those things happened. It was not in me to ignore that cry for help from the man I had once loved, and Thayer too felt some compassion for the obvious despair revealed in that cable.

I wasn't working, so I had no money of my own. It was Thayer who supplied the $200 for me to send. I can't really remember what my emotions were at his doing it, but I seem to recall a mixture of gratitude at my husband's readiness to spare me the need to say no to Tom, and a curiosity about what Tom would be like, when he did return to civilization and a steady job. His years in Tahiti must have changed him—but how much?

I do remember that I warned Thayer that the $200 would probably never be paid back.

———CHAPTER———
SIX

I HAD NEVER KNOWN a "real live magazine publisher" either, and whenever Harry Luce and his first wife Lila came to our house for dinner, or we went to theirs, I knew it would be a special evening.

Not a "special event," for in those days, even though Harry was already one of the famous people everybody talked about in the world of publishing, you could call him or Lila at eleven in the morning, and have a good chance of getting them to do something with you that same evening. Or, more often, Harry could call up at eleven in the morning, and invite you for that same night, knowing you would break some other date if you had one, and choose to be with him instead.

Even then, as a young man of thirty-two or thirty-three, he was a compelling presence, though never an easy one. He was a year younger than Thayer, but they had been at Yale together, both class of 1920, both on the Yale *News*, both Skull and Bones, one of Yale's three private societies that labeled you "big man on campus." His weekly newsmagazine Time was only about eight years old, with nothing like the circulation it was to have later on, but it was already a huge money-maker; his radio news show, *The March of Time*, was booming "Time marches on" in countless households, and he had launched a second magazine right into the teeth of the Depression, a business magazine, Fortune.

Henry Robinson Luce was not yet a "press tycoon," but he was already a power in the world of journalism and a very rich man. You would never have guessed it from the way he looked or dressed or acted. He had almost none of the social graces that go with success, no urbane good manners, no small talk. At a party, he hadn't the faintest interest in amusing anecdotes or the swapping of jokes, never bothered to make a complimentary remark to a woman about a new dress she was wearing—he didn't even see it—nor to a hostess about the superb dinner he was eating—he never knew what was on the plate before him. He would fire a question at you in a rapid-fire, almost gruff intensity, usually about one of his political loves or hates, and if you seemed ill-informed in your reply, or vapid or too casual, he would abruptly turn to somebody else.

But one night, at dinner at our house, a black-tie dinner for ten or twelve, Harry suddenly asked a different kind of question. Without preamble, without transition from what he had been saying, his voice raised to subdue other talkers, he suddenly demanded, "How many marriages and divorces at this table?"

One of the women tittered and Harry ignored it. "We've been reading about the divorce statistics in the U.S.," he said firmly, "and here we are, a pretty good sample of the U.S. best. So how many?" He never said, "America," or "the United States." He always said, "the U.S."

"I've been divorced once and married twice," somebody volunteered, apparently embarrassed to speak up.

"I've been married once and divorced never," the woman next him said, more easily.

"Good," Harry said. "Let's go round the table." Several people had been divorced and remarried, several had not been divorced. When it came to Thayer, he said, "Divorced twice, married three times." And then it came to me.

"Once and a half," I said.

"Once and a half what?" said Harry.

"I've been married one and a half times."

106

I said it lightly and there was a ripple of laughter, but everybody understood. Harry Luce, staunch Presbyterian that he was, son of missionaries, understood too. He didn't laugh.

I don't remember how the totals came out, but I was in a young hostess's paradise; the table had sprung alive, and it was Harry Luce, the serious guest, who had done it. Harry had a lot of enemies even then, or at least Time did, and any number of critics, but I was not yet a critic, and I never became an enemy. From the beginning I knew things about him that most people never got to know, and even when I did become a rather sharp critic of his publishing and political sins, I always knew there was something to admire in this strange, convoluted man.

Thayer told me, for example, that when Harry Luce founded Fortune magazine, he had asked Archibald MacLeish to come and work for him. MacLeish, already a published poet, had a young family and none too much money, but what he didn't have was any knowledge of the world of business. This he told Harry, and told him, furthermore, that he was immersed in writing his first long narrative poem, which was a long way from finished.

Harry, the hardheaded publisher, made him an offer anyhow, the sort of offer no sensible publisher in the world would ever have made: go ahead with your poem, keep on writing it, but when you need to earn some money come to Fortune for whatever hours you want to put in. The pay was to be good solid pay, even on that unconventional basis, and Archie MacLeish accepted. The poem turned out to be *Conquistador*, which won the Pulitzer Prize a few years later.

Another thing I heard about young Harry that put down a solid bed of affection, even admiration, in me was that a few years before, when Time was still struggling to make some money, it ran a story about a major shipping company that infuriated its president. The firm was one of Time's first steady advertisers and thus an essential to the business side of the magazine. Its advertising schedule wouldn't be important a few years later, for it was only a single column per issue; but it was for *every* issue, on a twenty-six week contract, which had already been renewed.

The offending story outraged the president to the point where he demanded retraction and apology in the earliest possible issue, in equally prominent space. Harry checked and rechecked the story with his writers, with the researchers involved, with his few colleagues. Then he tried to reason with the president of the firm and his executives. The story had proved to be correct. Time would have to stand by it.

The shipping firm's president was adamant. Retraction, apology or they would cancel their advertising schedule in toto.

Harry took it upon himself to go downtown to see the man. Nobody from the Time force of space salesmen would do. No subeditor would do; it had to be himself.

He showed all Time's research reports; he stated Time's case; he was at his forceful best. Then came the "or else."

"Or else we'll cancel next week's ad and all the others we've signed for."

Harry gathered his papers together, put them back into his briefcase and stood up.

"Then I guess Time has made its own enemy number one." There never was an apology, much less a retraction, and Time did lose the shipping campaign.

If the story is apocryphal, if it has been embroidered by time, I do not know it. I have never heard it denied, even by people who could never accept the barest possibility that Harry Luce had virtues as well as his manifold faults. I think I always saw those faults; at a much later time in my life I was to write a sixteen-page piece about the worst of Time's political and journalistic doings.

But there were certain traits in Harry Luce the person that all his life deeply appealed to many people who were severely opposed to Harry Luce the press tycoon. I was one of those people.

Not all the characters in the new chapter that had opened in my life were Nobel Prize winners, foreign correspondents and magazine publishers. Many of Thayer's personal friends were his Yale classmates and their wives, and many of them lived on Park Avenue, Fifth Avenue, and were in the Social Register, that small book bound in black and red that was supposedly the demarcation point between the upper crust and everybody else.

If you had to make a phone call while you were at one of their houses, you would find the little book sitting there on whatever table held the telephone, the only personal directory needed for their special crowd.

When you were invited to dinner, even just for four people and bridge, you hardly had to ask, "Do we dress?" for it was taken for granted that you did. In the date book that I began to keep at about that time, the notations scrawled at the bottom of the pages nearly all read, "Wallings—7:30 D." or "Farnols—7, Don't D."

The Depression was biting deeply into the life of the nation, but those D's continued. When you went to the opera or the theater, you usually wore evening clothes, and not only for opening night or gala performances.

Since I was not going to an office anymore, I soon found that there were more evening dresses in my closet than daytime dresses, and, in the style of the period, always with evening slippers dyed to match, and smashing costume jewelry to set everything off.

In a remarkably short time it became natural for me to say, "Black tie," when I was inviting people over to our house for the evening. Thayer thought we ought to catch up on our social obligations by giving a big New Year's Eve party, and it became a pattern for all our New Year's Eves.

On the morning after the largest of them, I counted all the people who had been there for some part of the evening, dropping in from other parties, or being there the entire time. There were two hundred.

I had invited my sister Alice and her husband to the first of these parties, but she had turned me down. She didn't have an evening dress, she said; I told her she could wear one of mine. Her next excuse was that Milton didn't have a dinner jacket; he could rent one, I said. Once they got there, I was positive, they'd enjoy themselves.

At last I persuaded her, and we chose a dress that looked as if it were meant only for her. But two or three times before the night of the party, she called me to give me this or that reason why it would be better all around if she didn't "try to be social."

Again I was persuasive, but as it turned out, I was not very wise to be insistent. It was soon all too evident that she was ill at ease, that she felt awkward and out of it and "wallflowery." After perhaps half an hour, she signaled Milton and they left.

I was to ask her to several more parties, but she let me know that she didn't feel comfortable "with that kind of crowd." I don't remember her ever coming to another one of our parties, and at last I gave up trying.

But dinners and cocktail parties for authors, and black-tie evenings were now an established part of our lives. It was a world I had known nothing about before meeting Thayer, except through reading or seeing drawing-room comedies imported from England. It was festive, it was glamorous, it set up your ego; I liked it. I have no intention now of being judgmental about that long-ago Mrs. Thayer Hobson who so enjoyed being "like everybody else" or a little more so, because to any writer or would-be writer, everything one goes through is part of one's development, sensible or silly, profound or snobbish—all of it is grist to the mill—or future mill.

And actually my very first piece of published fiction came right out of that new kind of life I had entered as the wife of Thayer Hobson.

It didn't happen right away. There's nothing one-two-three about getting your first fiction accepted and published. Anybody who has ever tried to write a story for publication knows what a rejection slip or letter of rejection looks like, knows what it feels like to get one, how you are confident one day and then in despair the next. Worst of all, many know how insidious is the notion that you should stop butting your head against the stone walls of editors' offices, and never send in one more thing to one more stupid, biased, ignorant magazine.

The notion came to me often enough, heaven knows, but I went right on butting my head. In my first year of being a wife, with no living to earn, no office to go to, I had sent forth stories titled "Kiss and Sell," "The Flawless Affair" and "The Joyous Swindle," and during one two-month stretch I was showered with nothing but rejection slips or letters like this from my agent:

Dear Miss Mount,

"The Joyous Swindle" was seen by Forum, Harper's, Scribner's, Good Housekeeping, McCall's, Chicago Tribune, Liberty, Redbook, Pictorial Review, Holland's and Ladies Home Journal.

Have you a new story on hand?

Yes, it was still Laura Mount. Thayer didn't mind, far from it. A familiar by-line was an asset, he said, not to be tossed aside. Writers had pseudonyms for a thousand reasons, anyway, pen names, noms de plumes. Look at George Sand, look at Boz, look at George Eliot and the modern Rebecca West. Over-the-transom stories, signed by unknowns wouldn't have half the chance of being read and considered—I should go right on signing my things Laura Mount, especially with editors who were stationed right in the city and presumably read the *Evening Post*.

So I did, and I kept on trying, and at last, at last, there came a different letter. It began, "Everyone thought this excellent and hopes you'll send us something else soon."

It was on the letterhead of The New Yorker. And a few weeks later, in the issue dated April 23, 1932, my first piece of printed fiction appeared. It was short, a sketch more than a story. Here it is, complete:

THE PERFECT MAN

"Lucia has an excellent new butler." (Pause.) "His name is Cohen," Lucia could hear her friends saying.

She stared thoughtfully at the tall and impeccably butlerish person before her. She had been so pleased when the agency had announced they had a perfect man for her, one who had been in the ménage of the Preston Talcotts for three years and who therefore must be well-nigh flawless. They were sending him, with full credentials, that very morning. They hadn't bothered to mention his name, nor had it occurred to Lucia to ask.

When the maid had brought him in, Lucia's first glance had told her everything. Even in ordinary clothes you could tell he

111

was perfection; in butler's dress he would be an angel. He looked like butlers in plays by Lonsdale rather than the ones you actually saw in real life, who all too often were plump, a little bald, oldish. This one was beautifully tall and straight and thirty and—oh, everything.

Before he had said more than "Good morning, madam," with the flatted "mad" that perfect butlers always managed and the deep, quiet voice, she had known the interview was merely a matter of form. She would take him at once.

"Good morning," she had answered pleasantly. "What is your name? The agency didn't—"

"My name, madam, is Cohen."

There had been a pause, there. It was then that she stared at him thoughtfully. In her mind she could hear herself addressing him with guests about, could hear her friends saying to each other, smiling. . . .

"I'm sorry, I'm not sure I understood," she said after a moment.

He cleared his throat gently.

"Cohen, madam." He had such a pleasant voice.

"Cohen?"

"Cohen."

Lucia coughed.

"I see." She watched the little arc her alligator shoetip made in the air as it swung back and forth. . . . Lucia has a new butler, a perfectly marvelous English butler; his name is Cohen.

"Did the Talcotts—"

"Yes, madam, they called me Cohen." Lucia felt herself suddenly uncomfortable. How absurd. Absurd, but she felt a little ashamed before him. He would think—

"My first name, perhaps?" he suggested, so quietly. Lucia looked up quickly. He gazed down at her, helpful and friendly.

"Oh, your first name," she repeated, not asking, merely wondering.

"Percival, madam," he said.

Lucia's voice sounded very dull. "Percival. . . . I see. No, I think perhaps . . ."

Lucia has a new butler, a handsome, very British new butler;

his name is Percival; Percival, my dear; his name is Cohen; his name is . . . No, there was something wrong here. She felt confused. She felt she would blush, with that tall and superior person watching, smiling just a little, understanding . . .

He uttered one of those little deprecatory sounds that make people look at butlers at the right moment. Lucia looked at him. His manner was perfectly impersonal, yet somehow conveying messages of reassurance about his attitude (with a flat "a") toward Lucia. She felt grateful to him. He was kind.

"Yes, ah, Cohen?" she asked.

"I should be glad, madam, to change it for you."

"Change it for me?"

"Yes, quite. Such things, you see, mean nothing to me." He said it so simply. Lucia sat very straight.

"They don't mean anything to—" She broke off. She had sounded indignant, defensive. To a butler. Oh, this was very humiliating.

He hadn't noticed. "Perhaps to, ah, Manning. Whatever you'd feel—"

She cut him off sharply. She said nothing, but her head snapped a clear enough gesture. There was a long silence.

"I'm sorry, madam. I merely suggested it. I suggested the same thing to Mrs. Talcott." Lucia looked up quickly, her eyes full of curiosity.

"Oh, really? What did she—?"

"They wouldn't hear of a change, madam. They said they loved it." He looked down modestly.

Lucia was suddenly furious. They loved it, did they? They were so superior, so sure of everything; they could have millions of butlers called Ginsburg or Paganini or anything and love it and gayly tell people about their superb name for a butler. The poseurs! The snobs! She had to say something to him, change the subject.

"Why did you leave the Talcotts, Cohen?" she said.

There was another silence. He was considering. He looked so imperturbably British.

"After three years?" she prompted. "Why did they—?"

"Oh, no, madam, they didn't dismiss me," he said, mildly

surprised that she had assumed it. "I left them."

"*You* left the Talcotts?"

"Yes, quite."

"But what . . . why?"

"If you will permit, madam, I think I should rather not discuss the matter."

Lucia gasped a little. He went on calmly and so pleasantly.

"Perhaps you'd like me to get Mrs. Talcott for you on the telephone," he suggested gently, "so you can reassure yourself that *I* did nothing?" She made no answer, simply stared. "You see, I feel that it would be bad form of me to discuss what it was displeased me. That is, if you permit—"

"I—of course, I—" She felt she could have killed herself for being so stammery.

"Perhaps you'd like to know, ah, I receive one and a quarter the month, madam; would that be satisfactory or—?"

"Oh, quite satisfactory," Lucia murmured. She couldn't do it. She could not take this butler, this butler named . . . He would have to change it after all. No, she couldn't do that either, simply couldn't admit—

"Would you like me to start at once, madam?" he was asking. "Tomorrow is the first. You'll find all the references you will want in this, I'm sure." He handed her an envelope. She took it silently. He bowed beautifully. The perfect butler. She couldn't take him. She simply couldn't.

"I think so; yes, of course," she heard herself saying, "ah, Cohen."

"Thank you, madam, I am delighted. I shall tell them in the kitchen? Good morning."

He was gone. She sat, still. This was appalling. Suddenly she got up and went to the telephone, dialled hurriedly.

"Hello, Lois? It's Lucia, darling. Just to tell you not to bother asking about your mother's—no, I just got one. Perfect; and, my dear, *what* do you suppose?" Lucia's laugh tinkled, high and sweet. "His name is Cohen . . . Yes, that's what I said, Cohen. He was the Talcotts' man, you know. Isn't it *precious*? . . . What? . . . Yes, I adore it too. It's *too* priceless. I couldn't resist it. I . . ."

—LAURA MOUNT

114

It is impossible to imagine myself writing that story if I were still living at home in Jamaica, or living in Greenwich Village with Tom Mount.

And at about the same time, I went through an episode that also could have come only from the new life I was leading. It happened at one of those black-tie dinners one night, and there had been news in the morning papers and on the radio that Hitler's Nazis were stepping up attacks on the Jews of Germany. During the night, storm troopers had invaded working-class Jewish neighborhoods, smashing store windows, harassing people coming out of synagogues, all to the general delight of good faithful Hitlerites.

At the dinner table, the men in their dinner jackets and some of the women in their evening dresses were talking lightly about "those awful Germans." One of the men conceded that Hitler was being a little extreme, but that extremism always crept into the start of a new regime. There was some offhand discussion of the point he had made, some light jesting, some wisecracks about Jews.

I sat there listening, knowing that any minute I was going to speak up. But nothing came to me in words, only in a buried quiver of knowing I wasn't just going to sit there. Everybody we knew knew I was Jewish, but generally it went unmentioned, perhaps as being too unimportant to mention—or possibly too indelicate.

Another man across the table remarked that Hitler wasn't merely being extreme. "The chosen people ask for it, wherever they are."

"Oh, come on," another man said. "Some of my best friends are Jews."

"Some of mine are too," I heard myself saying, slowly. "Including my mother and father."

Silence hit that table. A crazy elation boiled up inside me. You don't have to sit there and take it, I thought, you don't have to be the one embarrassed. Let *them* take it too, let *them* be embarrassed.

I glanced at Thayer. He winked approval at me. In a moment they began to talk again and the dinner party went on.

* * *

An enormous change came into Thayer's life and mine with the death of William Morrow, founder of the firm. His widow, Honoré Willsie Morrow, an author herself, no longer young, had neither the training nor the desire to take over in his place as head of the firm; instead she moved to England with their children and settled there permanently. She offered to sell Thayer her stock. It would make him president of the company.

The opportunity electrified him. To have his own publishing house! Before he was thirty-five! From the moment the offer came, nothing mattered more to us than finding the way to manage it.

Thayer had inherited some money, years before, when his mother died, as had his brother and two sisters, about $100,000 each, but a great part of that had vanished in the Wall Street crash.

He hadn't been one of those who had stubbornly clung to his stocks until they were worthless; he had taken a big loss but got out before he was wiped out. All this had happened before we were married, and at the time I was hardly aware of Wall Street, except for lurid stories of bankers jumping out of windows.

But I did know that several months later, while we were abroad on our honeymoon, when most of the experts, including Thayer's broker, thought the worst was over, Thayer, like so many other people, got back into the "recovering market" in plenty of time for future losses.

So when Mrs. Morrow made her offer, he was in no position to jump at it. The Depression was in its second year by then, getting uglier each week. It is true that none of our own friends were selling apples for a nickel on street corners, nor had anybody we knew been fired from a good job and been forced to hire out as a janitor or store clerk. But the Depression hung like a black oily fog over everybody's consciousness, over every plan that needed money. The notion of trying for a substantial bank loan would have been fatuous.

"I could sell out every last share," Thayer finally said, "and use it as a down payment. I probably could work out some kind of installment deal with Honoré for the rest of it." He shook his head despondently. "But then we'd have to live on just my salary. And we couldn't."

"I could try to get a copy job again."

I remember the feeling as I said it. Partly the old wonderful eagerness to help somebody I loved, and partly a reluctance to give up or even alter the happy pattern of our living. I had been taking piano lessons and studying French—not to speak it, but to be able to read easily in a second language—and I was working fairly well at writing what I thought might be a novel. I had written about forty-five pages of it.

"There must be some jobs in agencies even now," I went on. "The papers and magazines still carry ads—somebody must be writing them."

That old proofbook of my copy for George Batten Company and all my free-lance accounts stood me in good stead. Agencies were not taking on new staff, but in the end I got a half-time job at B. Altman, one of New York's long-established department stores. I was to write "high fashion" copy, something I had never attempted.

Macy's was running a clever campaign, right in the mood of the times—"It's smart to be thrifty"—and I would have felt far more confident if I had been given some such realistic assignment, but if copy on high fashion was what my new boss, John Clark Wood, vice-president and advertising manager of the store, wanted—then high fashion would become my new field. It was the middle of winter in 1932, and seventy-five dollars for an afternoon job could have had ten thousand people leaping for it. I felt lucky, and reported for work the very next day. At high noon.

In the evenings, I was still a publisher's wife and a hostess, though we cut back hard on the frequency of those evenings. But I was once again a job-holder, earning money on my own. It felt good.

Thayer's deal with Mrs. Morrow went through and we were happier than ever. We lived only on what he and I brought home as weekly salaries, and knew there could be no more sudden vacations for some time. On his necessary annual publishing trip to London, on one of which I had gone along, he would now have to go alone, but that prospect did not disturb us either.

And then Thayer devised a scheme by which we could earn

some extra money *together*. *Sure* extra money, what was more, free of risk, guaranteed safe.

We would collaborate on a book that would absolutely find a publisher even in those hard times for the book trade. How so sure? Because the new president of Morrow would publish it himself. And hard times notwithstanding, it would sell enough to earn us a few hundred dollars. For it would be the kind of book that always sold, a Western, complete with cowboys, hosses, saddles, saloons, fastest-draw-in-the-West and the lot.

Thayer ran the whole venture. The plot was his, the characters were named by him, it was he who parceled out which parts of the story I would write and which he would. He wrote the first chapter, I the second, he the third, I the fourth, and so on to the end. Then he did the final job of seaming all the locutions and scenes and dialogue together, editing it to make it speak with one voice.

We stuck to it; we spent evenings and weekends doing it; we really did come up with a full-length book. We signed it with a pen name, Peter Field.

I have no idea where the name Peter Field came from—Thayer thought that up too, just as he thought up all the other names in the book, the Lazy Mare Ranch, the Golden Fleece Saloon, Powder Valley, Pat Stevens, the hero, and Sally, the heroine.

I am suddenly glad, piously glad, that I can say so unhesitantly that all the names were Thayer's choices, for as I sit here now, decades later, I can hear all too plainly the happy jeer I recently endured from my son Chris, when I said I was at the point in this book where I was writing about Peter Field and the Good Old West.

"Do you remember the names of the horses in it?" he asked.

"Of course not—I haven't looked at it in fifty years."

"One was a black horse called Darky," he said gleefully, "and the other a bronco named Nigger."

"Oh my God, No!"

In perfect filial fashion, he guffawed at my horrified look. I kept on saying, "*No*, not really, oh heavens," but after he left the house, I fetched the wretched volume and looked for myself. Not only was he right about Darky and Nigger—he had read the book, he said, years ago at school—but there also was "a little Chinaman, Cholly Lee," who was Pat Stevens' cook and a cherished character, nearly always addressed by him as "Chink."

In a moment of pure honesty, I reached for the phone to call Chris and own up to this further outrage, but in the act of dialing, I cringed and decided that Chink could wait, unremembered, until Chris came across him in *this* book.

That western was called *Outlaws Three*. Inside the first copy, Thayer drew an elongated, angular beast, whether a longhorn or a hoss I now cannot decide, with its rear quarter branded in true Western style, a heart pierced by an arrow.

"To Peter from Field," he wrote in pencil. There's a yellowed clipping of a newspaper review pasted inside, that starts, "What happens in *Outlaws Three* is supposed to have happened in the 1880s . . . but Peter Field is the sort of writer who knows how to make it happen right before your eyes. You won't draw a calm breath from the first page to the last. . . ." etcetera, etcetera.

It sold for $2 and earned us about $500, and we were so tickled with ourselves, that we set about doing another one, also signed Peter Field, this one yclept *Dry Gulch Adams*. A year or so later, that too was published; it too earned about $500, and lo and behold, there were two books sitting there side by side on a shelf in our living room which I could look at and feel half-authorship of, plus some rave reviews for which I could give myself half a pat on the back. Maybe I had even learned a good bit about plotting a book and writing it and staying with it from start to finish.

But despite the two books and the two paychecks each week, we were pressed for money like everybody else. Thayer's first wife, Janet Camp, daughter of Yale's famous football coach, Walter Camp, did not remarry for a long time, and he was still paying her alimony. His second wife, Priscilla Fanzler, had married again before we were married, and her alimony had halted, but the child-support checks for Timmy still went on, more of a burden now than before. Thayer finally insisted on cutting down on those, in proportion to the drop in the cost of everything else, but they were never to stop.

119

Timmy was still visiting his father at the legally appointed times, but now that we were living on the seventeenth floor of a big apartment building, he could no longer be left at street level to come up by himself, not even at the elderly age of six.

Priscilla still wished to avoid any meeting with Thayer, so it was Timmy's stepfather who brought him over to us, riding up in the elevator and delivering him straight to our door. I was the one who would take Timmy home across Central Park when his visit was over.

And that was how I got to meet Alger Hiss, Priscilla's second husband. He was still in his twenties then, tall, handsome, and by all accounts a brilliant young lawyer, assistant to Justice Oliver Wendell Homes of the Supreme Court, destined for an illustrious career at the highest levels.

Indeed, after seeing Alger Hiss for a few times, despite the brevity of each meeting and the fact that our talk was largely limited to what Timmy had done, I was so impressed with his obvious intelligence, his charm and even his good looks, that I felt the first quiver of anxiety about Thayer's other marriages.

I had been told by somebody that Thayer had left Priscilla with a parting note on a pincushion—though that might have been the way he left Janet—but pincushion or whatever, I knew that Thayer and Priscilla had parted suddenly, with Thayer doing the parting, and now I began to speculate about their breakup, though I never had done so before.

If Priscilla was good enough as a wife, I wondered, for Alger, this superior, appealing young man, why was she not good enough for Thayer to stay married to?

But that quiver of anxiety was squelched by the reasoning process; everybody knew that some people are right for some people and wrong for others. Nevertheless I never did forget what little I saw of the young Alger Hiss, and years later, when the Hiss trials began in 1948, I could stop any conversation about it dead in its tracks by murmuring, "In a way, I used to be related to Alger Hiss."

"High fashion" as an adjective generally means high-priced, but at Altman I also wrote about clothes that were not so high.

Whether or not writing ads can be considered any preparation for real writing has been argued many times, pro and con, but in my opinion *any* kind of daily writing is an invaluable apprenticeship for anybody intending to become a professional writer, not just a hobby writer.

Good ads have to have headlines that catch the attention; some of them have a story to tell, a mood to set, but more important than any other consideration, they are there to be done every day. Whether you're in a mood to write or not, you go to that typewriter or pick up that pencil; you can't make excuses for skipping a day; you learn to ignore a headache and write; you learn to surmount sadness or worry and write; you grow out of all nonsense about "not being in the mood," or waiting until the spirit moves you.

At Altman I never spent an hour without writing. I didn't keep a proofbook of any of my work there, but there were several highlights that brought raises and advancement. Soon I had to have an assistant for odds and ends—a Vassar graduate, Carroll Whedon, who dubbed herself "the garbage girl," and who became the closest friend I had until her death thirty-five years later. At the end of my first year, my boss asked me to change to full-time and raised my pay to $135. (Why it was not double my $75, I don't know, but in the Depression you didn't haggle over raises, as he well knew.)

By then Franklin Delano Roosevelt was being inaugurated and telling us we had nothing to fear but fear itself. It was 1933. It would be absurd for me, or anybody else probably, to name one year and say, "That is when I became a political being as well as a private being," because underneath and behind that one particular year are all the subterranean influences and pressures of all the earlier years, from babyhood onward, but it if were not so absurd, I would say, "It happened in 1933."

But as his hundred days of the new deal began, with his talk of the forgotten man, the unemployed, the despairing old, the jobless young—every word of his compassion made my heart jump. The new measures he sent racing through the Congress, the National Recovery Administration, the Civilian Conservation Corps, the Public Works Administration, all his new bills with their melange of initials that made his detractors sneer about "alphabet soup," the N.R.A., the C.C.C., the P.W.A.—each time I read the news of a new support he was proposing, to prop up the staggering nation, a rush of grateful hope went through me.

I had never seen anything like it in big everyday newspapers. This wasn't something in the liberal or radical press, the New Leader, the New Republic or the Nation. This was right there leaping out at you from the front pages of the *Times* and the *Tribune* and every newspaper the country over.

I wished my mother were still alive. I could hear her say, "Oh, my goodness, imagine a government *caring* about its people that way."

I called my father right after the inaugural, and we had a meal together, as we did every few weeks. "They'll never admit it," he said, "not even Roosevelt himself, but this New Deal is what mama and I and the rest of us have been fighting for all our lives. Just think—some kind of old-age insurance, some temporary pay when you lose your job, new regulations to stop Wall Street from letting people get killed off on margin, government insurance of the money you put in your savings at the bank..."

But it wasn't only FDR that turned me into a person who devoured newspapers for more than their book and theater reviews. Hitler was now officially chancellor of the Third Reich; radio broadcasts gave us all his roaring and ranting to the millions who idolized *Der Führer*; the first official boycott of all Jewish shops began, evoking an international protest about the boycott; Jews had to wear special yellow arm bands to mark them in the streets, and had to sit on special benches in parks, railroad stations and all public places; eminent Jews were summarily dismissed from the universities and from the government.

And on the tenth of May, 1933, symbolizing for me all the other obnoxiousness of Nazism, was the public burning of the books. That perhaps more than any single event turned my own life outward, and my private life intertwined with the life of the world. Much later I was to think of that book-burning as the first holocaust.

In the world of fashion, the two highest points of any year were the Paris openings in January and July. At the start of 1934, my job at Altman hit its own high point because I came up with an idea that not only delighted my boss, but was to lead on to something much more rewarding than writing ads for a store.

Seven years had passed since Lindbergh showed that oceans were for flying over, but even then it was not possible to hop a plane and go in a few hours to Europe. The press, major dress buyers from every country's big stores, fabric manufacturers, magazine fashion editors all went a week or two ahead, by ocean liner, and though the daily newspapers and *Women's Wear* all ran cabled reports the following morning; it was a long wait for the immediacy of sketches or photographs. And the cabled reports inevitably had the tone and feel of news reporting.

One day I went to John Wood, saying, "It's a crazy idea, but I think we could scoop the whole city on the openings."

"Scoop how?"

"Scoop Vogue and Harper's, of course, they're weeks off, but scoop even the *Times* and the *Trib* and all the dailies."

"And just how do you propose to do that?"

"The minute Margery comes out of a Chanel opening, or Lanvin or Schiaparelli," I said, trying to sound matter-of-fact and practical, "we could have her on the phone, in a three-way hookup, with you and me listening. She could give me one or two highlights of what she saw, and I could write it that same day, and have it in all the papers the next morning."

John Wood got it immediately. Margery Castle was our own fashion representative in Paris and London; she would know what would make good copy, she would be precise and articulate, even leaping from the last mannequin in a Paris showroom to her telephone at her hotel.

Transatlantic telephoning was no ordinary little matter, either, in 1934, and a three-way hookup took planning and arranging — and money. It would be expensive, but John Wood didn't mind. There would be two such calls each day for the week of the openings, since Paris was five hours ahead of us, and nobody knew how long each call would last.

The first one we tried might be the last; I had no idea of how it would go, nor did my boss.

"Hi, Margery," I said, "What's the weather like over there?"

"Cold enough to freeze Kelsey's," she said. She and John Wood talked through a sentence or two and then we got down to business.

By great luck there was some real news right off the bat. One of the newer names in fashion, Elsa Schiaparelli, had gone in for big wide padded shoulders on women's suits, coats, even dresses and blouses. As I listened, I knew I could write about that in a tone of hot–new–exclusive–extra–extra.

Yesterday in Paris
Schiaparelli
showed fashions
that will put your shoulders
way out to *here*.

The headline must have gone something like that. The whole ad was done in enlarged typewriter type, widely spaced lines, lots of dots between items . . . lots of detail . . . with the two main openings covered, as if two women had been right there and were talking about them. With some judicious changes.

"Hi, Margery, what's the weather like over there?"

"I've just come out of Schiap's show and I'm frozen."

"How was the show? Anything exciting?"

"You're going to throw out any tight-fitting dress you have and wear one with great big new-looking shoulders."

"New-looking how?"

"Padded, and sort of square, and just stunning."

Et cetera. Of course I made up most of the phrasing, but there was nothing phony in the factual part of it, nothing that would show up as incorrect when the sketches and photographs did arrive ten days later. A big box of type explained the telephone arrangement between us and Paris.

Well. Even Time covered Altman's "fashion coup" in its business section that week, not naming me, of course, but praising John Wood for his promotional talent. There was a good bit of hullaballoo at most department stores and specialty shops. Never again would there be a dead spot of several days before any of those competitors managed to connect up with a Paris opening.

That summer, at an outdoor dinner party at some country club in Westchester, I was seated next to Roy Larsen, another of the bright young men in the highest echelons of Time Inc. Roy was devoting himself just then to developing radio's *March of Time* into a regular feature for the movies, where it was normal practice to run a selection of news items during the preliminaries of every program.

We talked about that, and then he asked what I was doing. I told him about Altman. He remembered Time's business story about "the Altman stunt," and asked about it, and when he heard how it came about, he really looked impressed. Then and there I got another crazy idea.

"Someday," I said, "I'd like to do promotion for Time."

Everybody knew that women were nothing but researchers at Time, and he looked at me as if I'd said that some day I'd like to be the First Lady.

"Does Harry know you'd like to work for Time?" he asked.

Of course he didn't—I hadn't know it myself until that very moment. I was sure Roy would tell him what I had said, but next day I did none of the live-wire things you're supposed to do with opportunity, like phoning, "How about it?"

We were going out West for a vacation, for one thing. I had never been west of Philadelphia and couldn't wait. Thayer was out in California already, on publishing business, and I was to meet him in Reno, where he would be waiting with a hired car. The idea of getting off a train at Reno, not for a divorce like the usual unhappy woman getting off there, but in a holiday mood, with my husband waiting for me, with plans to tour the Rockies, then see the great Salt Lake and the Painted Desert and the giant redwoods and the Pacific, and then Hollywood and movie studios and movie stars—all this seemed more immediate than phoning Harry Luce about a job.

We were both in need of some real rest and recreation. It had been a hard-pressed year. Thayer seemed at times to be working more intensely than ever, though things were going reasonably well at Morrow; he had a new mystery writer, Erle Stanley Gardner, whose first book, *The Case of the Velvet Claws*, was

125

such a bestseller that Thayer was signing him up on a long-term deal for other stories about Perry Mason. Even so, Thayer often seemed overtired or nervous about the future.

As for me, again and again I had to fight off remembering that I was still not pregnant, and that it was now the fourth year of my trying to be. I was still being faithful about my visits to Dr. Damon, still being encouraged about improvement. Once he even ventured a guess—"Maybe this coming year"—but still not pregnant.

We even tried artificial insemination, something far more daring in the thirties than it is today. It didn't "take," and Thayer and I decided that if, by 1935, we still had no success, we would adopt a baby.

All along I swore I would never become one of those sad, obsessed women who let their lives be wrecked because they couldn't have a baby. But whenever I saw my sister with her baby son, some of my old inferiority came over me; even when I looked at Dr. Damon's other patients in his waiting room, most of them in various stages of pregnancy, I began to look at them in a kind of helpless awe, wondering why they could all do so easily what I was now unable to do.

And just about then, before our vacation out West, something happened that made it even harder for me to stay clear of my obsession about having a baby. And who should bring about that extra element in my struggle but Tom Mount?

The return to civilization, which he spoke of in his cable from Tahiti, had turned out to be a return to France, specifically Brittany. He had been living in a French environment in Tahiti, speaking French, studying it, and in Brittany he enrolled in a lycée for advanced courses in French.

His teacher was a young Frenchwoman, Andrée Pommier, and soon they were in love. Also, pretty soon, Andrée was pregnant. But in the Pommier family there could be nothing for a pregnancy except a rapid marriage.

I do not know when or how Tom finally managed a divorce from Olive, but I do know there was what Andrée calls "a white wedding," complete with red carpet on the sidewalk outside the church, and on the steps leading into the church and up to the altar. There was also a *dot* for the bride of 100,000 francs. The following April their first son was born.

They had lived in France until their money gave out and then came back to America, settling in a small house in Woodstock, near Kingston, New York. In time we all four did the modern thing, and met several times. When it became clear that Tom still had no steady job, what with the Depression and his long absences from the advertising world, Thayer said that if he wanted to try his hand at writing a Western, the way we had done, he would help him along with suggestions and editing, and that Morrow might very well publish it.

Writing Westerns for Morrow became Tom's surest way of earning a living, albeit a sporadic one, for he still was not a man who could hold himself to a schedule of daily work.

And then, a few weeks before the trip to the Rockies and the Painted Desert and the giant redwoods, Tom telephoned me. Again he sounded desperate, again he was in crisis, again he had no one to turn to but me.

Andrée was about to give birth for the second time, and there was no money for doctors, hospital, anything. Could I lend him $300?

I told Thayer all about it, saying that since I was now earning money of my own, if I did agree to make this new loan, it would be my own $300, not his. For a day or two I tried *not* to agree; I tried to think of what I could say to Tom to turn down his appeal, and finally admitted that it wasn't in me to do it.

But it hurt. The sardonic paradox in the situation haunted me. During my life with Tom there had had to be that brutal abortion, and then another one. And now, while I was unable, because of them, to have a baby, he was asking me to pay for the birth of *his* child.

I sent the $300.

And I'd been unable, too, to get anything more accepted by the New Yorker. I tried another sketch, "Central Park Pan," about a music student with no place to practice, and received a printed rejection card. I tried another about a lonely woman who sends herself flowers and gifts so her friends won't guess the extent of her solitude. Another printed card.

I tried nonfiction. A profile of Yehudi Menuhin, then a boy in his teens, at least brought a letter; it was too full of admiration, they told me, without that faint touch of skepticism they felt it needed. I did another profile, of a famous attorney, Samuel Untermeyer. That too earned a letter with a firm No, thanks.

Rejections are never easy to take. In addition to all this, or perhaps because of all this, we were going out more than usual, to the movies, to the theater, to parties. Now my datebook often had evenings a step removed from publishers and editors and authors. I had begun to jot down not only *D* or *Don't D* and the time and where, but also, the morning after, the names of the other guests at parties, against future New Year's Eve invitations at our house. These datebooks I did save year after year.

One particular page in April 1934 pretty well dazzled me when I came upon it recently. It was a party at Beatrice Kaufman's house, the wife of George S. Kaufman, the playwright, given for the founder and head of Viking Press, Harold Guinzburg, and his wife, Alice.

"Bon Voyage to G's—11:30 *D*." Then, in an unusual move for me, a few jotted comments.

> Theatrical mostly—dull—beautiful clothes—nothing more boring than a roomful of determined beautifully dressed women...
>
> Margalo Gilmore, Ellin Mackay Berlin, Clare B. Brokaw, Noel Coward, Harpo Marx, H. B. Swopes, Geo. S. Kaufman, Geo. Gershwin, Walter Winchell, Pulitzers, etc.

And the very next night, another party, this one a literary one for authors and publishers and critics. The next night nothing, but the night after, another party at Roy Larsen's in River House.

But parties pass and vacations end, and one morning in early autumn, during some irksome talk at Altman about what would be the "big number" this season and what the "Fords," my own voice echoed in my mind. "Someday, I'd like to do promotion for Time."

This time I did pick up the phone and call Harry Luce. I acted on impulse, without first rehearsing some diplomatic way of putting it, and told him I had an idea about me and Time, and could I talk about it with him when he had a free fifteen minutes.

"Sure," he said. "Where are you? Come on over."

Half an hour later I had walked the eight blocks from Altman to the still-new Chrysler Building, and gone up to his office very near its ornate pointed top. And once the preliminaries were out of the way, I was saying things I hadn't known I thought, until I put them into words and heard how true they were about my point of view.

"I've often wondered, Harry, why it is that Time always writes with so bright and clever a touch *in* the magazine, but turns sort of banal and stuffy when it writes about itself in an ad or piece of promotion?"

"Is that what you think?" His big eyebrows shot up and he shot the question at me in his usual abrupt style, but he seemed more interested than annoyed. He was always game when he was challenged. He knew all about the work I did, knew I was no amateur. "I suppose you can give me some example of how bad we are?"

I had been sure he would challenge me too, and my good memory let me be specific. In those days Time's promotional efforts were mostly done by mail, in sprightly, well-done letters, but I talked about two or three announcements they had recently run in the papers. "They have an institutional air," I said. "A little pompous."

He didn't like that final word. He stared at me. But at last he said, "Well, we might give it a try." He asked how much pay I'd want.

"I'm getting seven thousand."

Now he was annoyed. "Nobody here would go for that," he said crisply. "We don't pay people more than five thousand."

He meant they didn't pay women more than five thousand. Later I learned that only one woman there earned as much as five thousand at that time; she was in charge of the *Letters* department, deciding which letters should be printed, editing them, answering some herself as spokesman for the editors.

"I couldn't agree to five," I said slowly, careful not to sound

129

hurt or disappointed. "Taking a step backward in salary is so demoralizing."

"For a trial period," he stated. "To see how it works out. Perhaps for six months." He still sounded annoyed.

I sat up straighter. "What about a trial period with *no* salary? Then after six months, you would know whether I'm *worth* seven, and it could be retroactive."

"Nobody works here for no salary!" He was silent for a moment and then gave in on the seven, still sounding gruff. He would discuss it with a few of the people I'd be working with, and I'd hear from him soon.

It wasn't soon; it was December, but two weeks before Christmas, I became the first woman hired not as a researcher, not as a secretary, not for letters, but the first woman taken on for a major job on Time, the weekly newsmagazine.

SEVEN

AND THEN, SUDDENLY, CAME divorce. I put it that abruptly because that is how it came to me. There was no warning, no preparation.

It was like a drawing room comedy by Noel Coward or Frederick Lonsdale, the two of us sitting together on our sofa in our lovely living room, having after-dinner coffee from our small black Wedgwood demitasses, and Thayer quietly saying, "I have something to tell you."

There was a long pause, me looking attentive, expectant. "I've fallen in love with somebody," he went on. "Somebody else. I've tried to fight it for a year, all this past year, but I couldn't. So I have to tell you—I'm so sorry to hurt you, but I want a divorce."

Falling in love at first sight may be a myth, but annihilation in one moment is not. It was like a bomb dropping, a bullet to the inner brain.

I didn't behave well. I wept, I grew hysterical, I couldn't speak in sentences, my breath tore out of my throat in gasps. As he told me—off and on through most of the night—how it had happened, I went through layer after layer of shock, of disbelief, a shuddering away from this sudden explosion of everything my life had come to be.

It had begun a year ago, he said, one night in January, when he had sailed for England and his annual publishing trip on the S.S. *Manhattan*. I had gone to the pier to see him off, behaving well enough then by showing nothing of my longing to go with him.

Just three days before he had written me a short note, which later went into my safe-deposit box with all the legal documents connected with divorce. I could never in my life let anyone else read a love letter, new or old, but there comes the perfect exception to any rule.

> Laura my beloved. Five years—a terribly long time and isn't everything lovely. You and I have such a grand marriage, and I have grown to regard it as part of life itself. Imagining life without you is as fantastic as thinking of living without a head.
>
> So remember all day today that I love you and that I thank all the powers that be that we found each other five years ago today.
>
> THAYER

But three days later, on the S.S. *Manhattan*, there was a young woman, Isabelle. She was on her way to France, Thayer told me during that night, to marry the man she had been engaged to for some time. She was a platinum blond, "a little theatrical looking," he said, and for three days she would have nothing to do with him. Then he sent a note to her table, and their affair began.

When he came home a month later, she remained in France for a while, but broke off her engagement to the man she had gone over to marry. Thayer was determined, he said, to renounce this new love, and I am sure he meant it. But he couldn't, or at least he didn't. As he kept on talking, I realized that all through our wonderful vacation through the Rockies and the Painted Desert and Hollywood, he had been in love with somebody else, all through our continued efforts to have a baby. My worry that he seemed overtired and nervous about the future, hadn't been merely a thing of my own imagination.

Early in November, despite money problems and the Depression, he embarked again on a publishing trip abroad, the second that year, highly unusual in itself, and more so because it was on the much larger, more expensive S.S. *Majestic*.

There was a bon voyage party in his cabin, with the Wallings and lots of other friends, lots of champagne, all the smiles and quips usual at such gala moments.

All those smiling laughing guests knew one thing I did not know: Isabelle was in the next cabin.

This too Thayer told me during that long night of revelation, along with many details of mail-forwarding of my letters, prearranged cable addresses and the rest of the paraphernalia of deception. He seemed to be under some compulsion to confess all, as if to acknowledge guilt, to emphasize it, were to eradicate it.

And I seemed to be under an equal compulsion to hear all, like a suicide taking sleeping pills, swallowing another and another and then another, to be sure the deed is done. "If it were done when 'tis done, then 'twere well it were done quickly."

I said I did not behave well—none of that lovely grace under pressure people talk about, usually when it is somebody else under the pressure.

The next morning, after perhaps an hour's sleep, I went to my new job at Time—I had been there only three weeks and to call in absent was impossible. I had packed a suitcase and left it at the Wallings, where I was to stay for the next nine days, unable to return to our apartment while Thayer was moving out. Bill Walling was one of Thayer's closest friends, and had become one of mine, and now was to be more than that, my comforter, my adviser, the go-between in any necessary dealings with Thayer.

Eight days later I wrote a seven-page letter to Thayer, a frantic letter filled with desperate suggestions about trying to save our marriage, suggestions that make me boil with fury now that any woman (most women?) should feel her life exploded into shreds and shards because a man leaves her.

Perhaps Thayer and his new love could just have an affair for a year, to see if it was only an infatuation? Perhaps he could leave New York with her for a year, for some place like Arizona, pleading illness as the reason for his absence—he had been wounded in the war and still carried splinters of shrapnel in his lungs. I even implored him, now that Dr. Damon seemed so sure that this might be the year—implored him to let us try artificial insemination again, so I wouldn't be losing that part of my life too. It could be done without my even seeing him in the doctor's office.

Thayer's reply was pretty frantic too, longer than my letter, filled with *I am guilty*—"None of this is your fault—you're so good and I'm such a rotter—this just eclipsed everything I've ever known—"

And the next day came a briefer letter setting forth an offer he had made me that long terrible night—the offer of nothing less than William Morrow & Company.

That too went into my safe-deposit box. It would take time to arrange the transfer, he wrote, perhaps a year, to pave the way with his partner Charles Duell and others in the firm, but it could be done. He knew how I hated to give up the whole world of publishing that I had grown to love. He wanted to live in the country, anyway, and write stories.

> This is just an informal note, putting into writing our understanding about Morrow. You understand that I've got certain financial obligations to take care of there, but as soon as is possible for you and me, I'll fix things...so that you can go into the company and so that your interest in the company and control will be substantially what mine is now...your position as far as Morrow and Morrow stock and Morrow control will be what mine is now.

It ended, "I'm sorry about everything. Forgive me if you can."

Just imagine! I might have had a life as a publisher, filled with Perry Mason bestsellers (Gardner wrote over a hundred books) and all the other successes Morrow was to have. And when the firm finally was sold, some forty years later, for about $75 million, the biggest share might have been mine!

But of course my answer to Thayer was the equivalent of "you don't have to bribe me; if it's over it's over." And alimony went against my Zametkinish principles, so I said no to that. My lawyer did nothing to dissuade me; I had never had a lawyer, and scarcely knew this one. Some time later, through Bill Walling, I did say that since about $20,000 of my earnings through the past three years, had gone into our common life to help Thayer acquire his Morrow stock, I ought to get at least half of that sum back.

What I got was not cash, but a certifcate for 134 shares of Morrow's preferred stock. A few months later, I tried to make a bank loan of $500, offering the stock as collateral. The bank said it was of no value as collateral and rejected the application for a loan.

But some time after that, the vice-president of Morrow, Charles Duell, who had invested some $30,000 in the firm when he became a partner, offered to buy the preferred stock that was in my name. I talked to Bill Walling about this proposition, uncertain whether this might diminish Thayer's margin of control in the company, and not willing to act behind his back, in any case.

But the very name *Morrow* still opened wounds afresh for me; the idea of hanging on to a stock certificate that maintained any connection to the life Thayer was still leading was chilling, even repugnant, as if I were indulging in the self-flogging of mnemonic reminders.

Bill took it all up with Thayer. In the end Thayer offered me fifty cents on the dollar of the face value of the stock certificate, and when I received his check for $10,000, I invested it in Time stock, and severed that last connecting thread to the world of book publishing—never dreaming that one day I would enter it on my own from the author's side of the royalty statements.

One of those storybook coincidences that make for such great anecdotes years later when all pain is spent, tied Harry and Lila Luce's divorce to Thayer's and mine.

That was a Thursday night, when Thayer told me about Isabelle, the third of January, 1935. He had intended to tell me the night before, waiting only through the New Year's festivities, settling on the second night of the new year to say, "I have something to tell you."

But on the morning of that second day, a Wednesday, Harry had called me on the office phone, asking if we were free that evening, and how about dinner and the opera with Lila and himself? I checked with Thayer and told Harry's secretary we'd love to. Thus my marriage lasted one day longer, courtesy of Harry Luce.

The Luces were living in a rather grand apartment on East Seventy-second Street, just off Fifth Avenue. Though we were just four at dinner, it was all very formal, with a couple of footmen in livery behind the dining-room chairs. (I'm sure this was Lila's doing, not Harry's.) We dined and went off to the old Metropolitan Opera House on Broadway, below Forty-second Street.

The opera was *Manon*, not anybody's favorite. During the intermission, going to the bar for drinks, we paired off, Lila with Thayer, Harry with me. Harry was bored with the music; he seemed nervous; he fidgeted, and talked about the diffuclties of launching *The March of Time* in the nation's movie houses next month.

"Harry," I said after a bit, "what with all the extra work on *The March of Time* and everything else, you look sort of bushed. Maybe you could do with a little vacation."

Lila, I later learned, was saying to Thayer, "You've been driving yourself too hard, Thayer, you sound tired out. Why don't you take off for a while, not on another publishing trip, but just for a vacation?"

The intermission ended and we all went back to our seats, two young couples in evening dress at the opera, living the fashionable life of New York. The next night I got the news from Thayer, and Lila got her news from Harry. He had fallen in love with somebody else and he was sorry to hurt her, but he wanted a divorce.

The someone else was Clare Boothe Brokaw, and he had met her a few months before, at a party at our house. We had known Clare for a couple of years; we had met her at a literary cocktail party at the Alfred Knopfs, and had become friends. In those days she was not political at all. She was a wealthy woman because of the huge settlement her lawyers had won for her when she divorced the millionaire, George T. Brokaw, whom she once described to me as a sadistic drunk who would force sex on her the very night she came home from the hospital after each of her several miscarriages. But "leading an alimony life" was not for her; she had recently become managing editor of Vanity Fair, one of the city's smart magazines. Her first book, *Stuffed Shirts*, was a success, full of barbed wit. She was amusing and clever to talk to, and one of the really beautiful women. She spoke with animation, and had an odd little trick of clipping off certain words and phrases. It gave her speech a staccato brightness, and today, when I hear her on television, I often catch that same little clipping-off.

Many a hostess thinks an extra woman at dinner is a handicap, a load, a drag, but no hostess ever thought that about Clare. She had been at our house several times, and then came the night the Luces were there too. When I invited her, I told Clare who the other guests were to be, and I still remember her entrance. People were standing around in the living room, drinks in hand, chatting, waiting for whoever was missing to get there.

At last she came through the arch that led from the hall to the living room, and paused, waiting for Thayer or me to come and introduce her. She stood there with her blond head slightly tilted to one side; she was wearing a black evening dress with lovely jewels, but instead of the usual corsage at her shoulder, she was carrying a small nosegay of white flowers in both her hands. As she waited, she seemed to be looking demurely down at them.

Maybe she hadn't intended to make an entrance, but make it she certainly did. The only other thing I remember clearly about that night when the future Mr. and Mrs. Henry R. Luce first met, is that after dinner they stood a little apart from everybody, talking by themselves, she leaning back into the curve of the piano, facing the room, and Harry, ignoring the room, turning his back on it, holding forth intensely, and then listening intensely.

Clare was too clever to appear impressed with him; she would say something light and laugh, then change moods and seem totally absorbed by what he was saying. Some of our other guests told me she was baiting him about his beloved Fortune, tossing out little mots about how bad it was and how easily it could be made better.

When Clare herself was a hostess, she never regarded an extra woman as a drag—if it was the right kind of extra woman. She invited so many men to her dinners and parties that she was delighted to meet women who would fit in.

"What I want," she told me once, "is a woman with intelligence and brains, who gets her clothes at Bergdorf Goodman."

It appears that I met her requirements when *I* became an extra woman. On two successive Mondays while Thayer was off on that second "publishing trip," she invited me for the evening. She had an apartment high up in the Sherry Netherland Hotel on Fifth Avenue, across from the old Plaza, a large six-room affair on an annual lease, whose rent, her brother David told me, was $6,000 a year, which today would be about $30,000. It was furnished with her own things, and each room could have been photographed in full color for any of the upper-bracket magazines.

Her dining room is the one I remember best. It had raspberry-colored walls, white carpet, draperies and chairs also in white, and the long roomy table was a gleaming oblong of blue mirror. My datebook tells me that on one of the nights I was there the other dinner guests were Bernard Baruch; Sir William Wiseman; Sam Behrman, the playwright; Rayond Moley, one of Roosevelt's "brain trust"; a Somebody Wiggin, first secretary of the British embassy; Mark Sullivan, the author; Marya Mannes, who would become an author; and Dorothy Hale, who was to become deeply involved with Harry Hopkins, another member of the brain trust.

But it was not anybody's brains that impressed me enough that evening for me to be writing about it now. It was something Clare said when we were alone after dinner. I had gone to her bathroom, and as she opened the door to it for me, I took one look and blurted out "Ye Gods," or possibly "Gee Whiz."

It was twice the size of an ordinary bathroom and the bathmat covering its large rectangle of floor was not your ordinary bathmat either. It was not of terrycloth or shag or carpeting; it was white fur, white ermine, with the little blackish brown paws attached at intervals, in the way ermine was often done at that time.

But the bathmat was not the whole story. The same white

ermine with the dangling dark paws had been made into a cover for the toilet seat.

Clare laughed at my astonishment, delighted at my disbelief.

"It used to be a coat," she said. "My mother-in-law, Mrs. Brokaw, gave it to me and I hated it. While I was married I had to wear it and wear it, but I always knew that once I was divorced, I'd find a perfect use for it."

Clare already knew what Harry was planning; I had yet to learn about Thayer. I had cabled him happily about starting at Time, and he had wired back the most loving congratulations. He was to get home in time for Christmas—it had been his longest trip ever, well over six weeks. Christmas should have told me something; all the price tags were left on the gifts he brought me from Europe. I ascribed it to the hard-working schedule he described and thought nothing of it.

There was something else that might have told me something, and didn't. I had never had my "wedding present" from him; whenever we talked about it, I said I didn't really crave any jewelry, except for my wedding ring with its circle of small square-cut diamonds, but that the one thing I truly longed for, something that would cost less than any jewels and give me far more joy, was a Steinway piano to replace my small battered old baby grand.

For obvious reasons, we had kept putting it off, but before he left on this long arduous trip, he urged me to go to Steinway Hall and select the piano I wanted, and have it in place to greet him on his return. He had already arranged the payment for it. One of his cables included a reminder about the Steinway.

I might have wondered at all this insistence about the wedding gift so long and amiably delayed, but it never entered my mind that there was any symbolism in this new determined haste about presenting it to me at last.

Of course after that Thursday night, I couldn't go near it; it was a drawing-room grand, gleaming and beautiful, but I could not open it nor touch its keys. It stood there, locked and silent; I stopped taking music lessons; it was months before I could go to a concert, and longer before the thought finally worked its way through to me that Beethhoven and Bach and Mozart were a little bigger than one's private pain.

Some people get over shock and grief with enviable celerity. In others the tenacity of pain can be astonishing. I am one of the latter kind. But on the other hand I am fortunate. For me there is one analgesic that can actually cut me away from that area of pain for hours at a time, can give me surcease, make me so absorbed that I don't know what time it is, don't remember to eat, don't know when it is time to go to bed. The name of that kindly drug is writing.

I had been vaguely aware of it many times before, but now after that third night in January, I turned to it with a kind of ferocity. My new job provided one kind of writing, but the deepest absorption came from what I began to call "my own writing."

That was for the nights when I was alone, at home in that lovely apartment I had moved into as a bride. The lease had nine months more to run, and once Thayer moved out, it was all mine, with its terraces and large rooms, with the door permanently closed to the bedroom where we had slept, in a kind of inevitable imitation of the closed piano.

But the office was its own kind of analgesic—from my first assignments, doing promotion for Time itself, under the aegis of the regular promotion director, to my first special task for Harry Luce.

The first of these had come the very week I had arrived there. Late one afternoon, his secretary, Miss Thrasher, asked me to come up to his office. As I entered, he was reading proof of a double spread ad for that week's Time, called a house ad. It was the announcement of *The March of Time*'s February first debut on the movie screens of the nation.

He handed it to me, a rather long piece of copy in smallish type, mostly all text, and waited while I read it. Before I could read the panel of additional information that ran down its side, he demanded, "Well, what do you think of it?"

I hesitated. I was still so new there, my very first week. I had not yet let myself volunteer one word of opinion about anyone else's work, even in my own department, and whoever the copywriter of this ad had been, wasn't going to be too happy with what I thought about it.

It had no illustration, no artwork, with the staid look of a formal corporate announcement. Its headline spanned the two facing pages.

TIME announces a new V E N T U R E
THE MARCH OF TIME
—A NEW KIND OF Pictorial Journalism

Journalism is defined by the dictionary as the business of managing, editing or writing for a journal or a newspaper. That definition is, of course, obsolete. It is just another example of the lexicographer's inability, in these days, to keep up with the facts of life.

The copy went on to newsreels and talking moving pictures and led to the charge that journalism as practiced in newsreels had thus far "achieved comparatively little significance." *The March of Time* was going to change all that, in a series of twenty-minute moving pictures, produced under a special organization set up by Time.

"Yes?" Harry demanded again, after giving me what he deemed sufficient time to read and reach an opinion. "Well, what do you think of it?"

"Why, Harry, I think it's what I said during our first interview. It's pretty pompous. And pretty dull."

"Fine. I wrote it myself," he said briskly. "Do you think you can do any better?" Before I could answer, he added, "Let me have something in the morning, for the next in the series."

"Tomorrow morning?" I glanced at my watch. It was four P.M.

"We're late as it is."

"I'll try to have something."

He turned back to his work and I picked up the proof and departed. Before I even faced my typewriter I knew I was going to try something radically different. I wanted a whole new idiom, colloquial; I wanted short copy in a large legible type, and I also wanted a big smashing illustration that would have to catch the eye.

I phoned Jane Miller, a young illustrator whose artwork for Lord and Taylor had long ago made me persuade John Wood to get her to do some drawings for Altman as well. We had worked together well for a couple of years.

"Hey, Jane," I began, "how would you like to make me some layouts in a rush, on something that might mean a big new connection for you?"

I told her about my new job and my overnight assignment. We worked until midnight. After she left, I worked on for another few hours. At nine in the morning I phoned Harry's secretary and said, "Whenever he's ready."

I had one piece of copy complete, short, addressed right to the reader, and several headlines and first paragraphs of other copy. The first layout, on white transparent paper, was also for a double spread in the magazine; nearly the whole left-hand page held a big bold drawing of a movie camera, tilting across the entire page, with a swirl of cables that ran over to the right-hand page, all done in slashing black strokes of India ink. Four short headlines staggered across the expanse of white space, all in informal lower case.

what happened?
why did it happen?
what's back of it?
what does it mean?

The last line was twice the size and heaviness of the others. The right hand page said:

TIME seeks new ways
to give the answers—
turns to pictures, to sound, in
THE MARCH OF TIME

Something big happens in the news. The man who actually saw it happen knows he was especially alive that day. He can't stop talking of his experience—he was brushed by NEWS. News, happening, is the stuff of life.

Time has been experimenting with motion pictures to give you that eye-witness feeling about those events of our time that can be caught with a camera.

For Time feels that moving pictures and recorded speech are parts of a new and more vigorous journalism (a journalism that may well turn into the most potent instrument of reporting yet devised in the long evolution of news-handling).

The copy went on with the story of the year's experimenting, and two panels of smaller type across the bottom gave necessary details about theaters and dates, all in the same general tone.

When Harry sent for me, I simply put the big layout Jane had made, with that camera and those cables and those headlines all drawn in—put it down on his desk, offered him the copy I had written, and went to the window, so he wouldn't think I was watching for his reaction.

For a few minutes there was not a sound from him. Then came a sort of jerked-out, "Well!" A long pause. I turned back from the window, but kept on standing there. Then he said, "Yes, I see. Yes."

The sound of it made my pulse jump. "Oh, Harry, I'm glad." I returned to his desk and handed over other sketches Jane had made, with headlines I had given her to draw in. He raced through everything. Then he returned to the finished one and read it once more.

"We'll run it," he said. "Get it into production."

From there on, in addition to my regular ads and folders for the promotion department, I had had the special assignment of writing the promotion campaigning for *The March of Time*. There was a new double-spread every other minute, it seemed, and it was to Harry or Roy Larsen that I submitted them all, not to the head of my own department.

I was in a deadline rush for one of them the very night that Thayer told me he wanted a divorce—it was, in part, that deadline that kept me back from phoning the office the next morning to say I was ill and couldn't make it. That kindly drug of writing and work was waiting for me right then, and it was never to be in short supply.

That morning I managed—how I do not know—to write a first draft of another *March of Time* ad that was approved and ran. Jane again made a dramatic layout for me, and did the artwork for it; this time the left hand page was one huge coil of movie film, with my headline running through it.

Pictures are eye-witnesses...
TIME plans to cross-examine them

Pictures by themselves can be demons of obstinacy. They can show you something happening—and clamp their mouths shut about why it happened, what was back of it, what it means, what it portends.
TIME is not to be put off any longer...

I was grateful to be overworked at my new job. I stayed late every day, long past the usual office hours of all of us on the business side, often going down to Schrafft's on Forty-second Street in the Chrysler Building, to eat a hurried dinner, and then go up to my desk again, unwilling to go home to that silence and emptiness.

I had kept our maid, a slender black girl about my own age, who had been our maid right through our whole marriage. Every day now she would urge me to come home for my dinner, saying that she felt awful when I did not let her cook for me and take care of me. Occasionally I had done so, just to find myself unable to eat in that beautiful dining room, find myself weeping distractedly as I leaned against her, her arms around me, assuring me that it would get better. I had always ended up a little comforted, but dreading another such breakdown.

So most nights I stayed at the office until ten or later. On my desk was a bottle of clear white medicine. I told everybody that it was for a stubborn cough I couldn't get rid of. Today it would be a bottle of Valium or Miltown. Then it was some sort of chloroform mixture my doctor had given me to sip when I began to fall apart in pain.

I have already reached the limits of what I can write about my own despair and grief. I cannot write in the first person about the intimacies of suffering, any more than I can write in the first person about the intimacies of love.

In adolescent letters and diaries, it is inevitable to find, "Then he put his arm around me," or "Then he kissed me," but in maturity, first-person revelation about sex strikes me as un-thinkable.

So it does when it comes to writing about despair and shock and deprivation.

Perhaps that is one reason I found such release in writing fiction—to have a surrogate about whom I could write freely when it came to sex and love. By "freely" I do not mean with those clinical details I find so offensive in many modern books and plays and films; I merely mean *freely*, without constraint except for the inner one of taste or reticence.

And when it comes to setting down for others' eyes the clinical details of pain, again I find it unacceptable unless the sufferer is a surrogate. Where there is no surrogate, then the bursts of weeping in the night will have to be surmised by the reader, the loneliness, the bouts of anguished memory, the pillow wet with tears, the nightmare of waking from dreams of reconciliation, only to find the zero of reality.

But of all the analgesics, the most potent was not to be found in a bottle of colorless liquid on my desk, not from overwork and long hours at the office, but from my own writing.

The closed door, the locked piano, the silent apartment—whenever I had no recourse but to be at home for the evening or the weekend, I wrote. Never yet had I sold a full-length short story to one of the big national magazines; now I made it a specific goal, a short-term objective that I could keep my eyes on, if I just put blinders on for an hour at a time, shutting out the shattered terrain of my exploded marriage.

I began a story, "Hands Down," about a beautiful girl of eighteen, Francesca, whose ambitious parents train her to be-come a concert pianist, despite her own desire to play a mean jazz piano. She meets a handsome and very rich young man, Tim, aged twenty-three, who knows not a note of any music earlier than "Alexander's Ragtime Band," but who pretends to be a worshiper of all classical music to impress her. When he learns that in the Depression, her parents cannot yet afford a proper debut for her, he promptly declares himself a patron of the arts, who will arrange a dazzling debut for his protegée, with all society attending.

Of course, to have this debut work splendidly would have been no story at all, but since the misery of failure wouldn't make popular happy-ending fiction, there had to be a neat twist out of the abyss for all concerned. There were also sundry subplots and ramifications, including Tim's fiancée and a young Lord Ottley of London, with his jazz band made up exclusively of other young lords or, at the least, Honourables.

I had a hard time writing it; managing all the subplots was beyond me, and I kept telling it first from Tim's point of view and then Francesca's, and within the tight scope of a 5,000-word short story, that didn't work at all.

Just as I was about to give up and try something else, I told Clare about it. She liked the way I wrote; she had once paid me seventy-five dollars for a travel piece I did for Vanity Fair, called "Mediterranean Cruise." When she heard the plot of "Hands Down," she said, with absolute authority, "You can't kill it. It's such a good idea, an editor will rewrite it for you if he has to. You keep at it."

So I kept at it, and finally Collier's bought it for $500, changing its title to "Play Something Simple." To be sure it wasn't a flash in the pan, I set to work almost compulsively on another story of the same length, "The Wrong Job," and just three weeks later Collier's took that too for another $500.

I didn't sign either story Laura Mount.

I am not sure when I first began to think seriously about my by-line on something I wrote, or when I first began to ponder the general question of my own name. But for some time, flowing along in the unseen river of my unconscious mind whenever I had to sign a manuscript was a tiny current of discontent about what I called myself in print.

I had been born Laura Zametkin, my father's name; I had used my mother's name, Laura Z. Keane when I got my first jobs; I had gone to college as Laura K. Zametkin; I had used Tom Mount's name as a reporter and for my first articles and fiction. And then I became Mrs. Thayer Hobson.

Where was *I* in all this? I was Laura, yes, but Laura who? To my friends I was simply Laura Hobson, but when I sent that story to Collier's, it wasn't going off to a friend, and this time I did a good deal of wondering about how to sign it.

I didn't want to go back to Laura K. Zametkin—to be called Miss Zametkin by an editor or anybody else. I was no Lucy Stoner, like Jane Grant, the wife of the New Yorker's famous editor, Harold Ross, who believed in a woman's sticking to her own name all through life. I didn't want to be *Miss* anything. I was nearly thirty-five and I felt that to become a "Miss" again would have been a purposeful denial that I had ever been married.

By itself, Laura Hobson was a good name for an author, but it was stripped of *me*. The initial *Z.* would put me back, right into the middle of it. Instinctively I knew that everybody would forever ask me what the *Z.* stood for, and I also knew I would always tell them not just, "My maiden name, Zametkin," but also, "It's Russian and it's Jewish."

So back there in 1935, my first real story to appear in a national magazine was signed Laura Z. Hobson, and I was back in touch with my own beginnings.

Because of that odd juxtaposing of events in that one month of January 1935, and because I knew both Harry and Clare, I was to have a more concentrated friendship with Clare for a while than I was to have for the rest of my days.

Like most of the world I still knew nothing about their plans to marry, but within three weeks, Clare herself chose to let me in on the secret. Being Clare she did it in her own special way.

At the end of the month she was leaving for a vacation at *Hobcaw*, Bernard Baruch's vast country estate in Georgetown, South Carolina. She gave herself a going-away party and I was one of the people she invited.

My datebook for the entire month is blank, except for three brief entries: the first about the Luces and the opera, the next night's, "Thayer tells me about Isabelle," and a final one nine days later, "Thayer departed."

Clare knew about that, and when I declined her invitation, saying, "I just can't," she said, "You just *can*," and gave me a little lecture about showing the world not only that you could take it, but that you were alive and free and available for something new and attractive.

I went, and it was one of her usual gatherings of the affluent and clever. Toward the end of dinner, she tapped her fork against a glass until she had everybody's attention. Then she said, "I have a big secret, but I'm only going to tell you a part of it."

"What secret?" The whole table said it, in various forms, and after suitable suspense, she said, "I'm going to be married."

"To whom?"

"When?"

"Why is it a secret?"

She obviously enjoyed the commotion. "I told you it has to stay a secret for a while, but I'll give you a clue." She looked mischievous and happy. "He's connected with the movies."

"Douglas Fairbanks?" somebody asked.

"Robert Taylor?"

"Clark Gable?"

Names of handsome movie stars tumbled about the table, with Clare shaking her head at each one. "He's not an *actor*—I never said he was an actor." Whereupon the name of every movie producer was mentioned, with the probable exception of Sam Goldwyn.

At last she put a stop to it, acknowledging that she had been having them on, just for the fun of keeping them guessing, but that it was no fabrication, and they'd all hear about it in due time.

But when we were alone, fixing our makeup in that ermined bathroom, she said, "You ought to know who it is—you know him."

"I *know* him? I don't know a soul in the movies."

"You know him quite well." I looked blank, and she added, "I'll give you one more clue—he's powerful and he's young and he's rich."

I still didn't catch on. Then she exclaimed, "Laura! It's Harry!"

"Harry Luce? But you said—"

"*The March of Time* is connected with the movies, isn't it?"

My astonishment must have delighted her. "I just had to tell somebody who knows Harry," she said, "or I'd go mad not being able to talk about him for the next few months."

She swore me to secrecy and I gave her my pledge. Only later did I reflect on the order of those three adjectives she had used to describe her new love. Powerful and young and rich. And the greatest of these is—

It was only a few days before she showed she really did need to talk about Harry with somebody who knew him. She called me from South Carolina and asked me to come down to *Hobcaw* for a week.

I couldn't possibly ask for a vacation seven weeks after I'd started at Time, I said, but she already taken care of mundane details like that. She had already told Harry she had confided in me, that she *needed* to see me; he had already agreed; all I had to do was to go through the motions of saying to him I would be grateful for a little time off.

That was the first time I ever felt that an invitation from Clare had something of command performance about it, and heaven knows, the vision of a week away from that empty apartment was temptation enough.

I did see Harry, each of us deadpan, with no mention of Clare or where I was going. I had to put it off until the weekend, to attend the gala black-tie party, celebrating First Night of *The March of Time*, but the very next morning I took the train for South Carolina—and ran into one more Clare-typical episode, the most bizzare of anything else in this period of our concentrated seeing-each-other. At the time it shocked me out of my wits, though I see it differently now.

I was met at the railroad station the next morning by Mr. Baruch's car and chauffeur, driven to the dock where Mr. Baruch's yacht awaited me, and when we arrived at *Hobcaw*, though it was still very early in the morning, there stood Bernard Baruch himself to welcome me. Clare was nowhere in sight.

There had been a large house-party in progress for several days, with various senators, generals, writers, all well-known, but the guests were all leaving that morning or afternoon, including Mr. Baruch himself. Clare and I were to be alone.

Thayer and I had, on occasion, been weekend guests on a

millionaire's estate, notably at the financier Frank Altschul's in Greenwich, Connecticut, where fine tennis courts, swimming pools, croquet courts and a stableful of splendid horses all awaited your pleasure, but this stay of mine at *Hobcaw* enlightened me a little further about some of the habits and foibles of the very rich.

In my bathroom, every single morning, I found untouched bars of imported French soap, still in their handsome wrappers, and sealed—the new bars I had used the day before had vanished. I soon wondered what they did with all that expensive day-old soap. A new fire was laid in the fireplace every morning; my riding clothes and boots were brought back, the boots polished, the riding habit newly pressed; the nightgown, underwear and evening dress I had worn the day before were collected while I was having my breakfast from a tray in bed. More impressive to me than any of this was the fact that in the bathroom, exactly five sheets of toilet paper had been removed from the roll, and then placed back ready to be plucked—presumably to save me the effort of yanking off the sheets myself.

I never saw Clare until we met for luncheon. She was writing a play; I think the title was to be *Napoleon Slept Here*. (This was before her first smash hit, *The Women*.) We would part again after luncheon, and she would go back to her play. I was also trying to write one, about newspaper reporters; mine was to be called *Thirty-Thirty*, because the symbol—30—or—XXX—was the journalist's sign of the end of a story.

Then we would meet at five, dressed for a ride, our horses brought to us by grooms. She, I was sure, had had a productive afternoon—she looked happy and satisfied. I had spent most of the time weeping over my lost marriage, writing half a scene on my play to try to partake of that helpful drug, and endlessly splashing my face with cold water to hide the telltale signs.

Each evening we dressed for dinner, the two of us, and then Clare would read me what she had written on her play that day. I don't remember much of its plot, but I know that separate lines were witty, acidulous, and that many of them made me laugh. Then we would part and go to our firelit rooms—and while she went back to her happiness of being newly in love and waiting for marriage, I went back to my nightly struggle for sleep.

One evening, just after dinner, we were in the living room, and Clare was talking about Harry and their plans. I was standing near the mantel, I remember, one arm propped up on the corner of it. Clare was telling me about some letter she had just received from Harry—she never read any of his letters aloud, but she would paraphrase and tell me bits that amused her, and tell me things she had written to him.

Quite suddenly, she said, "Do something for me, will you?"

"What? If I can—" She was looking at me speculatively.

"Take your dress off, Laura. I want to—"

"My dress off?"

"Off." She made a sweeping gesture, indicating something tossed away. She was smiling. Nothing about her voice or expression had the slightest hint of sexual interest—the notion never even entered my head. She was up to something mysterious, and I couldn't imagine what, but it must have been instantly clear that sex or attraction had nothing whatever to do with it.

"Come on," she urged. "I'll say why in a minute."

I shrugged and dropped my dress to the floor. I wore no bra and stood there in my brief silk underpants, my evening dress making a silken circle around my ankles. I was still near the fireplace.

Clare was gazing at me, at my breasts. She cocked her head to one side and stared for a moment. Then she said, equally calmly, "Would you lie down on the sofa? On your back?"

By now I was thoroughly intrigued myself. What was this crazy woman up to? What was behind all this? She was scheming something; I could almost feel her mind planning ahead. I lay down on the sofa. For a moment she didn't move.

She knelt beside me, about three feet away from me, her eyes now on a level with my own. It became clear she was interested not in my entire body, but only in my breasts.

"Put your arms over your head, would you, just for one more minute?"

That I did too. I had never been particularly proud of my

151

breasts, though in that day, long before the new fashion had arrived for large opulent bosoms, I had never needed to worry about them either. But as she continued to kneel there on the carpet, motionless and gazing, as if at a portrait in a museum, Clare managed a look of pure approval.

"Thanks a million," she said then, and turned away. I arose, slid into my forsaken evening dress in one swift movement, and then said, "Okay, let's have it—what the hell is all this about?"

She laughed a little, a laugh of mischief and private self-approval and, I think, gratitude for a favor well done by me. Then she laid her hands over her own breasts and made a slight grimace.

"After five pregnancies," she began slowly, "and four miscarriages—"

She didn't finish the sentence; she was shaking her head in a kind of dismay. I remembered what she had told me about her marriage to George Brokaw; I knew that only one of her pregnancies had ended in the birth of a child, her daughter Annie. I understood what she meant by that look of dismay.

"You've never gone through a lot of miscarriages and pregnancies," she said then, "so I wanted to see what virgin breasts looked like. I'm going to get myself fixed—I want to be perfect for Harry."

As I said, at the time of this little directorial performance of Clare's, I was shocked speechless, especially by the cool collectedness with which she brought it all off, sans apology, sans explanation, except for that telltale gesture and little speech at the end. I kept the whole episode a secret for years and years, from everybody except my analyst.

But nowadays, and indeed for the past two decades or more, with half the movie stars and countless other well-heeled women on the stage or in television or in business, having their faces lifted, their buttocks tightened, bosoms raised, fat hips surgically shaved off, it merely shows me that fifty years ago, in 1935, I was being useful to Clare the Pioneer.

Remembering that astonishing night now, finding myself smiling over it, I kind of admire the nerve and resolution she had then, and discover myself half-wishing that she had never gone into politics, because it used to be such fun, knowing anybody like her before she did.

Neither Clare's play about Napoleon, nor mine about newspaper people ever came to anything, and I went back to trying to write short stories. That first one of mine, with its first use of my real name, Laura Z. Hobson, was never seen by the one man who would most have liked the way I had to decided to sign anything I ever wrote, my father.

He knew about it but he never saw it in print. He was ill, and facing an operation, so I withheld the news about Thayer's leaving me, lest it unduly upset him.

He had at last given up trying to live alone in the house in Jamaica; it had been rented to a depression-stricken family for about twenty dollars a month, and he had moved into a two-room corner apartment high above East Broadway and the offices of the *Jewish Daily Forward*, where so much of his life had been spent.

The building was a workingman's cooperative society, partly owned by the *Forward*, and it was open to all elderly or old people who had been connected with the labor movement on the East Side. The moment he moved in, he was treated like a king, with everybody in the neighborhood soon knowing that the great Zametkin was living there, and everybody in the building proud of his presence. He had old cronies to play chess with, people to talk to, people who looked up to him and did him honor.

I drove downtown once or twice every month to see him; he was always glad to see me, and I tried to be glad when the day came for my regular visit.

But time spent with a father as positive in his opinions as he was could not be easy, and I was never reluctant to have him look at his watch and say, "Well, I'm getting tired," or "It's very pleasant when you come to see me," which I read as a signal that my visit was over.

He had his operation at Beth Israel Hospital, for his long-standing prostrate trouble, not a life-threatening situation in any sense. But for years he had had high blood pressure; it was four years since my mother's death; it is doubtful whether he had any powerful will to keep on living, and early in March he died. He was seventy-six.

There was public mourning for him and a memorial service arranged by the *Forward* Association. Many of his old colleagues eulogized him, including the man with whom he had so often been at loggerheads about the newspaper's policy, Abraham Cahan.

My father's death brought me one final letter from Thayer, the last one I was ever to receive.

> I am terribly, terribly sorry, my dear, that this had to be added to all the other pain and unhappiness. It seems too much...I was really fond of him, and I admired him and his life tremendously. He was strong and honest and devoted to something far greater than himself. He left a real mark on the world, and a good mark, which very few of us will...
>
> You, Laura, will remember all your life that it was you above all who contributed to the happiness of his last years. You did everything for him. It was you he turned to.
>
> And again...although there's nothing I can say to you that will help you, Laura; that's one tragedy of this nightmare, I who am more anxious and concerned to help than anyone in the world, can do nothing that would be any use to you—try to forgive me for the pain I've caused and the things I've shattered for you.

That is one letter I was glad to find in my safe-deposit box a thousand years later.

I never saw Thayer Hobson again for the rest of his life. There was that Thursday night when he told me, there were the frantic letters, and one or two notes about specific things like doctor's bills, and that was it—all of it.

We never met again. There were no sessions in a lawyer's office; we did not meet in the divorce court at White Plains. He had ruled out Reno as the place for our divorce as too slow and too expensive, but for a larger reason as well.

154

He had Bill Walling explain to me that only a New York divorce would serve the truth; a Reno divorce on grounds of incompatibility would be a lie, and he insisted on the truth. He wanted it to go on the record for all time that I was in no way to blame for this divorce, that the single cause of it was his adultery, nothing else.

To select adultery as the sole reason for divorce was, and still is, beyond my emotional ken, but I do not know what I thought then of Thayer's insistence on this official *mea culpa*.

Bill went with me to the courtroom on a day in early summer that same year; after being sworn in and agreeing that I was suing for divorce, I was allowed to retire to some sort of ante-room, where I was completely alone. I remember that there were a lot of wooden chairs around, and the smell of mayonnaise and food, and that I sat there, dully wondering if it were near a cafeteria. It seemed a long time until Bill and my slightly known lawyer came to tell me they had gone through the formalities and that my marriage was over. Bill drove me to New York. I went back to my office and worked.

Thayer died in 1967 at the age of seventy. Perhaps he was justified in everything he had done to achieve his own happiness. He and Isabelle stayed married until her death in 1960. Whereupon, in the same year, he married for the fifth time.

His obituary in the New York *Times* ended, "A funeral service will be held tomorrow . . . in the Roman Catholic Church of the Sacred Heart . . . Mr. Hobson became a convert to Catholicism after his second marriage."

And thereby hangs a strange little postscript to the worrisome *thirdness* of his marriage to me nearly forty years before. Whether the fourthness of his next marriage also bothered him I never knew, but the first time he appeared in *Who's Who*, and in all his other entries thereafter, the only marriage he listed was the one in September 1935, to Isabelle. In editions after 1960, he added a second marriage.

Janet was deleted. Priscilla was deleted. Laura was deleted.

When I first discovered this, I thought he might have wished to dissociate himself from Priscilla and Alger Hiss. But that first entry was in the 1944 edition, four years before the Hiss case, so that couldn't have been the motive.

Whatever the motive, we three earlier wives were scrubbed off the record. I don't know about Janet and Priscilla, but for me this was to cause some awkwardness.

Not only because, five editions later, I too became an entry in *Who's Who*, appearing alphabetically ahead of him, with my vital statistics including, "m. Thayer Hobson, July 23, 1930, (div. 1935)," but because Thayer's entries, in listing names of his three children, always began, "children Timothy (by prev marriage.)"

It was inevitable that many of our old acquaintances should think that the prev marriage was the one to me, and that Timothy was our son. When Timothy married, it was equally inevitable that some of them would send me congratulations on the marriage of "your son Timothy."

Ah well, by then everybody knew the phrase, *revisionist history*, and I managed to bear it with some equanimity.

EIGHT

I WAITED NEARLY TWO years and then I set about the wonderful and scary business of trying to adopt a baby. I waited that long because I wanted to be certain that I wasn't using some tiny baby as a prop, as a pet, as a companion.

I had been thinking about it for God knows how long, but during the first cataclysmic months after my sudden singleness, I set it aside as a forbidden possibility until such time, if ever, that I myself felt whole again, free of any need for *this* kind of surrogate.

Today the "single-parent adoption" is nearly an everyday matter, but in the middle thirties, it was almost unheard of. Many of my friends said it couldn't be done at all, that I would just risk another period of frustration and heartbreak if I even attempted it.

But I thought there must be some adoption agency somewhere that wouldn't take such a doctrinaire position, some agency headed by people wise enough to make an exception to the rule. I knew that any applicant must be reasonably young, and reasonably well-off, and that there must be some solid reason behind the request for a baby to adopt, not just some frivolous whim or fleeting fancy. I made a serious study of all the better known adoption agencies, and finally set my sights on The Cradle, out in Evanston, Illinois.

Then I did something I never would have done to help me join a club or visit a foreign city—I asked people for letters of recommendation, or letters of introduction. Marshall Best, an editor at Viking Press, wrote a letter saying I cared about people and children, and Carroll Whedon wrote another, saying she had known me and worked with me for four years, and that I would make a reliable and good mother.

I don't remember why I didn't ask either Clare or Harry, but it never occurred to me to turn to either of them on this sort of thing. The only well-known person I did ask was Dorothy Thompson, and her letter ended with something like, "If I had to leave my only son in another woman's care, I would be content and at ease if it were Laura Hobson."

As for me, I could not have been clearer about why I was embarking on this quest. I had first begun to think about it and talk about it while I was still married; when it ended, I had of course stopped my visits to Dr. Damon; I was sure I would not marry again very soon as some people did—look at how long it had taken me to get over Tom. And I was positive I did not want to go through life without the basic human experience of bringing up a child.

At thirty-six I was reasonably young, and with my job at Time, I was reasonably well-off and secure. I had sold a third story and begun another, and Kenneth Littauer, the fiction editor at Collier's, had sent for me to tell me this spare-time hobby of mine could make me into a successful short-story writer who would always find a market.

At the office, it seemed that every new assignment given to me was the sort I had some affinity for. Shortly after my campaign for *The March of Time*, I was asked to try my hand at some promotion for Fortune, once again, "a house campaign," to run primarily in the magazine's own pages.

By then anybody I worked for at Time Inc. knew that no matter how sober and important Fortune had become in the world of business and industry, I would feel that any tone of solemnity in the promotion would inevitably turn into self-importance and pomposity. Just the same I handed in my first copy with some diffidence.

But my business is different.

That was the first headline in the series, and the copy began, "I make locomotives—why should I advertise to the general public?" or something to that effect. Of course it went on to discuss the invisible values of public recognition and good will, and the editors as well as the "business side" liked it. One page of the campaign ran in every issue of the magazine for two years or more.

On most of my assignments it was not Harry Luce to whom I reported, but I knew he saw everything I did—he saw everything *anybody* did. As my first year was drawing to a close, he had sent for me.

"Well, the trial period is well over," he had begun. He never smiled openly at you, but he seemed pleased at what he was about to say.

I had forgotten all about the trial period we had talked about in my first interview. It was supposed to be for six months. By now I had been there for eleven.

"So now, I suppose," he went on, "I either have to fire you, or give you a three-thousand-dollar raise and a thousand-dollar bonus. What should it be?"

He always hated any outward show of emotion; it would have irritated him to death if I had jumped up and seized his hand to thank him. But he must have known I was overjoyed. If I still could not use the word happy, I could at least use the word self-assured. About work, anyhow.

I was a survivor.

At that time I had no political compunctions about working for Time or any of Harry's ventures. For one thing I was on the "business side," with no voice about editorial matters, with nothing to do with the content of the magazines, except to deplore what offended me.

There was a group of important people in the top echelons

of editorial command who were fighting against those things, and I quickly became a lesser devotee of the group. Archibald MacLeish was one of that group, Ralph Ingersoll, Russell Davenport, Eric Hodgins, Dwight MacDonald and half a dozen others.

Time kept referring, for example, to Leon Blum, then premier of France, as "Jew Blum." Harry would listen with a kind of polite inability to get the importance of what people were saying when they spoke up in protest. He simply could not see that there was anything repugnant in the phrase. It was merely a descriptive, he said, an implied tribute to the man—how superior he must be, with all the antisemitism in the very country of the Dreyfuss Affair, to have achieved the status of prime minister.

"It's *interesting*," he insisted. "If I called Roy Larsen Harvardman Larsen, to point out he wasn't a Yaleman like the rest of us, would that reveal any prejudice?"

"But, Harry," I once said to him. "Has there ever been a pogrom of Harvardmen?"

However, it may be that something else was operating in me to free me of any trepidation about working for Time and Harry Luce.

My father had spent years on the *Forward*, despite his deep disapproval of many things Abraham Cahan did in the paper and to the paper. He felt that Cahan was so intent on circulation and financial success that he was adopting some of the tactics of yellow journalism in general, and Hearst in particular.

He too was part of a group of critics and dissenters. At one point, while the paper was still young and struggling, when Cahan returned as editor after a five-year absence, they grew so vociferous in their disapproval of what they termed Cahan's sensationalism, and "lowering himself to the masses," of his "making a frank appeal to Jewish nationalism. . . . and chauvinist sentiments" that they decided that Cahan would have to be replaced.

In those days they still had annual elections about the editorship. "The only problem was where to find a strong candidate to replace him," and their choice was "Michael Zametkin, the most resolutely radical of the old guard to stand up in opposition to Cahan."

The quotes are from Ronald Sanders's book, *The Downtown Jews*, and they lead into an epsiode that was thoroughly characteristic of my father.

> Unfortunately Zametkin was not present at the meeting... and the committee sent out to find him.... He was "not at home..."and the committee members scoured the cafés until they found him in one of them, playing chess. When told he had been nominated for the editorship, Zametkin replied that this was a superfluous gesture, since the *Forward* already had an editor, Cahan. He went back to his game.

My father must have known that Cahan couldn't be dislodged, not with the circulation jumping day by day. He and all the other disapprovers remained on the staff, exerting their influence, maintaining their opposition.

My guess is that if my father had accepted the editor's chair, the paper would never have been the roaring success it was for so long. He would have thought of principles, not newsstand sales, and too often, principles don't make profits. In my childhood I sometimes heard him threaten to resign, but he never did. He knew that if you resign in a huff over policy, you yourself might feel ennobled by your action, but that you were leaving the fighting to the troops that stayed on.

I certainly wasn't noble enough ever to think of leaving Time, no matter how much I agreed with the liberal troops there, and it was one morning just as I was leaving for the office, that the postman finally handed me an answer to the letter I had sent to The Cradle in Evanston Illinois.

No interview in my entire life has ever meant more to me, or seemed more crucial, that the one I finally had with Florence B. Walrath, the head of the adoption process there. She had written that of course an exception was possible, suggesting that I arrange a personal visit. I called her long distance that same morning and we arranged a meeting.

It was a November day in 1936 when I entered what looked like an ordinary one-family red brick house in a small town. My first sight of Mrs. Walrath gave me hope—there was nothing of the institution about her, any more than there was about the house itself. She was well into middle age, and by way of putting me at ease, told me that she had stumbled into the world of adoption some twenty years before in trying to arrange the adoption of a baby for her own sister, who had just lost hers, and who was told she could not have another. She sounded like a woman of feeling and understanding; there was nothing of officialdom about her.

She began with practical matters then, about my age, my job, my income, my religion.

"Jewish and agnostic," I said. "My ex-husband was an Episcopalian and agnostic."

"What religion would you want your baby to be?"

"Either, any—I don't care. If we had had a baby while I was married, it would have been an intermarriage baby. I believe in intermarriage."

Then she suggested that I just sit back and tell her more about myself, anything I thought might help her judge the whole adoption issue. "What matters most to us," she said, "is the future of the baby."

"Do I talk to you as if I were trying to impress you with all my virtues?" I asked, suddenly a little uncertain. "Or do I just spill everything out, even if I shock you?"

"I've been talking for twenty years to people who want to adopt, and people who have to offer their babies for adoption," she said quietly. "I doubt if there is anything you are going to tell me that I haven't heard before."

So I told her. About Tom, about the two abortions, about my marriage and all the visits to Dr. Damon, and the abrupt *finis* not only to my marriage but to my growing hopes for a pregnancy that could go forward to the birth of a baby.

She hardly said a word, but the look on her face told me I needn't regret being so open with her. She asked whether I wanted a boy or a girl. I said I wouldn't dream of cutting my chances in two by specifying a sex—I would be happy with either a boy or a girl.

162

"If I'm allowed to make any 'specifications', " I went on, "it would only be about brains—a baby of intelligent parents—after all, it will be growing up in a world of writers and editors—so if there's any conceivable way to tell about a baby's I.Q.—"

She smiled, nodding. "Even at eight weeks of age, a baby can let you make a pretty good guess about native intelligence. Have you ever been to a kennel where there's a new litter of puppies?" I shook my head. "There may be seven or eight of them, and one puppy will crawl away from the rest and come sniffing at your shoes, examining you—that's the brainy one of the lot."

"And an eight-week-old baby?"

"That's the one who'll beat all the other babies its age, and make a grab for the bottle when the nurse comes close."

I got a mental picture of a tiny baby making a grab for a bottle I offered, and something tumbled inside my chest.

"It may take a long time," Mrs. Walrath finally said. "It's often as much as a year, even more." She put out both her hands and took mine. "But you can go home now, and know that one day you are going to adopt a baby."

A new element had been creeping into my datebooks during those two years. Notations had begun to appear at the top of their pages, as well as across the bottom. Phrases like, "Insert at page 10," or "p. 12, 13, 14," or "Began new story," were added to the entries that had appeared in the first months of my single state, when many of the pages carried only the legend, "Dined alone, movie, worked, read."

Not the majority of the pages, by any means. There were many jottings of names, nearly all feminine: "Betty H." "Ruth Mary," "Liz Woody," "Alice" or "Al." My sister was warm and loving during that time of dislocation, and I was grateful. Most of the time as we were growing up we were on good terms, despite the usual sisterly tiffs; during the summer session at Cornell that I had had to take for the extra credits needed for my degree, for example, I had asked her to come from Ann Arbor, where she had gone to college, and stay with me. She did, for the entire session.

Another time, still at college, after making myself a summer dress of red-and-white dotted swiss, sewing every stitch by hand, I decided to make one for her, in blue and white to go with her auburn hair, spending hours on it, envisioning the delight there would be on her face when I surprised her with it. And it was there.

So, like many sisters, despite our childhood rivalries and quarrels about whose turn it was to do the dishes, we had remained close, and it seemed natural for me to turn to her for help. And giving that help seemed natural to her too.

Mostly we saw each other alone, just the two of us, either at my house or at hers, Milton discreetly withdrawing as soon as he could, to leave us free for intimate talk.

When the three of us were together, the talk usually was about the news, and, as had been so true with my father, no matter what the headlines of the day dealt with; Hitler's ranting and raving on the radio, his Gestapo, Roosevelt's second term, the beginning of the civil war in Spain—somehow our talk soon veered to the Soviet Union.

Often it was I who did the veering, determined though I was to steer clear of the subject that so agitated me, yet helplessly drawn to it. Often it was my sister who shifted the subject. But whereas with my father I had been on the "same side" about Russia, with Alice or Milton, I was always on the opposite side, often to the extent of sharp irritation for each of us. Or less politely, of fights.

When I was young, I used to think that shrill rising voices in political argument must be part of a Russian-Jewish background; only later did I realize that family fights were just as shrill and loud in Italian or French or Spanish or Polish or any language on earth.

I also used to think that it was my mother's fault that I would burst into angry tears during these family harangues, because she had so often dissolved into tears when we were little and my father was in one of his shouting moods. Each time a visit with Alice ended that way, with me in tears and Alice comparatively cool, I would swear that I'd never talk politics with her again. She probably swore exactly the same thing, but by then we both cared too much about what was happening in the world to stay clear very long.

All those evenings with Alice or Betty or Ruth Mary or Liz

really did help with the adjustment I was trying to make to a new scheme of living, and after a suitable time, as if waiting only to give me a chance to get hold of myself a bit, many of the couples we used to see began to ask me again to dinners and parties, though they were now faced with the new problem of inviting an extra man for Laura.

They did face it though, and my date book began again to show evenings with the Wallings and the Farnols and other good friends, Harry Scherman, founder of the Book of the Month Club, and his wife Bernardine, Charles Poore, the *Times* book critic, and his wife Mary, Bill Whitney, an attorney, and his wife Dorothy, John and Carly Wharton, both connected with the theater, and of course, Clare, as before.

So the *D*'s and *Don't D*'s did not disappear as if being single again were an insurmountable social barrier. But weekends remained very nearly unbearable. By Thursday of each week I would begin to dread the emptiness ahead, of no office, no dates, no human contact. Some of the Saturday and Sunday pages did say, "Matinee, worked, read," or "Carnegie, worked, read," with occasional variations like, "Played tennis," "Went to movies," but they soon had begun to carry one other notation I myself would have been the last to predict.

"Woodstock" appeared on the last weekend in March in that first spring alone. "Tom and Andrée."

I had liked Andrée from our first meeting, and apparently she had liked me, but she was still comparatively a stranger, and I'm sure that if she had been living by herself, there would never have been that weekend in Woodstock.

But just as Tom had cabled from Tahiti, "no one to turn to but you," and used the same words on the telephone when he had appealed to me for a loan for the birth of their second son, so I now felt that of all my friends, even of all my family, it was Tom I could turn to most surely for that special understanding that takes years in the building, different from that between two sisters because of the added dimension of a man-woman insight.

And just as Thayer had been endlessly patient while I was compulsively confiding in him about what had gone wrong between Tom and me, so Tom was now kindness itself in helping me talk myself free of some of my buried feelings.

There was nothing left of any sexual impulse between us, but a solid residue of our old knowledge of each other made it possible to build a new connection of sympathy. Some sort of release does come from talking out one's pain, whether to a rabbi, a priest, an analyst, or a dear friend. Tom took on the role of all of these, and I sometimes marveled at how good he was with other people's problems, when he was so bad at managing his own.

He was still in touch with Thayer, because he was still writing Westerns for Morrow to publish. One or two had appeared under pseudonyms, and had done reasonably well, but for some reason he never wanted me to read any of these books of his, and I never even knew their titles. He was tactful enough never to mention seeing Thayer, and I was wounded enough never to ask for any news of him.

That March weekend up in Woodstock was not a solitary performance. Several more times during that summer and fall, I would call on a Thursday and ask if they were free, or Tom would call me and invite me up. Woodstock was by way of being an artist's colony; I met some of their friends, and in any social gathering with strangers, I found that I was a skilled dissembler—I could sound as cheery and bright as anybody, with no hint of the private fact below the sunny surface.

It wasn't long before Tom was again asking me for loans, small ones now, (Bank $33, Car $42, Dr. $10, Bank $33) but I was by then taking that for granted as part of any continuing friendship with him. Perhaps I was feeling that the one in debt was really me, relying on them as I soon did for their help with those Saturdays and Sundays.

Once Andrée herself had to call me, in a misery of embarrassment, to ask for a loan for medicines for the two little boys. Tom was in one of his nonworking spells; they were strapped; the kids were sick; the druggist had turned off their credit. I was almost happy at the chance to do something for Andrée, and told her so. She was having her own private problems with marriage; she was not given to easy confidences, but that was already clear.

At last other weekend invitations began to appear in my datebooks, and evening dates with men alone—Rogers Lamont, Howie Mayer, Marshall Best, and men from the office. But very often, somewhere above them were those new notations, in various combinations. "Worked 6 hrs. Finished 'Frankly Incognito.'" A few days later, "Rewrote whole beginning, 8 P.M.– 1 A.M." Several weeks later what must have been a climax was reached. "5,000 words in 2 days; 8,000 in last 10. Finished "City Doctor." Approx 14,000 wds."

That was my first attempt at a novelette, about three times the length of the ordinary short story, and rumored to bring several times the amount of money. I was going out to spend the weekend in Hopewell, New Jersey, with Bruce and Beatrice Gould, the new co-editors of the Ladies Home Journal, and my agent, Helen Everitt, the wife of an editor at Little, Brown, Raymond Everitt, and a good friend, gave me permission to bypass the step of having her make a formal submission, and take my manuscript out with me, to let them read it while I was right there.

Bruce was one of the friends I had made on the *Evening Post*; he had been one of their top reporters, and had made a marked impression on me the very first week I sat beside him at a neighboring typewriter. At one point, I had turned to him, and in the voice of a novice, had asked, "Mr. Gould, would you help me?"

"No," he replied pleasantly, shaking his head. "Work it out by yourself."

For all my chagrin, I had the sense to know it was a lesson in being self-reliant, and he and Beatrice and I remained friends for years. On this particular visit to Hopewell, I was disappointed to learn that because their little girl, Sesaly, had suddenly become ill, Beatrice had rushed her off to a doctor who had always taken care of her, but who lived far enough away so that they would have to stay overnight.

I told Bruce about my novelette, and when Beatrice phoned to say Sesaly would be all right, he insisted on taking my sixty-page manuscript up to bed with him.

Long after midnight, he thumped on my door and roused me. "Come on downstairs," he said. "It's great."

In bathrobes, we met in the living room. "City Doctor," he

said, was the best thing I'd ever done. He would buy it. They would run it in the first possible issue. The going price for a full-length novelette was $2,500.

I was staggered. Five times what a short story brought. It was two in the morning, but I telephoned Helen Everitt, and we both squealed with delight over the phone. Then I telephoned Alice, and she didn't mind being waked up either. As for me, I remained awake most of the night, too excited to sleep. Maybe the day would come when I could earn my entire living writing short stories and novelettes, instead of doing it only part-time as a hobby.

But, alas, morning came, and with it, Bruce's co-editor, Beatrice. Bruce and I both told her the great news; she said she would read it right away and went off to do it. I began to notice the tick of minutes on my watch, never dreaming that I was in for a new editorial experience.

For when Beatrice reappeared on the scene, after a two-hour absence and a long discussion with Bruce behind closed doors, she looked stern, her eyes aloof, while Bruce himself looked abashed, if not sheepish.

She had read "City Doctor" and she didn't like it. She was, in fact, un-buying it.

Again I was staggered. I had never imagined that anything like this could happen. Rejection slips I knew about; they were normal. But to have a manuscript accepted, with the price all set, with an editor hearing me make exultant 2 A.M. phone calls to my agent, to get on the phone himself with the agent and praise the work, and then to have a co-editor annul the whole thing—this was beyond my comprehension. It still is.

In the morning Helen tried to reason with Beatrice on all possible fronts: Laura would make any reasonable changes, Laura would cut it, Laura would write in new scenes. Nothing worked. Beatrice had made up her mind and my novelette stayed un-bought.

A couple of months later Helen arranged a "kiss and make up" party for me and her husband and the Goulds at the St. Regis roof, dinner and dancing and very black tie, and we all tried to act as if nothing too unusual had happened. None of us knew that in the end McCall's would buy "City Doctor" for

$1,000, in a truncated version, a hybrid in length between short story and novelette, nor that years later it would be remembered by a movie producer, Bill Dozier, and bought by him for a TV drama. And Helen had been very persuasive, in inviting me to the party, about the folly of cutting a major magazine off your list by staying sore at what its editors—or one editor—had done.

But often, when I hear Orwell's phrase, not to be written until a decade later, about some animals being more equal than others, I remember this particular episode of my writing youth, and I find myself thinking, "and some co-editors are more co than others."

On the very day that I was out there at The Cradle in Evanston, our old house in Jamaica was sold for the large sum of $2,800, with a down payment of $280. The sale included the plot of ground, 40 by 100 feet, and it was Milton who had taken the burden from Alice's shoulders and mine, found the buyer and arranged the deal, drawing up all necessary documents himself since he was an attorney.

My father had left no real will, just an informal signed statement that whatever money there was in his bank account was to go to his twin daughters in equal shares. His life savings came to about $2,400.

There was no need for him to specify anything about the house, for two or three years before he had already turned it over to us, making out the transfer deeds in my name for convenience's sake, knowing that if we ever sold it, I would turn over Alice's share.

We talked it all out thoroughly, she and I, hating to sell it, yet knowing that neither of us would ever live in it again. Though it had been lived in by our "Depression tenants" for about two years, its state of neglect kept worsening almost as much as if it were standing vacant.

Milton had reckoned up the cost of repairs, as well as taxes and other expenses, to give us some idea of what it was costing us to hang on to the old place. Minor plumbing repairs cost only $5 or $10 then, but the fives and tens kept being repeated; water taxes were $3.15 a month, fire insurance was $22 a year, and furniture insurance another $12. Worst of all were the real estate taxes to the city, about $290 a year.

Neither of us thought in terms of holding it as an investment in future real-estate values; we were united in our desire to end the burden of those repairs and taxes, and with our tenants often defaulting on their $20-a-month rent, we were only too happy to have Milton take on the job of listing it with several brokers in Jamaica and finding a purchaser.

Before too long we had one. For the nominal sum of $10, Milton had given Katz Realty Co. a sixty-day option, and very soon they found a client, Fannie Burke, who had offered to buy it for $2,200, "as is."

Small though the sum was, he thought we should accept it, and Alice and I agreed. As attorney for both of us on this matter, he drew up all the legal documents, and one day called me at Time, and asked me down to his office to sign them. Alice didn't have to go, since the house was in my name only.

I had never been to Milton's law office, and it surprised me. It was not the expansive establishment of many New York law firms, with four or five names of partners lettered in gold leaf on the door; it was a single small office, and rather unprofessional-looking, as if it were for somebody just starting out, though Milton by then was in his late forties.

But Ida Katz, the broker, and her client were there, and we signed documents and shook hands all around. The actual payment was to be made at the closing, in ten days.

But before the ten days elapsed, Milton called me once again. The Burke-Katz deal had just fallen through, but there was no reason to worry. Depression or no, there was enough interest evinced already among Jamaica's brokers, to make him certain of another offer before too long.

And sure enough, within another few days, he asked me down to his office a second time, to sign another set of legal documents, this time with the Bayside Construction Corp. in the sum of $2,800, with a down payment of $280. Our house was gone.

It was a melancholy task, as it always is, when one has to dismantle the house where one's childhood was spent, but Alice and I went out there and did it. That was when I, for one, found those college letters I had sent home to "Dear Family" from

Cornell, and Alice found a few things she wanted to keep. But nearly everything else was either thrown out, or sold to anybody who would buy it.

And was that the end of it?

About three months later, on an evening in February, I was at home, not alone, not writing or reading or practicing, but just finishing dinner with a man I had begun to see a good deal, both in the office and outside, Ralph McAllister Ingersoll, one of the vice-presidents of Time Inc.

The doorbell rang, and I opened it myself. There stood a messenger, asking, "Are you Mrs. Hobson?" At my nod, he handed over an envelope.

"Who sent it?" I asked. "What is it?"

"It's a summons, lady," he said, and rang for the elevator.

It was indeed a summons, the only summons that has ever been served on me in my entire life. It was a summons, what's more, for fraud in a real estate transaction. It was issued by the Supreme Court of the State of New York, County of Queens.

The plaintiff was Fannie Burke, and the defendants were Laura Hobson and Milton I. Milvy.

In the resonant language of the law, it alleged first,

> That at all the times hereinafter mentioned, the defendant, Laura Hobson, was and still is the owner in fee and possessed of the real property situate and lying in the County of Queens, State of New York, described as follows:

I could hardly take in the four pages of typed foolscap, with Exhibit A and Exhibit B attached, as well as another page about the official delivery to the Bayside Construction Company, in return for certified checks ... etc. ... etc. ... the deed to Premises No. 84–55 Parsons Boulevard. ... etc.

It was Ralph Ingersoll who helped me read the four pages a second time, and helped me decipher the piled up alleges and whereases.

But one paragraph, the clause labeled NINTH, was clear enough even for me and my astounded brain. On the date set for the closing of the first deal, the Katz-Burke deal, the defendants, Laura Hobson, and her attorney in fact and/ or duly authorized agent, Milton I. Milvy . . . refused to accept the said purchase money and refused, and still refuse, to deliver a deed to said premises. . . .

The first deal had not fallen through, as Milton had told me. He had had a higher offer of $2,800, and without one word to me, had thereupon backed out of the $2,200 deal with "the plaintiff, Fannie Burke."

A hot rage boiled up in me. The deed to said premises was in my name, only my name, and it was *me* being summoned to a court of law. The slightly dramatic phrase, *my good name*, kept thudding at my brain.

I went to the telephone and called Alice long distance. She and Milton were on a vacation in Florida; I called her there. Again I didn't behave well, if by "well" you mean polite chitchat about the weather and how are you.

"I've just had a summons served on me," I began, and I blew my top, my voice rising as I told her about it, shouting at her, not caring that Ralph Ingersoll was right there listening, dissolving into tears as I always did when I was furious.

She blew her top right back. "If Vincent Astor canceled one real estate deal," she yelled, "because he got a better offer, that would be just good business—Vincent Astor is a genius in real estate. But if Milton does it—you never liked Milton anyway, or anything he ever did—"

It was fairly true. I didn't much, though I kept on trying because of Alice. He and I were dead opposites, not only about Russia, though that probably was the sorest point between us—Russia in his view could do no wrong!—but about many other lesser things as well.

Milton, for instance, though I knew they were well off, owning their own house in Westchester, and having investments in tax-free municipals and in stocks, would get the license plates for their car not in New York State where they lived, but in Georgia, where he had some legal right to do so. It saved him about eight dollars a year, but I thought it was cheap, and probably was none too careful about letting him sense that I did think so. Alice certainly was subtle enough to sense it. I never was

172

the diplomat I should have been among people close to me, and possibly am not to this day.

Nor was I diplomatic on that long distance call to Alice in Florida.

"You tell Milton," I finally said in angry sobs, "that I am going into that courtroom, and tell the judge to cancel out that rotten second deal for twenty-eight hundred dollars and reinstate the first one at twenty-two hundred."

And that is just what I did.

These papers, too, went into my safe-deposit box, and now, going through them decades later, I find one minor matter to laugh about. Is there always one small point in human struggle that can seem hilarious years later, no matter how unlaughable the whole?

That small point is an item written in Milton's own handwriting, on his final calculations of the broker's fee and other expenses in the sale of the house.

"Litigation settled... $200," the item says. All costs came off the top, before the proceeds were split between Alice and me. So Milton had billed me for half the cost of that disgusting lawsuit.

The man I was dining with alone when the summons came was one of the major people at Time Inc. He too was a Yale alumnus, in the class following Harry's and Thayer's. He was a mining engineer and at twenty-four had published a book, *In and Under Mexico.* Then he joined The New Yorker as a reporter and before long was its managing editor. He had switched to Fortune when it began in 1930, and again soon became managing editor, for about five years. It was during that period that I first knew him.

He was married then, and the Ingersolls were one of the couples in that Yale crowd whom Thayer and I saw at dinners and parties, at their houses or ours. By the time he was having dinner with me alone, he was divorced and had moved on from Fortune to being vice-president and general manager of all Time Inc. He was one of the presiding powers, but was not my direct boss when I began to see him outside the office.

He was not noticeably handsome, having what I thought of

at the beginning as "thyroid eyes," slightly protuberant, but he was a pleasant-looking man, distinguished by being several inches over six feet in height. He was slim and wore a thick moustache, perhaps to compensate for being quite bald, to a degree that could no longer be called balding, though he was only in his mid-thirties, born the same year as I.

He was what Time called "a socialite," and in his case there was family tree to back up the label, for he was a descendant of that famous social leader of the Mauve Decade, Ward McAllister, who, back in 1892, had determined who in New York should be annointed as "true society," dubbing them, "the Four Hundred."

The first notation in my datebooks of my seeing Ralph Ingersoll alone, or "Mac," as most people called him, was for luncheon about a year after my marriage ended.

Despite all the trite admonitions about never going out with any man from your office, I have never once known one intelligent woman who ever refused to go out with a man for that particular reason, and I certainly did not.

Mac and I lunched together occasionally and I soon found that it was possible for me once again to be really drawn to, and interested in, and even happy with, an intelligent and able man who seemed to be drawn to me.

Some months of those lunches went by, and then, in the fall of that year I bought two orchestra seats for one of the hit shows of the season, *Yeomen of the Guard*, not knowing whom I would invite to go with me. Or perhaps I knew perfectly well, but kept thinking I'd had no special motive in getting those hard-to-get tickets, and kept putting off a decision. Then, a day or two before the performance, I phoned Mac at the office, said I had the tickets and asked if he would like to have dinner at my house and go with me to the theater.

He promptly canceled another engagement, accepting and saying we'd go on to "21" afterward, giving it all a gala sound. So began the next major experience of my life.

By then it was nearly two years since Thayer had left me. During those two years, or at least after some of the numbness and pain and anger had finally begun to recede, I had found that even without love or deep emotion, sexuality could not be exiled, and that it was good and natural and even essential to a rounded existence. In due course I had begun to have some experience with what goes by the name of affairs.

But an affair to me meant sex and little more, and even I who praise sex as one of life's dear, driving forces, knew full well that in an affair, there was an emptiness that one would soon long to fill. When it became apparent that I could not, that the sex was all, I always knew it would be a fairly limited encounter and little else.

There was nothing of the limited encounter with Mac, even before that night of *Yeomen of the Guard* and "21." To have luncheon with him was to have the fascination of shoptalk and the "inside dope" about people and problems on all the magazines; he was witty and could be biting, and there was plenty to be biting about.

For one thing there was now the rising uproar among Time's liberals about the way it was reporting the civil war in Spain. The editor of Foreign News was one Laird S. Goldsborough, the coiner of "Jew Blum" and other little gems, and now he was putting his nasty skills into his weekly reports about Spain. He never called Franco or his troops Fascists, for example; they were Falangists or Nationalists. Spain's Loyalists he wrote of as "the popular front" or more tersely, "the reds," as if they were not the duly elected government of the nation.

This outrageous slanting of the news had people like MacLeish and Ingersoll and Hodgins and the rest of the protesters in a steady rebellion, but again Harry seemed unable to see the importance of what they were saying.

Harry himself was changing. During the famous "Hundred Days" at the beginning of the New Deal, and for some time afterward, he had been fairly moderate in his criticisms of FDR and his government. MacLeish had written a major article in Fortune in praise of Roosevelt, and Eric Hodgins another, attacking the entire munitions industry, in "Arms and the Men." Harry Luce surely disagreed with both pieces, but took them in his stride.

But by now, a few years later, with Roosevelt recognizing the Soviet Union, with the second term beginning, Harry's distrust and dislike of everything Rooseveltian had tightened and hardened into a sort of fanatic enmity. It may be that this tightening and hardening was also strangling the life out of whatever flexibility he used to have about the opinions of the liberals around him, though it is true that his personal affection and respect for them as people never wavered. Nor did he ever fire one of them for disagreeing with him or calling him to task for journalistic blindness or bias.

Once, during an election many years later, one of his conservative friends challenged him. "How is it that you and Larsen and all the officers of Time Inc. are Republicans, but just about the whole staff of writers and editors are Democrats?"

"I don't know," he answered ruefully. "I guess Republicans don't write so good."

But he apparently thought his foreign editor wrote plenty good, for the snide reporting of the war in Spain went right on.

I was still only on the fringes of that uproar about it, but there was another uproar at Time Inc. at the same time that I was very much involved with. That was the approaching publication of Life, the picture magazine.

The most talented people in the organization had been involved with it for years, either directly or obliquely; the interest in the forthcoming new magazine was spreading across the nation; two preliminary dummies, one in August 1936, called simply Dummy and another in September, called Rehearsal had gone forth by the thousands to the press, the advertising agencies, all major advertising clients, to gossip columnists and feature writers, to radio stars and newscasters, to all word-of-mouth folk everywhere. The geyser of rising excitement about Time Inc.'s newest venture kept going higher and higher.

Many talented people had taken part too in writing the Life prospectus, which was sent not only to all the world of journalism and celebrity, but went directly into the homes of the entire list of subscribers to Time and Fortune, now numbering more than a million.

And it was Harry Luce himself who wrote most of that prospectus. Even now, when I read its opening paragraphs, I get a prickling excitement at the concept and purpose expressed in it, never mind whether the actual magazine could or could not, did or did not, fulfill that original concept and purpose.

To see life; to see the world; to eye-witness great events; to watch the faces of the poor and the gestures of the proud; to see strange things—machines, armies, multitudes, shadows in the jungle and on the moon; to see man's work—his paintings, towers and discoveries; to see things thousands of miles away; things hidden behind walls and within rooms; things dangerous to come to; the women that men love and many children; to see and take pleasure in seeing; to see and be amazed; to see and be instructed.

Thus to see, and to be shown, is now the will and new expectancy of half mankind.

This was Harry at his best, not Henry Robinson Luce, the world power in journalism, but Harry as a writer. And who could know how many people who read his words got the same prickling excitement and expectancy from them as I did?

What one can know is that 235,000 of them sent in their $3.50 checks that made them charter subscribers for the first fifty-two issues, and that another 250,000 swept the first edition off the newsstands within the first few hours.

Of course, long before the presses began to roll with those first copies, many of those same people who had worked on the prospectus and the magazine began to consider what the first public announcement should say, what tone it should take, how much it should tell. Many of them wrote drafts of possible headlines and copy.

It was to be a full page ad in all metropolitan newspapers throughout the U.S. A streamer across the top would say OUT TODAY. The illustration would be Life's first cover, in actual size, a stunning photograph, not of a pretty girl or a movie star, but of the great work-relief project, the dam in Fort Peck, Montana, taken by Fortune's famous industrial photographer, Margaret Bourke-White. Down one side of the full page would run a narrow panel, a table of contents of everything in the hundred pages of that first issue, and its price: *10¢ every week.*

But that left a big space open for headline and copy. What should the headline say? What the copy?

As usual, Harry asked me to try my hand also. I read all the preliminary drafts by other people, and though I didn't find anything pompous or stuffy, I did feel vaguely that they were trying to stay within the idiom of Harry's prospectus, and that the results were, perhaps, all too lofty for a newspaper ad, too complex, almost too well-written.

And too long. I began to write, and rewrite, and tear up and start again. What I finally handed in was forty-five words long, the shortest piece of copy I had ever written in my life.

WITH THIS ISSUE, LIFE BEGINS

Sending out Volume I, Number 1 of a new magazine must always be a momentous event to the editors who finally say, "This is it." Yet Life's editors refrain from saying it. All they say, as yet, is "With this issue, *Life begins*."

That was the copy that ran. Harry pulled me off all the other campaigns I was doing, for Time, for *The March of Time*, for Fortune, and for the next fifteen months I wrote nothing but Life promotion, three separate campaigns, working with and reporting mainly to him and to Roy Larsen.

And at the end of my second year at Time Inc., they gave me a $2,000 raise and a $2,500 bonus.

I really *was* a survivor, as far as my daily living went. If ever I did hear from The Cradle out there in Evanston, I could say even more confidently that I was reasonably well off, and surely able to support myself and one small baby.

___CHAPTER___

NINE

I WAS ON A month-long winter vacation early in 1937 when I got a telegram from The Cradle, re-telegraphed by my secretary from New York.

I had spent the first ten days in Cuba with Dorothy Whitney, then in the process of starting her own divorce, and from Cuba I flew to Key West to meet Ralph Ingersoll who had flown down from New York for another week. The night the wire came, we were back in Miami and had been out dancing. I got to my hotel room at 2:00 A.M. And there it was.

> WE ARE READY FOR YOU
> CAN YOU COME AT ONCE

Even now I can remember the sweep of feeling that raced through me as I read those ten words and read them again and again.

But I have something sharper and newer than memory to set down here about that sweep of feeling, something I wrote before the next month was out. My old instinctive need to "write it down" that had made me keep a diary when I was fifteen must have seized me again, but this time it was not just in a diary or journal that I wrote, not for myself alone. Three weeks later I began to write how it had happened, what I did, what I felt, began to "write it down before I forget, before it gets ordinary," as I said in the first paragraph of what I wrote.

It turned into a manuscript, the only anonymous thing, apart from promotion, that I ever wrote for publication. Here is the part that tells about receiving that telegram:

> I don't remember the first few minutes very well. I think I just sat on my bed and stared. I remember a sort of spasm of tremendous excitement, surprise, possibly joy; I'm not really sure. And then a spasm of frightened panic.
>
> *Alone*—that word which had long since lost its power to frighten me or hurt me—came back. I sat there. It had really happened. So soon? Suppose I wired it was *too* soon, I wasn't ready, that maybe it would, after all, be wiser to wait until I married again—would they think I hadn't really meant it and then ignore my next application?
>
> I began to wonder whether it was a boy or a girl, how old it was, what its parentage, what it looked like. I knew I was going.
>
> It was a Thursday; I knew the courts closed over the weekend...I called the airport...Then over the phone I dictated a long telegram to the head of the nursery. I'm used to dictating and it came automatically—details of my arrival, and could they arrange for a nurse to return with us to New York, and could they supply enough layette for traveling.
>
> And then I heard my own voice saying into the telephone, "Inexpressibly grateful to you and terribly happy and please be good to my baby until I get there," and something real happened inside me. "Be good to my baby?" Already something in me that was protective, that wanted this one special baby to have some special consideration, something more than just any baby?

The anonymous piece was called "I Just Adopted a Baby," and it appeared six months later in the Ladies Home Journal. I would not let Bruce and Beatrice Gould use a picture of my own baby—they knew that before my piece was sent to them—but more than half the first page was devoted to a delightful picture of two children adopted by George Burns and Gracie

Allen, and on the next page they used smaller pictures of the adopted daughters of the Jack Bennys and the Wallace Beerys. "The pictures on these pages aren't pictures of my baby," I wrote. "He isn't as beautiful as that—he's more beautiful than that—I don't know. I know it doesn't matter." I went on to give some brief background for the reader of the anonymous woman who was writing the piece, so that there'd be some basis for understanding. Swiftly I roughed in some essential facts about my life—middle thirties, with a good job at a big magazine, divorced, childless "because of some bad operative technique thirteen years ago," and I even gave a summary of my motives for trying to adopt a baby, single though I was.

After writing about the telegram, I went on to the long-distance call I put in to Mrs. Walrath the next day before taking the plane.

"Tell me about my baby. Is it a boy or a girl?"

A boy. I hadn't cared, but I was glad. Two months old, perfect health, every test excellent.

"What about his parents—I mean as much as you'll tell me?"

Within the rules, the information was given me. It was good. College graduates both...the father British, of Scotch, English, Protestant ancestry, the mother an American, of Russian, Jewish—

"What's his birthday? What does he look like? What color are his eyes? Has he any hair?"

And then my piece told of the hours of waiting for my flight, and the ten hours in the plane to Chicago, and finally of my early morning arrival in Evanston, at the small red-brick house called The Cradle.

Somewhere inside was my baby. Nobody was around downstairs. I heard the imperious, hungry yah-yah-yah of the babies upstairs and I raced up. I saw a nurse and said, "I'm Mrs.——: where's my baby?"

She smiled, told me I'd have to get into a hospital gown and gauze mask. I did, washed my hands in antiseptic, and then went into the "showroom" to wait. I went into a tiny

181

sunny room, where there was one beribboned bassinet in all that scientific place.

I waited and realized that my heart was hitting pretty hard against my ribs, and once again I knew a fragmentary panic. But I had no thought of getting out of it now.

Then the nurse came in and put my baby into my hands. Not my arms; I didn't know enough to offer my left arm. She put him into my two hands, and by some accident—I know perfectly well it was an accident—as I looked down, he grinned up at me. And my eyes filled with burning and I stood there and wept into my fine gauze mask until I couldn't see him. And the nurse didn't say anything.

Though I didn't use Mrs. Walrath's name in my piece, or name The Cradle either, in the interests of anonymity, I did write about her arrival.

I flew down the hall to meet her. She opened her arms and kissed me and congratulated me on my fine baby.

She told me a little more about his parents, but only shook her head when I begged for details—were they married, weren't they (I didn't care either way), their reasons for giving up the baby? She explained, as she had with a thousand parents, that though that day I was so sure I'd rather know everything, in six months or two weeks, I'd be truly grateful she hadn't given me precise facts I could visualize for all time into a painful or bitter story connected with my baby. I could see that.

But then, unexpectedly, she gave me a little word picture of the girl who gave birth to my baby, and ended, "And in general, a person you'd like to know, to have as a friend— she sat there, in that chair where you're sitting now, and told me why she thought it best to give him up, and she was fine and brave and admirable."

But then she warned me I couldn't take my baby out of the state if I missed court that day, and I rushed back to the city to the lawyer The Cradle had arranged for me. His legal fee was $25—that was all the money that was involved in the entire business.

And before the day was out, I had sworn in a court of law to "shelter, educate and protect" my adopted son until he "should attain his majority." Twenty-one years.

That same day, accompanied by a Cradle nurse who had permission to stay only for six weeks with me, I left for home on the Twentieth Century Limited, with my son Michael Z. Hobson, named for my father, "sleeping in a basket, for all the world like a marketing basket, except for its blue stripe and two hinged handles."

When we returned to New York, amidst all the congratulations and visits from my friends, receiving silver rattles and silver pushers and silver cups for my baby, I didn't forget to make an entry in my datebook for February 13, 1937:

> Adopted Michael
> born Dec. 8, 1936
> now: 22½ inches long
> 10 lbs. 15 oz.

Now, reliving that experience that brought my son Mike into my life, and reliving it through the words I wrote when I was young, I cannot help a twin vision of what once was and what now is, a montage of youth and old age.

Who could have thought then, as I held that eight-week-old baby in my two hands, that as a man of forty-five, married, a father, a successful publisher, he would one day be having luncheon with another successful publisher who would ask him . . .

But let me be a little oblique and set down not my own words here, but the first paragraph of a letter I received a year ago from that other publisher.

> Dear Laura Hobson,
>   At lunch the other day with Mike Hobson, an old and good friend, I was asking, as I usually do, about your work, and he told me . . . that you had a new novel coming out. He also asked me what I thought of the notion of you doing your autobiography, and I reminded him that we had talked about this notion on a couple of other occasions and that of course I thought it was a wonderful idea. I still very much do. He said, Well, why don't you write her and say so? So that's what I'm doing.

The letter was signed by Donald I. Fine, the president of Arbor House, the publisher of this book.

I wish Mrs. Walrath were still alive, so that I could telephone her at The Cradle and tell her about that.

My baby served as a peacemaker between my sister and me, and the quarrel about the summons was fast forgotten. She was wonderful about the news, and her small son Paul, now five, seemed delighted when I told him, "Now you have a little cousin. I just adopted a baby; his name is Mikey."

I was practicing a big new lesson, how to handle the "adopted" theme—without concealment from the first. Mrs. Walrath had made a special point of "no surprises," during my visit, had given me books to read about adoption. For the sake of the baby there should never be "the moment of revelation," when parents finally told their child that he or she was adopted.

Long before the baby knew any words at all, while it was only hearing spoken sounds that would later turn into words like milk or diaper or bottle or love, so it should be hearing the sound of the word *adopted*. "Before I adopted my baby," or "when I adopted Mikey," or "the greatest thing I ever did was adopt my little boy."

Whatever surprises and moments of revelation there were, were my own, at the way supposedly sophisticated people behaved at the news of Mike's arrival.

Ralph Ingersoll opened a savings account, "in Trust for Michael Z. Hobson," with a twenty-dollar deposit; Marcia Davenport sent over a great rocking-horse he couldn't use for at least two years; the Wallings sent over a sterling silver cup, engraved "Bottoms Up, Michael," and Dorothy Whitney, on receiving my wire from Evanston, which I had sent from the railroad station to everybody I cared about,

ADOPTED MIKE MOTHER AND CHILD DOING NICELY,

had stocked my house with bottles and nipples and pacifiers and tons of baby food.

And Clare, now famous all over again as the author of the smash Broadway hit, *The Women*, set about making a special blanket for his carriage. Expert with a crochet hook, she made great white daisy-shaped medallions, of a soft powdery wool, perhaps three dozen of them, which she then turned over to a needlewoman to be stitched together in a panel, lined and bordered in pale blue satin—a coverlet fit for a prince's pram.

I was still seeing a good deal of Clare, either alone or with Harry in their new apartment. Three weeks after Evanston, for instance, three consecutive days in my datebook say, "Cocktails—Luces—5:30," "Clare here to see Mike—5," and "Luces, *The Women*—Buckminster Fuller, C.D. Jackson—7 D."

There was still no political rift with Clare—she had voted for Roosevelt in 1932, just as I had, though not when he ran a second time in 1936—and she was still so much fun to talk to, though I never made a confidante of her about any man I was seeing, and certainly not about Ralph Ingersoll, whom she knew through Harry.

Just after my divorce, she had counseled me about people making assumptions about any single woman seen out on a date.

"The minute you start going out again," she had said firmly, "everybody who sees you with a man will leap to the conclusion that you're having an affair. Just ignore them. Let them guess. Never say a word. Because all the time you'll be happily sleeping with the doorman."

Ralph was not the only man I was seeing, though the others were all in a different category, people I liked and enjoyed but would never think of as anything but good friends. By now my datebook virtually never held the notation, "Practiced, worked, read," nor were the solo names always feminine, though the masculine ones usually held a tag like "tennis," "bridge," "backgammon," even "chess," though I never became very good at it.

Still there were hardly more than two consecutive pages without the initial *R*, or *M* for Mac. The hour next to that *R* or *M* varied markedly—often it was the conventional 7 or 7:30, but it might also be 11:30 or 1 A.M., meaning we each had had separate engagements elsewhere but had agreed we would be together later on.

Ralph owned his own airplane, and once he flew me up to Woodstock and met Tom and Andrée. (Was I always to know men with a passion for having airplanes?) His was not a tinny relic from anybody's wartime air-fleet, as Tom's had been; it

185

was a modern Fairchild four-seater, and he was as proud of it as a woman with a diamond necklace. Or with a new baby.

For the summer, because I wanted six-month-old Mikey to be in the country for the hot weather, I rented a house in Silvermine, Connecticut, near Norwalk, from Richardson Wright, the editor of House and Garden, a place so famous for its plantings of delphinium that tourists would come by on Sundays to wander the seven acres of gardens. (The rent for the entire summer was $750.) It was also near an airport.

Though Ralph usually spent weekends at his own delightful place further north, in Lakeville, Connecticut, he often flew up to Silvermine, either en route, or during the week. It was there one night in July that he asked me to do some promotion that had nothing to do with Time or Life but with the war in Spain and Ernest Hemingway, and a film Hemingway was making, *The Spanish Earth*.

At the office, the uproar had heightened about Time's reporting of the war, and something else was happening there too. Factions had developed among the protesters themselves—they were not only angry at Time; many of them were now angry at each other.

With the bad news from Spain, with Franco victories, there had also come clarification. Germany and Italy, rushing arms, ammunition, thousands of troops in on Franco's behalf, were determined to win for the future of Spanish fascism, and the Soviet Union, rushing arms, ammunition and thousands of troops was determined to win for Spanish communism.

The duly elected government, the Loyalists, was a coalition of democrats and socialists and liberals and communists, and the Soviet Union intended not only to win the war, but to win control of the government in the process.

And among us protesters, among all the supporters of the Loyalist cause, there were many who wanted neither fascism nor communism to be the future of Spain; what *we* dreamed of was a democratic Spain.

So the factions formed, as they nearly always do. The Spanish-American Anti-Facist Committee, already the best-known of all the new groups in the nation, was actively recruiting members in all large cities, raising contributions, doing propaganda, staging meetings and rallies. A great many people at Time heartily endorsed it and believed in it.

And right there, I first found myself in clear opposition to a "good cause," or what was ostensibly a good cause. For somehow I felt from the start that there was an interior purpose in that Spanish-American Anti-Fascist Committee that was not *my* interior purpose.

"They're not doing all that for the Loyalists," I began to say out loud. "They're doing it for the C.P."

I began to get into lots of hot water with some of my friends, but I would end each argument by saying, "There are other ways to help Spain."

And there were. Harry Scherman was one of the leaders of the Medical and Food Campaign for Spain, to raise funds for ambulances, hypodermics, drugs, bandages and all kinds of medical supplies for the Loyalist forces, and I wrote leaflets and letters and even a pamphlet to be sent through the mails to vast lists of Americans—perhaps his own Book of the Month Club list.

"That's *only* for Spain's good," I used to think, "not Russia's."

And rightly or wrongly, I felt the same way about *The Spanish Earth*. It was to be a short documentary about the war, about the Loyalist camps, about the people supporting them, about the living and the wounded and the dying, and Hemingway himself was writing it. *The International Encyclopedia of Film* says that he was writing it "with a new style of reporter-type commentary," and it says that Archibald MacLeish, John Dos Passos, Lillian Hellman and others were also involved with it. A man named Joris Ivens, born in Holland, was its cinematographer, and the musical score was being composed by Marc Blitzstein.

MacLeish must have brought Ingersoll into the project, though it might have been Lillian Hellman—Ralph and she had been friends for a long time. And when Ralph asked me if I would do one or two small pieces of promotion for *The Spanish Earth*, I was not only happy to try, I felt honored to be connected, even so tangentially.

I met Hemingway only once—"how-do-you-do," and all I can remember of him was that I thought how big and stunning-looking he was. The hundred pictures I have seen of him since then, of "Papa" Hemingway as a much older man, have thoroughly overlaid whatever primary memory of him I might otherwise have kept of him as a young man barely out of his thirties.

But I do remember that during the few nights I sat up late working on the small promotional pieces I did—they could spare very little money—I did every once in a while think to myself, "It's for Spain, not Moscow."

I don't know why I never went through a communist phase in my youth, not even in the Depression, not even in my rage against nazism and fascism. Many of the other people I knew, even those who might, in later years, reject everything they had once believed so ardently, were then communists or communist sympathizers.

But not I. It may well be that it was my own father who fixed it so that I would never go through that communist phase. There was never any doubt about where he stood. In a book called *The Forging of Socialism in America,* by Professor Howard Quint, and published by the University of South Carolina Press, there is a section about how my father "and a group of oppositionists" broke away from the Socialist Labor Party and founded the *Jewish Daily Forward*, with Michael Zametkin as editor of its first issue in April 1897, how he then affiliated with Social Democrats and "vigorously opposed both the reactionary right and the revolutionary left."

And so, always, did I. I called myself a socialist, a radical socialist, sometimes even an anti-communist socialist, I thought Marx was one of the great original minds, but I felt sure that any nation that tried to transmute Marxist socialism into communism would only succeed in defeating nearly every decent value of free men.

There was always something in me that insisted that there could be nothing in a life that was not free, that nothing on this earth could make it up to you if you could not say what you wanted to say, write what you wanted to write, vote as you wanted to vote, protest right out loud when you thought your government was wrong, strike for better conditions and higher pay.

Sometimes a friend would say bitterly, "What good is freedom to a man with no food and no work?"

"What good is food and work," I would retort, "to a man in a prison camp with no freedom?"

By then, of course, I was talking of Stalin's prison camps, and all too often it was my sister with whom this angry exchange took place.

But Alice had had the same father and the same childhood environment as I—how could we be at such dead opposites? That was one of the puzzles that I never solved, and cannot truly understand even now. As our feelings deepened, on either side, I began to feel that it was as impossible to argue about Russia with her, and with some of my own friends, as it would have been to challenge devout nuns and monks about the infallibility of the Pope. Sometimes I wanted to shout out loud to all of them, "You call yourself an agnostic, but really you're a religious fanatic, and your religion is communism."

One of the ugly fights with Alice about communism came in the fall of 1937, not about the war in Spain, but about a pair of stockings she was wearing.

She had long slim legs and slender ankles—Liz Woody had once said to her, "If I had ankles like that, I'd run for president."

Though Alice had little interest in clothes, she always wore the finest silk stockings—rayon was sleazy, and nylons hadn't yet taken over—but on the day of this quarrel, I suddenly noticed that she was wearing what looked like heavy cotton stockings, though it was a warm day. I asked her why.

"It's the boycott," she said.

"What boycott?"

"The silk boycott. Because Japan invaded China."

I began to feel agitated as if I knew what was coming.

"Most silk comes from Japan," she went on. "So Stalin ordered a worldwide boycott."

"And if Stalin orders it, you just obey?" Before five seconds could pass, we were at it. "Look at that scar," I stormed at her, pointing to the scar on her hand around the joint of her thumb, from an accident in the chemistry lab at the University of Michigan. She'd been a science major. "It's an honorable scar, a sign that you're a scientist. How can anybody with a scientist's mind and scientific training just accept orders from on high, the way you're doing about those damn cotton stocking?"

She stormed back at me and we parted in anger. I've never known why I couldn't remain calm and judicious-sounding in arguments about politics with my own sister, when I usually managed to with other people.

I used to hate those fights with her and perhaps she hated them too. I often felt afterward that it was all my fault, but intellectually I doubt the validity of that singleness of guilt. When can anybody tell who said the first inflammatory words in a quarrel, or decide whether there were fewer than two culprits?

Looking back at it now with the distance, or possibly the wisdom, of age, I feel sure that just as I had a secret scorn for her slavish following of the party line, so she must have had a secret scorn for the life I was leading, the friends I had, the parties, the evening clothes, my attractive apartment on Park Avenue, and most of all my working at Time.

But even that analysis may be too simplistic. She was a teacher, member of a noble profession; I was a promotion writer, a few echelons above the despised trade of advertising; she earned a teacher's salary; I earned thousands more.

And once again, even this double-layered analysis may still be too simplistic. Could it be that the deepest and most fundamental of all layers had been set down long before, in our infant years, when she had to listen to my mother say again and again that she was too weak to roll off the edge of the kitchen table, and when she had to sit there on the carpet and watch me proudly walk across the room to hand her that lump of sugar my father had ordered me to take to Elsiebus, who could not yet walk a step?

I have my own convictions about all these matters now, just as she must have had her own in the years before she died. But life was to arrange itself so that in those final years, we never got to talk out any of these deep schisms before it was forever too late.

As always, in the rushing days of youth, something soon came along to help Alice and me patch up our quarrel, or put it into the background. Last time it had been Mike's arrival; this time it was nothing so felicitous.

A few weeks after that business of the cotton stockings, I was at home one night working on a short story, "Marry Me for My Money"—McCall's was getting first look at my stories since the "City Doctor" debacle with the Goulds. I had had an early dinner with some friends, and as I often did when I got home early, I'd thought, Well, just to finish that scene, and had gone to my portable typewriter in my bedroom.

It was about ten when the phone rang. It was Ralph asking if he might come over right away. "I am replete with bad news," he said, and it didn't sound as if he were joking. "I'm in a phone booth," he said. "I'll be right there."

Replete with bad news. I was to keep hearing those four words for a long time to come. As I waited for him I thought, Trouble at the office? He had enemies there, some people who thought him overbearing and ego-ridden, but that happens with all people in command. Could it be about a woman?

In our growing intimacy, Ralph had told me of various affairs he had had in the past, even naming the women, some of whom I knew, just as I had told him everything, not only about Tom and Thayer, but also of the infrequent and brief affairs I had had since my divorce.

"I always swear," I once said to him, making him laugh, "that now that I'm single, I'm going to be absolutely promiscuous, but I just can't seem to live up to it. All that lost opportunity! It makes me mad."

I hadn't laughed when he told me of the women he had had affairs with, but I hadn't been shocked, or even surprised. He had been separated from his wife for a good time before their divorce, and by now he had lived alone for over three years— of course he had had affairs.

As I opened the door to him a few minutes after his call, he actually looked replete with bad news. He was pale, tense, almost silent. He poured himself some whiskey, not bothering with ice or soda, and then said, "It's Ruth. I've just come from her house."

Ruth is not her real name, but she was one of the women he had once had an affair with. She was not one of the ones I myself knew, but I did know a bit about her and the work she did and her parents.

"She's pregnant," he said abruptly. "It was that weekend I

told you about. Everybody got pretty tight, and stayed over, and it happened."

He had told me of the Yale football-weekend with a couple of classmates and their wives, and of the impromptu drive afterward to Lakeville. One of the Yale wives had invited Ruth as his date for the game.

He hadn't seen Ruth alone for years, he said then, not once since he and I—

I could barely listen. The great hook of jealousy lodged in my entrails, yanking, tearing. Pregnant—that word pregnant, that thing that happened to everybody else—I had stopped thinking about it, and here it was again, deep at the core, a wound of envy and longing.

"She doesn't want to have an abortion," he said then. "She knows we're not in love, she admits it, but she doesn't want to have an abortion."

He began to talk about children and love and marriage. He had never had children; he wanted children; if he were to marry again, it would have to be somebody he really loved, it would have to be somebody who wanted to have children too, who would plan with him to have children.

He wasn't talking about any specific marriage, just marriage in general, and about children in general, even about love in general. I had never seen him so unhappy, nor so uncertain of himself.

"In that phone booth, I could hardly make myself dial your number, hardly bring myself to tell you you about it, or hope you might understand."

At that time of my life, and perhaps even now as well, I always managed to understand and forgive men who hurt me. I think I was glad then that I didn't bear grudges—look at the way I'd found an entire new level of friendship and warmth with Tom Mount. The only exception was Thayer; I still could not accept his sudden tearing up of our marriage, like ripping a small bright Persian rug out from under my feet.

But that was in the past, and this was now; this was watching a man I cared about—I didn't use the word love yet either—watching him going through a dreadful time. In the end, of course, I said I did understand.

I don't remember how we got through the rest of that night, but exactly two days later, on December 31, 1937, the entry in my datebook says, "Dr. Damon, 11:30. R—Lakeville."

I had not gone to Dr. Damon's office for three full years. Now I was starting all over again.

We drank no champagne to a Happy New Year that weekend in Lakeville, and the first seven pages in my new little datebook for 1938 hold no R's nor M's. But Saturday, January 8, does say, "Theater, *Golden Boy*—R. 7. D. El Morocco dancing."

Ralph talked about Ruth only once that night, saying, "Everything will be all right." He sounded relieved, and I understood that she was in the process of arranging the abortion, or perhaps had already had it.

There were happier matters for him to talk about. He had already begun to plan one of the greatest steps in his professional career: the creating and launching of a new afternoon daily newspaper in New York City, a liberal paper to be called *PM*. Millions would be needed to start it, but he had already begun to talk to people like Marshall Field and other millionaires who showed themselves receptive to the idea and the first rough plans he was developing.

He was busier than ever. He had just been appointed publisher of Time, and for the first time became my direct boss. It made me a little apprehensive on my own behalf—would I have to wonder from here on if I got a big raise, whether it was, in part at least, because of our relationship? By now people had begun to guess about it, not only among our friends, like Clare, who now invariably invited Ralph as the extra man for me, but even at the office, among the people we knew best. But I dismissed that worry about raises; nobody could be harder-headed in business dealings than Mac Ingersoll; some people who didn't like him too much thought him ruthless, and an egomaniac.

One of his first policy decisions as publisher was to set up an Executive Board of Senior Portfolios for the several divisons of the magazine, and one of these was to be Senior Portfolio of Promotion.

There was a $50,000-a-year expert in the field, not on Time's staff, a Leo McGivena, who was chief contender for the new title, but Ralph discussed the whole matter of hiring an outsider with Harry and Roy and others, and then offered the $14,000-Mrs. Hobson as second choice, again on a year's trial, and with a token raise of $1,000.

This despite the fact that I had recently had my first flop on a special assignment for Harry. He had sent for me and showed me a headline he himself had written for a full page of what was called "prestige promotion." This meant promotion not designed to sell subscriptions to the magazines, nor to persuade advertisers to buy space in them.

It was like a "position paper" on some public matter, to be signed by Time Inc. In this case the public matter was nothing less than the entire economy of the United States.

The country was still struggling to get out of what the Republicans were happy to dub "the Roosevelt recession of 1937." Though the GNP, the Gross National Product, was no longer as deadly sick as the $55 billion it had been when FDR took office, it had recovered only as far as an anemic $65 billion after a year of the New Deal, and still rated intensive care. (In case you've forgotten, the GNP for 1982 was $3,059 billion.)

The headline Harry presented to me was

YES, WE CAN HAVE
AN EIGHTY-BILLION DOLLAR
ECONOMY

"Do you think you can write copy to go under it?" he asked.

I thought for a moment, trying for phrases, trying to measure my own capability in this murky area of economics.

"Not if I have to blame everything on labor," I said.

"You don't have to blame everything on labor." His tone was sharp.

"Or on the unions."

"Or on the unions. Did I ask you to pin the blame on labor or the unions?" He was more irritated than I had ever heard him.

"I was just thinking out loud."

"Suppose you try writing a piece of copy about the whole

194

U.S. economy, not any one part of it." He turned away, dismissing me.

I tried. And did some cram reading on economics and tried again. But when I presented it to him, he read it through without a word, with no change of expression, and then took his pencil and drew a cross through all of it, from the farthest corner of the paper on the upper left side, clear down to the farthest corner on the lower right, and upward from the lower left to the upper right. They weren't lines; they were vexed slashes. Then he wrote two words, "Try again," and signed it, "HRL." Without dots in between. (Years ago, when Time Inc. was just getting started, there was a major corporate decision, never to use a comma in the phrase "Time Inc.")

I did try more copy, but I never did get anything that was okayed to run. Harry never said anything further to me about one more attempt; I never knew whether he himself tried to write it, nor whether he assigned the task to anybody else in the organization. I do know that that one particular piece of prestige promotion never appeared in the public prints.

But except for this fiasco, everything else I was doing was still going so well that I was given the Promotion Portfolio, and I was busier than ever too. For fifteen solid months I had been concentrating on the three major campaigns for Life: now I was not only to write all of Time's promotion—including its first full-page automotive campaign—I was also officially in charge of its sixteen-person Service Division, a collateral department of people who prepared material for salesmen's presentations, did special assignments of mailing pieces and the like.

I was no longer just a copywriter; I was also a boss. I could hire and fire. I couldn't belong to the newly formed Time chapter of the Newspaper Guild; I was Management.

How I managed to keep on writing short stories in my so-called spare time, I no longer know, but energy is limitless even at the advanced age of thirty-seven, and manage I did.

One Wednesday page of my book says, in early February, "R—5:30–8; worked on story 9–mid." The Saturday says, "worked aft. and eve. R—10." On the day of rest that same week, it says, "worked all day, 7 hrs."

So when my annual month's vacation came around in the middle of February, I was more than ready for it. I was going to Montego Bay in Jamaica, in the West Indies, and after a while Ralph was to meet me at Kingston, at the main airport, and we were to go off somewhere from there. He wasn't sure when he could get away from the office—he would wire me the moment he knew.

Vacations and evenings out were possible for me still, even though I was a parent, and not the unattached woman I had been before. For I had searched for and found the perfect person to help me with my baby, now over a year old.

Again the jottings in my datebook had taken a new turn. One says, "Mike stood up alone—8½ mos." And in December, "Mike 1 yr. old—$100 donation to Cradle." But much earlier than that, six weeks after adopting him, just about when the interim nurse from Evanston had to return, a new name appeared that was to be of great importance for a long time. "Rosie started today."

She was Rose Miller, not a British nanny-type, nor an American governess. I had met her when she was working for Tom and Andrée up in Woodstock; she was their general cook and maid, not assigned to care for their two boys, but I'd noticed how good she was with the kids, how patient, how inventive about things for them to do, how genuinely fond of them, and they of her.

She was an American, of Czech descent, still in her twenties, a high-school graduate, and reliable as morning. The Mounts had had to let her go during one of their periodic poverty spells, and they didn't have an address for her.

But at my insistence, Andrée did dig out the name of the employment agency that had sent Rose to them, and I finally reached her, after following one or two false leads. She was working as a kind of slavey for a family in Brooklyn, with six children and in a house with five flights of stairs. She seemed timid about taking a call on the phone, and all I dared do was tell her about Mikey and ask if she could come and see him on her day off.

"How would you like to live here and be a baby nurse?" I asked her after she'd seen him. "And wear a white uniform and white shoes and—"

196

"Oh, Mrs. Hobson."

"I have a good maid, so no housework or cooking, except for the baby, and—"

"Oh, I'd give anything. You can't imagine what it's like at this job."

"What do they pay you?" She told me; she was working at Depression wages of sixty dollars a month. "I'll pay you seventy-five—"

Before the "five" was out of my mouth, she had accepted. My one stipulation was that she would promise to take her cue from me about bringing up my baby, in the way I thought best—I'd been reading books and I felt that it was right that she follow my lead—and my pediatrician's—about picking up or letting cry, and all such matters.

Rosie was one of the lucky finds of my life. Each year I raised her pay, always a little beyond the going level, before she had to ask me for more money. She stayed with us for nearly ten years, until she married and was in the middle months of pregnancy with her own first baby.

So an evening out, a weekend, a vacation—all these were possible, and this one to Jamaica began without tension about leaving Mikey, without further distress about Ralph's being replete with bad news, and with an eagerness for the sun and and beaches of Montego Bay, plus the anticipation of that coming rendezvous in Kingston.

Travel alone when you're young is no risky undertaking of possible loneliness; before the first tennis game with the hotel pro is over, you've met six other tennis players; your first hour of sunbathing on the beach yields one of those tennis players who introduces three or four other people, and so on in merry progression from day to day. After about two weeks, I gave a cocktail party at the hotel where I was staying, to repay my social obligations, and over thirty brand-new friends came to it.

But when at last the wire came, telling me what flight to meet at Kingston, I left them all behind with alacrity and was there at the airport to watch Ralph come through the open door of the plane. That same afternoon we flew on to Barranquilla, in Colombia, and it was there, after dinner and dancing, that he told me about Ruth and the abortion.

"She had it two days ago."

"Two days ago? Only two days ago?"

"That's why I waited so long to fly down," he said. "I wanted to stay until it was over, and I knew she was okay."

"But I thought it was over long ago, when you said, 'everything's all right.'"

He was astonished. "What I meant when I said that was, 'It's all right, she's changed her mind, she will have an abortion.'"

Why had she waited so long, I wondered. Long after the evening was over, after Ralph was asleep, I lay there wondering. She had known back in December, just before New Year's, and this was the first of March—that meant she had put it off and put it off, for one whole month, and then another whole month.

Why? Had she been afraid? After she had told him it was all right, that she agreed that an abortion was necessary, had she gone through week after week of indecision, eight whole weeks of wanting to go ahead and have that baby?

For some reason, my eyes stung and I couldn't swallow. I thought of this woman I had never seen, lying in bed up there at this very minute in the bitter winter weather New York was having, wearing that napkin filling with blood from a newly scraped womb, perhaps weeping in regret, and something in me seemed to swell with sorrow for her—over what I didn't know.

The next day we flew on to Panama to stay at a famous ocean resort just beyond the city limits. I had never been so near the equator; the trees, the flowers, the soft air—all of it was tropical, creating a new kind of sunlight, a new starlight.

A few days later, Ralph chartered the *Caiman*, a fishing vessel that could sleep six, and hired its owner to take charge of it and of us, while we went deep-sea fishing in the waters off the Pearl Islands.

When we'd been at Key West, I'd had my first experience of deep-sea fishing, going for sailfish, and I had loved the new experience, though the only trophy I have of my prowess is a snapshot of me standing on a dock between two very dead and very big barracuda that were suspended from hooks on a rigid horizontal steel rod a couple of feet above my head.

We spent two weeks down there, at latitude 9 degrees, and it was there that we first talked about getting married. Almost in the same breath I was saying that before I dared to say yes, I would have to find out whether or not I was now able to be pregnant. Ralph was thirty-seven too, and there had been no children while he was married. He had taken to little Mike from the moment he saw him, but I knew with a perfect sureness the primitive instinct to have a baby out of one's own body.

I had already told him, of course, that I had again begun regular visits to Dr. Damon. Now he said he would ask Dr. Damon to send him to a physician whose patients were men who might have sterility problems, "just to be checked out."

It didn't occur to me then to wonder why he would even think of being checked out when he had only a few months ago made Ruth pregnant, nor apparently did it occur to him.

But when we returned to New York, he did go to Dr. Damon, and on to the specialist he recommended, who pronounced him perfectly normal. As for me, Dr. Damon was telling me that with these past three years of further healing, and perhaps more importantly, with the adoption of my baby, ending all the old despair and frustration, the prognosis for a future pregnancy could be more optimistic than ever. I remembered what he had told me just before Thayer's announcement that he wanted a divorce—"Maybe this coming year," and felt, Maybe *this* is the year.

Hope again, renewed hope. Both our lives were changing, deepening. We both knew now that what we were involved with was not only a love affair, but love.

TEN

IT WAS TO BE a fateful year for me in four distinct ways. One was political, and for the first time I was not to be on the fringes but in the very center of something that was to make the front pages of the *Times* and the *Herald Tribune* and the inside pages of many other newspapers, especially in the East.

One day Dorothy Thompson asked me to lunch. I had remained in touch with Red, and Dorothy, being invited to their parties, more than ever intrigued by the differences between their personalities, their points of view, their friends, Red's nearly all Americans, Dorothy's nearly all German and Austrian refugees, writers, artists, scientists, professors, diplomats.

She was no longer a foreign correspondent, having been banned by Hitler from Berlin. Since 1936 she had been writing a three-times-a-week political column, *On the Record*, in the New York *Herald-Tribune*, alternating with Walter Lippmann. She called herself a liberal-conservative and was anti-Roosevelt, but she was fiercely anti-Nazi and anti-Fascist and anti-Communist, and the core interest in her life and work remained foreign affairs. Her views and columns were striking, often pugnacious and always popular.

Her *Tribune* column was syndicated in 130 papers across the land, and she was known as the First Lady of American Journalism by people who liked her, and the Lady Pundit by people who did not. As a political expert, she also had a regular program on NBC radio, and a monthly column in the Ladies Home Journal. Apart from all this, she was in constant demand as a lecturer, and was forever en route to appear on the dais somewhere at some important function.

So when she asked me to have lunch, I knew it was about something she cared about deeply. It was. America was planning a great World's Fair to open in the spring of 1939 in Flushing Meadows, in Queens, and though nearly every nation in the world was planning to have an exhibit there, Nazi Germany was not.

But a great many of the most illustrious refugees from Austria and Germany, she told me, had been banding together for several months, together with an American contingent, to arrange some sort of massive propaganda pavilion at the fair, aimed at dramatizing for Americans what the Nazis had cost Germany in the arts, science, education, medicine, religion.

"Humanities in Exile" was the tentative name of the group, and their leaders had already persuaded Mayor Fiorello H. La Guardia and the World's Fair Corporation to donate a tract, 30,000 square feet in size, for whatever their exhibit was to be.

Much of the early organization of the proposed pavillion was done before that day Dorothy asked me to lunch. The American group was illustrious too, including Samuel L. M. Barlow, the composer, and his wife Ernesta; Dr. Frank Kingdon, president of Newark University; the Nation's Oswald Garrison Villard; Connecticut's Governor Wilbur L. Cross, assorted people well-known as historians, attorneys, writers, publishers, and of course, Dorothy herself.

This American group was basically the administrative and executive branch of the project. They had sought—and received—official permission from the Secretary of State, Cordell Hull, in Washington to go ahead, provided that the enterprise be of "an entirely private nature and does not in any way attempt to represent a foreign nation."

The real creative group that had spent endless months working on the exhibits that were to go into the pavilion, had grown until there were nineteen subcommittees, each under the leadership of an expert in some specialized field.

One of them was Erika Mann, representing her father, Thomas Mann's active interest as well as her own; another was Dr. Paul Tillich of Union Theological Seminary; another, Dr. Karl A. Wittvogel, the famous orientalist, and another was Dr. Max Moericke, an art expert.

When the two groups were about to join forces more formally, the refugee people felt the need of having some American who was a recognized technician in the matter of promotion, to act as their "trustee" among the American members, and to give them professional advice about public reaction to their ideas and plans, who might write a "white paper" about their motives and aims.

Dr. Wittvogel went to Thomas Mann, who sent him to Dorothy Thompson, who invited me to lunch, and I was in.

Soon major people from both groups formed an administrative committee: Dr. Kingdon, Ernesta Barlow, Erika Mann, Dr. Wittvogel and others. The only salaried member was a Mrs. Brandes, our secretary and coordinator. We began to meet regularly and often, usually once a week, usually at my house, and as usually happens with people absorbed in an idea, far into the night.

We needed a name, a shorter, more colloquial name than their working title, "Humanities in Exile." A dozen were suggested, five dozen—we finally chose "Freedom Pavilion." We needed a permanent chairman; Herbert Bayard Swope, for years executive editor of the *World* and one of the "big names" in New York, had been asked months before by the Barlows to serve as chairman, but thus far he had agreed to act only as temporary chairman.

We needed a striking poster and a pamphlet, a printed thing that could be sent out to the press, to possible sponsors and donors. We needed to raise $275,000, of which less than half had already been pledged, about $50,000 promised by various Jewish donors, whom we knew about largely through Harold Guinzburg of Viking Press, and another $50,000 of "non-Jewish" money through Victor F. Ridder, publisher of the *Staats-Zeitung*, a German-American newspaper.

Why there had to be this careful balancing act between Jewish

202

and non-Jewish donations was very nearly beyond me, but I was assured by certain practical minds that it was an imperative for the sake of public relations. Of course I knew what the implication was, but it left a nasty taste in my mouth just the same.

Another nasty taste was the need to remember that America was already torn between people who called themselves "America Firsters" and people who felt that isolationists were, in effect, saying "Hands off Hitler—whatever he does."

So our poster and our pamphlet had to find the ways to be strong and effective, and ignore all the imaginary pitfalls of the balancers and the cautious.

I spent many nights writing that pamphlet. For the poster, which would also be the cover of the pamphlet, I appealed to Lester Beall, one of the leading art directors of the time, and he soon produced a dramatic piece of work as his contribution. His color scheme was a vivid red and blue with touches of white and yellow.

FREEDOM PAVILION
GERMANY YESTERDAY
—GERMANY TOMORROW

Superimposed on that bright background were two photographs in a whitish grey, one of a refugee woman in a sweater, her left hand holding a handkerchief to her sorrow-contorted face and weeping eyes, her right arm raised high in the Nazi salute; the other, larger, taller, the Statue of Liberty, her right arm also raised, parallel to the saluting arm of the weeping woman, but holding aloft that torch.

When I showed the pamphlet to the committee at our next meeting, you could almost hear them gasp. After a while they asked me to read the pamphlet aloud:

Six years ago, they burned the books—and up in that bitter smoke went the freedom of Germany.

There were more than books in those savage bonfires—though few could believe it then.

The free test-tubes of medical research were there, though,

and the batons of great conductors—the research notes of scholars and the designs of architects and inventors. There were canvases that had not yet been painted and religions that had endured for thousands of years.

What really went up in those flames was the right of German men and women to think, to teach, to write, to sing, as free men and women everywhere may think and teach and write and sing. What really went up in those appalling flames was freedom.

The purpose of the proposed Pavilion at the World's Fair is to show Americans everything that fell to ashes in Germany as the Nazis rose to power...to show how great, how many-sided, how enduring a contribution to humanity was the contribution of those Germans now outside Germany—be they Protestant or Catholic or Jew. How great it was, is and will be again—perhaps one day in Germany; until then in new lands, in new ways.

The pamphlet went on to tell what would be exhibited at Freedom Pavilion, "a great exhibit of art and science and music and books." It told of the famous people who would appear there, "writers, playwrights, stars of the theater, screen and radio...special shows, concerts, lectures, public readings....by Max Reinhardt, Lotte Lehmann, Bruno Walter, Dorothy Thompson, Thomas Mann."

And it ended by saying,

So much for what there will be at Freedom Pavilion. What there will not be is the propaganda of denunciation—in the sense of burning effigies or violent exhibits.

But every fine book—every fine name on that roster—every Viennese fiddler in the Café—the very fact that the whole undertaking is sponsored and created by groups of men and women of all politics, of all faiths, Catholics, Jews, Protestants, working together in harmony and respect—

All of that will be propaganda, forthright and creative.

Call it propaganda—call it human protest—call it what you will. Americans will understand it.

When I came to the end, tears stood in the eyes of some of the people there, and as I then read out the list of the notable sponsors we of the American contingent had persuaded to lend their names publicly in support of our pavilion, there was surprise and gratitude and even applause.

There were fifty names in all, our own committee names included. Among the others were Hamilton Fish Armstrong, Nicholas Murray Butler, Henry Seidel Canby, Marc Connelly, Walter Damrosch, Marshall Field, Harry Emerson Fosdick, Harry Guggenheim, Otto Klemperer, Fiorello H. La Guardia, Henry R. Luce, Archibald MacLeish, Henry Morgenthau, Condé Nast, Alfred E. Smith, Herbert Bayard Swope and others.

I don't remember why Ralph Ingersoll's name was not there; I must have asked him, and he must have declined. I do know that when I asked Harry Luce if he would sign, waiting anxiously while he read my copy for the pamphlet—I remember the shaft of pleasure that went through me when he came to the final paragraph and reached for his pen.

There were still miles to go, of course, between reading that pamphlet to our committee and seeing our pavilion go up at the World's Fair. There would be money-raising and protracted effort, there would be problems and disappointments and again problems.

But all of us in that meeting that night shared a common knowledge that we were ready to send something tangible out to the press and to the people who read the press. As for me, I felt a good sense of being useful in a cause I believed in.

In actual life, major events rarely come in neat compartments, tidy little pigeonholes of happenings. Nor do they often come in consecutive sequences, nor obey the Greek unities of time and place. Instead they often overlap or intermingle, in a sprawling tangle of good and bad, or good and good, or even bad and bad.

So it was with me in that year of 1938. The whole nation seemed to be in a state of anxiety and agitation, as the whole of Europe was, not only about the war in Spain, but about Hitler's march into Austria in the spring and the disgusting Munich pact for "peace in our time" in the fall.

And in my own private life there was plenty of agitation and effort. During the early months of Freedom Pavilion, I was also hard at work on a big study I had voluntarily undertaken at the office, a complete review of all Time's promotion efforts from 1923 onward. It meant endless hours of reading, research into the past, writing the manifold results and conclusions into a cogent document as the platform for recommending new approaches and bolder experiments. And that entailed writing first-draft copy and headlines to show the ultimate nay-sayers or yea-sayers just what I was driving at.

I was also beginning to help Ralph with the prospectus he was working on in his off-hours, for the newspaper he had set his heart on. He would write a section and ask me to read it; I would try to read it as if I were a potential investor, and we would discuss it. Sometimes I would turn to the typewriter and try my own version and offer it to him as a kind of sounding board.

He was grateful, and again I felt the good sense of being useful in something I believed in. We were both overworked, what with all our extracurricular activities, tucked into our hours at the theater or in restaurants or out dancing, as well as our scheduled work at the office, and by late spring, I, for one, had my first acquaintance with an exhaustion that wouldn't go away with a night's sleep. I had a cold I couldn't shake; I had lost a little weight. I asked for, and received, an extra week off, and flew to Bermuda. I took along the last two volumes of Proust's *Remembrance of Things Past*, and read my eyes out between swims and sun-bathing.

It was while I was down there that I missed my period. I never needed to wonder when a period was due; it was twenty-eight days and never anything else. I waited a day, then another, then a third. And I knew. I didn't need to have any rabbit tell me; I knew. Once I had said, "You could set the moon by my periods."

On that third day I was flying home. I had wired Ralph at his apartment,

MIGHT HAVE SOME NEWS LOVE

and he was at the airport to meet me.

As soon as were in his car, but carefully warning him that it was only the third day and might mean something else, I told him. It was a big custom-made Lincoln he had bought, scarcely used, from one of the Vanderbilts, and he loved it so much that I once had thought indulgently, He might not be especially house-proud, but he sure is airplane-proud and auto-proud too.

Now a pride I had never seen seemed to glow in his face. We were headed for New York, but at my news, he turned the car around and began to drive at random through the summer-green countryside of Long Island. We hardly knew where we were driving; it seemed to me that he, like me, needed motion and space, to match the exultation that had come to us, and somehow we ended up, an hour or so later, at Jones Beach of all places, a public beach open to one and all, a place I would never expect Ralph to select as a destination for any celebration.

We sat there on the sand, and soon we were talking possible names for this baby. If it were a boy, his first son, he would want him named Colin Macrae Ingersoll, after his father. We were so taken with the new delight of naming, I don't think we got around to a name for a girl. I was happier then than I had ever been in all my life, and so, he said, was he.

The very next morning I was at Dr. Damon's office. It was too early for clincial indications, but he ordered the tests and told me he'd see me in a week. The results of the tests came before that and he called me. It was true. I was pregnant.

I felt that until now I had never had any conception of what joy could be, and I didn't mean it as a pun. Of all the happinesses and triumphs I had experienced throughout my years, winning that scholarship to college, earning my first money, getting my first raise, falling in love with Tom, my marriage to Thayer, being published for the first time, everything—except only the moment when they put Mikey into my cupped hands—all those earlier joys and triumphs fell away before this rising, curling breaker in a new ocean of thankful joy.

The days passed, and the nights, and I kept on counting, even though I knew. The fifth day, the sixth, the seventh, the eighth.

The eighth day was a Monday, June 13, a week and a day after I flew home from Bermuda. I had already rented a house for the summer, this time in Greenwich, Connecticut for $1,200, and was to move in two days later. Mike was now eighteen months old; I remember the arrangements I had hurriedly made with a local carpenter to have a gate installed across the top step of the stairs, so he couldn't take a tumble in all his racing around.

At the office on that Monday, my phone rang and Ralph's secretary asked me to come in to his office. It was a large corner office; unofficially I had helped him decide how to decorate it, in beige and dark browns, with built-in bookcases. I went in and the door closed behind me.

"We have to talk," he said. He looked troubled.

I waited. He seemed to be studying some papers lying on his big desk blotter, looking down, frowning a little at them. Was it some copy he didn't like? A new assignment he was considering for me? Or was it about *PM*—the private part of his life that was by now absorbing all his chief abilities.

"I've been thinking and thinking," he said. "It's simply the worst timing there could be."

My heart began to thicken in its beat. Timing?

"For this next year," he went on, "for the next several years, more likely, my whole life has to be devoted to the paper, just to the paper, *only* to the paper."

I waited, staring at him, not able, not willing—

"It's impossible," he said, "for me to fit in getting married, having a baby—I just can't go ahead with it—"

I don't know what I said. I can't even recreate any cohesive speech here that I could feel was real. All I know for sure is that again it was annihilation, a bomb exploding, a bullet to the inner brain. He kept explaining why he couldn't go ahead now, kept trying to find ways to make me see it.

Moments later, I was leaving his office, going straight to the ladies' room, kneeling down to the bowl of the toilet and vomiting in great convulsive gushes of this new grief.

But even there, kneeling on that cold tiled floor, with both my arms encircling the rim of the toilet bowl as if seeking support, something in me thought, I'll do it anyway, I'll never void my body again, never.

I moved to Greenwich, I kept going to the office. I kept counting the days. I couldn't eat, I couldn't sleep. Dr. Damon prescribed a double dose of Nembutal; the two yellow capsules would give me two hours of drugged dreaming, and I would spring awake in sobbing anguish.

The first weekend, I drove to Woodstock, and told Tom and Andrée, and blessed them both for their instant sympathy. Tom asked if I thought analysis might help me; he had often talked about his going into psychoanalysis, not yet an everyday undertaking in those days, but he had never done anything about it. Now he urged me to seek help; it might prove a positive help, if I were really intent on going ahead alone with this pregnancy. He would get the names of some good analysts from some of his friends who had been in analysis themselves, and I could at least have a preliminary discussion with one of them.

I said I'd consider it, that I'd consider anything that might help me bear things better. I had a vision of shrapnel splintering disbelief and pain inside my mind and body.

At the office, Ralph had the grace not to send for me for any meetings. I did not hear from him by phone. I did not see him. He did not write to me in any further effort to explain.

The thirty-sixth day passed, the thirty-seventh and thirty-eighth and thirty-ninth, the fortieth and forty-first, the forty-second and forty-third. On the forty-fourth day, June 21, two days past my thirty-eighth birthday, I was on the train to the city from Greenwich, going to the office.

Usually I commuted by car because I loved to drive, the Merritt Parkway was so new and newly landscaped, and the garage at Rockefeller Center charged only eight dollars a month for all-day parking. But that day my car was being serviced for the summer, and so I had taken the train.

It was a lovely summer morning, and I was trying to relax, to look out at the fresh green of the trees and the blue-white of the June sky, and empty my mind of thinking or anger.

As we neared the city, I suddenly felt a hot rush of blood down my thighs. I sat paralyzed, and then stumbled to the train door. I had a large manila envelope with me, filled with copy and layouts, and I held it behind my dress, awkwardly, in case the bleeding should show. My mind, numbed though it was, took in the fact that we were nearing 125th Street, where there was a station. I got off the train, went down the long flight of stairs to the street and hailed a cab.

"Doctor's Hospital, please. As fast as you can." I was crying, and the driver sped through traffic.

Dr. Damon was summoned from the emergency room. It was a total miscarriage, and he tried to comfort me. At least I now knew I could indeed get pregnant. He must have called Ralph to tell him, for in the afternoon he came, bearing beautiful yellow roses. I couldn't really talk to him for the sedation they had given me, and the crying, and I was relieved when a nurse came in and suggested that I needed to rest and possibly sleep.

How could I guess, as I lay there convulsed with grief in that hospital bed, that this tragedy was to lead me, however indirectly and slowly, into the life of a full-time writer, no longer of light romantic short stories and novelettes for popular magazines, but of serious full-length novels, all of which were to become published books?

Five days after I left the hospital, before the month of June had ended, I did seek out a psychoanalyst, one of the three Tom had found out about from his friends in Woodstock. He was Dr. Lawrence S. Kubie, one of the highly regarded analysts in the city, with an office on East Eighty-first Street, a few steps from the Metropolitan Museum.

"What do you do when you can't *bear* it?" I said almost at once as he seated me in a chair beside his desk. Then I wept so fiercely that I couldn't go on.

But soon he was leading me through the large outline of what had most recently happened to bring me to his office, and then began to ask further questions about the past, my childhood, my schools, what sort of work I did. There was no suggestion that I use the couch at the side of the room; this was the first step, an inquiry into the larger structure of my life, into which this specific trauma had fallen.

At the end of the allotted "hour," he gave me two further appointments, three days apart, still calling them "preliminary," the better to let him decide whether I seemed a patient he could help, and the better to let me decide whether I believed him the right analyst for me to remain with. Compatibility was an important element in analysis, he said; apart from the inherent and acceptable problem of resistance, even hostility, that might develop from time to time, there had to be an overall compatibility of temperament between analyst and analysand. If we both decided to go ahead, he would see me five times a week and his fee would be ten dollars a visit.

I already felt that he would be right for me. Heaven knew I had had no difficulty in talking to him, even on this first visit— it had all poured out of me, almost incoherently at times, and yet with a sense of order and sequence. And he was nothing like my notion of what an analyst would be: he was no bearded Viennese of the stage, with a heavy accent and odd mannerisms of speech; he was an American, in his early forties, rather good-looking, with a quiet easy voice, a direct gaze from dark eyes, and I had been told that he had had many articles published in psychoanalytic magazines, so I thought he would be sympathetic about writing.

On my third visit, he told me he had come to a certain conclusion that might temporarily confuse me, and even cause me some distress and a sense of frustration, since he would be unable, at this time, to proffer an adequate explanation for it. Faintly he stressed the phrase, "at this time," a promissory note that at some future time he would provide the full reasoning behind what he was about to tell me.

"Distress me?" Apprehension began to rise.

"I have come to the conclusion," he said with some difficulty, "that I am not the proper analyst for you, and I have here the names of two other analysts, both excellent."

"You won't take me as a patient?" Unexpectedly, a new sense of desolation seized me.

"I have thought this step out most thoroughly," he said gravely, "and I have consulted two of my colleagues about my decision. They agree that due to certain circumstances—"

"*What* circumstances? Why?" I covered my face with both my hands, and I could hear myself sobbing the way a child sobs. "It isn't fair not to tell me why."

Dr. Kubie went on quietly, speaking to my covered face about the two names he had written on a card he put down on his desk before me. Each of the two would be a better choice for me, he said, and he had already discussed my situation with them, withholding my name, but offering enough information and situational data so that each had felt certain—as indeed he had also—that I could be helped. Whichever of the two I went to, I could feel myself in expert care.

"How can I tell which one?" I said. "I'm a layman—I can't judge. I should think you'd at least get me out of any guessing game, and recommend the one *you* think would be right." I sounded angry; I had read somewhere that it was all right to be angry with your analyst, that it merely showed normal resistance, not bad manners or petulance.

He seemed to regard the point carefully. Then he reached for the card with the two names on it; I hadn't even looked at it. "You have a point," he said, writing on another card. "This is Dr. Raymond Gosselin. If you will allow me to, I will phone him now, and set up an appointment. He is one of the people I have already talked to about you."

Silently I nodded, and heard him do it. Dr. Gosselin would see me at noon the next day.

I went out of his office more forlorn than ever. I walked toward Fifth Avenue, facing the entrance of the great museum, its white stone facade and great windows shining in the summer sun, and slightly shimmery through the tears in my eyes. This official dismissal by an analyst was, it seemed suddenly, what I should have expected. Tom had gone off to Tahiti and left me to stand it and find a new way of life, Thayer had walked out on our marriage and left me to get over it, Ralph Ingersoll had gone back on me in one of the deepest crises of my whole life; and now, even this Dr. Kubie had turned me out and away. What was *wrong*?

The next day at noon, in Dr. Gosselin's office, after some preliminary talk was over, I suddenly challenged him. "Are *you* going to see me three times and then say you can't take me on?"

He didn't answer that. He didn't shake his head for no. He merely waited for me to go on. I didn't know enough about analytic technique to realize that this was to be his normal procedure ninety percent of the time I was to spend with him, didn't guess how perceptive and instructive the other ten percent was to prove.

Dr. Gosselin was entirely different in looks and personality from Dr. Kubie, about the same age, and also an American, minus beard or accent, but somehow less intense in mien, fair in coloring, with calm gray eyes. After a pause, I asked if it were proper for him to tell me a little about himself, and how he came to be an analyst, because I'd had the rather general idea that analysts were either European or Jewish.

As I said it, I thought Dr. Kubie was probably Jewish, though I hadn't thought about it while I was with him—I never seem to think whether somebody is a Jew or not a Jew.

He was a lapsed Catholic, Dr. Gosselin said. "Medical students," he said, in a tone that told me my question was entirely legitimate, "all have to decide at some point what they are going to specialize in, if they are to be other than general M.D.'s. Some choose pediatrics, perhaps because they love children; others choose surgery, perhaps because they want the most dramatic ways to cure people; others may choose psychoanalysis because they have known depression or rejection in their own childhood, and therefore know at first hand how powerful a wrecker's ball either one can be, smashing through the most solid walls of self-worth. Maybe their own experience predisposes them for the one branch of medicine concerned with ending depression?"

He inflected it into a question at the end, and instinctively I knew that this was no exploratory visit, knew that we would go on, knew he would not see me three times and then send me away.

"Many students," he added, "who happen to be Jewish learned all about rejection in their childhood."

"Of course, I never thought of that."

"Being a lapsed Catholic can create a lot of rejection between a teen-ager and a devout family."

He smiled for the first time. I didn't realize it then, but I had just heard the longest speech I would be hearing from Dr. Gosselin for at least the first year of my analysis, and perhaps the only direct replies.

"Could you tell me why Dr. Kubie wouldn't take me as his patient?"

Now he did shake his head. "It was nothing that could be construed as being your fault. Later on, when you are told why, you will see that."

Then he turned into the doctor-in-charge: beginning tomorrow at 8:00 A.M. (since I had an office to go to at 9:00,) I would be on the couch; he was a practitioner of classic Freudian analysis; I would be encouraged to pursue the classic methods of free association; I would write down brief notes about my dreams; he would urge me not to make any major decisions—changing jobs, getting a divorce if I were married, breaking off with close friends—no important life-determinations for the first period of the analysis, perhaps for more than a year. It would take a long time to get to the end of the process we were now initiating. At any time that I found myself unwilling to continue, I would be free to leave, and it would be me and nobody but me who would decide when the analysis had reached its conclusion.

"Will it be a happy ending?" I managed to sound a little less somber as I said it.

"There are no simplicities in analysis," he said, and glanced at the small clock on his desk, placed so that a patient could see it too. The fifty minutes were over.

He had promised nothing, and I went off with no diminishing of grief, but with a new curiosity suddenly alive. This might be *interesting*.

I said it was to be a fateful year for me in four distinct ways. One was centered in Freedom Pavilion; another was my pregnancy and miscarriage; a third was going into analysis; and the fourth was my first experience of going into action against my own government—or at least against some of my government's bureaucrats.

It all started so simply. I was at a literary cocktail party one afternoon when a woman named Agnes Crane, author of a detective story or two, asked me if I was "doing anything about affidavits for refugees?" I barely knew her, though I had known her husband Ned Crane during my years in advertising agencies.

"No," I told her, "though I've sort of wondered how you go about it."

"Would you be willing to try?"

"I'd like to, if I could." It was an answer casually given, though no reluctance lay concealed within it. I really had wondered how an ordinary citizen, not in the government, could possibly do anything about the growing crisis of helping refugees escape from Germany.

This was long before there was any talk of a "final solution" for Jews in Germany; it was just after *Anschluss*, with the Nazis marching into Austria, in the spring of the year. I had not yet had my week in Bermuda, nor my miscarriage; it was before Dr. Kubie and Dr. Gosselin. (I said things overlapped and intermingled! There was certainly no pigeonhole in my life marked *affidavits for refugees*.)

"Well, in Vienna," Agnes Crane went on, "there's an analyst named Richard Sterba. He's not Jewish—"

She went on to tell me she had known him there because her niece had been a patient. He was one of the leading psychoanalysts there; when Freud was forced to flee the Nazis, Dr. Sterba was offered the presidency of the Vienna Psychoanalytic Society, but he refused out of hand. If the father of psychoanalysis had to leave Austria, how could any analyst choose to remain?

I was at once eager to be of use to this unknown Dr. Sterba. Then she went on to say that Frau Doktor Sterba was also an analyst, a child analyst, and that they had two infant children and a nurse who would have to travel with them. But if I really meant—

"Oh, yes, I'd love to try."

She gave me the name of an attorney who was specializing in these affidavit applications, and told me some more about the Sterbas and what signing affidavits entailed; it meant blanks to fill out, and guarantees and the usual delays that arose when dealing with officialdom, but I made some light remarks about the delays and paperwork that forever arose in any office.

I saw the attorney the next day, and listened carefully as he explained that signing an affidavit meant that you were guaranteeing support, if it were necessary, to the prospective immigrant, so that he or she would never become a public charge upon arrival in this country.

I told him I knew that the Sterbas had laid aside money for just this emergency, and assured him they were so well-known professionally that they were bound to do extremely well wherever they chose to practice.

Nevertheless, he told me, by signing affidavits for these five people, I was guaranteeing my willingness—and my financial ability—to spend $50 per week for each of them, should it be necessary. For a moment that fazed me—$50 a week for five people would be $250, and I was earning $300.

But I knew it was only a technicality, and in the next week or two, I busied myself happily with writing to the Sterbas, filling in documents, signing them, supplying photostatic copies of my income tax checks for the past year, front and back copies, and finally sending off everything to Richard and Editha Sterba, who were already in Switzerland, in a pretty town called Ascona.

Naively enough, I thought that was it, except for the pleasure I would have in welcoming them when they got off the boat in their new country.

The first exchanges of letters between me and Richard Sterba began on a high note of optimism. He explained almost at once that for some time, he and his wife had been asking their patients to send half of their fees to a colleague of theirs in Switzerland, a sum of 30,000 Swiss francs, about $7,000; the equivalent today of nearly $50,000, so that I need be under no tension about any financial problems to come.

I liked his letters; it felt good to be doing something about refugees from Hitler instead of just talking about the tight quota systems that seemed to have replaced America's old tradition of asylum—"Give me your tired, your poor," and all the rest of the lovely words. The Sterbas weren't poor, but they needed to be taken in as much as any others in flight.

The first snags showed up early. Official letters from the consulate at Zurich—I wasn't a relative; why then was I taking on this sponsorship? Further letters—I had sent only photostats of the checks used for my income tax; what was needed were copies of the tax returns themselves, and not only for the year 1938, but for the previous year as well.

Each letter took a week or more in transit, by ship mail, of course. Each time, I would reply the same day or the very next. Weeks elapsed between replies just the same.

And the Sterbas, over there, were soon to lose their confidence that they would soon be in transit. Every phone call to the

American consulate in Zurich, every letter, finally every visit in person by Dr. Richard Sterba seeking the latest news about the status of their applications for visas merely uncovered new demands for "essential material" before definitive action could be taken.

One week he would be asked for actual proof that his 30,000 francs existed; another, he would be told that since I was not related by blood, I could not be accepted as their sponsor, nor my affidavits held valid, and still another, why he had "concealed" his 30,000 francs when he had first made application for papers from Vienna—though officialdom knew full well, presumably, that under the new Hitler regime it was a capital crime to send money abroad, and that to say blandly on his applications that he had been doing just that would have been like turning himself in to the Gestapo. The moment he was safely beyond the borders of Switzerland, he had declared every franc of it, naming the colleague who had helped him bank it, naming the bank that held it. Officialdom knew this too.

After each of these new setbacks, Dr. Sterba would write me, and I would write back, astonished that in times of such emergency, any American consular office could behave with such grinding coldness, could keep erecting such tight high barriers. With each new demand from Zurich, my outrage grew.

In September, the visas were denied. The news stunned them and stunned me. They were in Switzerland on temporary visitor permits, which were to expire in a few weeks. To be sent back to Austria would have meant arrest, possibly concentration camps, because by Nazi standards, for "Aryans" to emigrate as a protest against Hitlerism was nothing less than treason to the Reich.

That was when I began to write Washington, to wire Washington, to write Zurich, to cable Zurich. The chief of the visa division in the State Department in Washington was Avra M. Warren, and though I tried to maintain a civil restraint in my letters to him, I did let some of my true feelings about the closing doors in Zurich show through the decorum.

I always wrote not on my private stationery, but on the letterhead of Time Inc. Perhaps that little ploy helped, for at least

I did get prompt answers from Mr. Warren, and was taken at my word when I said that I would gladly pay for cables to Zurich instead of the usual sea mail.

He could not "order" Zurich to produce visas, Mr. Warren told me, but he could ask for a complete review, and assured me the cases were still open, and made suggestions about what I should do on my own. I cabled Zurich directly:

WARREN WASHINGTON ADVISES ME TO ASSURE YOU OF MY READINESS TO SUPPORT STERBA FAMILY HERE STOP AFFIDAVITS SHOULD CONVINCE YOU OF ABILITY TO DO SO STOP STERBA WILL PROVIDE ADEQUATE PROOF OF HIS THIRTY THOUSAND FRANCS STOP FEEL DEEPLY RESPONSIBLE STERBAS GUARANTEE MONTHLY SUPPORT IF NECESSARY. HOBSON.

I wired my thanks to Mr. Warren and of course cabled the Sterbas that same day. Other letters and cables followed in what seemed an incessant stream.

And still no visas. Reading through those old letters now, looking at those cables, going through that dossier which grew to be a mile thick, I am astonished that it could have all gone on, in the interstices of everything else going on in my life, my hours with little Mike, my work load at the office, my miscarriage, my private misery over Ralph, my entry into the first critical hours of analysis, all the meetings on Freedom Pavilion—

Yet somehow, in the insistent warp and woof of the tapestry of a life, somehow it did all go on, strong, urgent, persistent.

And then in October, the visas were denied a second time, now with only two weeks more left on their temporary permits. This time I sent a multiple-page telegram, at fast rate, to the chief of the visa division in Washington, whose replies to me had held what I thought to be a note of understanding:

JUST WHEN ALL SEEMS PERFECTED...ZURICH NOW REFUSES VISA TO WIFE BECAUSE SHE HAPPENED TO BE BORN IN BUDAPEST ALTHOUGH PARENTS AND HERSELF ALWAYS AUSTRIAN CITIZENS. ZURICH NOW BALKS AT INCLUDING HER IN AUSTRIAN QUOTA, WISHING TO SEPARATE A FAMILY WITH TWO SMALL CHILDREN POSSIBLY FOR TWELVE

YEARS. STERBA SAYS VIENNA, PARIS, LONDON CONSULS ALL RULE WIFE UNDER HUSBANDS QUOTA, THE ZURICH CONSUL BEING ALONE IN INSISTING ON SEPARATING FAMILIES...COULD YOU NOT TELEGRAPH ZURICH AT MY EXPENSE TO CEASE THIS APPARENTLY ENDLESSS SEARCH FOR NEW RED TAPE?

It went on into November, into December, the Swiss permits were extended; but early in the new year of 1939, the torment was at last over, the visas came through and the Sterbas sailed to a new life in the United States.

I gave them a party of welcome, where Richard, a superb amateur violinist, good enough to play occasionally with great orchestras, played Mozart and Bach and Beethoven for my guests, and the long ordeal was over.

But our own private meeting a few days before, of Richard and Ditha and me, was the meeting of people who had grown close through difficulty and despair and the will to win out over the forces of inertia and unwillingness.

We have been friends for all the years ever since.

ELEVEN

TODAY WE TALK a lot about deterrents, the death penalty as a deterrent to murder, vast nuclear armaments as the only deterrent to war, and I, for one, cannot put my faith in either one. Nor do I believe that there is anything powerful enough to deter neurotic love.

Looking back on myself through the distance of four decades, I can see that so it was with me. I did not know then that there was anything neurotic in the way I could keep on longing for, and being in love with, a man who had hurt me, or who would hurt me again, but I apparently was missing that particular ingredient of insight and strength then, which could have made me say, "Enough—that's it. I will never give you the chance to hurt me so again."

Oh, I could say it, and I did; said it to myself in a fantasy rehearsal, over and over, of how I would with dignity and courage refuse ever to see him again. I said it to Ralph when he telephoned to ask if he might see me, wrote it in answer to his letters. But of course, in due time, I did see him again . . . and again . . . and again. I did tell him that I couldn't really have any trust in any future for us unless he too went into analysis, to find out what made him do things that other people so often called ruthless, and he actually did go, to a world-famous big-shot analyst named Gregory Zilboorg. Perhaps that contributed to my willingness to go on chancing it.

It is not easy for me now to have to face that missing ingredient of so much of my youth. I have to fight myself away from thinking, How could I have been such a ninny, how could I have been such a spineless fool, as to go ahead and again put my trust in anybody who had showed himself capable of dealing out such pain?

But chagrined or not, I am remembering that in the first pages of this book I wrote, "nothing will be made up, nothing invented, no special pleading to exonerate me in some quarrel or misfortune."

It was not lightly written, back there in chapter one, and though I also said, "I don't mean that I will permit myself no reticences," I have thus far fought down any impulse to hide or gloss over those facets of my behavior that in later years I came to regret.

And yet, on balance, I am not so sure how justified that regret is. What is the opposite of a readiness to trust again and believe again? Skepticism? Cynicism? A calculating streak that makes you weigh everything on the dull scales of caution? That wouldn't have been right for me either.

In any case, about a month after I had begun my daily 8:00 A.M. visits to Dr. Gosselin, I did begin to see Ralph Ingersoll again. Perhaps I took too literally my analyst's injunction that I make no major decision for a year or more, no changing jobs, no breaking off with close friends, no important life-determinations. The R's began to dot my datebook once again—lunch at "21," dancing at the Stork Club, the theater, and finally just "R." After a week or two, all was as it had been before. I thought I was completely happy once more.

Neurotic as a modifier for the word love must mean varying things in varying circumstances. It seems to me now that it indicated that being hurt intensified my longing to be unhurt, that it eradicated the stain of the bad times and intensified my memory of the good times, so insistently that I thought mostly about recapturing them, and needed to believe that we were doing just that. With one new complication.

As the summer in my rented house was ending, I had a phone

call one Sunday afternoon from Dr. Kubie, saying he was driving to town through Greenwich, and might he stop by for a half hour? I was surprised, delighted and somehow intrigued—this was an *analyst*, a special breed of human in the eye of a new analysand, an analyst wanting to see *me*!

He was a charming guest, full of praise for Mikey's ready, outgoing friendliness toward a stranger, an engaging talker, an easy visitor. He stayed for dinner, and as the evening lengthened, the country-house tradition came into play and it was agreed that he stay over and drive me to town in the morning.

We both understood that all this was platonic, yet driving to the city at seven o'clock on a bright September morning, to take my eight o'clock appointment, the car radio brought on not the news, but one of the hit songs of the day, and we both sang along with it in a kind of larky amusement.

> Let's fall in love,
> Why shouldn't *we* fall in love...?

We laughed, the way teenagers laugh, hilarious at our own sense of naughtiness, as we sang it all the way through, and then repeated it.

When I reported all this from the couch in Dr. Gosselin's office, there was the usual listening silence and nothing more. Just as there had been when I told Dr. Gosselin about seeing Ralph again. And the silence was to greet my subsequent reports of dates with Dr. Kubie and dates with Ralph.

By now Dr. Kubie was Larry, and there was an alternating pattern to my evenings, a kind of lunatic seesaw. In one week during September, for instance, I spent three evenings with Larry, platonic as ever, dining with him, going to the theater with him, having him to dinner at my house. The other four evenings were with Ralph, whom I had of course told everything there was to tell about seeing Kubie.

And I told Dr. Gosselin everything too. His private judgment of what his fellow analyst was risking in the way of lousing up my chances for clarity in the early stages of a supposedly classic Freudian analysis, I did not know. He never said.

But I myself must have realized pretty soon that something

Perhaps my graduation picture at Cornell; it is dated 1921.

My mother and father; undated photograph, probably in their fifties.

At age two and a half, my twin sister Alice standing, me seated, complete with fist.

One of the evenings when my datebook said "D," 1937.

My first photograph for a book jacket, *A Dog of His Own,* 1940.

Skiing, Sugar Hill, New Hampshire, 1938.

The jacket picture by Halsman for *The Trespassers*, 1943. It was also used for the jacket of *Gentleman's Agreement*.

For Laura
with Love and Kisses,

James Thurber

1932

SIMON AND SCHUSTER, INC.
Publishers

ROCKEFELLER CENTER · 1230 SIXTH AVENUE · NEW YORK
Telephone CIRCLE 5-6400   *Cable Address* ESSANDESS

September 26, 1944

Dear Laura:

Yesterday -- the day before your letter of September 24th
arrived -- Arthur Schwartz came to New York, and Andrea and I had a
wonderful time with him last night hearing a lot about you and the
good things that have been happening to you in Hollywood.

Schwartzie thinks that you may have been unhappy through
living at the beach -- so far from the center of things. I can well
see that you did this for the sake of the kids, and I must say I applaud you for doing just that. At the same time if, between now and
your return East, you feel you ought to be spending some time nearer
the center of things, I hope you will relax discipline and take the
gang to a place like the Beverly Hills Hotel, or whatever those nice
and pleasant places are -- particularly the one that Henry and Gerry
Souvaine lived at.

The pictures of the kids are beautiful and I am taking them
home tonight to show Andrea.

I have read all the letters you have had from people about
the novel. I am impressed by some and less impressed by others.
Perhaps the letter that makes most sense to me is the one from Carol
Whedon -- even though she disagrees with me. To a certain extent
she says what Harry does: that if you are going to write it, you'd
better write it regardless of what other people say or think.

SIM

ROCKEFELL
Telephone CIRCLE 5-6

Norman Cousins' heart is so definitely in the right place
that I hesitate to disagree with that wonderful letter of September
13th that he wrote to you. Norman is a dynamic guy and definitely a
force for the good, and I sound like an awful old stuffed shirt when
Dear Laura:
I don't
know what (concomitant of other ideas that aren't so good, even though the ones
RLS said
at this point. that aren't so good again come from a man with his heart in the
I'm sure
it's not this. right place. An instance I recall is an evening last winter when we
Love
Nina went to see the preview of a movie called -- as I remember it -- "A
Candle in the Wind." It was the story of a refugee pianist from
Czechoslovakia (not Rudolf Firkusny!) done by a Czech refugee and
some movie guy from the state of Maine. I forget both their names.
After the show was over Norman and I didn't see eye to eye at all.
He felt it was a wonderful picture, that it might have some chance
of success -- but what of it if it didn't. I agreed only with the
last part: what of it if it didn't. I thought it was definitely bad
and, in so far as it was, would not at all help the cause of the
refugee. As it turned out, this picture made no splash at all, and
it probably did not help or harm the cause of refugees from Czechoslovakia. But I bet my bottom dollar on the fact that it was a
second or third rate picture no matter how much it had its heart in
the right place.

I do know this about the outline for your novel -- not the
novel itself -- that Lee and I as well as Arthur Schwartz all think

it would give you some form of heartbreak.

Heartbreak possibilities:

1. (Prelude) A letter like this

2. If it is sent to Essandess, and Essandess tells you they like it, but really don't, and publish it anyway.

3. Essandess tells you they don't like it and don't publish it.

4. Another publisher tells you he likes it and publishes it. Then if the book doesn't go you will wonder whether he really liked it or whether he just wanted an author who was (a) extraordinarily personable and (b) had a sale of 25,000 copies on her first book.

5. No publisher tells you he likes it and it isn't published at all.

I admit there is a chance that Essandess might like it and publish it and that it might be a success or, that if Essandess doesn't do it, some other publisher will. But I do think the cards are stacked terribly against this project.

You know yourself how much a writer wants not only success but the knowledge that his publisher or editor is with him heart and soul.

I have a lot of other thoughts along these lines -- some of them perhaps not as heartbreaking as what I have outlined above. And since you will be in New York in six or eight weeks, I think we ought to reserve discussion of them until we see each other eye to eye.

By all this I do not mean that we are against publishing books about refugees or Jews or Negroes or any of the other problems which

so many people would rather not face or think about or hear about. But we do know that in order for those books to do any good they have to be extraordinarily well done and plausible. "The Trespassers" did not achieve the hundred thousand or more which we had hoped for because not enough people found that -- for whatever reason -- it rang a bell in their hearts. On the other hand "Strange Fruit" did ring that bell and so did "Native Son" and so did "Under Cover."

The great Jewish book corresponding to "Strange Fruit" has yet to be written. Perhaps you are the one to do it.

Well, more of that in New York.

Always yours

Dick NB

(RLS was gone by the time this letter got typed. Nina)

Mrs. Laura Z. Hobson
18718 Malibu Road
Pacific Palisades, California

RLS:nb

In uniform for the AWVS—American Women's Volunteer Services, the Motor Transport Corps, 1945.

At last a coed at Cornell, 1919.

Eric Hodgins, in his thirties; he later wrote *Mr. Blandings Builds His Dream House.*

La Baule, Brittany (my first trip abroad) in 1929.

With Clare Boothe
Brokaw and Gen. Hugh
S. Johnson, head of
N.R.A., at *Hobcaw,* in
South Carolina,
February 1935.

In Bermuda, with
Rosie and Mike, 1938.

Mike, at five and a half, Chris at six months—what sibling rivalry?

Tom Mount, in his late thirties, 1935.

My first dude ranch, the
Bar B.Q. near Jackson
Hole, Wyoming, 1934.

Biking in Bermuda, 1937.

My first publicity photograph, for "City Doctor" in McCall's, 1937.

Prompted Michigan's Republican Clare Hoffman: "Who is he?"

Replied John Rankin: "The little kike I was telling you about the other day, who called this body the 'House of Reprehensibles.'"

This was a new low in demagoguery, even for John Rankin, but in the entire House no one rose to protest.

Everybody knew where Rankin stood, which was four-square against a federal ballot for soldiers, eight-square against the Administration, and, of course, 16-square in favor of the poll-tax, white supremacy, and Southern womanhood. John Rankin, master of old-fashioned oratory, counted on his corn to hold the House's attention. He was not wrong.

The Time article that inspired *Gentleman's Agreement*.

was all wrong in the "transference" department, which I was just hearing about from Dr. Gosselin, for I spent a couple of chuckling hours writing what I thought was a delicious comic poem, with the refrain, "Gosselin and Kubie and Freud." Words that rhymed with Freud made me clap mental hands in self-approval, like *destroyed*, *annoyed*, *cloyed* and *void*, plus Brooklynese renditions of *thoid*, *hoid* and *boid*.

I gave a copy of my comic poem to Dr. Gosselin, I sent one to Larry and showed my own to Ralph. I'm sure nobody liked it as much as I did . . .

I never was too clear about what ended the seesaw, but after about a month everything was back on level ground once more, with me seeing only Ralph. Perhaps a remonstrance to Dr. Kubie from Dr. Gosselin did it, or maybe it was my terrifying operation for a breast abscess, with all the attendant fear of cancer, and the glory of relief when it wasn't, an operation that brought Ralph as my first visitor after surgery and Larry virtually passing him in the hall as my second.

Or possibly that comic poem of mine carried a Freudian message directly to Dr. Kubie himself, especially those rhyming words, *annoyed*, *cloyed*, *void* and *destroyed*.

Who's to say? But he did stop calling me, and I was not to see him again as a "date" until long after my analysis had finally come to its end.

Just about the time I was feeling so triumphant about the visas for the Sterbas, I went through, with so many others, a harrowing public defeat, the sudden death of Freedom Pavilion.

It began with a combination meeting and cocktail party at the exclusive River Club in River House on East Fifty-second Street, with all sorts of prominent New Yorkers invited, and it ended four days later with our bright brave idea a corpse.

I was to write my first political exposé for publication about that death, write it a few weeks later, with all our committee members urging me on in their desperate need to let the world know how this disaster had come about.

I wrote from my own notes, from letters, from their notes and memoranda, and from the official record of the party itself, set down by stenotype—there were no tape recorders then.

My piece turned into a 7,000-word article, a seven-page insert in the Nation, and was almost denied space, because the never-wealthy Nation could not afford seven extra pages of newsprint.

But those extra pages were made possible by my friend Dorothy Whitney, who was soon to marry the actor Raymond Massey. She was nothing like a liberal; she would never have known about Freedom Pavilion, except that she knew me. When I told her the Nation wanted my piece but couldn't afford the additional paper, she promptly donated $200 to pay for it, and "FREEDOM PAVILION, The Missing Exhibit at the World's Fair," ran in the issue of April 29, 1939.

Just before it was to appear, I went up to Harry Luce's office and offered him my manuscript. "The Nation might say something about me being with Time Inc.," I said, "so I thought I ought to let you read it before it goes to press."

He waved it aside. "I'll read it when it's on the newsstands," he said. "Not beforehand." I liked him for that.

It had been a hard piece to write. The first third of it had to give the reader all the background, the idea itself, the various groups involved, the sponsors, our permission from the State Department, our plot of ground, Lot N–14, granted by the World's Fair Corporation. Only then could I get to the cocktail party and our very first meeting, just three days before it, with our temporary chairman, Herbert Bayard Swope.

The big do at the River Club was his idea, selected by him as the surest way for us to "go public" about raising the big money we needed. He had come to none of our planning sessions, had heard none of our developing ideas, except in reports from our paid secretary and brief talks with Dr. Kingdon.

But in this first meeting he proceeded to take charge. He had already sent out telegrams to 100 people, so prominent that their very names assured us huge press coverage. His wire hadn't said exactly what it was about, just "to discuss a matter of high cultural and international importance at the World's Fair." He hadn't brought us a list of his prominent names; that was his province and we'd be sure to be impressed. Their RSVPs were already coming in to his office and all was well.

But all was not well in some other areas. He didn't like the poster; we shouldn't use it as the cover of the pamphlet. It was antagonizing; it was provocative; it was political; it would alarm people.

Freedom Pavilion was all wrong as a name, too; it was also antagonizing and provocative. "Old Germany" would be better—the building could be a sort of Old Heidelberg inn.

As he left, Mrs. Brandes gave us nine names he wanted deleted from our list of sponsors on the back of the pamphlet. Every name was Jewish, every one of the nine. He had also removed Dorothy Thompson's name and Thomas Mann's name from the other people signing his telegram of invitation—she couldn't say why.

A few days earlier she'd told us in a letter that the only German names he wanted in the text of the pamphlet were Thomas Mann, Albert Einstein and Sigmund Freud. "These are so great that the fact that two are Jewish can be discounted."

We yielded about leaving off the cover of the pamphlet for the cocktail party, but voted down everything else. Waiting through the next three days proved pretty tense for all of us.

Pretty tense? From the moment Mr. Swope made his benign opening remarks to his hundred prominent people, it became more like being on Death Row. "The root of the idea," he told them, was "to indicate the enormous part . . . Germany played in the progress of civilization and the betterment of humanity."

He didn't mention Freedom Pavilion by name. He didn't mention Hitler or Nazis or the burning of the books or the flight of refugees. He said not a word about smashed careers or dismissed professors or arrests in the night or concentration camps.

The nearest he came to it was: "There is a sense of resentment that occasionally manifests itself against certain activities of the existing government of Germany. . . ."

As I wrote in my Nation piece, "That is not set down from memory, long as I shall cherish it. It is taken from the official stenographic record of the proceedings."

But all of us on Death Row got a reprieve with the next speech, from Dr. Kingdon, in which he spoke eloquently and to the point. A brief following speech did nearly as well.

And then Mr. Swope got an idea. Instead of introducing the next scheduled speaker, he suddenly called upon Monsignor Michael J. Lavelle, rector of St. Patrick's Cathedral.

225

"I don't think I would care to vote for anything that would be likely to provoke trouble, or get us into war," the eighty-two-year-old monsignor said. "It was a side issue . . . that brought us into the last war . . . I beg of you to be careful not to provoke conflict . . . some of the smallest things have caused war between nations. . . ."

Mr. Swope was on his feet. "It is precisely with that in mind that this meeting was called . . . it is a very sound caution . . . I share his attitude precisely . . ."

Governor Al Smith also endorsed the idea of caution; and so did several others, from the floor or on the platform; there were a few further speeches, the pamphlet, minus inflammatory cover, was handed around, drinks were served, and the great party was over.

"We are finished," Dr. Paul Tillich said to me. Dr. Reinhold Niebuhr, also of Union Theological, echoed him. Erika Mann said, "But *why* did Swope suddenly call on Monsignor Lavelle, who would surely kill this?"

It was killed all right, and despite last-ditch efforts by all of us to raise money anyway, despite trips to Washington and meetings and telegrams, it stayed killed.

One final grotesquerie occurred when some of us went to Swope's office for his reports of "reactions" from the prominent people—virtually all "dubious" or "opposed." He had two candidates for permanent chairman, in case we did go ahead, and one was Thomas J. Watson, president of IBM, International Business Machines, who had been decorated by Hitler on behalf of the Third Reich.

When I told Erika and the others about this Nazi-decorated candidate, I could scarcely look at their faces. And four days later the final electric shock was sent through the struggling body of Freedom Pavilion.

"Whalen won't let us do it," Dr. Kingdon reported. "They've been getting to him. He won't let us have the site."

They've been getting to him. Who, exactly, was that they? In the Nation I purposely assigned no specific blame, but it must have been pretty clear. It wasn't just Mr. Swope, nor even just Monsignor Lavelle; it was also all those who called in "dubious" or "opposed." It was one of my first public encounters with that

226

"they"—and all through my life, I have, in one way or another, tried to do battle with those nay-sayers, those cautious ones, those people in foreign consulates who close the doors, those senators and congressmen who vote down the good strong laws that could save lives done in by hunger and illness and pollution, those cliques and demagogues who deride the young on their protest marches for civil rights, about Vietnam, about nuclear bombs...

But way back then, perhaps I wasn't quite up to it, despite my Nation exposé. When we were forced to say farewell to Freedom Pavilion forever, I, for one, felt a new kind of acid etched into me by those letters R.I.P.

It was in that same month of April that Ralph Ingersoll left Time Inc. for good, to launch the final campaign for his newspaper *PM*.

He had become obsessed with it; he thought of little else, talked of nothing else, planned for nothing else. More and more of our evenings were spent in the homes of the wealthy, whom he had approached for investments, the Gimbels, the Fields and many others; when we were alone, he would be working on the development of this or that department in the paper. Even on those evenings when we went to the theater or out for dinner and dancing, our in-between talk was nearly all of *PM*.

His absence from Time had little effect on my working life. By then I had been raised to $20,000 a year, and my responsibilities were wider than ever. But something else had been added. Harry and his cohorts on the executive floor had established a profit-sharing plan for what was called the Senior Group, thirty people selected out of the thousand employees of the organization, who were to "help guide Time Inc.'s destinies for the years to come."

I was the only woman among the thirty. The extent of profit-sharing would vary from year to year, but for 1939 it was to be about 51 percent of your salary. Thus my pay that year was to total not $20,000 but about $31,000, which I've just been informed by an inflation-reckoning friend of mine, would be about $125,000 today.

Only half-jestingly, Harry explained at the first meeting of the new group, "I want every one of us to have the chance of becoming a millionaire in the future, or at least a half-million-aire." Maybe there was nothing jesting about it at all.

Apart from the dazzle of the dollars, there was now a new dimension to my life at the office. I, who was to discover much later in life that I was no public speaker or lecturer, that even the prospect of standing up on a platform to address an audience meant a preceding week of damp palms and wobbly knees—I could just sit at that big conference table among all the major editors and executives of the entire company and talk as I always talked, never flustered, never tongue-tied. "Let me sit down," I used to say, "and I can talk my head off, no matter who's there."

Yet the sum of my life did indeed change. Though the paper occupied more and more of Ralph's time and mine, it also separated us more, and the stresses of raising millions of dollars of investments stretched his nerves to the squeak-point, and mine right along with his.

We again had bad times, tensions, differences, bouts of misery, to be made up, vows offered about more considerate behavior. Once, about a month after my Nation piece, I jotted down in my datebook the terse note, "Letter to R. *Finis*," obviously not yet having absorbed the possibility that in neurotic love, *Finis* does not necessarily remain *Finis*.

But that same day, as was by then typical behavior for me when I was unhappy, I began to search for an idea for a new short story. This time I came up with not just another light love story, but the most somber one I had ever attempted, "If He Were Mine."

It begins with Schuyler Barrett, a Wall Street financier, about forty, waiting on a dock at the Hudson River for an ocean liner from Germany, on which is a small boy of ten, Otto Rosenberg, son of one of Germany's greatest violinists.

Sky Barrett has scarcely ever given a thought to refugees from the Nazis, either adult ones or ten-year-olds, but on a vacation with his wife and son, Frecky, for a music festival three years before, the two boys had met and become fast friends, writing to each other afterward, Otto practicing his schoolboy English,

planning future trips, sending get-well cards and holiday greet-
ings.

Through a set of circumstances all too possible in the ensuing
three years, Otto has lost both his parents, his non-Jewish mother
now disowned by her family because of her dreadful marriage,
and his famous Jewish father "shot while trying to escape" a
concentration camp.

> "What must I do now, Herr Barrett?" Otto had written
> him. "I live with the gardener who is too poor to hold me
> more than a little. I know you will not let me off, so what
> must I do now?"

Sky Barrett had begun the search for suitable adoptive parents,
and had arranged through business connections in Berlin to ship
Otto over to him in New York while he searched. There had
followed the joyous reunion of the two boys, and then the
maddening delays, plans almost completed for adoption and then
blasted, Otto oblivious of all the difficulty and changing his
name to Oliver. "I sound more like America."

At last, the inevitable happens, when Frecky, two years older
than Oliver, finally asks, "Why can't *we* adopt him ourselves?"

> "Your name would be Barrett," Sky tells Otto, "just like
> Freck's and mine."
> "Barrett." Oliver tried it thoughtfully. "Barrett. Oliver
> Rosenberg Barrett. I couldn't forget my father?" His voice
> had barely a question in it; he was so sure.
> "No, son, you'll never forget your father," Sky said and
> thought, Damn it, this kid makes you want to cry. "Oliver
> Rosenberg Barrett it is."

The rest of the story concerns not only the two boys during
the next two years, not only the changing of the little German
Otto into the American Oliver, but the slow metamorphosis of
Sky Barrett from a man who had never thought of the needs
and deprivations of anybody beyond his family and his own
relatives and friends into a man who is subtly forced to do so.

The adoption, when it becomes official, makes a good story

down on Wall Street; it gets into the papers, and soon his morning mail takes on a new coloration.

> "...and because you yourself...have by your actions, shown where you stand in the matter of thousands of the world's children, made homeless and insecure..."

He is asked to be a sponsor of a group setting up camps for Spanish child refugees; a day or so later, he is asked to sign on to subsidize professors and scientists fleeing from tyranny; he is asked to do this, urged to do that, join here, contribute there...

At first he resents these letters. He's no crusader, no do-gooder, by nature he is no signer or sponsor. But then the time comes when he does sign one pledge of support, to an academic group, and finds that it feels right to set his name down along with others for something that matters. And to sign a check for it as well.

Interwoven with all this about Sky is another story that arises when Oliver and Frecky, the two top seeds for the boys' tennis tournament at the country club, sign up on the bulletin board for the annual matches. One of the two scrawled signatures reads, "Oliver Rosenberg Barrett."

Everybody at the club knows all about what Sky has done, knows that his wife has gone along indulgently enough too, but to have that bulletin board staring at you each time you go by it...

Soon the president of the board of governors takes Sky aside to ask if he could explain to Oliver, and get him to enter his name simply as Oliver R. Barrett.

Suddenly Sky Barrett of Wall Street finds himself shouting. No, he won't explain to Oliver; no, he won't ask him to make a change on the bulletin board. The name stands, all of it, every syllable of it.

The ending of the story strikes me now as a touch sentimental, with Oliver in a knockdown, nose-bleed fight with another boy member of the club, and Barrett's heart contracting with rage as he understands what his kid had been called.

> "What did he do, son, say you were a Jew?"
> "No—he said—he said I wasn't an American."

Like Sky Barrett's morning mail, my own daily batch of letters soon took on new meanings. It had started with my piece in the Nation, actually, but it widened when this story came out in McCall's just a few weeks after World War II started, a rush of mail from liberals, individuals or in groups, the ACLU, the NAACP and many others. The letters brought not only comment, not only appeals for money, not only invitations to meetings and rallies, but even, in a few cases, for the use of my name.

It seems likely now that "If He Were Mine" must have welled up from my feelings about the visas for the Sterbas or from my wrath about Freedom Pavilion, but wherever it came from, writing it gave me a pleasure quite different from the pleasure of doing a romantic little love story.

Something deep inside me had spoken out through this story, and I knew an elation I had never known before. Not only when it was finished, but while I was leaning into my typewriter night after night writing it.

As I said, the word *Finis* doesn't necessarily remain *Finis*. I wish I had never thrown away all my letters to Ralph, but that one, with all the rest, is gone. Ten days after I sent it, another terse note appears in my datebook. "R's letter," and we were back together again.

I had rented a house for the summer in Paget, Bermuda, and had gone down, at first for only a weekend, not only to get Rose and Mikey settled in, but to be the one to launch my little boy's aquatic life. Rosie was nervous about the water, and I didn't want her to communicate her fears to my two-and-a-half-year-old son.

Then in August, when my month's vacation took me back there, Ralph abandoned his money-raising and his wealthy investors and flew down to live with us for two whole weeks. And when we got back to New York, we were engaged to be married, officially, publicly, ring-on-the-finger engaged to be married. Up at Lakeville, Ralph's father and his stepmother, whom he called Tante, gave us a big outdoor engagement party to announce our news, and introduce me to all their friends and neighbors, and back in town, we were guests of honor at parties given by just about everybody we knew.

A telegram from Archie MacLeish stands out in my memory. It was addressed to Ralph, and congratulated him on his "finding the perfect help meet for your life." I had never heard the two separated words, *help meet*, used in ordinary speech anywhere, certainly had never seen them in any telegram, had never even read them except in the Bible, when I searched and found them in Genesis, but Archie was a poet and used words as a poet uses them.

There was a touching overtone to them that filled me with pride and resolve. I wanted to be a perfect help meet when I married again. I would try to be a perfect help meet. For all his faults, and despite all of my own, Ralph deserved a perfect help meet.

It didn't even occur to me to wonder what kind of help meet Ralph would be to me. That kind of thinking wasn't usual, as far back in my life as that. Indeed, one of my terrible handicaps had always been—my analysis was beginning to reveal some of my own buried problems—one of my own handicaps had always been my conviction that all men drew back from able women, didn't like it if a girl or woman had more talent, if she earned more money, that the man wanted to be the strong one, the superior one, and if not, so long, farewell.

I used to say to Dr. Gosselin that one reason I was so happy with Ralph was that he was so successful himself, he could look at my promotion job and my short stories as a sort of cute act he loved to watch. Today I would be saying that he never felt threatened by me.

But I am positive that way back there, when we read Archie MacLeish's telegram, we would both have thought it absurd even to raise any rude question about help-meet-in-reverse.

It took quite a long time before I realized that I too would have to leave Time.

Our engagement put a formality to what must have been a tentative doubt for some time to everybody in the Senior Group. I was now the fiancée of a man starting a rival publication, a man whom many of the group were none too fond of. They knew that no daily afternoon paper could conceivably be considered a rival of Time, The Weekly Newsmagazine, but they also knew that I was privy to some of the innovations Ralph was planning, and that I was bound not to say a word to anybody about them.

Conversely, they must have begun to consider what innovations or new departments being planned by any of Time Inc.'s various magazines might better be left undiscussed at our weekly meetings.

I was, of course, bound not to tell Ralph anything that was confidential at Time Inc., but what needed to be confidential often stayed hazy in its first stages. I began to feel an awkwardness in the basic situation.

One night during the winter, at dinner with Ralph and Harry Luce, I raised the question myself. Was it now indicated that I should resign?

It was not an easy question for me to raise. I had to earn a living, and nothing thus far had led me to feel certain I would have a great big beautiful job on *PM*.

Far from it. Four years before, when Harry and Clare were just married, Ralph and a couple of others at the office had urged Harry not to consider letting her play any role in the creation of Life, no matter how good she had proved herself to be in running Vanity Fair. In private, they phrased it, "not letting her get a foot in the door," not for Life nor for any of the other magazines. And she never did, at least not officially.

But I had never been managing editor of Vanity Fair nor any other publication; all I knew was the relatively subordinate area of promotion, and it had not once occurred to me that Ralph might feel the same way about me and my foot. Nor did he ever imply anything of the sort.

But from time to time he would tell me he had offered a permanent job on the staff of *PM* to people I knew, like Elizabeth Hawes, a famous dress designer for the rich, who had written a best-seller, *Fashion Is Spinach*, and Lillian Hellman, and many others, men as well as women.

None of this worried me. Publication day was still months off, set for June, 1940. But when I began contemplating the rather scary act of resigning from Time, where I had spent five such solid years, I did ask him what sort of job I might have at *PM*. The only place he could think of for me was a labor column, at a salary of seventy-five dollars a week.

But, of course, that might change before pub day.

Only it didn't. I did resign, and still it didn't. Nor did much of anything else work out the way I had wanted it to—perhaps I should say, the way *we* had wanted it to, for I cannot believe, even now, that Ralph didn't share my regret over the growing realization that a few months after the public engagement and the ring-on-the-finger certainty, we once again were doomed.

To assign blame in private troubles is something I have always been as wary as possible about; I am sure that if he were writing now about that period in our lives, he could say that I was too sensitive, too easily hurt, too demanding, anything and everything that human beings can seem to be when things go deeply wrong between them.

There were still high spots, like the day the paper was fully subscribed—with merrymaking and celebrating and a renewed sense of unity between us. There was a January vacation to Cat Cay and then Nassau, and on our return the most exciting visit of my life, to the Oval Office in Washington, for an audience with President Roosevelt.

It had been arranged by Archie MacLeish, who was then Librarian of Congress, so that Ralph could tell the president about the new liberal newspaper that would be supporting him in New York if he should decide to run for a third term because of the outbreak of war in Europe.

It was in anticipation of that august event that Ralph decided to give me my wedding present early, my first mink coat, and Tante and I went shopping together in time to have it made to order for me to wear when we went to the White House. (My wedding present to him was to be a tennis court for his house in Lakeville.)

But the high spots grew less frequent, and the spells of contentment and joy less frequent too. We had begun to have fairly hot arguments about politics, never like the shouting bouts between me and Alice, but pretty heated just the same. The fiercest had happened just nine days after we had become engaged the preceding August, the night the news hit the world that Hitler and Stalin had signed a ten-year non-aggression pact.

Ralph could find it "understandable" that Stalin was playing for time against the Nazis; this had brought forth the anguished cry from me, "But it means war—millions of people will die," and a storm of invective against Stalin and all his deeds for years back.

Ralph had maddened me by remaining calm, logical. "You don't trust Stalin," he finally said. "I do."

It was two o'clock in the morning; we had been out dancing, and had gone to his place, and now I was too agitated to stay the night. I began to fling myself back into my clothes, miserably ashamed that instead of remaining cool and collected as he was, I was weeping bitterly.

Those final words of his about trusting Stalin broke through my control and I did something I had never done in my life—I took the slipper I was putting on and hurled it across the room at him. I am a poor shot; it missed him. But though I apologized the next day, I wasn't truly sorry about that flying shoe.

I never for a moment thought Ralph Ingersoll was a communist, but in those days there were many people who had a kind of eternal readiness to "understand" or accept just about anything Russia chose to do. Ralph often seemed to me to be one of them.

This was long before the days of McCarthy but even then, liberals so hated "red-baiters" and "red-baiting" that we often muzzled ourselves rather than denounce the Soviet Union outright, and risk being labeled red-baiters ourselves.

It was a sort of self-censorship, I see now, and at times, in social situations where one didn't get into heated protests about what people were saying, I was often enough snared in that trap of polite murmur rather than forthright dissent.

Since our engagement, Ralph and I were often invited for weekends up to Lillian Hellman's luxurious farm at Pleasantville, where there always was a gathering of talented people, including Dashiell Hammett who lived there, and among those people I nearly always found myself alone on one side of a great gulf, with Ralph on the other, during all the talk about "the imperialist war."

They all hated Hitler and Fascism and the Nazis as much as every decent person in the world, but they still could speak of "the imperialist war." And I, perhaps intimidated by them because they were friends of Ralph's and famous to boot, would cram back what I really wanted to say—only to burst out with it to Ralph later on, as we drove back to the city. And so, as it had been during that final blur of misery with Tom nearly twelve years before, when we were reaching the end of our life together without yet admitting it, there were increasing tensions between Ralph and me, more frequent quarrels, more tears from me, more silences and impatience from him, and finally the knowledge that it was all over.

I became ill. Once more it was a breast abscess, and once more the hospital. It was to become a pattern, that when I was depressed enough, something went wrong with my body.

This time there was nobody sailing off to Tahiti, no one person leaving the other. If anything was ever mutually arrived at, this parting was it, even though it would be I who would put it into words in a final letter.

From the hospital I called Dorothy Whitney, confiding in her, telling her it was over, breaking down while I spoke. She was by now Dorothy Massey and she and Raymond were out in San Francisco, where he was playing in the road company of one of his smash hits. She told me to get myself onto a plane and get out there to the coast and stay with them a while, and I went.

From their hotel I phoned Red Lewis in Beverly Hills, where he had rented a big house, and took him up on a long-standing invitation to drop in if ever I was in California, and once again I was told to catch a plane.

He was not yet divorced from Dorothy Thompson, but they had been living apart for some time. He had developed a new infatuation, for the stage and for being an actor. He had been playing in summer stock, once in Thornton Wilder's *Our Town*, and also in Eugene O'Neill's *Ah, Wilderness!* In the theater he had met a very young actress, Marcella Powers, and when he met me at the airport, Marcella was with him. He introduced her as his niece.

I hadn't known about Marcella, but nothing of that sort concerned me. What did upset me was that his house was also full of a lot of young hangers-on, many of whom struck me as deadbeats, young actors using him to try for a foothold in the theater, and only too glad to eat Red's free food and drink Red's free wine and free whiskey and swim in his pool and use whatever connections they could dig up on the grounds that they were friends of Sinclair Lewis.

It saddened me to see him so far removed from what he had been. His last few books had been badly received, and on the plane coming down the coast from San Francisco, I had skimmed his newest, *Bethel Merriday*, and had been so dismayed by it that I presented it to the stewardess before landing, just so Red wouldn't see me carrying it and expect me to say something about it.

After a few days at Red's, I flew to Sun Valley, the new resort in Idaho. I still couldn't face New York, where the first issue of *PM* would be appearing on the newsstands in three weeks, on a Tuesday, not the usual Monday, but a Tuesday, a day long ago selected, Tuesday, June 18, my fortieth birthday.

I had known despair before, over Tom, over Thayer and my divorce, but this seemed to be even more unbearable, perhaps because of that fortieth birthday so nearly mine. To Dr. Gosselin, I had once cried out, "It's all *my* fault—I always fall in love with a man who's going to kill me."

There I was in the grandeur of those mountains and I felt crushed and lost. I had no job, no office to go to, and though Time Inc. had given me a year's pay as a farewell bonus, I would have to begin searching for a new way to earn a living.

What I did have to keep me going was my wonderful little son, who was now three, and ten published pieces of fiction, and my own sense that my tough daily sessions of analysis were helping me at last to follow that ancient maxim I had learned so long ago in Baby Greek at Cornell. *Gnothi seauton*—"Know thyself."

If the dreams of marriage and love were over, these three realities were not. I kept clinging to them as I spent days and nights trying to write a letter to Ralph to explain why I knew we had broken apart for good.

I wrote it and rewrote it, and finally, just eighteen days before *PM* first rolled off the presses, I went to the post office myself and slipped it through the slot.

And this time, the *Finis* remained *Finis* forever.

TWELVE

IN A CONVOLUTED WAY, it was President Roosevelt's decision to run for a third term that led a publisher, a major publisher, to suggest to me that I could write a novel, not a short story, not an article, not promotion or pamphlets but a full-length novel.

He not only suggested it, but made an amazing offer, an advance of $5,000 if I would do it.

A published book? Not a Western, signed by a pseudonym like Peter Field, but a real novel, with my real name on its spine. I was flabbergasted. I had never once thought of writing a novel. Nor had I written the first line of the first paragraph of the first page of this book he wanted, yet he was offering me a contract, with $1,000 on signing and $500 a month for eight months, to say, "Yes, I'll do it."

The publisher was no visionary, but Richard L. Simon, of Simon & Schuster, and the convoluted route that led him to his astonishing offer, had run along a dozen different main roads and byways in my life.

We had first met while I was still married, and meeting just about all the younger publishers in New York, like Bennett Cerf of Random House, John Farrar of Farrar, Straus and Dick himself.

One of Dick's own interests had always been promotion, not

only book advertising, but promotion in general, and he had read just about everything I'd ever written for Time, Life and Fortune.

But it was one special piece of promotion, a thing I did on a voluntary basis, that fell right in with an idea he had been developing on his own.

It was a full-page ad on a political theme and it had been in the papers a few days before the 1940 elections, as a rebuttal to another ad on behalf of FDR's opponent, Wendell Willkie. The Willkie piece was written by one of my dear friends, Harry Scherman, and I had to keep reminding myself, as I wrote my ad in reply, that he was too big a man to let it mar our friendship.

His ad, addressed to the well-known "undecideds" of the polls, said that if they voted for FDR in this time of a declared national emergency, they would produce an "inescapable and disastrous paralysis" in Congress, because of the opposition to a third term. It was a warning of a house divided, a nation unable to act in "opposing the march of the dictators." It was signed by Harry himself and eleven conservative authors and editors.

Mine was written almost overnight, in opposition. I no longer remember who approached me and asked me to write it, nor do I recall who put up the money for the newspaper space. But it was signed by twenty-five of the best known writers in America, including Sinclair Lewis, James Thurber, Dorothy Thompson, Thornton Wilder, George S. Kaufman, Edna Ferber and nineteen others.

IT SOUNDS LIKE A THREAT, MR. WILLKIE,
—AND AMERICANS DON'T LIKE THAT

They wrote an ad for your side, Mr. Willkie... and it's running in about forty papers clear through to Election Day.

Maybe you didn't get around to reading it... maybe you'd better... and denounce it fast.

For in effect it threatens this nation... with a sit-down strike in Congress.

Oh yes, it does. Slyly, cleverly, concealed under the eight-dollar words...

The copy went on from there to talk to the undecideds themselves. The Willkie ad had asserted that it was "presented in no spirit of partisanship." Mine said, "This ad doesn't pretend that. This ad is as partisan as anything," and went on to urge the 5 million undecideds to vote for FDR.

Dick Simon had read the ad and had asked around among all the literary signers until he had found out who had written it. He was especially intrigued because he knew Harry Scherman had done the Willkie ad, and he and Scherman were not only business friends but good personal friends as well, sharing their love of music, playing bridge together, visiting each other.

And he knew me, and wondered whether to mention Harry's ad to me when he phoned to say he liked mine, and whether to mention mine when he phoned Harry. It may be that this double awareness helped keep me in his mind as he kept mulling over the startling publishing idea he was developing.

He didn't say anything to me about it for quite a while, but then one day in the spring of 1941, he phoned me and asked me to lunch. He wanted to talk to me about a proposal he had been considering for some time. He reminded me of the "Mr. Willkie" ad, and that he'd said it had a fresh, pugnacious tone he'd liked. He also added that he had read several of my stories and the piece I'd done on Freedom Pavilion, as well as lots of my regular promotion copy.

I was pleased by all this, and eager to see him, thinking it was all background for some promotion he wanted to discuss for his firm, probably on a free-lance basis.

But what he wanted had nothing to do with promotion. "We've always been successful at S & S with nonfiction," he said, "but not so much with fiction. I want to change that."

He was determined, he said, to build up a fiction list. He had put forth a plan to his partners to find and develop novelists. He wanted the firm to set aside a total of $25,000 for advances to five people who could write, people who were not already tied to another publisher, and offer each of the five a $5,000 advance, to get them to write a novel for Simon & Schuster to publish.

I was one of the five.

"But, Dick, I never even thought of writing a book."

"But you *could* write one. I know writers when I see them. You know how to tell a story, you get a lot of emotion in what you write—"

"But a book! A story takes a few weeks, but a book?"

"What about your storybook for kids?"

"That was kind of a lark—it took me forty-five minutes."

"It's a published book just the same."

It was true. During the fall I'd had an idea for a story for children. I was forever telling my son stories, and this one came from the fact that he had just been given his first pet, a black spaniel named Inky, and was out of his head with love.

So my story was about a little boy named Mikey—who else?—who wanted a dog of his own more than anything in the world, so on his fifth birthday his daddy and his mommy gave him a floppy black spaniel, whom he named Inky, and took out to the park on a leash and was happier than he'd ever been in his whole life.

But one day, he thought, If it's such fun to have one dog of my own, it would be *twice* as much fun to have two dogs. His parents were on vacation, but he begged his Aunt Lulu to get him a Scotty, and Aunt Lulu—a very foolish woman—did, and he got another leash and was twice as happy. And then, one day—

The story went on in a rapid crescendo until Mikey had ten dogs of his own, on ten separate leashes, and was *ten* times happier—until various disasters began to strike.

Forty-five minutes was not just a figure I pulled out of the air. With about ten words to a page, and no more than thirty pages in all, with most of the invention already done as I kept telling my little boy various installments of this horrendous saga, it really did take me less than an hour to write the first draft. Then while I was reworking it, I'd called my old colleague, Jane Miller, for the illustrations, and she'd done wonderful comic pictures of a bright-eyed kid and slightly askew spaniels, Scotties, terriers, poodles, Dachshunds, all the way up to a great big tremendous Great Dane.

I'd showed the text and sketches to Marshall Best of Viking Press, and they had just published it at a dollar a copy. *A Dog of His Own* was on sale at all bookstores, and though it was a

"Juvenile," consigned to the company of children's books, it was indeed a published book, its bright cover bearing the legend, "Story by Laura Z. Hobson; Pictures by Jane Miller."

I had sent a copy to Dick and his wife Andrea, to read to their two little girls, Joanna, who was Mikey's age, and the baby, Lucy. (Their third daughter, who was to become the famous popular singer, Carly Simon, wasn't on the scene as yet.)

So here was Dick Simon talking seriously to me about trying to write a real book, an adult book, a full-length book, a novel.

But I couldn't do the simple thing and say yes. Suppose I signed the contract and took the first thousand dollars, and then couldn't think of an idea good enough for a real book? Suppose I kept trying and trying, month after month for eight months, and still hadn't written a book fit to present to a publisher, all the while receiving $500 a month from him? That would leave me $5,000 in debt!

Nor could I drop everything else and live on $500 a month for most of a year. I would still have to keep on writing short stories, to earn what we needed to have, and perhaps do freelance promotion as well.

So I asked Dick to let me think it over for a while. I was tremendously grateful, and told him I was, and I was moved as well at this show of confidence from an established publisher. And the notion that perhaps the time had come when my writing would move up to an entirely new plateau—this gave me a vision of happiness that I had not had in all the months since I had written that letter to Ralph in Sun Valley.

Dick Simon's offer could not have come at a more propitious time. Just about a year had passed since I had resigned from Time, and though my farewell bonus had prevented any acute worry about money, the experience of joblessness was demoralizing. Finally I had begun to search in earnest, not among other magazines, knowing instinctively that on none of the others could I duplicate, or even approximate, the pleasing conditions of working at Time Inc., where so many of my colleagues and bosses were also my friends.

Two interviews were noted in my datebook before I found a job, one with Niles Trammel, then president of NBC, and a second with William Paley, head of CBS. That still meant radio, in 1940, not television, and I had landed in the promotion department of CBS in August at $15,000, on a trial basis for half a year. I didn't mind the cut in pay, for it overlapped my farewell bonus from Time, and if everything worked out, I'd be going up to my base pay of $20,000 in six months. Nobody even talked of profit-sharing at CBS.

Of course everything would work out, I thought, only it didn't. From the start there were personality differences with my immediate boss, Vic Ratner, perhaps exacerbated by the fact that he believed strongly in using facts, figures and statistics in promotion, and I didn't.

My first major assignment there was for their hour-long weekly religious program that went out across the whole network, and instead of using a bunch of statistics about its ratings, I pinned it all on a simple headline, "It is Sunday morning."

Or maybe he just took a dislike to my personality, as well he might. I was still tense with misery about breaking with Ralph Ingersoll, nearly unable to pass a newsstand where his still-new *PM* was on display, without feeling an inner twisting of memory and loss, and also tense with comparison—unable to stop my mind from comparing working at CBS to working at Time.

At Time I had had all kinds of work and overwork, but also all kinds of leeway: I could tack on an extra day to any weekend for my secretary and myself, without asking permission; I could ask for an extra week's vacation and know that I'd receive that permission. At CBS, I was just an employee.

And not *enough* of "just an employee" to keep Vic happy with me. I was right there at CBS when I was writing my election ad to Mr. Willkie, first informing Vic that I was doing it, working after-hours, of course, but getting phone calls from and having lunch dates about it with many of the people involved with it.

Everybody at the office talked to me about it when it appeared—feelings were running hot and high during that election—but from Vic there was only silence. And two or three weeks later, when the Christmas issue of McCall's appeared with my story about Otto Rosenberg Barrett, lots of my co-workers, and even some of the higher-up executives, made a sort of fuss over it, but again Vic said nothing. Not one word.

So I guess it was inevitable that in another month or so, Vic wrote a "Dear Laura" letter, five single-spaced pages in length, and wrote it just in time to hand it over on New Year's Eve. Buried in verbiage was a simple fact: I was fired. A month's notice, of course, but fired.

Talk about a propitious piece of timing! As I asked once before, is there always one small point in human struggle that can seem hilarious years later, no matter how unlaughable the whole? I wonder if Vic ever asked *his* analyst why he simply had to hand over that "Dear Laura" letter on New Year's Eve.

So had begun the year of 1941. I had been invited to a black-tie party at Dorothy Thompson's who had moved to Central Park West, and I made myself go, all dressed up, alone in a taxi, embarrassed to death, as most women in those benighted days would have been, at appearing at a party without a man at my side, and wondering, almost as soon as I got there, who would offer to take me home once the Auld Lang Synes were over.

I escaped, by myself, just after midnight, without saying good-bye to my hostess, so she wouldn't worry about it, went off alone, wretched, trying to kill off memories that kept coming at me of other New Year's Eves when I was in love and happy. At my apartment house, when the doorman opened the door of my taxi, I was embarrassed once more, that he should see me in all my finery but alone.

Upstairs as I undressed, I glanced over at my desk, my eye caught by my new datebook for 1941. Beside it lay the old one for the year just gone. Idly I opened this one, back to those days at Sun Valley. From there on, with just four exceptions, all the pages of all the weeks of all the months were blank.

Two entries were about my job interviews, the third said, "Started working, CBS," and the fourth was Dorothy's party on the last page of all.

I can only speculate now about why all those pages were untouched. I must have seen people during those seven months, heard music, gone to the theater, had dinner with friends, and most of all, begun or worked on a story, but the pages from May onward are void. Not even on the day when I wrote my storybook for kids did I make a note of it, not even a follow-up line to say, "Viking took *Dog*." Most inexplicable of all, is December 8, empty of the expected, "Mikey is 4." There at least, I have a theory: December 8 was also Ralph's birthday; we had always made much of the two birthdays coming together.

As for the rest of the dead pages, I can only guess that I must have been too dispirited, too heartsick over what I held to be my third failure in my private life as a woman, first Tom, then Thayer, then Ralph, too depressed to want to keep track of those days and nights. That had happened in my early twenties, when I kept a journal, that same instinct to delete from the record, by the simple trick of not setting anything down, those parts of whatever suffering seemed to me indescribable.

So it was not a festive time for me. Being fired shakes you, even when the timing is not as sadistic as Vic's, and on the first business day of the new year, I had reached for the telephone to call Time Inc. Everybody had known for months that I was no longer engaged to Ralph—I could go back. Probably not to the same old job, which had been filled by somebody else for just about a year, but to something.

I never even considered calling Harry Luce; that would have been a kind of nepotism, a step removed. We had begun to see far less of each other, anyway, partly because I was no longer with Time Inc., and partly because my first political distance from Clare had begun during the 1940 election, distance and disapproval.

Not that she had become more and more conservative, more and more Republican, more and more a public figure in the arena of politics. Lots of my best friends, as the saying goes, are in that same arena, and we remain friends, if only when we both stay clear of the arena.

But Clare had begun to use her acerbity and wit in ways that I found unacceptable. One of the most egregious examples was her gibe at Dorothy Thompson, when Dorothy announced in her syndicated column that she, Dorothy, who had always voted as a Republican, who had ardently supported Wendell Willkie through most of the 1940 campaign, had now changed her mind and shifted her allegiance to Franklin D. Roosevelt, and would campaign for him and vote for him.

The two women had debates in public and on radio in the weeks leading up to the election, and neither of them was shy about the use of sarcasm or wisecracks. But it was Clare who at last went beyond what most people thought was acceptable in any public slugging match.

"Dorothy Thompson," she once proclaimed, to the delight of every gossip columnist in the land, "is the only woman I know who's having her menopause in public."

After the campaign, she sent Dorothy a pleasant message of friendship, and Dorothy replied in kind, so they remained "friends," and indeed Clare and I were, to a certain extent, to remain friends too, though at greater distances and longer intervals.

A year later when *A Dog of His Own* was published in London by Hamish Hamilton, Clare wrote for the jacket blurb, "It gave the most awful pain in the heart, longing for a small boy of my own to go with the book," while Dorothy, printed directly above Clare, went in for a little political fun, unusual for her. "It preaches the only moral, social and economic lesson, namely: that too much of a good thing is too much. Only think how well-off Mr. Hitler would have been if he had been satisfied with a Dachshund and a Pomeranian, but no, he also had to have a Scotty and a Great Dane, and I give you my word, if we are not careful, he is going to go after a Mexican hairless. And with them all on a lead, he is going to be exactly like Mikey— praying for a policeman to save him."

So there they were, publicly united on an inner leaf of a book jacket on behalf of a friend's little storybook. But as far as my own friendship with Clare went, and with Harry as well, a very large diminishing had taken place.

By now, she and Harry had become world figures, not just famous in publishing circles, but famous among diplomats and foreign embassies and royal courts, not only all over Europe but in General Chiang Kai-shek's China. And most of their friends dwelled in those lofty realms as well.

In any case, when I reached for the telephone on that first business day of the new year to call Time Inc. about Career No. 2—Harry and I had once actually discussed a possible Career No. 2 off in some distant future—I was going to call Allen

246

Grover, whom I liked a lot, a vice-president, close to Harry, and a friend during my years there, but not part of my life in the years before.

I began to dial the old familiar number, Judson 6–1212, but I stopped with the third twist of the dial. Did I really want to go back to my old life at good old Time Inc.? Once, in my analysis, by now in its third year, I had heard myself say, in a sudden outburst, "I don't want to spend my one life in a big plaid office on a payroll, being a big shot, with a super-secretary and a sofa to take a nap on if I'm tired."

"Then you will have to put an end," Dr. Gosselin had replied calmly, "to the battle you've been waging."

"What battle?"

"The Thirty Years' War between the Zametkin conscience and the Hobson budget."

I had laughed, the kind of wild guffaw that means recognition. But it was no joke, and I knew it. Now I sat holding the telephone, not dialing beyond the 6. Wasn't this perhaps the perfect time to end that war, or at least declare a truce for a purposeful while, testing, searching? Could I possibly earn a decent living as a short-story writer, not as a spare-time hobby, but as my regular work, my principal work?

And what would it be like to work at home where I could see ten times as much of my little boy?

I had always managed more time with Mike than most mothers who had jobs, because I could so often leave the office early, and because I didn't have to do the marketing and cooking when I did get home. But now he was getting out of babyhood and into being more of a distinct personality, and I had a growing longing to fix it so that there were no great gaps in the day when I was not there.

I had begun to give him a weekly allowance, five cents every Sunday, and I had assigned his first household chore, emptying all the ashtrays. I had laid down the first "rule of limitations" between the two of us, to wit; "If my door is closed and you hear my typewriter going, you can't come in—unless you've cut your finger. Because it means I'm earning a living for both of us." (For years afterward, even when he was at Harvard, if Mike needed to call me on some minor matter, he might well begin by saying, "I just cut my finger.")

But back then, as I held that telephone receiver in midair, all that mixture of feeling about my little boy and my being at home and my longing to try myself as a full-time writer seemed to sweep through my mind, and I put up the phone at JU 6— thinking, Al Grover can wait.

I had a month to go at CBS, but my datebook once more began to have frequent entries: concert—David; theater—Brett; dancing, Stork Club—Hugh, D; lunch—Eric.

David was a friend of Dorothy Thompson's and very political, Brett was a minister, away from home and eager to see everything on Broadway, Hugh was a writer, not well known, who loved night clubs and dancing, and Eric was Eric Hodgins, now managing editor of Fortune, and soon to be its publisher, author of the by-now-world-famous blast at munitions makers, "Arms and The Men," and one of that long-standing band of protesters at Time Inc. who had kept after Harry Luce for years about "Jew Blum," the "Franco Falangists" and other such editorial iniquities.

I would have lunch with Eric and talk about the world's solemnities and then go out in evening clothes with Hugh and forget them. Each of them encouraged me to give myself one great big chance at writing short stories for my living, at least a whole year of it, and I would listen only too gladly and feel sure that in a year I could bring it off.

February 6 in my datebook says, "Left CBS." The next page, "My first day just writing! I'm very happy," and contains a few rhymed lines below it, with the notation, "Words & music by me." I can still sing it, to a jingly little tune:

> Mommy what's this? Mommy, what's that?
> Mommy, how *do* you keep on your hat?
> Where is Rose? When are you going?
> What are those? Why is it snowing?
> Why can't a kitty bark like a pup?
> How can I hang a penguin up?
> It's when and what and why and who
> And how and where and—WHEE—
> I'm four years old and want to be told,
> And that's why you love me!

Across the bottom of the page runs the explanation, "Song I made up for Mike after he asked, "How do you hang a penguin up?" He had a toy penguin, and Rosie was strict about his putting away toys or hanging things up.

I began a story about the reverse side of adoption, not about the joyous parents receiving their baby, but about the weeping young woman who had had to give that baby up. I called it "Pink Is for Girls," and wondered if it could possibly sell. I also was launched on research for an article on Pasteur, which my agent thought she could sell to Reader's Digest.

It was clear to me, and to Dr. Gosselin as well, that I had again come back to the business of living.

And then, a few weeks later, before I had had time to test out my ability to earn a living as a magazine writer, there was Dick Simon and his offer. And there were, also, all my question marks about accepting it. He'd said there was no need for a hurried decision, that his offer would stand, while I did whatever thinking and weighing I needed to do.

I thought and weighed a lot. I discussed it with Dr. Gosselin, I talked it out with Alice, with Tom and Andrée, with Hugh and Eric, but all these discussions with friends had an amateur status.

One evening with the Schermans—I had been right about Harry bearing me no ill will because of my Mr. Willkie ad in direct opposition to his—one night, I told him and Bernardine about Dick's offer, and they both urged me to go right ahead.

"Don't you worry about that $5,000," Harry said. "You know I believe in risk capitalism, and that's what it is, *his* risk. Your only obligation is to turn in the best manuscript you can write, by the date you promise it."

But I still didn't say yes. I was swamped with unfinished work, and felt my own obligation to finish all of it before starting on a new path. I had already begun what I noted as "very long story, really a novelette," which indeed would turn out to be 109 pages long. "Pink is for Girls" was still making the rounds, a slight shock, since my last ten stories had been accepted, with nary a rejection slip, and I felt compelled to send this new one out quickly, as an antidote to the possible disappointment awaiting the other. "You Always Make Me So Mad" was the title for the new attempt, and I couldn't even consider dropping it halfway. The sale of a novelette would really give me a chunk of new income, and the reassurance that goes with it in the first tentative weeks of free-lancing.

I was also involved with nonfiction. Reader's Digest had turned down my piece on Pasteur, but an editor there, Rondo Robinson, who later wrote a big best-selling novel, *The Cardinal*, had liked it well enough to offer me $1,200 for a 2,200-word profile of an unusual woman, Justine Johnson. She had been a star in the Ziegfeld Follies, had won prizes in beauty contests, had married the head of Paramount Pictures, Walter Wanger, and then, to Broadway's total disbelief, had turned away from the life of a beautiful blond to devote herself to scientific research in medicine, as assistant researcher to two well-known doctors who finally found what the press headlined as "A Five-Day Cure For Syphilis," and "the greatest step since Ehrlich and Salvarsan."

But the pressure of unfinished work was not the only enemy I had just then in my battle to reach a quiet, sure decision about Dick and his offer. Like everybody I knew, like the whole country, I was seething with emotion about the war in Europe.

Roosevelt had just succeeded in getting Congress to pass the Lend-Lease Act; he was stepping up the "limited national emergency" to the status of unlimited national emergency; German troops, so bitterly successful the preceding year in invading Poland and the low countries and France, were now marching into Yugoslavia and Greece; Britain was under savage bombardment from the skies...

Nobody could talk about anything but the war, about Bundles for Britain, about the isolationists in our midst, whose leaders included that world celebrity, Charles Lindbergh. And then, just at that time, came the blazing success of the Lindbergh rally at Madison Square Garden on behalf of the growing "America First" movement in the nation.

The movement was founded in 1940, with General Robert E. Wood, head of Sears Roebuck, as one of the co-founders, and grew among the nation's isolationists and noninterventionists so that it became a roaring force of propaganda against the idea of any involvement of the United States in the war against Hitler.

It was widely held to be not only anti-intervention and anti-British, but also antisemitic, so much so, according to many reports, that the name of J. Lessing Rosenwald, also of Sears Roebuck, was added to the board of directors as a strategy to counter those charges of antisemitism. In its early days, even some liberals joined in and became America Firsters, notably my old friend William Benton; also unexpected people like Chester Bowles, Kingman J. Brewster, then a student at Yale....

I had gone to that Lindbergh rally—and walked out on it—not knowing yet that the Lone Eagle himself would prove another roadblock on my way to a decision about Dick Simon's offer. But soon I was called on once again to set everything else aside and write copy for a full-page protest, written right at him and his movement. Reading it now I wonder that I had the gall to write as I did.

HOW ABOUT TELLING THE WHOLE TRUTH,
MR. LINDBERGH—
NOT JUST PART OF IT?

That "81% against war" which you harp on so incessantly was paired with another question *in the same Gallup Poll.*

But you have found it convenient—and also honorable?—to keep silent about the other question... The one limps and lies without the other.

My copy gave both questions, the first asking whether you would vote yes or no about the U.S. entering the war against Germany and Italy, and the second asking that same yes or no "if it appeared certain that there was no way to defeat Germany and Italy, *except* for the U.S. going to war against them." To this second question there was an overwhelming yes of 68 percent. It was this 68 percent Lindbergh was keeping so silent about, and the rest of the copy was pretty pointed about the ethics of that silence.

This time the ad was signed by a well-established nationwide group, Fight for Freedom, Inc. By a coincidence that touched off many emotions in me, its national chairman was the Right Reverend Henry W. Hobson of Cincinnati, Thayer's brother, whom I had not seen since my divorce, and whom I had always been not only fond of, but impressed by.

Once, years before, he had described himself, in some private family joke, as "bishop of the Proctor & Gamble Diocese of Southern Ohio," and during a long weekend we had spent with Henry and his family at their summer place on Fischer's Island, we had somehow got talking about religion, and he had made it clear enough, in his gentle and lucid way, that what bothered him was not my being Jewish but my being agnostic.

Years later, when my name too began to appear as one of the signers of full-page ads in the newspapers, in protest about civil rights or nuclear war, our two names always ran in alphabetical sequence, Henry's first, and mine directly after. Every time our names were coupled in print, somebody would ask, "Is that your ex-husband?" and I would always reply, "No, he is only my ex-brother-in-law, and I think the world of him."

This Lindbergh ad ran in late May, and it served as one extra little prod to Dick Simon, earning me another reminder by phone that he still thought his idea was sound, and still thought I was a sound choice as a candidate for it.

And I said, "I'm beginning to feel surer, Dick—I want terribly to try it. We'll talk up in the country."

What I did not know, what I could not suspect, was that there was already in motion a new train of circumstances which an approaching weekend in the country would reveal, circumstances that would virtually make my decision for me.

On the first of May, I had taken what I called "a dump of a place" up on Noroton Bay, in Connecticut. Until the middle of June I would be there only for weekends, because of my 8:00 A.M. schedule with Dr. Gosselin, but Rosie and Mike were already settled in on a full-time basis.

One thing my analysis had freed me from, even more surely than my liking for "a big plaid office, a super-secretary, and being a big shot," was the compulsion to rent only the smartest of summer places, like the one in Silvermine, with its seven acres of delphinium, or the following year's place in fashionable Greenwich.

This time I had taken a quite ordinary brick-and-stucco house

252

with hardly any ground around it, because it was right on the water, on an inlet of Long Island Sound, with a narrow sandy beach where Mike could play, plus a dilapidated old rowboat he named the *Lickety Split.*

Nearby in Norwalk were Dick and Andrea and their kids, and not far off were John and Carly Wharton with whom I was, by now, close friends. The Wharton children were already in their teens, and thus no prospects for play with Mike, but my proximity to them and to the Simons robbed me of my recurring tinge of fear of being lonely away from the city.

And then came the Memorial Day weekend, the weekend I was never to forget. There had been a party at the Whartons and a dinner with the Simons, and I had vividly described my little dump of a place, with its one small extra bedroom for house guests, its blocky overstuffed furniture and its skimpy plot of ground.

That was enough to bring Andrea over by herself on the Sunday morning, sure that she could devise ways to rearrange furniture and make it more attractive, or at least a bit less dinky, dull and drab. Andrea was one of the most outgoing people I had ever known, full of ideas about how to improve your cooking, your parties, your decor—she once told me that my dinner (I was never a good cook)—that my dinner was tasty but "too white," and quite right she was, since it consisted of sliced chicken under a creamy wine sauce, of tiny pearl onions, of braised celery chunks and the like. I never afterward prepared a meal without checking with a mental color chart, and sometimes making a small obeisance to Andrea.

On that Sunday she had ideas aplenty, and we began shoving the sofa and overstuffed chairs around the living room, shifting floor lamps, heaving the upright piano from one corner to its opposite number; we tied back heavy drapes, rolled up the dark carpet and carried it up two flights to the attic, bringing down a pale beige shag from my bedroom to replace it. She even drove off to Norwalk for a couple of bright flowered cushions, presenting them to me as a house present as she set them into the corners of the dark, discouraged sofa.

After a couple of hours of playing moving van, I was ready to call an exhausted halt, but Andrea was still going at full tilt, ready to tackle my bedroom, the guest room, even the furniture on the porch.

And she had her way—with me weary but willing, and admitting gladly that the dump had become lots more tolerable. People who didn't like Andrea's proclivity for taking charge said she was trying to be "everybody's earth mother," but I always liked her energy, her interest, her readiness to help, strenuous though it might be.

I drove back to New York that night, thinking ahead to the middle of June, when I'd move up to Noroton for good. I was bone-weary, but I knew why. It was a hot sticky night, almost like midsummer, and I looked forward to a cool bath in my silent apartment, and a long night's sleep.

As I was stepping out of the tub, I glanced at the floor-length mirror in the bathroom door, and stood still. Something was different.

I was different. I dropped my towel and moved closer to the mirror. Nonsense, nothing was different. I had imagined it.

I looked away, and then quickly looked back, as if to trap an elusive phantom before it could again escape.

Something's changed, I thought. My breasts are a little fuller. I felt them; they were faintly tender, but that nearly always happened before a period—

When had I had my last period? I no longer kept track the way I used to do during all those deprived years of longing, and as I had approached forty, the clockwork precision of those twenty-eight days had occasionally faltered.

Anyway, it was nearly three years since my miscarriage, and four since Mikey became part of my life, so that I no longer felt robbed of the experience of bringing up a child, and I scarcely ever thought any more about pregnancy or periods. No wonder I was not so conscientious about making little crosses on the calendar on the inside cover of my datebook.

But I went to my desk, naked, still damp with cool water, and opened to it. I had made no cross in the month of January, none in February; the first one was March 15, and then, absurdly enough, there was another cross already entered in advance, for every fourth week to the end of the year, ten little crosses, ten months right through to December.

I certainly hadn't missed two periods in January and February without noticing it. Oh, of course, I thought, that was when I'd just been fired from CBS, while I was wondering whether to call Al Grover about going back to Time Inc., or whether to take a stab at just writing full-time—no wonder I'd forgotten the little crosses. Then on March 15, I'd apparently made up for my lapse by putting them in all at once for the rest of the year, like predictions in an almanac, or ETAs, expected times of arrival, in railway timetables. So that streak of crosses could tell me nothing now.

I went back to the mirror. And this time I knew. I had imagined nothing. It was true.

That other time, even on the forty-fourth day, there had been no visible change in my breasts, none of this faint extra heaviness as I cupped them and lifted them. So this must be past the forty-fourth day, maybe past the fiftieth, even the sixtieth. Then this must be the start of the third month, and nothing had gone wrong; I hadn't miscarried. It was true and it would stay true.

I knew it with a calmness I had never known; knew it with a perfect serenity and with a leaping primitive pride.

In nineteen days I would be forty-one, and I was pregnant and this time my pregnancy would go forward to the very end until I gave birth to a baby.

This time nobody but me would have any say about that pregnancy or that birth. Nobody could back out, nobody could fill me with the anguish of rejection; there would be no sleeping pills and drugs and weeping nights, there would be no miscarriage. *This* was me alone, and I could rely on me.

There was no moment of quandary—shall I go ahead? There was no doubt, no dilemma. The start of the third month—then it had happened back in March. Back in March I was still seeing Hugh.

Hugh is not his real name. Just as Ruth was not the real name of the young woman whose misfortune Ralph Ingersoll had translated into the phrase, "I am replete with bad news," so now, for the second time, and the last, I choose to borrow a name.

Earlier in this book I wrote that in the two years between my sudden divorce and the beginning of my years with Ralph, I had at last "begun to have some experience with what goes by the name of 'affairs'."

One of those limited encounters had been with Hugh, and it had lasted for a few amiable weeks, ending without even a subtle damage to anybody's ego. That had been about four years earlier.

But just about the time I got Vic Ratner's New Year's Eve epistle saying I was fired from CBS, Hugh and I ran into each other again, and he asked me out for dinner and dancing, and soon we resumed our light, uncomplex affair. Again it lasted for only a few weeks, but after the emptiness of my private life during those dead pages in my datebook, I must have been vastly reassured.

Hugh was not married then, but later on he did marry and have children. Though he is no longer alive, his widow and children are. And that is the reason for his pseudonym. Unlike Tom or Thayer or Ralph, he never was, and never became, an integral part of my life, so keeping him anonymous in this context in no way distorts the completeness of what I am telling now about that life.

As I said, our relationship once again had been brief, a supple, lithe pleasantness for a few weeks in winter, nothing more, and over long before that electrifying night when I stood there before that panel of mirror in my bathroom.

Was I now to dig Hugh out of whatever he had been up to in the past two months, to tell him what had happened? It would be absurd. He knew all about my adopting Mike when I knew I was unable to have a baby; I had even said there was no need for contraceptives, because I couldn't have children. He had begun to seem distant, "part of the past," as I am sure I had begun to seem to him.

How far in the past? Again I went to my datebook, riffling through the pages backwards. No Hugh in May, no Hugh in April. I had seen him only twice after March 15, on the twentieth and then on the twenty-eighth. And this was already the first of June.

No, I had no obligation to Hugh at all. Here too was a total lack of quandary or dilemma. This was my last chance to give birth, this, after all those years of trying and failing, and I need not jeopardize it by offering any human being on earth the power to say yes or no about it.

I still remember the small thud of decision that sounded flat and hard in my mind, flat and hard yet somehow warm and happy. There would be no problems about this pregnancy except my own problems about how to manage it.

March 20 or 28—I began to count on my fingers in the age-old way. That meant around Christmas. If it were not nearly midnight, I would have called Dr. Damon, with some crazy message about working me into his schedule right around Christmas.

I slept fitfully, waking each time with a start of pure congratulation to whatever in me had at last managed this marvel of the pregnancy that was not going to go wrong. Each time I went straight to the mirror in the bathroom, lifting my nightgown high over my shoulders, studying my naked body once more.

And never once did I doubt it. I was pregnant, and this time I was going to have a baby.

THIRTEEN

I THINK DR. DAMON was as happy as I was. And as sure. He ordered tests, of course, but this time, the clinical evidence yielded by my own body, something about the cervix, as well as the faint engorgement of my breasts, plus that date of March 15 I told him about—all this let him tell me then and there that most probably I was already at the start of the third month.

And when the magic word *positive* came in from the laboratory, he summoned me back and opened his desk calendar toward the end of the year.

"The theoretical delivery date," he said, turning it toward me so I could see. He had already marked in a light H on December 28. I had told him of my last two evenings with Hugh; March 28 appeared more likely, he said, and I didn't ask him why it did—I was no longer clear about things I used to know by heart, like ovulation dates.

We began to plan how to manage this great secret project. We never even discussed the secrecy aspect; we assumed it. Back in 1941 there was no such thing as being open and casual about a pregnancy out of wedlock, no liberated attitudes about a woman or girl being unmarried and pregnant and happy all at once.

My own impulse was to shout it from the rooftops to all the world, but I knew I could never permit myself that luxury. I had, of course, already told Dr. Gosselin, and would tell my regular physician, Dr. Katherine Butler, but apart from these three doctors bound to silence, I would have to select two or three of my friends who could be trusted to keep a secret for years, perhaps forever.

Thirty or forty years later, nobody like me would even be considering making a secret of a pregnancy, with or without the benefit of clergy or marriage certificate. But back then only one or two famous writers and actresses had told the world of their unwed pregnancies, and I have often wondered whether their brave avowals were not undertaken more to feed their own egos than to proclaim a principle. And reading, in some cases, about their damaged, neurotic children, I have wondered about their mothers' scale of values.

In my case there was one further consideration, more immediate and more powerful than all the rest, and that was my son Mike. He would be just five years old when the new baby arrived in his life, and apart from the usual sibling hardships of moving a step off center-stage to make way for a newcomer, was he to have the extra burden of learning that though he, Mikey, was an adopted child, the new baby was not? Never.

I knew perfectly how to protect him from that possible hurt. For some time I had been telling people I meant to adopt a second child. Way back, during my first visit to The Cradle, I had told Mrs. Walrath that I would be applying for another baby when the time seemed right. "I don't want my baby to have an only-child problem as well as an adopted-child problem," I had said, and she had promised that when I gave her the signal, she would begin the process for me once again.

So the crux of my plan came readily to mind. I would adopt this baby too, perhaps through The Cradle. I would give birth secretly, under some assumed name, and the first birth certificate would give the baby that same assumed name, and then I would adopt it publicly under my own name and the new birth certificate would give its own new name, just as Mike's did.

I asked Dr. Damon if that could be done, and he assured me that it could. He went on to say I didn't have to go through that elaborate scheme with The Cradle.

"We can have a private-doctor adoption," he said, "right here in New York." If I wished he would take charge of the entire procedure, not using some small out-of-the-way lawyer, as if there were something furtive about it, but going straight to one of the most prestigious law firms in the city, where he knew one of the partners, and where all the papers would be held *in camera* for all time.

"But is it all right for *you*?" I asked him. "I mean all this on top of everything else? You'll be admitting me to a hospital under some assumed name, and then signing a birth certificate that has that assumed name—if you were to get in trouble yourself—"

He cut me short with the raised finger of admonition. He was a short stocky man, middle-aged, slightly overweight, with a face as simple and good as a new loaf of bread. "All *you* have to think about is this baby," he said firmly. "Suppose you let me think about any other risks."

It turned out that he had already done a good deal of thinking about the medical end of it. When the time came for my confinement, he didn't want me in some small out-of-the-way hospital, either, nor in some city hospital. He wanted me in a private room at Harkness Pavilion, where wealthy ladies went to give birth to the heirs of large fortunes—expensive Harkness Pavilion, where nobody would ever expect an illegitimate birth to take place. There was a sort of audacity to it that I liked.

He almost grinned as he said it, as if he were already enjoying this bit of intrigue. That would be my only major expense, he ended, the hospital and the private nurses he would select for their discretion as well as their efficiency. His own fee would be his usual $750, which I could pay years later, if I found it inconvenient because of hospital bills and legal bills that I would be expected to pay promptly.

I said I'd manage somehow, no matter how major any expense, and I tried to thank him for his readiness, almost his eagerness, to achieve this special end to all the years of treatment he had seen me through. I found myself gulping, and he dismissed me with an appointment for two weeks hence.

I remained calm about possible financial hassles in the future—there was plenty of time to solve everything. The rest of the planning need not be hurried either, like where I would go to "hide out" when I began to look big—there was lots of time to decide that too.

Never had I felt so free of tension, my nerves so steady. It was as if I had lost the capacity for anxiety; whenever a new aspect of necessary planning occurred to me, I would tell myself, I'll think of the right thing sooner or later.

Apart from my three doctors, I had already told Tom and Andrée; they were delighted with my delight. I told my sister Alice and she was happy that I was so happy. And I told Rosie, because she would be in it with me right along, taking care of little Mike when the time came for me to leave home and go off somewhere.

There was one other person I told that very first week, and that was Eric Hodgins. Through the winter and early spring those lunches with him when we talked about the world's solemnities had steadily climbed in their value to me, perhaps partly because they made so large a contrast with the light, uncomplex hours with Hugh.

There was nothing light and uncomplex about Eric Hodgins, even in a friendship with a woman where there was no sexual involvement. He was blessed with an ironic sort of wit that was later to make him famous, but it was always clear to me that he was a complicated and troubled man.

Part of his trouble was alcohol. This was not another case of my deciding that somebody "drank an awful lot," a decision that often arose falsely because my measurement of how much people drank was exaggerated by my own trait of one-drink-and-that's-it.

Eric not only drank an awful lot; he was being damaged by it, and knew it, and until he faced it later on and joined Alcoholics Anonymous he was from time to time incapacitated by it.

But when he was not, he offered something unique to any friendship he valued. There was nothing smart or sophisticated about him; he never would dream of asking a woman out for an evening of dancing; I was to find that he never would dream of asking a woman out anywhere, though he had long been living apart from his wife. He had a homely face, a good face, and when he confided something painful, as he rarely did, he let his suffering appear in his face, without guile, with no effort to dissemble or diminish it.

And one of the causes for his suffering had been, some ten years before, the death of his first wife, Catherine, in childbirth. He often ascribed his heavy bouts of drinking to that terrible period, when his son was born. He had remarried several years later, and had stipulated, he told me, that there should be no children in this second marriage.

I found myself responding by telling him of my own miseries in the past, and as summer approached our friendship at last took the inevitable turn where it did include sexual involvement. That inevitable turn had come only two weeks earlier, in the middle of May.

Yet the moment that word *positive* became mine, I felt honor-bound to tell Eric. It might awaken painful old associations with that death-in-childbirth of his beloved first wife Catherine, and if so, he might depart from my life for a year or forever, but I was impelled by some precautionary impulse to warn him straightaway and straight out.

I did just that, told him everything except who Hugh was, told him about Dr. Damon's willingness to help me, told him of my plans to go away somewhere for the three big months, pledged him to secrecy, and said that if he found it disturbing to see me, I would understand completely and that we could declare "a couple of sabbaticals" and then see how we felt after it was all over.

The sabbaticals he rejected out of hand. He was at first stunned by what I was telling him, but there was no vestige of shock or disapproval in what he said, only an attempt to tell me that if this was needed to make me happy then he was glad for me.

There certainly was no stab of wonder, whether this could be his child. I had told him my third month had already started, and our own affair had begun only a fortnight ago.

And yet, he was obviously rocked hard by this news, no matter how much he meant it when he said he was happy for me. Much later he was to tell me that though I was sure I had at last overcome my tendency to "neurotic love," and that I was by now able to have maturer emotions, he himself was not so blessed with restraint about me, and this jolting news had just about shattered him.

I am afraid that I was thinking far more about what I was feeling than about what Eric was, and that may be why I am now so vague about how he really reacted to this astonishing—and to him, ill-timed—news, but the most vivid impression I do have is that his most immediate questions were why I had to "go off somewhere" and where that somewhere would be.

Out of state? Out of the city? Some place where we could not see each other?

"I had crazy ideas," I admitted, "about going out West or to Europe, but they were just all wrong. I have to be near Dr. Damon, I want to be right here if anything serious happens to Mike. It will probably be up in the Bronx in a furnished room, or in Brooklyn—any old place where nobody knows me."

I could see a look of relief, and I remember that he said something like, "As long as you don't hide out from *me*."

That I would have to hide out somewhere when I began to look good and pregnant, I had no doubt. I was sure my little house in Noroton would serve nicely through the whole summer, but by October 1, when I'd be coming back to New York for good, back to my apartment house, with its doorman and elevator men and neighbors all seeing me huge with child, as I would be at the start of my seventh month—that obviously could not be, not if I really meant it about maintaining my secret.

And suddenly, all tangled with this early thinking about going off to a happy little hideout, all at once a new certainty stood clear in my mind: *that's* when I'll start writing the book Dick wants.

I was still loaded with work-in-progress. Reader's Digest had offered me another $1,500 to rewrite my piece about Justine Johnson, from a different angle and under a new title, "Blonde Beauty," and I had already begun the first pages of yet another story, "False Witness."

But by the time I was in my furnished room, all that would be out of the way. I would be alone, separated even from Mike and Rose, tucked off somewhere for three solid months, unable to see people, unable to meet an editor or my agent, free of all conventional demands for my time, for lunch dates, meetings. How marvelous a chance to start writing my first novel.

I called Dick at his office and said that at last I could say yes, I wanted to accept his offer, I wanted to try to write a novel. He was delighted.

"But Dick, even if we have a contract right away, I won't want that first thousand until I come up with an idea I feel is good enough, that I can tell you about. Is that okay?"

"You mean an outline?"

"Not a real outline, just the idea itself, what the book will be about."

He said that the moment I knew, the moment I really began writing, the contract and first payment would be taken care of in a week. He hoped it would be soon.

I did too. I never worked from an outline, not even from a plot already completed in my mind. I would get an idea for something, what I thought of as "a good start," and then let it develop from there as I went along.

I never doubted that some idea would hit me sooner or later— I never knew, nor do I know now, where ideas come from— but I knew that one would.

And that contract and first big check! If ever a new source of income was well-timed, this was one of the times. For a few silly moments I felt that all the benign and smiling Fates were conspiring not only to make this pregnancy happen, but also to arrange for it on the practical plane of finances.

I did think of what this big undertaking was going to cost. After all, I was out of a job, with no salary check at a nice stated interval, my farewell bonus from Time Inc. had been given me nearly a year and a half ago and was very nearly used up, and for some mysterious reason, my short stories were not selling the way they used to do, when they were just hobby-writing, nor was my long 109-page novelette.

Perhaps I was trying too hard, I thought, stiffening up, pushing too hard, pouncing on any idea for a story, instead of waiting around in a leisurely fashion until a sure-fire one came along, the way I did when they were spare-time things.

And I had had some unexpected expenses too, just before I knew that I would soon be in need of special funds for doctors and hospital and pregnancies. In the spring, when the limited national emergency was promoted to being *un*limited, meaning among other things that Detroit would be barred from manufacturing any more automobiles for the foreseeable future, I had rushed out, like everybody else, to buy a new car. It was a Packard roadster; the list price was $1,580, my turn-in allowance was $505, but that meant using a thousand dollars of my receding savings. So my funds were at a low ebb.

Again I remained oddly calm; I would find the way to solve what had to be solved. I would have to borrow; very well, I would borrow. And borrow with some audacity while I was at it.

I had always been a pretty responsible person when it came to being in debt—my father, with his irritable quarrels over every dollar of extra costs for things my mother wanted when they were building the house in Jamaica, had instilled that trait in me in my childhood, and my years with Tom Mount must have reinforced it for life—but if I had to borrow for *this*, I would borrow with no guilt. And because I did not want to allow money worries to build up at the last minute, I felt it wise to lay the money problem to rest well in advance.

And that fitted in with another decision. Who else should know I was pregnant? I thought for only a moment or two. It would be the Schermans. I would tell them and I would ask them for help. They had been so splendid in their pleasure at my other news, about Dick Simon and his "risk capitalism" of a $5,000 advance for a book that I felt sure they would feel only pleasure in my news, and some willingness to lend me some money.

The Book-of-the-Month Club had made millionaires of them long since, but they had never lost their simple human warmth in the way they lived and for the people they held to be their close friends. I was lucky enough to know that I was one of them. So I phoned to ask if I could see them some evening soon, alone, just the three of us.

"It's about something more important than writing a book," I said, and of course they had me over at their first free moment.

I didn't just blurt out the immediate news. They were half a generation older than I, and though we differed about Mr. Willkie

265

and such, we were united in most of our beliefs and attitudes. That they might be shocked about what I was about to tell them never occurred to me—that sort of narrowness in either of them was unthinkable.

I felt that I owed them the full background for it, and I gave them just that, asking first if I might tell them of certain deeply private events in my life, and if I might ask them to share a large secret.

They both listened with that intentness which is the outer skin of deep feeling and even approval. They knew all about my adopting Michael, but now I told them of the two early abortions, of the years of trying to have a baby during my marriage; I told them of Ralph and the miscarriage, and when at last I told them that I was again pregnant and going ahead by myself, their response couldn't have been purer or more generous. It was wonderful, they said, could they help, was there anything they could do, anything at all? For the first time, my throat jammed into a knot and my eyes filled. I think theirs did too.

"So I wondered if you would be willing—if anything went wrong," I said, "if you would lend me money, maybe a lot of money—" They both looked *yes* as I faltered. "Maybe five thousand—"

"We'll lend it to you now, without waiting to see if anything goes wrong." That was Bernardine, with Harry nodding his agreement.

"And we'll do it right through the office," he said, "so it's out in the open, an ordinary business loan, with interest, and formal papers, signed and notarized." For collateral, I could specify the first $5,000 of the life insurance policy I had taken out with Aetna when I adopted Mike.

I had never known that borrowing what I regarded as a huge sum of money could be so comfortable. Bernardine asked me who else was to know about my news, and we talked on and on, as if we had suddenly become one family. Within days, the check was in my hands, complete with proper documents, an open-ended note at the going rate of six percent, I believe, with no time for repayment specified. I opened a special account at my bank, so the sum would remain intact, earmarked for this one purpose. Never would I use a dime of it for anything else.

In those first days I was still bursting with the need to tell my news to at least one other friend who would care, who would be happy about it. If the Masseys were in New York, I would have told Dorothy, but they were now living, for the most part, in Beverly Hills. I thought of Andrea, but something held me back. I had at long last given Dick my answer about his offer— it would be a mistake to become too intimate a friend, now that I was to be his author.

And then I thought of the Whartons, whom I'd also known for a long time. We lived in the same apartment house now, one of the Vincent Astor "luxury buildings" on East End Avenue, overlooking the East River and Gracie Mansion, and we had been seeing even more of each other because of that shared address.

They were connected with the world of the theater; apart from the Masseys, I knew nobody whose lives were centered in the theater, and the Whartons' constant activity with plays and playwrights fascinated me.

John actually was an attorney with another of the renowned law firms in New York—the one Adlai Stevenson was later to join as a partner—but as counsel to some of the most famous playwrights of the day he had conceived the brilliant idea of forming the Playwrights Company so that the talented people who wrote the plays would also be the producers and controllers of their work all the way through. Robert Sherwood was a member, author of *Idiot's Delight*, *Abe Lincoln of Illinois*, and many other plays; so was Maxwell Anderson of *What Price Glory?* and *Winterset*; so was Elmer Rice, of *Street Scene* and *The Adding Machine*, as well as Sidney Howard, author of *The Silver Cord* and *Yellow Jack*.

Carly Wharton, too, was deeply involved with the theater in her own right, producing and backing plays with a young producer, Martin Gabel, who several years later was to marry Arlene Francis. In 1939, John and Carly and Martin, with the backing of Jock Whitney, another client of John's, had formed a producing company, Wharton and Gabel, and had been among the backers of *Life With Father*, by Lindsay and Crouse, which was to run for years and make mints of money for everybody concerned. Carly and Martin themselves put on a smash revival of *Charley's Aunt*, produced *Café Crown* and other hit shows.

So one day, shortly after telling the Schermans, I asked John and Carly if I might see them alone. The same thing happened, the same warmth, the same pleasure, the same offer to help—with one brand-new suggestion. I had just told them the Schermans were in on this secret, that they were lending me some emergency money, and now I said I hoped to sublet my apartment for October, November and December, for enough to make me rent-free in whatever hideout I finally decided on for "the big bulging months."

My rent in my nine-room, three-bath luxury apartment was $275 a month, but because it was so attractively furnished, there was little doubt that I could sublease it for $500 a month, giving me enough profit to pay not only for some small apartment but for the live-in maid Dr. Damon wanted me to have as a precaution.

"Precaution against what, I don't know," I told them. "I haven't had one minute of anything wrong."

"Will you be taking Mike and Rose there with you?" Carly asked.

"Oh, no. That would be all wrong for Mike—by then he'd be asking me all sorts of questions—that's when they'd be bound to start." I told them I had checked out this entire matter with Dr. Gosselin, of hurting Mike or not hurting Mike, and that for once Gosselin had come out with a big thumping positive answer, instead of greeting me with the usual Socratic—or Freudian—device of the counter-question, "Why do you feel so sure it would hurt your son to know the new baby came not from The Cradle, but from your own body?"

"I'll find some temporary place for Mike and Rose," I ended. "Rose will start room-hunting a couple of weeks before we leave Noroton and come back to town."

Carly looked thoughtful. "Why can't she and Mike just move in with us for those three months?" she asked. "Mike would still be in the same building, he'd still be a block away from school—"

"Oh, Carly." Mike had begun nursery school, a progressive school, the Home School, just a block from where we lived.

"They could have our guest room," Carly went on.

Their apartment was a twelve-room affair, taking an entire floor. It would mean that Mike wouldn't have to be dislocated for those months I was absent; it would mean he'd be with friends he knew and saw more frequently than he saw my own sister and her son Paul. I had already told Alice I would need a place where Rose and Mike could stay, but she had made no offer. I don't remember whether they had an extra room or not.

"Oh, Carly," I said again, "I don't know how to thank you." And I didn't then, but I must have thought once more about those benign and smiling Fates.

Intense cravings for pickles or sardines or sweets are supposed to be inevitable for pregnant women, and though there was one thing I began to crave in the early weeks of my pregnancy, that one thing did not fit the usual mold.

But then, nothing about this pregnancy did fit the usual mold. I had always known about morning sickness—I had not had one moment of it. I had heard about the dread of childbirth with one's first child—I had not an instant of it, my forty-one-year-old first notwithstanding. When Carly or Bernardine asked, as they did, "What will you do if the baby is the very spit and image of you?" I said, "It won't be—God won't let it." When Dr. Damon told me about the abdominal stretch-marks many women were left with after pregnancy, I said, "But I won't have any—God won't let them happen."

Everybody knew I was an agnostic; they all took these replies for the sounds of optimism, which is what they were. I was sure nobody had ever before had so peaceful and happy a pregnancy as I was having.

But there was that one craving I could not banish. At first it was a mere thought, a wanton notion that came at me once in a while. Then it grew stronger, more persistent. I wanted Ralph Ingersoll to know that I was pregnant and that I was going to *have* this baby.

It was perhaps a need for revenge, that ignoble word. It was perhaps the need to restore my psyche, to make a statement that I was after all a complete woman like all women. I did not know what it was; I talked it through with Dr. Gosselin, and still I could not put a name to it. But it would not go away.

269

I thought of writing him, but a letter would not serve. I wanted to tell him myself, I wanted to face him and hear my own voice saying the wonderful words. I knew he was still unmarried, and therefore still childless, and I freely admitted to myself that there was something compulsive in my wish to let him know I was going to give birth before the year was out.

But what reason could I give for wanting to see him? If I phoned and asked him to come to my apartment—I was still slim enough to be seen in public—what could I say was creating this sudden necessity to see him as soon as he could arrange it?

There had been no single word between us for more than a year, no phone call, no letter, no message through a third person. I had returned my engagement ring, I had returned my mink coat, that premature wedding present—much to the bewilderment and disapproval of practical people like Dorothy Massey. If I had kept them, I would have hated myself.

But that had been the only communication between us, a matter of things, not words. Ralph's newspaper *PM* was struggling—everybody in publishing knew that much about it, struggling as most publications do in their first year. If it was not yet an outright failure, it was a vast disappointment to its staff, its backers, and undoubtedly something more acute than that to Ralph himself. I was certainly not saintly enough to be sorry for whatever he was feeling about his paper, nor hypocrite enough to think I ought to be.

So my craving persisted, and finally, in late June, I suddenly thought of a "reason" I could proffer him for this pressing need to see him, and I telephoned him at the paper. I said something had come up that was important; he knew it must be or I would not be asking him to come. We agreed on six o'clock that very evening, and I said I had an early engagement, to assure him it would be a brief visit, with a time limit already set.

Off and on all day, I rehearsed the way I would put it, and in some attack of vanity, I dressed in a favorite evening dress of mine, long, with tiny pink and blue polka dots on a thin flowing fabric. The excuse I gave myself for this vanity was that I wanted to look as if I actually did have an early date.

When he arrived, my rehearsed words went out the window, as I might have known they would. For in the world at large, in that very week, actually on the day before, something so explosive was happening that all ordinary life seemed changed overnight: Germany was invading Russia.

And as Ralph came in at six, even as we were uneasily greeting each other at my front door, both tense under our attempt at sophisticated ease, his first words were the latest war news off the ticker as he had left his office.

So we talked about the war, during the first moments of offering him a drink, and fixing it for him. Despite the despicable nonaggression pact between Hitler and Stalin, which was supposed to last for ten years, Nazi troops were already inside Russia, and a new horror had begun.

Overnight the "imperialist war" of so many people we both knew had become "the people's war," and Ralph, inadvertently using the new phrase, suddenly took it upon himself to pay me a compliment.

"You always had more clarity than I did about politics," he said, and for a moment I wished that all the people I had ever argued with, Lillian Hellman and my sister Alice and her husband and lots of the people at Time Inc. who used to be so scornful of me when I wouldn't join some of their committees— I wished that all of them could hear Ralph Ingersoll say it.

And at last we got down to my reason for asking him up there. "It's about money," I said. "I need to make a loan, a big loan, and I thought you might help me."

He looked startled, as I had known he would. "Is it—what's wrong? Are you in some financial bind?"

"Nothing's 'wrong'," I said. "But it would be—I could be in a terrible financial bind if I didn't borrow some money to prevent it." He said nothing; he frowned in the concentration of waiting to understand. "A lot of money," I went on carefully. "Several thousand—maybe ten. Not all borrowed from you, of course."

I waited a moment in silence, and so did he. Then, quite simply, I said, "I'm having a baby—look."

For the first time I leaned back instead of standing or sitting as if I were leaning forward. My shoulders pressed into the upper edge of the sofa cushion behind me, and I looked down at myself.

Under the flowing fabric of my dotted dress, there now appeared a slight curving roundness, still tentative but a perfect orb. I spread my fingertips lightly around its rim, outlining it.

He was looked at my fingers and at my body. He said nothing beyond some syllables of surprise, possibly of pleased surprise—I cannot be more exact. He reached for his pack of cigarettes—he still smoked mentholated Spuds—and lighted one.

"Next week I'll be starting my fourth month," I said. "I'm awfully happy about it, but I need to set aside enough money and I got thinking whom I might ask for some part of it, and thought you'd probably understand better than anybody else."

"The fourth month?" He looked startled once more. "As far as that? You don't—"

"I haven't married," I put in. "It's got to be kept a real secret. You will keep it secret, I know."

He nodded, said something vague about his surprise that I could be in my fourth month, asked something about whether I wanted to tell him more about it, and I shook my head.

I don't remember much more of that encounter beyond those early moments of my revelation and his abashed response, but I do know that it had never occurred to me that he would do anything more than tell me he would have to think about the money, mention the vast expenses of *PM*, and then a day or two later let me know he couldn't manage the loan.

Which is what happened. One more thing I do know about that encounter is that when a craving is at last slaked, there is a lovely sense of release. In the slang of today, we would say, "Mission accomplished."

And then on a summer day, a few weeks later, something else was suddenly accomplished. Out of nowhere came the idea for the novel I would write.

Some magazine editor once told me that if you got an idea for a story, you could know whether it was any good if you could tell it in one sentence. I have always regarded that as too feeble a yardstick—try to tell the idea of *Pickwick Papers* in one sentence! But sometimes that inadequate measure can serve as a minor clue, and this sudden idea of mine could be told in one sentence.

It would be about one man's attempt to get American visas

272

for his family to escape the Nazis in Austria.

I would show scenes at the consulates, show the indifference, the delays, show scenes of frozen faces, the demands for new documents, for new proof, the passing of time, the rising fear . . .

I would base it on the Sterbas' dossiers, on our letters and cables to each other, as well as on the dossiers of other people I had done affidavits for after the Sterbas—in the three years since I had entered the world of visas and affidavits, I had been involved with a total of eighteen, not eighteen separate cases, but eighteen people in several families desperate for asylum in the country so famous for granting asylum. I would write the Sterbas for permission to use our cables and letters.

I suddenly thought of a first sentence. "The migrations had begun." I went to my desk, rolled a sheet of paper into my little portable typewriter, and began to write.

> The migrations had begun. At that point in time, the trains, the ships, the rutted dirt roads, the cement highways, the vaulting air lanes of the earth and skies were beginning to carry again the ones in flight.
>
> From the early thirties onward, the flow of the migrations swelled and thickened. In nineteen thirty-seven and -eight and -nine, two millions of Europe's people were moving, flying before the bitter fact that they were not wanted, not safe on the ground they knew and loved.
>
> Movement, flight, the roots uptorn, the dear belongings left behind, the unknowing roses abandoned in the garden— gone forever the beloved view from the kitchen window, the comfortable smile of a twenty-year-known neighbor.

Something stirred deeply inside me. I could write about it because I *knew* about it, because I had absorbed it, had suffered over it, had lived it. You could write light fiction that was made up out of thin air, write romantic nonsense or murder mysteries or a tale of espionage, all made up, all concocted, but you couldn't write a serious novel unless you had lived through some basic part of it.

I would have to invent a lot of "story line" to round it out, to make it a novel, not reportage. It wasn't to be journalism, but a novel; that meant I would have to create a good deal of plot, especially concerning the American part of it, invent some sort of developing involvement between the American girl who tries to help get those visas and the Austrian man who needs them. Oh, there would be lots of need for making up the rest of a rounded story, with people you would care about, with motivation you understood, with that insistent line of rising tension that holds the reader to the end.

All that would take work, hard work, lots of work. But the basic idea was suddenly there. Once more I was sure.

If ever in my life there was a summer of tranquility and a sense of self-worth, that was the summer.

In early August my analysis ended. For three years it had gone on, five mornings a week, except for annual vacations for Dr. Gosselin, which I at first resented as a sort of sign that he really didn't care enough about his patients; whenever I had asked how I'd know when the analysis was over, he always had replied quietly, "You will know."

Some of the time he would make no answer, and wait until I made some fatuous remark like, "How do you know when you're really in love—it's like that, is it?" And he would make no reply to that either.

But now I saw that he'd been right all along. I did know. No longer did it seem possible that I would ever rush into an analyst's office crying out, "What do you do when you can't *bear* it?" No longer did I find myself weeping into my pillow at night, the hair at the back of my neck wet. For four years I had not felt a spasm of longing when I saw a little boy playing in the park or on a beach, and now, when I passed a pregnant woman on the street, I no longer wondered why every woman in the world could manage what was so impossible for me.

One morning I said to Dr. Gosselin, "People always ask if analysis works. Just look at mine. It started with me writing promotion on a salary and it's ending with this contract to write a book. It started with me unable to have a baby, and it's ending with me five months pregnant. Does analysis work?"

He probably said nothing to that either, but when I left his office for that last time, thanking him for all the help I had had from him, he took my hand in both of his, and his smile wasn't remote or analytical at all. He wished me well for the rest of my pregnancy, wished me and the new baby and Mike everything good for the future and, as he opened the door for me, he added, "If ever you need me in that hideout of yours, and can no longer come here, I can go to you there."

I could hardly believe it was my last visit. But they would have had to stop before long anyhow, because by midsummer, I could no longer wander around among people and hope they wouldn't notice that I was pregnant.

Up at Noroton, only one problem began to develop about my secret. I did not let it rise in daily life for I saw nobody up there but Eric, when he could come up from the city for a night, and Carly Wharton, when she drove over for an afternoon to me at my place. Whenever Andrea Simon phoned about a dinner or a party, I would make some excuse and ask for a rain check. The Schermans' summer place was an old stone house from the days of the American Revolution, out in Bernardsville, New Jersey, and though we kept in touch often, it was now only by telephone.

The daily business of driving to town to do the marketing was no problem either, for though Rose could not drive, the new Packard roadster luckily enough had its seats slung very low, like today's bucket seats in some sports cars, and its big doors came up high, so that even when I waved to somebody passing by, all that showed of me was shoulder level and up.

As for my visits every other week to Dr. Damon, on Park Avenue in New York, he had planned that minor matter to perfection. His office hours began at nine in the morning, but after the middle of July he merely told me to be there promptly at 8:30 so I would be in and out before his first regular patient arrived. He even arranged with his doorman, on those special mornings, to let me double-park, if necessary, as an "emergency patient," so I wouldn't have to search for some empty curb, blocks away, and walk back through the most fashionable part of town. (Since I was leading a charmed life, no traffic cop ever noticed my double-parking. Undoubtedly God didn't let him.)

But there was one problem developing, nevertheless, and it began to seem major as the weeks of summer went by. It arose from my dear outgoing friend, Andrea Simon, in her big house only a few miles from my little dump.

My repeated need to turn her down when she asked me to a party, or when she suggested that I bring Mike over for some kids' picnic, got by at first, but inevitably she began to grow suspicious about all the polite refusals and great excuses I was forever dishing out.

One day she came right out and said, "Say, Hobby, what's going on over there? I have a feeling you're up to something. Are you okay?"

"I'm just wonderful, Andy, I'll call you back."

And I faced up to this emerging little dilemma. Do I let her keep guessing or do I come clean? This was no idle curiosity, this was part of Andrea's warmth and caring about a friend; what I was doing was all wrong.

The way to keep my secret was just the opposite of what I was doing—what I should do now, was to take her into camp with me and the Schermans and the Whartons. *Then* she and Dick would never tell a soul.

So I asked them over. I was still fairly compact, though Mike, sitting next to me on our little beach one day, leaning against me, had recenty said, "Say, mommy, you feel kind of fat." I had taken to wearing loose smocks, the kind painters did in their ateliers in Paris, and I put on my prettiest one, of Liberty cotton in a bright flowered pattern, to receive the Simons in.

As I opened the door to them, I had no need to make any proclamations about my news. Andrea simply boiled over with congratulations, and even Dick was satisfactory in his astonishment and pleasure.

And after all the why's and wherefore's and telling them the whole background of it, including the fact that the Schermans and the Whartons were in on it already, after telling them my plans for the next four or five months, I then suddenly said, "Now I can tell you what my book's going to be about."

I told them in general and then went to the oak table that was serving as a desk, and picked up the six or eight sheets that were lying there, with words crossed out, other words written in, in pencil between the typed lines. I had been writing yet another story, "The Promise," but I was also working just a little on my book, and by now my opening paragraphs had become the opening pages, indeed the whole first opening scene of the book.

I began to read them aloud, and as I glanced once in a while at Dick's face, I saw there that unmistakable look of approval that can make any budding author's heart leap high.

The rest of the evening was not about pregnancies or hideouts, but about books and writing and publishing. And always, at the center, there was this particular book, which was to appear some two years later as *The Trespassers.*

Dick kept coming back to it, drawing me out, asking questions I had not yet the faintest answers to, questions I would have to solve when the time came, solve well or poorly, but solve somehow.

Looking back on that novel now, from the perspective of nine published novels, I can see that some problems were indeed solved well, but that there were others that were done poorly.

I reread *The Trespassers* about two years ago, after a week's vacation with the Sterbas up in their summer place in the hills of Vermont, and I thought that if I were writing it now I would know enough to reduce sharply the American half of the story, and be content with the truth and reality of the European parts.

But way back then in 1941 and '42 and '43, I had not yet learned my new craft of writing a serious novel. I had not yet learned that though it was right for me to use the stuff of my own experience for the main materials of my story, I needed to be far more subtle in inventing the people whom I would choose to act out those experiences in my manuscript.

The flaw came, I think now, not with the Austrian analyst and his wife, whom I called the Vederles—the Sterbas had settled out in Grosse Pointe, Michigan, and we saw each other only at rare intervals when they were in New York, so they had to be pure inventions as I wrote of them, and so they were.

And the girl I called Vee was, inevitably, largely myself, or an idealized girl I would have liked to have been. But the man this Vee loved, Jasper Crown of my novel—there I can now see flaws which I would today know how to steer clear of.

I had thought to make him a composite of several of the male figures in my life, for one, of my father, who talked and wrote so much about equality and freedom and who could, at times, be such a despot at home; for another, of my brother Joel, who could make such promises to me about Cornell and then go back on his word; and lastly, of Ralph Ingersoll, the brilliant man who could be so ruthless when it suited his own needs and ambitions.

I see now that in that major character of Jasper Crown, the mysterious alchemy between fact and invention that I so much needed was all too imperfect in my hands, and that what came out was a sort of sludge that might look like a symbol of spite or malice about Ralph.

And yet, that cannot be the whole of it, for I had many letters from readers saying that Jasper Crown was a perfect portrait of some powerful man they knew. "Did you ever know our American ambassador So-and-So?" went one letter. "Your Jasper Crown caught him to a tee." Another said, "You really must know human nature among those at the top—Jasper Crown is exactly like my boss."

Many times, in the years since then, I have read novels by beginners and, with a kind of rueful forgiveness, thought, Oh, well, in the next novel he will have learned, or she will have learned how to make use of basic material without seeming to make use of actual people.

But it seems clear now that long ago, on that summer evening in 1941, when my first novel was in its first chapter, and my first successful pregnancy in its fifth month, I myself had not yet learned enough of that fundamental lesson.

What I did know then was that it was one of the headiest evenings I had ever spent, with life widening out into new dimensions, *my* life at the beginning of its second half, at the start of its fifth decade, suddenly seeming to me a newly rushing river, filled with two incomparable strong new currents.

FOURTEEN

EARLY IN SEPTEMBER, Charles A. Lindbergh crashed through the tranquility of my summer. Out in Des Moines, Iowa, he made a speech at another America First rally, which assured the world that England could never win against Hitler, and that there was a plot in America pressing to get us into the war. The plotters were the Roosevelt administration, the British and the Jews.

He said he "could understand why the Jewish people desired the overthrow of the Nazi regime," but "advised however, 'that instead of agitating for war, the Jewish groups in this country should be opposing it in every possible way, for they will be among the first to feel its consequences.'"

"'Their greatest danger to this country,' he said of the Jews, 'lies in their large ownership and influence in our motion pictures, our press, our radio and our government.'"

The quotes are all from the New York *Times,* but the outcry was worldwide. Every paper in every country of the globe—including Germany's and Italy's, of course—reported Lindbergh's speech, every magazine, every radio broadcast told of it.

And there was I alone in a little house in Noroton with no access to the Fight For Freedom Committee or any other group

I could appeal to, to raise money for a public protest in even a few major newspapers.

If I telephoned the people I had begun to know in such groups, they would ask me to a meeting, and I would have to dig up some excuse not to go.

So I seethed with a helpless inactivity. I telephoned Eric, who was as incensed as I was, I phoned the Whartons and the Schermans, and Andrea Simon. I tried to work Lindbergh out of my head by denouncing everything he stood for. And I failed.

I had failed the year before with a book written by his poetic wife, Anne Morrow Lindbergh, author of *North to the Orient* and *Listen! The Wind*. I had read the new one the day Paris fell to the Nazis, called *The Wave of the Future*, the wave being fascism and the book being what most critics called an apologia for it.

But this time the national hero himself so repulsed me that for once my new-found talent for handling pressures evaporated, and left me filled with a necessity to *do* something, to decide something and do it right away. In my sleep I dreamed sentences and phrases and headlines.

And in the morning I did the one thing I could do. I went to my portable typewriter, in my old need to try writing it down. And soon I was writing something that, at least, felt right to me.

CHOICE . . . FOR GENTILES

Listen, it is good to have this out in the open at last. Let us look at it, see the choices, then take one stand as a nation.

There are over 130 million of us Americans. There are 122 million Gentiles — you are strong, you are many. There are 7 or 8 million Jews, of which I am one. You can drown us, shoot us, poison us all and have done forever with the Jewish problem.

Go ahead, get on with it. You have the armies, the arsenals, the power to do it. Don't do it in the clumsy Hitler way, letting half of us escape or endure in concentration camps. Be efficient as Americans are, clean us out neatly, nicely, with no quiet weeping in the night.

And then pay your price, like men. Pay it fully, pay

without whining or regretting. Your sons and daughters will pay it with you, and their sons and daughters...

Say farewell forever to your beautiful phrase about life and liberty and the pursuit of happiness. And to that other, that all men are created equal.

Say farewell to your noble Preamble to the Constitution. Tear up with firm hands your Bill of Rights.

Erase from your nation's memory the purpose of the Revolutionary War and the Civil War. Never mention again without unease the names of Lincoln and Thomas Jefferson, Walt Whitman and Patrick Henry and all the strong or gentle others.

Among you let all Catholics or Mormons or Seventh Day Adventists quit feeling safe, secure. For never again could *any* religious minority feel secure to worship their God as they wish.

Among you let all talk stop about the great freedoms— at least those three, freedom of religion, freedom of speech, freedom from fear. Never again tell your child he is every other child's equal, that tomorrow belongs equally to him as to any other. For the granite pendulum of persecution might swing against *him* before he is a man.

Yes, the price would be big. The price would claw to bits America's monumental history, lay waste her simple, noble concept of democracy. The full price would break most American hearts.

Either pay it like men, or have done with the tawdry torture of antisemitism.

For I say you can drown or shoot or poison me—but you cannot ask me to walk humble and afraid.

You cannot tell me where to live, what to say, what to work at.

Nor can you direct whether I shall be powerful and famous, or weak and unknown.

You cannot urge me to keep silent on the majestic questions of war or peace for my country; you cannot counsel that I should never write, debate, hold high office, work or pray for my country's welfare.

You can still my heart and muscles and nerves, but you cannot mute my lips or my pen. If I am to live on in America, I shall live and work and sing as an American, full and free.

> I say you can kill me just once—but you cannot make
> me die a thousand deaths of apology or fear.

I showed it to Eric that same night, when he came up. I told him I had sent it to Harry Luce to see if he would print it in Life's next issue, or in Time, in connection with Lindbergh's speech. Eric said he would talk to Harry about it.

I mailed a copy to Dorothy Thompson; I let the Whartons read it, and sent it to the Schermans. With one exception, the response to it was profound; the exception was Dick Simon, who felt that Jews should not raise their voices on this sort of thing, because it was sure to be taken as special pleading.

Harry Luce wrote me at once.

> Dear Laura,
>
> Like Eric, like anybody who thinks he knows good writing when he sees it, I greatly admired your *Choice—For Gentiles*.
>
> There was no chance, physically, of getting it into the issue going to press today... We will take another look-see when the next issue shapes up next week. Frankly, though, I hope that Mr. Lindbergh will seem, for the moment, at least, a dead bunny.
>
> It may, alas, become necessary to become hotly belligerent on the tolerance issue. But I hope not.... Tolerance is at its best when it can be taken for granted—for it is not an end in itself but one of the deep assumptions without which other ends are impossible.
>
> One should have watch-dogs against intolerance—and, thank God, the dogs barked plenty last week. But we don't want a perpetual dog-fight.

His letter went on to a second page, ending with the suggestion that we might see each other on his return from a cross-country trip he was starting on at once.

But neither Life nor Time printed my piece. By the next issue, Eric told me, they were saying they needed "a news peg" to hang it on.

Dorothy Thompson wrote me immediately too. She was up at Twin Farms in Vermont.

Dear Laura,

    I think your little blast is marvelous. I am keeping it for an opportunity to publish it. I think with Harry Luce that it ought to have a news item to tie it to. Like him, I hope we are not going to have one, but I think we are.

Hers was a short letter, ending with the news she had bought a house in town on East Forty-eighth Street and wanted to see me there in October. But she didn't find any opportunity to publish the piece either.

I thought to myself, Do they both really think that a few days afterward, Mr. Lindbergh's speech is no longer news peg enough? That it's just yesterday's newspaper and not worth another comment or a few more lines of newsprint?

I folded up my piece and put it away in my files, knowing it would never see the black and white of a printed page. But I was wrong. Over forty years later, here it is. And, with all of today's reports about a new tide of antisemitism the world over, it may, alas, still seem valid.

Two weeks after Mr. Lindbergh so enraged me, I moved back to New York, to the hideout that had been found for me to live in until after the baby was born.

My only distress was that I would be separated from little Mike for a long time, that I would not see him for his fifth birthday, that I would not be there for Christmas. But as I settled into virtual retirement from the world at large, I was more confident than ever that all would go well.

Perhaps there is some sort of primitive bond between women who have borne children and a woman who is having her first child, a willingness to help, even an eagerness to encourage and reassure.

And perhaps because I was already forty-one and "at higher risk" in the eyes of many, there came from the women who were in on my secret an unceasing flow of support. There were exceptions, of course: Andrée Mount lived in Woodstock and my sister in Croton-on-Hudson, so they could do nothing, but it was as if the others had banded together to see me through.

It was Carly Wharton who arranged for the sublease of my

apartment at $500 a month for four months; it was Andrea Simon who helped find a suitable maid to live with me, and it was Dr. Katherine Butler, overworked as all dedicated physicians are overworked, with their hours for free clinic patients, tacked on to all their regular hours—it was Dr. Butler who included some house-hunting on her rounds of the city and came up with a perfect hide-out.

It was a one-room studio apartment, furnished, with kitchenette and bath, at 128 West Seventy-eighth Street, right near the Museum of Natural History, renting for $60 a month. What made it so perfect was that it was in a remodeled old brownstone, and on the ground floor, so there was no doorman, no elevator, no need to run into neighbors on the stairway.

The one drawback was that there was no room for the live-in maid Dr. Damon was so insistent about. But there was another empty apartment, identical to mine, right behind it on the same ground floor, and after a phone call to me, Dr. Butler rented that one too, even arranging for a buzzer system to be set up between them.

Mine faced the street, but the rear one was on a backyard, a twelve-by-twelve square of concrete, where I could pace up and down for exercise, as in a commodious cell, but open to the sky.

The suitable maid Andrea found was a country girl, big and blond, a cleaning woman and plain cook, with nothing of the skilled city maid about her, and thus unlikely to turn up later in some friend's house where she would recognize me as "the pregnant lady from West Seventy-eighth Street who had a different name."

She of course would never know me as Mrs. Hobson, would never see any letters addressed to Mrs. Hobson, would never see any stationery with the name and address of Mrs. Hobson on it, never answer any phone calls for Mrs. Hobson.

All of which meant I had to choose a new name, the false name that would later take me to the hospital, that would go on the original birth certificate, and be the surname the baby would bear until he was adopted and legally became a Somebody Hobson. I had begun to think of it as a boy, because of the strength of the kicking, but I had no preferences at all.

I didn't have to go in for any extended search about the false name—it came collaterally, as it were, because I had to borrow a suitcase to move in, a locked one in which I could keep letters addressed to me, my Hobson checkbooks, canceled Hobson checks and the like from the eyes of Rita, my buxom blond maid.

My own suitcases were initialed *L. Z. H.*, so I asked Rose if I could borrow hers—it was initialed *R. M.* "I'll be Mrs. Rose Miller," I told her. "No, that's too real. Then Mills, Ruth Mills."

But from detective stories I knew that in a moment of crisis, you never answered to anything but your real name, so I amended that to Ruth Laura Mills, called Laura.

I would be Ruth Laura Mills at my new neighborhood bank, I would be Ruth Laura Mills at the hospital, and I'd be Ruth Laura Mills on the birth certificate. My absent husband, off in the Air Force, would be Captain Andrew Mills. I would arrange to get occasional letters from Captain Mills, with an A.P.O. return address on it, and a distant postmark yet to be selected.

What postmark? And what about an out-of-town postmark on letters I might have to send to people in New York during the months I would be absent? And where was I supposed to be, anyway?

Again answers came as collateral gifts. When I wrote the Sterbas, asking permission to use part of our visa letters and cables in my new book, I suddenly thought, I can tell everybody I've gone to Grosse Point for a few weeks to do research with my Austrian friends, the Sterbas. And I'm sure they'd let me mail them a batch of letters once in a while, for them to mail for me out there, like a criminal's mail drop.

Of course they said yes to both my requests, and accepted without question what I said in explanation. "It's not a clandestine love affair," I wrote, "but I can't say more than that about it, except to thank you."

And so everything fell into place as the final months began, and there in my ground floor room, diagonally across Central Park from my son Mike and from my own home, my pregnancy drew to its close while my first novel was getting off to a firm beginning.

I wrote every day, wrote with an energy that surmounted all

the hesitancies and misgivings any first novelist must go through. I never felt a moment of illness, I never felt lethargic, I was never lonely, though I was grateful for visits from the few people who knew—I saw Eric in the evenings more than I saw anybody else, and at times even read him a few paragraphs of what I had written that day, and clung to his encouragement for the pages that lay just ahead.

I daresay that any author who has ever written a book knows the inner excitement that comes when the first chapter is ended and the second begun, knows the pleasure when the pages begin to mount up to thirty or forty or fifty, a visible little sheaf of pages lying there on the desk, and even now I seem to relive my own surprised sense of accomplishment as I reached page sixty and seventy and eighty as those weeks of October and November went by.

And Dr. Damon shifted to house calls, and encouraged me further. Everything was going perfectly; I was a good strong patient. And an obedient one. I never failed to carry out orders on all the strenuous calisthenics and daily three-mile walks he had prescribed, to build up muscles—striding around my concrete twelve-by-twelve cell during the morning hours and taking my brisk walks in Central Park every evening. In those days it never even occurred to anybody that you might get robbed or mugged in Central Park after dark; there were no signs posted, as there are today, Park Closed between Nightfall and Dawn, and I marched into it for my nightly three miles, alone and serene, wearing no disguise, except for the low-pulled brim of an old sports hat and a big scarf coming up around my chin.

And even while I walked I was working, thinking in terms of sentences and scenes for my book. It was an exciting preoccupation I had never known before, on a larger scale, about a larger theme, and at night, as during the hours actually at the small desk in my room, my mind seemed to be bursting with ready ideas and images.

I didn't let myself think up fancy phrases about being creative in a double sense, and yet, looking backward now through all the years, I recall vividly that stirring current of creativity, that intermixed phenomenon of body and mind creating, so simple, so complex.

My son Christopher was born on December 27, 1941 at 10:40 in the morning, weighing eight pounds and two ounces.

He looked nothing at all like me. My first glimpse of him brought an image of Hugh, but only vaguely, and only for a moment. When my eyes cleared a moment later, he looked like nobody but himself, red and new and wonderful.

The name on his identification bracelet was Mills, as was the one on my wrist, and his birth certificate would say Charles Andrew Mills, Jr.

It was twenty days after Pearl Harbor, and the nation was at war. For the three final weeks leading up to the night just past, I had been as shaken as everybody else by the news from Hawaii, Luzon, Guam, Wake Island, had listened to the incessant warnings on the radio of possible air raids over New York, had blacked out my windows every night, and been informed of the bomb shelter designated for my street—the basement of an old hotel half a block away to which I never went, even as a drill.

So cataclysmic are the first days and nights of war that one feels almost obligated to regard everything else as unimportant, yet I cannot honestly say that the war actually did dwarf my own awareness of what was so soon to happen to me. It was only later that I could think and write of those vast antonyms, death and life, dying and giving birth.

But there in my ground-floor room, alone for hours upon hours, counting off my own days as well as straining for every scrap of news about the war, I could scarcely measure true priorities. I don't remember now that I made any real effort to try; I think that I accepted them as some kind of inevitable equation. I do know that I couldn't sleep soundly then and seemed to be waiting all night for the *Times* and its terrible dispatches; I know that I never turned off the radio until I had heard every communiqué three times over; I know that I clung to the telephone each morning, just to hear what the Whartons or Schermans or any of my friends had heard, what they felt, what they thought would happen next.

But each day, if only for a few hours, interrupted many times by my bulky need to rest, to walk around the room, to turn on the radio, each day I wrote another page or two of my book.

On the night the pains began, my manuscript was at page 142, and as I locked my suitcase for the last time, I put those pages in and carried them along with me to Harkness Pavilion, up at Columbia-Presbyterian Hospital, that same hospital where I had been ten years before for so different a purpose.

It was the night after Christmas when I knew it had begun, about one in the morning. I remember a fierce shaft of joy as well as that first shaft of pain; remember the business of timing two or three pains and then telephoning Dr. Damon, and telling him not only "how often" but also how happy.

Then I called Carly Wharton, who had long before made me promise that I would, no matter what time in the night. And then I called Eric, who was living at the University Club, who had also made me promise.

Dr. Damon said he would call the hopsital and appear there in due time, but the two of them came to take me there. In the taxi I sat between them, each of them holding me by the hand. Carly looked confident, Eric shaken.

At the admissions desk, I said, "This is not my husband, Captain Mills, but Dr. Damon said my friends could go up with me for a while," and received a ready nod. Dr. Damon had kept his promise to set it all up for me.

In my room on the maternity floor it was not long before a nurse came in to say they would have to leave. Carly left first, leaving Eric alone with me. He had been trying to hide his inevitable memories, but now he looked even more stricken. Some impulse made me grasp his hand and say—this I remember word for word—made me say, "*I'm* not going to die, Eric, don't be afraid."

When it was over the next morning and I was back in my room and awake, Carly and Andrea were leaning over me, saying all the usual happy things. Eric had just left; he had stayed all night through, for nine hours, unwilling to leave the hospital and not *know*. Among the three of them, they had arranged to have a stream of telegrams arrive at spaced-out times in the next two days—including one from San Francisco ending, PROUD AND HAPPY AND ALL LOVE TO BOTH OF YOU. It was signed ANDY and had some military-looking rigmarole of letters as part of it. I think the Schermans had a friend or colleague out in

California at one of the many army bases there.

Down the corridor, a room or two away from me, also having a baby, was a delightful woman I knew, Jean Poletti, wife of the lieutenant governor of New York State, and if either of them reads this book, they will learn for the first time that their old friend Laura was right there too, about thirty feet away, wishing them well with their new baby. As for me, I had no fear of running into either of the Polettis, because Dr. Damon had given my private nurses specific instructions that I was not to be required, as all maternity patients always were, to walk the long corridors for exercise. What walking I did was done right in my own room, whose always-closed door carried the white card, No Visitors.

I had to remain for the unusual length of sixteen days, on Dr. Damon's decision, so it was nearly the middle of January when I left, with my new baby in my arms, and Carly carrying the suitcase and escorting us. But not back to West Seventy-eighth Street, nor back to East End Avenue. Nor to the reunion with Mike I had been looking forward to for so long.

It was still not over. If I were going to "adopt a baby" I could not be arriving home after a long absence, bearing him in my arms. The Cradle had always insisted on an eight-week period of observation for any infant, before letting him leave with a new parent or parents, and we were going to follow all the traditions of the best adoption agencies and arrange for a two-month stopover for this particular baby.

Rosie had searched for and found another one-room apartment, this one, blessedly, on the East Side and much closer to home, when I finally did reach home. That would be the first of February when my subtenants moved out of my apartment on East End Avenue.

For about two weeks I would live at the Hotel Barclay, but I couldn't take my baby with me there either, without ruining the entire arrangement right at the end. But the last of the many arrangements were now in place, and where that taxi took the three of us as we left the hospital was to this "halfway house" at Fifty East Sixty-sixth Street, where the name on the brass plate in the entrance hall would still read Mills, and where an expert and discreet baby nurse, sent me by Dr. Damon himself, would live for eight weeks with little Andy Mills.

I went there every day, for at least three hours, for two bottles, for the required number of diapers—went there each day, no matter what, to give this tiny baby that unconscious knowledge that somebody called mommy was a constant presence in his life. To the live-in nurse, I was, of course, Mrs. Mills, a rather mysterious lady who had to sleep elsewhere, but who was reachable day or night by telephone, first at a hotel and then at an apartment high above the East River, the precise address of which she was not to know.

On her days off, I slept overnight, sleeping in the single bed she had vacated, with the necessary number of bottles and sterilized nipples in the small Frigidaire, and a rented crib occupied by an infant I would not yet let myself call Chris or Chrissie, for fear I would trip up and say the wrong thing when she was there.

The only entry in my datebook for those weeks of the halfway house was on the day they began, January 12, 1942, and all it says is, "50 E. 66."

I knew I would always know what those numbers stood for, just as I would always know what the brief entry really meant that I jotted down for the momentous day of December 27, 1941: "10:40 A.M.—8 lbs. 2 oz."

My reunion with five-year-old Mike just about did me in. I had to contain myself, I knew, had to hold back too much emotion, lest I waken in him too sharp a realization that this wasn't just mommy coming home from a trip or a vacation, nor rouse in him too keen an awareness of how long it had actually been.

I had called him "long distance" about once a month from West Seventy-eighth Street, each time saying I'd be seeing him "in a few weeks."

With casual friends or acquaintances you could always say you'd been away for a few weeks, and they always accepted it; in reality they never knew how long it had been since they had last seen you, a month or six months.

But did Mike accept it as a few weeks, or did his young

unconscious mind tell him it had been a quarter of a year? Or, if not in those precise terms, at least tell him it had been a very, very long time? I had never really been sure while I was away, and the insistent nibble of doubt had at last made me phone Dr. Gosselin to ask if he would indeed come over to West Seventy-eighth Street.

That one visit had differed from all the office sessions. Dr. Gosselin permitted himself to comfort me, instead of asking me why I was so sure that Mike at five had an accurate sense of calendars and passing time? If I were at ease, he assured me, Mike would be easy; if when I saw him again, I was free of doubt, Mike would be free of doubt. Had I left my little boy to go gallivanting around Europe having affairs, that I need have guilt about leaving him?

And now Mike proved him right. He knew I was coming and when I opened the Whartons' front door, he leaped up at me and flung arms and legs around me. He didn't have to say, "Gee, mommy, you're kind of fat," and for a moment or two as we kept hugging each other, he even ignored the bright boxes of toys I had set down on the floor.

I had presents for the Wharton girls and for John and Carly and Rosie, and if ever I felt like a favorite member of the family returning home, that was one of the times.

By then I had been out of the hospital for three days, living at the Barclay, seeing Andrea and then Carly and then my sister and then the Mounts, and in the evenings Eric. One day, as a luncheon guest, I had Frau Doktor Sterba over; she was in town and I had told them in one of my last letters to Grosse Pointe where I would be, "when I leave your charming house at Grosse Pointe, where I've had such a happy stay doing research for my novel."

When she came to my room, she could tell nothing by looking at me; I was very nearly—not quite—slim again. I had had a permanent wave and had bought one new dress, a loose one, a size larger than my usual dresses, but no maternity outfit by a long shot. I wanted to meet people in something they had never seen me in before, so nobody could compare the way it used to fit me with the way it did now.

Ditha Sterba is not a particularly cozy woman to talk to, but there was a special look in her eyes as she greeted me that made me say something like, "I'm sure you and Richard know everything I haven't told you."

She nodded. "We hope we did guess correctly."

"You did. It's a boy and he seems marvelous." And I went over and kissed her, for the first time in our lives, and said, "Thanks for helping. Thank Richard too."

But all the visitors at the Barclay and all my pleasure at being in a big spacious luxurious room instead of in a ground-floor studio apartment on West Seventy-eighth—all was forgotten when I again saw Mike.

I told him one final lie about my visit to Grosse Pointe. For the rest of my life, though I often withheld certain matters from my two children, as all adults do, I never lied directly to either of them except about that gorgeous matter of adopting Christopher. The time might come—might—might—who could know then if it ever would come, or when?

But the second or third time I saw Mike—I saw him every day after school—I dropped in a phrase or two about Grosse Pointe and about "going to The Cradle, while I was out there in the Middle West, where it was so near, to see about adopting another baby, so let's hope we're lucky all over again."

"A baby brother? Or a baby sister?"

"I don't care either way. Do you?"

"A baby brother would be more fun—we could play catch."

"But a baby sister can play catch too—you could teach her."

And two long months later, weeks after we were settled back together in our own apartment, I told Mike, and everybody else in the world, that through Dr. Damon I was going to have what was called a "private adoption" of a baby boy eight weeks old.

And a week later, I locked the door for the last time on the small apartment at Fifty East Sixty-sixth Street, and brought my infant son Chris home for the first time. My big son Mike was at the door.

I showed the baby to Mike, let Mike hold him, talk to him, feel whatever he felt about having a brand-new brother. All was well, more than "well," all was better than having a brand-new

292

toy, exciting, important, the best fun in the world.

Or so it seemed for that first day. As Rosie began to take care of the new baby, bathing him, changing him, as I began to show him off to my friends who came to see him, Mike began to shade his first rapture into a slight aloofness, and before too many days had passed, he produced a question for me that was to be repeated in many variations for quite a while to come.

"What would happen, mommy," he asked one evening as I kissed him goodnight, "if the new baby went to sleep and never woke up?"

I do not remember whether I was dismayed or philosophical, whether I proved myself up to the new problems I saw opening before me then and there, or whether I was inept. I do know that for another considerable while, it seemed impossible for me to lean down over the small sleeping creature in the bassinet without thinking, It's true, it happened, it's really over and it's really true.

Technically it was not completely over, and would not be until I had been to court for the legal adoption proceedings. In New York, unlike Evanston, that could not take place the same day—six months had to elapse, with various routines to go through first. One of the preliminary steps took place very soon— the first of two visits by an accredited social worker of New York City to inspect the surroundings where the prospective adoptive baby was to live, and to pass judgment on the fitness of the prospective parents or parent—single parents were still considered an "exception" to be considered most carefully, even skeptically.

Whether the social worker was more impressed by what she could tell of me and my character in a brief interview, or by the attractive apartment, with its large rooms and smart furniture, I could not know, though I remember that she seemed very taken with the floor-length fully lined white chintz curtains in the long windows of the living room, with their bright red carnation motif, and with the gleaming black Steinway.

But her report, and the following one a few months later, must have been satisfactory, because in early July I went down to the Surrogate's Court in lower Manhattan and had my first official meeting about adopting young Chris, still officially known as Andrew Mills, Jr.

And in that same court thirteen days later, where everything was legally *in camera*, but where the presiding judge did, in fact, know the whole story behind this adoption, I was to have one more unexpected bout of tears, one more time of a throat so constricted that I could hardly speak.

After I took my oath to "shelter, educate and protect" my adopted son Chris until he "should attain his majority" twenty-one years in the future, the judge suddenly took both my hands in his own. He was a family man himself, he told me, with six children, some fully grown, some quite small, and he was a deeply religious man as well. He talked with that mixture of sounds that were part Brooklyn, part Bronx and part brogue, sounding more like one of New York's finest than a presiding judge in the Surrogate's Court.

"It's a fine and lovely thing you have done, young lady," he said solemnly. "God bless you and your son."

That was July 22, 1942, well over a year since that Memorial Day weekend. Of course I made an entry in my datebook.

COURT—adoption proceedings
for
Chris!!! At Last !!!!!

There it still is, exclamation points and all. I remember that as I wrote it down, my pencil blacker than usual, as if I were engraving in metal or stone, I was seized by some obscure impulse to dig out the datebook for the preceding year, and turn the pages backward and backward till the day it all began, March 28, 1941.

The whole top of the page was torn off, as I knew it would be. That very day that Dr. Damon had made his guess about the "theoretical delivery date," I had gone home and torn out half that right-hand page bearing Hugh's name. In a lifetime's worth of datebooks, or as I was soon to begin calling them, "work-logs," that is the one and only mutilated page.

And yet, gazing at the remnant of that page now, as I write this so many years later, it amuses me to see that, straggling under the remaining notation, "7:30 D," there runs the legend, "worked 2 hrs." On the reverse side of the torn page it still says, "worked 3 hrs."

I'm not sure that *amuses* is the word I secretly mean.

FIFTEEN

THE TRESPASSERS *WAS NOT* to be finished until March of the following year, and not to be published for half a year beyond that.

I had not been able to get back to writing it for nearly six months after I had put my 142 pages of manuscript into the suitcase I took to Harkness.

My abandoned pages remained in my desk drawer, shut away as if it were painful for me even to look at them. There were about 35,000 words in all, I knew—I had calculated that before leaving them—35,000 words of first draft, all needing editing, rewriting, cutting, improvement. But I was not able, as I had hoped I would be the moment I got home for good, was not able to get solidly back to regular daily writing.

I had begun to worry about money.

Soon I asked Dick Simon to halt my monthly advances of $500, because it unsettled me to receive that continuing check in the mail when I wasn't working on what it was supposed to be for.

All those hideouts and halfway houses and hospital bills and private nurses and hotel stopovers that I had been so cavalier about taking on and paying for, had managed to pile up into the largest list of "unusual expenses" I had ever entered on an annual budget, and quite suddenly they had turned into a sort of gigantic red light holding me back from starting forth again on my manuscript.

I had not yet used a dollar of the Schermans' loan; perhaps I should have done so then and there. But the loan was specifically earmarked *Baby*, and I had promised myself I would not use it for anything else.

So one thing I did was to go and see the Schermans. They had had many reports from Dick about my early pages of the book and from the letters I had sent him on its theme, and they knew enough about me to feel sure I wanted nothing now except to go back to it.

I told them about my unpaid bills and worrying creditors. "Could I—?" I asked, "—would it be ethical for me" to use their five thousand dollars that I had not touched for having my baby, would it be all right for me to use it, or some of it, for clearing the decks until I could finish my book? They never hesitated with their yes.

But even that did not seem like enough preparation for all the time I would need to give to writing the novel, and I kept thinking of other ways that might add to my peace of mind. I sold my Packard roadster for about what I had paid for it, and paid off a few of the more pressing bills—gasoline was rationed to three gallons a week per car, so a big one was not much use anyway. And then at last I did one pretty peculiar thing I thought would make *me* truly comfortable. I went to each of my creditors and asked *them* to be understanding and nice!

I went first to the Vincent Astor office, my landlords, and explained about my book that was to be published next year. I even took along my S & S contract and let them see for themselves about that $5000 advance. Then I asked if they could possibly let me give them my promissory notes for the rent for several months, so that I could manage financially until *The Trespassers* was finished and turned in.

They agreed to let me pay half the rent and give them notes for the rest. I then went to Bergdorf Goodman, where I had a bill of over a thousand dollars from the preceding year, when I was doing all that interviewing at N.B.C. and C.B.S., and at Bergdorf, I did the same thing, saying that their monthly reminder was driving me crazy, and could they let my bill slide until my book was done. They agreed—in those days there were no finance charges on unpaid bills to department stores.

Then I told Dick that I would have to take a little time out and earn some extra money as quickly as I could—which meant going back, temporarily only, to promotion. Not in an office job, but as a free-lance. Maybe he could recommend me to some good big prospects.

So my first assignment came from S & S, to originate a campaign for their subsidiary, Pocket Books, on a thousand-a-month basis for a few months, from which I would be paying two hundred a month to Lester Beall, the art director who had done the Freedom Pavilion poster that had so unnerved Herbert Bayard Swope and a host of other "prominent New Yorkers." He was in it not only to give me layouts for whatever copy I wrote, but also because part of my assignment was to come up with some new ideas for the general format for all Pocket Book covers, and I wanted him to work those out with me.

This was no simple little task, but in addition to it, I turned back immediately to some of my rejected stories, first of all "The Promise," which still seemed possible of rescue. I cut it by half, shifted scenes, added some new material and then persuaded my agent to submit it once more, hoping for some quick income.

But before I could start rewriting another, I became involved with two new war-engendered groups that were to claim much of my life for a very long while. One was the Writers War Board, with people like Clifton Fadiman, Rex Stout, Katharine Brush, author of *Young Man of Manhattan*, the painter Reginald Marsh, McKnight Kauffer, a famed illustrator, a few people from magazine and newspaper staffs and many others, summoned together to contribute what we could to the war effort, at first largely for posters and slogans. From the first, the meetings were long, and the special assignments plentiful.

One of these was my first acquaintance with anything labeled Top Secret. This must have come at the suggestion of Archie MacLeish, who was now associate director of the Office of War Information in Washington.

I was to do the necessary research and then write a thirty-page booklet for our troops who were to be assigned to strange lands for war duty. My booklet was to deal with, of all places, Burma, its coinage, its language, its people, its mores; it was to be delivered to a special messenger from the Office of Strategic Services, headed by Bill Donovan, and known as the OSS, which at that time, I firmly wish to believe, had none of the characteristics it was to have by 1947, when it evolved into the CIA.

Presumably my assignment was classified so that nobody would suspect any activity planned for the Burma Road, and I remember being so impressed at being in on anything top secret, that I never asked a solitary question about the government agency that had so indirectly enlisted my services.

But there was another new group that also shoved aside my notions of working for monetary gain. It was Friends of Democracy, with members like Rex Stout, its president, Louis Bromfield, Van Wyck Brooks, Morris Ernst, Will Durant, John Dewey, Eric Hodgins, Dr. L. M. Birkhead, its national director, and many others. National headquarters were in Kansas City, Missouri.

They didn't all come to meetings, of course, but the New York contingent that met often at my house included Ernst, Stout, Eric, Dr. Birkhead and several more. What they wanted of me was once again full-page newspaper promotion, but now it was no longer called political ads or public protests; now it was known as "part of the war effort."

And the purpose of this new effort was nothing less than taking on some of the most powerful leaders of the American press; William Randolph Hearst, Colonel Robert R. McCormick of the Chicago *Tribune* and Captain Joseph M. Patterson of New York's *Daily News*. All were so isolationist, so anti-Roosevelt and anti-Churchill, that they struck most liberals as being dangerous propaganda forces against the waging of the war.

WHAT DO *YOU* CALL
"AIDING THE ENEMY," GENTLEMEN?

ran one of the headlines I wrote, under large pictures of these three lords of the press, followed by pernicious quotes from their newspapers, each dated precisely and attributed exactly.

What about inkpot "aid to the enemy,"
Col. McCormick?

ran another full page. In each case we were careful to quote scrupulously, in full context; in a prominent box we also were careful to point out that the terms "aid to the enemy" or "inkpot sabotage" were "not used in any legalistic sense. We are not talking the language of lawyers but of the man in the street."

For anything as bold as this, there were again meetings to hold, funds to raise, everything checked for possible libel. To our astonishment we also had to face downright refusals from many newspapers, their editors or front offices too wary to permit our ads to appear in their pages. Their turn-downs came with curt explanations like, "not our function" to make judgments of other newspapers.

It is hard to believe today, that some of these nay-sayers were the New York *Times* and the *Herald Tribune*. The first paper to accept our full-pages was the San Francisco *Chronicle*, and after that a few other papers became willing, too, and a few braver radio commentators and columnists gave our war effort a much wider trajectory.

Each time there was a let-up in all this war-begotten work, I turned once more to my own mundane needs to do fiction or promotion. Ultimately I did land some assignments for the circulation department of Time, writing renewal letters on a sort of piecework basis, with good pay per piece, and before the year was out, Time's promotion manager, Nicholas Samstag, offered a steady $100 a week for a few months, to be on call for special material for use in his department, mostly presentations for the space salesmen. In those days, "space" meant only white space in magazines or newspapers, available at a price for advertising.

So for month after month, my 142 pages of manuscript stayed untouched, one of the dreariest things in the world, an unfinished novel. But I thought of it, thought about scenes, wanted it, began to feel tense about staying so long away from it. Was I going to turn into one of those people who start writing a book and never complete it?

I must have thought of Tom Mount, still talking about the serious novel he was going to write, still with no book published except his Westerns, under those assumed names he would never tell me. He had reentered the armed services; he would soon be Captain Thomas E. Mount of the United States Marines, and going off to Quantico. He was proud of himself again, and I happy to see that renewed pride. By then Tom was forty-six, back in uniform at forty-six; no wonder he was proud.

But nothing could give me a restored sense of myself until I was once again at work on my book. All along I had kept on with the massive amount of research that I had found would be needed for it, writing universities and government offices for documents on immigration quotas in various countries of the world, studying intricate tables, poring over published books about changing laws and regulations, new restrictions, greater requirements.

But that was not what I could call "working on my novel." And it was not until June 10 that I was at last able to jot down in my datebook, "Began seriously on book again—3 hrs."

Now there were daily notes of progress: June 20, "sent 70 p. to typist, all edited." That meant the first half of the manuscript I had left for so long, not "not writing forward," as I was soon to put it when I began to achieve brand new paragraphs, new pages, new scenes.

By July first, I had finished the rewrite and could begin to write forward. "Turned in 142 p. to typist." Next day said, "142 to S & S. Also Curtis Brown." Curtis Brown had become my agents—Ray and Helen Everitt had moved to Massachusetts.

It was about that time that I began to think of those daily notations as going, not into my datebook, but into my work log, or, more simply, my log. Somehow, though I continued my old habit of putting down the names of people I saw, parties I went to, concerts, theaters—as well as the occasional headline entries, printed all in caps, MIKE HAS MUMPS, to be followed a few days later by CHRIS HAS MUMPS, or MIKE HAS MEASLES and its inevitable sequel, CHRIS HAS MEASLES—somehow, from that mental shift from datebook to work log, I sensed that a basic change was taking place in the recording of my life.

To write, "Insert 188 A,B,C," or "something all wrong—started Chap. over," or even just plain, "9–11 AM; 2–6 PM; 10–mid."—all these ticks of the working clock began to measure off for me the sense of accomplishment or lack of accomplishment that suffused me each time I left my desk.

Also about that time, I made a big mistake with my son Mike. Because of the sad state of my finances, I had rented no summer place for that year, and when the Sterbas, stopping off in New York on their way up to Vermont for July and August, heard of my city-bound plans, they invited Mike up as their guest for a month at the children's camp they ran in the mountains, not far from Manchester.

There would be a swimming pool, ponies and horses to ride, lots of new friends—at the word *ponies*, Mike was transfixed, and would have started forth then and there. And a few days later, after our long, hot, cindery all-day train trip to Vermont, the first thing he wanted was to see the ponies. By my train-time for home the next morning, he seemed interested only in the stables.

Alas, it took just about a week before his infatuation with ponies had worn thin, and the Sterbas and I all knew we had made a blunder. Mike's initial rapture with horseflesh had given way to homesickness, and soon it became clear to the Sterbas, as they finally told me by phone, that it was not just the routine first bout of homesickness of most children at camp. Analysts though they were, and good mother that I was supposed to be, we had all overlooked one special factor we should not have overlooked for a minute: the new baby.

To little Mike, they finally realized, the real reason he was off there at camp was that mommy wanted to be alone with the wonderful new baby, sending *him* away from home so she could be. He grew silent, ate almost nothing, was often weepy, looked hurt and abandoned. He began to talk about a daddy—all the other kids kept talking about their daddies.

The Sterbas were quick to diagnose the inner meaning of his behavior and various remarks he tossed off, and blaming themselves for what had happened, called me to let me know all about it. We decided I should get up there fast, to take him back home. I talked to him on the phone and told him I was coming for him right away.

I dropped everything and went by the next train. And in Mike's delight at seeing me again, knowing he was going home with me, he did something that only sharpened my distress. He called me daddy.

I let it go the first time, but during the hours before we could leave for the railroad station next day, though he had reverted to mommy, he also said daddy once or twice more.

"I'm mommy," I said at last, as calmly as I could. "You haven't any daddy, Mikey, just the way millions of other kids haven't. Especially now, with the war, and so many daddies getting killed."

"I know," he said matter-of-factly, as though I were telling him something I needn't bother to mention.

"Just wait till we're on that beach at Fire Island," I said, and saw his eyes light up. Before I had left home, I had already evolved a plan I hoped might counteract this whole blunder and set things right again. Through a friend of mine, Bonwit Teller's designer for their made-to-order department, Fira Benenson, I had rented, sight unseen, a one-bedroom bungalow at Ocean Beach on Fire Island, and Mike already knew he and I were going off to the seashore all by ourselves for two whole weeks. No, not the baby. Not Rosie. Just Mike and me.

It worked wonders. I cooked our meals, I played with him, swam with him, taught him how to dive under the waves. I told him stories, read to him, ate all three meals with him, and made him dry the dishes when I washed them and help me make our beds.

All his waking hours were spent with me or with the kids he soon met on the beach. He was too young to play on the beach alone, or go into the water, but all the mothers took turns at beach-watching.

Once in a while I'd take him into the village and let him hear me phone Rosie for reports on Chrissie, telling him afterwards that the baby was okay and that Rosie missed him and wanted him to hurry back, but he accepted these references to the baby as no great matter, and soon I felt that his old sunny feeling of being the kingpin was reestablished once more. Or *a* kingpin.

I could write only at night, after he was asleep. But what I lost in new pages and new scenes was as nothing to what I regained from *this* sense of accomplishment with my older son.

Once at home again, July was nearly over, and I wrote forward in a kind of demented rush. By Thanksgiving I was turning in over 190 new pages to Dick, sending it in batches of about 50 pages at a time, having editorial sessions with him by phone, at lunch, even by letter, and always writing forward for one part of the day while I mulled over the changes he suggested, and then doing the rewrite at some other part, often at night.

We were on wartime rationing then, for meat, sugar, coffee, everything, and my awareness of the coffee I would be needing at night became a minor obsession. I was lucky in my rations, since officialdom asked only "How many members in the family?" never bothering about their ages, which gave me not only my own coupon books for coffee, but also one for Mike and one for Chris.

Even so, I would ask my maid to save the coffee grounds from the morning percolator so that I could superimpose a few fresh grains at lunchtime and new grains again during the hours of the evening, when more and more I was at my portable, writing forward or going backward and thinking forward.

I still had a social life, tucked into the interstices of that day and night writing rush. I saw Eric often, I saw the Simons and the Schermans and the Whartons. Fira Benenson and I had become increasingly good friends; she was absorbed not only in her high-fashion job at Bonwit Teller, but far more so in politics and the people active in politics.

She was Russian-born, a bit older than I, daughter of a man whose large holdings in the Lena gold fields had been confiscated in the revolution. The Benensons had fled to Paris, and later she married "outside her religion," a Polish Catholic, and became the Countess Ilinska. She used her title only in private life, never in business. She could walk into a gathering in a long mink cape, wearing an astonishingly high mink hat with it, and then, as she removed cape and hat, find half a dozen straight pins still stuck in the lapel of her suit, left-overs from her hours in her workroom.

In the European tradition, her evenings were "a salon," where her guests were people in government, writers, editors, professors; one of her close friends was the liberal Senator Bob La Follette, Jr., and I met Lawrence Spivak and his wife at her house, he who was to be, for a decade, first on radio and then on television, the impressario and anchor of "Meet the Press."

Another frequent visitor at Fira's was Alexander Kerensky, who had been, so briefly, the Premier in Russia in 1917. It fascinated me to see a historical figure in the flesh; he was in his sixties, and his Russian accent was so thick I could barely understand what he was saying, though Fira kept up a running accompaniment in English when she could. I remember that the first evening I met him, I thought, If only Kerensky and the moderates had prevailed, Papa could have gone right on being happy about the Russian Revolution.

But of all Fira's guests, the one who was to remain one of my good friends, on a political level, for the rest of his life, was Louis Fischer. He was an American journalist, a disciple of Mahatma Gandhi, author of many books on Stalin, on the Soviets, on Gandhi and Stalin; he was to be editor of *Mahatma Gandhi*, the autobiography of the Indian leader, one of the sources used, decades later, in the making of the film, *Gandhi*.

Louis had himself been a stout Communist, until the trials and purges of the thirties, when he, like so many others, had gone through the harrowing experience of repudiating so much of what he had long believed in. In 1941, as a favor to him, I had written a full-page advertisement for his *Men and Politics*, in which he was formulating his basic principle of "The Double Rejection," meaning fascism on the right and communism on the left.

"They'll call him a traitor," my headline went, "a turn-coat . . ." I was right; he was savagely attacked by many erstwhile colleagues and friends. Much later, together with Arthur Koestler, André Gide, Ignazio Silone, Stephen Spender and Richard Wright, Louis contributed to *The God that Failed*, that book on the painful theme of disillusionment, political disillusionment.

That thesis of the double rejection reminded me of what Professor Quint wrote about my father, that he "vigorously opposed both the reactionary right and the revolutionary left." No wonder I valued the inscription Louis wrote in one of his books: "To Laura, my favorite double-rejectionist."

There were many other friends and many other interests to give me breathing spells and pleasure during that rushing spell of daily writing; not all of them were on such high intellectual levels. About once a week, I stayed up at all-night poker sessions, at those low stakes that can run up to a few hundred dollars by the end of the year if you are in a losing streak. When I was married, Thayer and I would occasionally play bridge, not very good bridge, but our true love in card games was poker, and I seemed to have had more of a flair for that, and certainly liked it much more. Nevertheless, by the end of the year, adding up my wins and losses, I found that I was out nearly $800, and wrote on the last page of my datebook, "Quit until novel finished." And I stayed quit.

By New Year's Eve of 1943 my manuscript was at page 420, and I began to feel that the ending could not be far away, perhaps another couple of hundred pages. But going as I was by then, writing with a fluency I had never known (and, as it was to turn out, was never to know again), the expectation of another two hundred pages gave me little pause. I was writing about eighty pages a month.

The day after New Year's I went to a stationery store to buy something I had long wanted, a different kind of datebook or work log. The ones I had been using were of assorted sizes and textures; the first two had probably been sent to Thayer—they were marked "Colonial Press"—and the next seven had been sent free by my insurance agent, medium large, their pages edged in gilt, in fake green or black leather. Already the earlier ones looked shabby, their ersatz covers shredding off at the corners, the gold leaf in which my name was printed on them looking like tarnished tinsel on a discarded Christmas tree.

The new one I bought would remain uniform year after year—I visualized the next ten of them side by side in precise alignment. Ten of them side by side? My God, I would be fifty-two by the tenth one! I bought the first of the series anyway; it was a tidy

7-by-4½ inches in size, free of gilt-edged pages, bound in red cloth, costing about a dollar. Strange new names began to appear in its pages, not social names, but names connected with my still untitled novel.

"Kay Brown, Selznick, wants mss." was the first of these, and soon, "Bertram Block, 20th-Century Fox. Lunch, Dick, Collins of C.B." My publisher, my agent, Hollywood! Who had sent copies out there? Not me!

A month later, "Leland Hayward office wants copy." Another few weeks, "Kenneth McKenna, MGM phoned re mss."

I can remember again that mounting excitement and anticipation caused by this new cast of characters in my working life. Sad to relate, I did not handle all the clamor with any judicious evaluation but let it fuel up the flames of hope—or ambition—or whatever it was. Best-seller ahead . . . movie sale . . . money worries vanished . . .

There were, too, the first reader's reports and editor's comments, many of which I saved in a special folder, to be transferred later on into my first press portfolio of reviews.

One such came from Dick's partner, M. Lincoln Schuster, called Max. I barely knew him in a personal way, but I did know that he was not noted for restraint in his pronouncements. His first memo to Dick about my book said, ". . . the mass migration theme is magnificent, worthy of a Homer or a Virgil . . ." The second, after he'd read 142 pages, went on single space for an entire sheet, pointing out some flaws I "would surely repair," but including such fanfares and flourishes as "the basic conception is really superb" and "The good, the exciting, in fact, the noble, predominates."

To wind up this flow of hyperbole, there was a P.S. "Incidentally, a sure movie."

Heaven be praised, retroactively at least, that even then I had the wit to burst out laughing. Simon & Schuster, on that first contract of mine, not only had the sliding scale of royalties dished out to beginners, but also a goodly share of the movie rights. I took a mean delight in showing this encomium and its practical postscript to Eric, who ridiculed it with me.

I surely wasn't wise enough back then to wonder whether there was any danger in all that praise and all that movie interest;

it takes time and experience to recognize how insidious an attack it can be on any author, and I never paused to get into a decompression chamber, or even to think, Maybe it's a pipe dream.

But I did go on working, and at last at 1:15 in the morning on the night of March 11, 1943, after the final paragraph on page 605, I set down the remarkable words, THE END.

I had written nearly 140 pages in the preceding month; since November first I had done over half the book. Taped into my work log for the next day is Dick's engraved card, which he had sent with flowers. He had printed one word on it. *WHEE!!!*

And it was only on that following day that I suddenly realized that there was a coincidence about my finishing this particular story of migration and flight on March 11. That was the fifth anniversary of *Anschluss*, Hitler's march into Austria.

In those days you could turn in a big manuscript and see your work in galleys two weeks later. What's more, you could hold the first copy of a bound and jacketed book in your hands in about two months.

But there would be half a year of waiting before publication day, and I had no intention of giving in to that "post partum depression," the let-down that most writers feel, so I had been told, upon coming to the end of writing a book.

Again the way out was work—giving all my energy to earning a living for my small family. My Time arrangements were soon to lapse, and my work for Pocket Books was completed and done with.

So I returned to short stories and my old standby, promotion. But this time I was interrupted by nothing less awesome than the United States Army.

Just two weeks after that exultant *WHEE*, I was asked to a special meeting of the Writers War Board, clearly labeled top priority. The army had requested that a group of writers, particularly women writers, be sent on a tour of WAAC camps. The Women's Army Auxiliary Corps had been started in the First World War, and had been reactivated during the past year for this second one. Now the army wanted publicity—and enlistments.

In April off we went, Kay Brush, Alice Hughes, a syndicated

newspaper columnist, various women feature writers on newspapers and magazines, several men, and lots of army brass, including Colonel Oveta Culp Hobby of Texas, newspaper publisher, public official and now director of WAAC.

We travelled in several DC–3 bombers, led by General Somervell's transport plane, and stopped over at WAAC camps in Fort Custer, Michigan; Des Moines, Iowa; Fort Knox, Kentucky; Fort Oglethorpe, Georgia; Fort Chattanooga in Tennessee and Fort Jackson in South Carolina.

Our tour lasted for four days and nights, taking us to at least two camps a day. We ate in the mess halls, talked to the recruits and their officers, slept in officers' quarters but mostly mingled with the WAACs themselves.

I remember how shocked I was, naively and stupidly shocked, the first time I went to one of the regular latrines, and saw the dirty words, lewd remarks and pithy suggestions scrawled on wood or plaster walls, as if I had assumed that only males were capable of such vocabulary.

And I remember how fatigued I was each night, after a twelve-hour day of tramping, inspecting, interviewing, talking, asking, watching the uniformed women on parade and at their regular duties. But when I returned home at last, with a raging cold, I at least had a ready answer for those who asked the cliché of the day, "Say, don't you know there's a war on?" And even in bed, I started a story about a shy, prudish girl who joined the WAACs.

But the very next morning I had my private reward—a messenger brought the elongated galleys, slippery as eels, of *The Trespassers*, and at last I could see my book in print.

Something happens when typed lines become printed lines; they gain an authenticity in the mind of the person who sat there at that typewriter for so many days and nights; they take on an importance, as if the linotype machine itself were some final editor, saying, This is it.

I began at once to read; even before I reached page 1, I was stopped by the title page, by the copyright page, but most of all by the dedication page. I had had no dilemma about whom to choose for this, my first book; without his help I never would have come to a point where I could even think of writing an entire novel. Indeed I had first thought of using the phrase,

"Without whose help—" as part of the dedication, but had rejected that as coy or cute. So the page simply said:

To
Raymond Gosselin

He was no longer in practice; he too was in uniform, at Camp Peary, Virginia, in the medical corps. As soon as I received a few bound galleys that didn't slide and slip all over you, I sent him a copy, as I had so long ago promised I would.

Once the corrected galleys were turned in to Dick Simon I again set myself to the need for income. I rewrote "False Witness" and this time it sold, to Cosmopolitan, for $1,250. I sold another to Liberty for $500, and a wartime novelette, *The Girl I Left*, for a large $1,750 somewhere else. I began "The Sleepless" and soon wished I hadn't; a notation says, "Damn thing's punk— start again," and for some time other notations on "The Sleepless" said the same thing in varying terms of irritation.

All the while I kept on searching for promotion assignments, and finally landed three magazines all at once, The American Mercury, no longer H. L. Mencken's, and on a less lofty plateau, Mercury Mysteries and Ellery Queen's Mystery Magazine. All three now published by Lawrence E. Spivak, whom I'd met at Fira's. He was a hard taskmaster, demanding about changes, often irascible, but his demands were intelligent, never petty, and I could cope with that. I don't recall the definite terms we agreed on, nor for how long we were to go on, but my income tax files for that year show $1,500 for several months' work on the Mercury, and $1,000 each for the other two. Mr. Spivak must have been reasonably satisfied, for the files also show, "E. Q. bonus, $250."

During the summer I also had one of the oddest little writing assignments ever, with one of the strangest "employers" ever. This was to turn out "short-short stories," a few hundred words each, for the nation's thousands of newspapers—three short-shorts every week—whose plots were to appeal especially to women at home or "women at war." They ran perhaps six or eight inches down a single newspaper column, and were paid for at a munificent $20 per.

I saved none of them, but in my log are some of the first titles, "Yellow Envelope," "Visitor's Pass," "V-Mail letter," "4–F Girl" and others such—the titles themselves tell me I must have had to put in almost as much time thinking up a "plot," or basic situation, as I would have for a real piece of fiction.

My employer was no newspaper, no magazine, nothing other than the United States Treasury. With an assist, of course, from the Writers War Board.

Taken together, these various sums, picayune or large, let me begin paying off some debts. I sent Dr. Damon $200 on account, the first fee I had paid him for my confinement. I sent $300 to Bergdorf Goodman, and I even redeemed all $750 of the promissory notes I had given Vincent Astor's real estate company the year before.

So I was writing almost as intensely, if not as eagerly, as I had been during those quickened months of getting back to and developing and finally finishing *The Trespassers*.

And during all the assorted assignments and tasks and stories and novelettes, despite all the seductive early reports on my book, for all the prepublication activity of press releases and interviews, there was one hidden preoccupation of mine which I never spoke of to a soul.

I had already begun to wonder what my next novel would be about.

This summer there was no blunder about camps in Vermont or separated family. Remembering Mike's daily joys at Fire Island, I took a rambling three-bedroom house at the bargain price of $550, again at Ocean Beach, and this time we were all going out for eight weeks.

Just before we moved, Mike did something that had me beaming with pride.

The headmistress of the progressive school he went to had asked if I would stop by for a year-end talk. "Michael is one of our best pupils," Miss Watson greeted me solemnly when I was seated before her desk, and I knew at once that "but" was to follow. "He gets along with all the students, he is alert and responsive, obedient, though he has a mind of his own. But—"

"What is wrong, Miss Watson?"

"But he is behind in his reading skills, woefully behind all the others, I'm afraid."

I must have looked astonished. They didn't send out report cards with numbers or letters, no plus or minus signs, just phrases like "alert and responsive." I could have had no warning.

At home Mike could take up *A Dog of His Own* and read it aloud page for page. I had wondered if this was because I'd read it to him so often that he had memorized the look of the words on each page, but he hadn't limited himself to *A Dog of His Own*. He was forever asking me to type out his name on my portable, and had long since learned how to pick out MIKE HOBSON on it himself. He kept poring over comic books, magazine ads, even newspaper headlines, sometimes reading words aloud to Rosie or to me.

I had an inspiration. The morning's *Herald Tribune* was lying on Miss Watson's desk, and I asked if we might have Mike in for a few minutes. I discussed everything right out in front of him, I said.

Dubiously, she sent for him. When he arrived, surprised to find me there, I said, "Hi, Mike, would you do me a favor?" I handed over the *Trib*, folded to the front page. "Would you read me something? Anything at all."

He took the paper, scanned its columns and then began. "The in-vent-or of this heely-copter," he read with gaps between the syllables, "is a student in Brook—Brookl-lyn Tetch-nical high school—"

"Thanks, Mike," I said. "That's fine." I turned to Miss Watson. "Can he go now?"

She dismissed him and I had a moment of pure happy spite, to see how abashed she was. I held on to my manners, but did make the point that it might have occurred to somebody on that progressive staff that perhaps Mike was too damn bored with Dick-and-Jane, See-Jane-run, to comply when they asked him to read the stuff aloud.

Then and there I decided to switch Mike to an old-fashioned school with specific grades and report cards. It meant moving to a different school zone, but without a car, living way over by the East River had become difficult anyway. Despite the wartime shortage of housing, I began apartment-hunting that same day.

So it was a summer of various upheavals. New school to find, new apartment to locate, the mounting tension of that approaching publication day, and running below all of it, like a dismal counterpoint, a thudding fear that I would never again come up with a book idea as good as the one for *The Trespassers*.

And at last, on a Tuesday in the middle of September, the moment that knowing people called pub day arrived, the day I had waited for, tried to imagine, daydreamed about.

Simon & Schuster had done an extraordinary amount of advance advertising, to the trade, of advance publicity to book reviewers, columnists, the press in general. It is true that back then it cost only $1,300 to buy a full-page ad in the Sunday book section of the *Times*, while today it would cost $9,000; true that a quarter-page on the daily book page was only $600 then, whereas it would be $3,000 now. But my book was to sell at $2.75, not at today's lofty prices.

And Simon & Schuster went right ahead and spent what it took to tell the world about my book. No author could ever accuse them, as so many authors could so often and so justly accuse so many publishers (I among them with some of my books in the years ahead)—could ever accuse S & S of "just printing it and then dropping it down a well."

Their prepublication activities had been aggressive and generous; preliminary notices and reviews in Publishers Weekly and the Kirkus Service were good; they had sent out advance copies to the grandest list I could imagine—Eleanor Roosevelt, Carl Sandburg, Pearl Buck, Dorothy Parker, Janet Flanner, Sigrid Undset, all leading columnists from Walter Winchell onward, as well as to all organizations interested in refugees, and just about every book critic in the land.

I loved the book jacket; they had my picture taken for it by Halsman, already famous. The first printing was 20,000 copies, and the sales staff kept reporting strong orders everywhere, from book jobbers, major bookstores, small bookstores. Each phone call from Dick, telling me some bit of news, was like Christmas Eve.

313

The evening before pub day I spent with the Simons. At eleven o'clock I took a cab, by myself, up to the all-night newsstand at Madison and Fifty-ninth to get the *Times* and the *Tribune*. I had been warned that many books are not reviewed for what seems like eons, and that most are never reviewed in the largest papers at all, but nobody at S & S gave any impression that such a fate was what they expected for mine.

And standing under a street light, I opened to the book pages of each paper, and there they were—reviews in both, right on pub day, a publisher's hope, an author's dream.

Lewis Gannett's review in the *Trib* was wonderful. . . . "this powerful and painful novel . . . a kind of tragic majesty . . ." The piece did touch on the "flaws I would surely repair," according to M. Lincoln Schuster's remarkable memo, about Jasper Crown and Vee, but the warmth of most of it lifted me right off the sidewalk.

But Orville Prescott in the *Times* flung me right back down. "Miss Hobson's account of the ordeal of the Vederles is written with such passionate indignation, it frequently bursts the bounds of fiction into the hortatory, rhetorical regions of sermonizing and pamphleteering."

As for Jasper Crown and Vee: ". . . that this kind of man . . . could drive his way to the fame and power he craved, you never doubt. What you doubt is that a woman as intelligent and fastidious as Vera could find him lovable . . ."

That wasn't enough for Mr. Prescott in his little slaughter-house. "If I give the impression that I am reviewing two different novels at once by mistake . . . that is the impression made by 'The Trespassers,' . . . two novels grafted together by main strength and awkwardness."

It was much longer than the usual review in the *Times*, with every other line a lancet. How long I stood there bleeding I never knew.

Sinclair Lewis used to boast that he didn't read his reviews any more, "just measured them." I never believed that, and I discovered what many other authors know, that deny it though you may, the review you remember most is not the good one but the one that kills you.

When I bought that press portfolio, I had also signed on for my first clipping service, and now I began to watch for the mail and what it might bring, good or bad. There was plenty of each. Masochistically I pasted in the worst ones as well as the others.

And in those innocent days before huge bookstore chains and vast paperback deals, a book could make the best-seller lists even with 20,000 copies. Soon mine did just that, albeit on the lowliest rungs of the ladder, in the *Herald Tribune*, the Washington *Post*, other out-of-town papers, and finally in the nether regions of the weekly list in the *Times*.

S & S put another edition of 5,000 on press, and the ads announced, "30,000 copies in print." (My work log notes, "really only 25,000.") Fan mail began to come in—nearly every letter stirred me. Soon Victor Gollancz, Ltd. of London signed up the British rights and a firm in Sweden signed up too.

I think I was happy. But before the month was out, I wrote, "Dick seems discouraged—selling slowly in new orders."

And by the end of the year, that most dreaded commodity of publishing, "return copies," began to appear from jobbers and bookstores. Not in tremendous quantities, but enough to pull those sales figures down a bit, and then another bit, until they came to rest at something just under 20,000.

That was not what you could call a failure. Dick was not just comforting me when he said that most first novels sold only a few hundred copies, rarely more than several thousand.

But I had to face certain realities, including the rude one that the two and a half years that had gone into writing my first novel and waiting for it to appear had earned me the grand sum of $7,000, all in advances. The $500 monthly checks had resumed the moment I resumed work on it, and then in the spring, after I had turned it in, I had asked for another $2,000 advance and had received it.

Therefore my first royalty statement the next year would show that no new money was due me. There was no movie money—Hollywood was still making gestures, but as for any sign of a sale, or even an option, nothing.

So all the misty fantasies of Instant Fortune dissolved and I faced the same old necessity to earn a decent living. But I also knew some lovelier things.

I had found that I had never been as absorbed, as eager and as happy at any work as I had been writing a book that moved *me* while I was writing it.

Promotion could give your ego a boost; short stories perked you up at your own cleverness about plot and dialogue. But nothing compared to the perfect state you were in while you wrote something related not to business, not to imaginary romance, but to the needs and hopes of real people in a real world.

I knew I would write another book, and then another, no matter what this first one had earned or not earned. I began to think, perhaps defensively, that if you were going to be a writer, you'd better keep one sort of writing away from the idea of money and income, keep it off somewhere in a special place, keep one area of your life intact for writing only what you wanted to write.

As I began to search seriously for an idea for my next novel, my new precept seemed to grow sturdier in my mind. And when, in the spring of 1944, I finally did come up with one, I had an immediate chance to test my new resolve.

For Dick Simon unequivocally disliked it, and did his best to persuade me not to waste time on it.

That was *Gentleman's Agreement*.

SIXTEEN

EVERY AUTHOR ON EARTH, I suppose, has been asked, "How did you get the idea for it?" I have been asked it for each of my novels, but never more frequently than for *Gentleman's Agreement*.

There is always a kind of simplicity in the asking, as if the questioner were sure you could answer with a neat declarative sentence, the way people could always answer the question, "Where were you when you heard about Pearl Harbor?" or "What were you doing when you heard Roosevelt had died?" Or, for younger people, "How did you hear Kennedy was shot?" And, for still younger, Reagan and the Pope?

With *Gentleman's Agreement*, strangely enough, there was to come one moment, one particular moment, late on a March evening in 1944, that I *could* name as the precise moment when my basic idea suddenly struck me. But the path leading toward that moment was long and winding, filled with detours and cursed with dead ends.

Gentleman's Agreement is about antisemitism in America right after the Second World War. Its principal character is a young writer who does research on antisemitism by saying he's Jewish when he isn't.

But that was a long way down the road. One of those detours, which for a while fooled me into thinking it would lead to my next book, had a sort of perverse war theme. "A nation is *happy* during a war," I wrote on the last page of my 1943 log. "Idea for a novel?"

It is almost impossible for young people today, to whom the word war means Vietnam, or for the middle-aged who also think of Korea—almost impossible for them to accept the fact that there could ever have been a war that most decent people in most countries called "a necessary war," or even, "a good war."

Those same people, however, hated warfare, hated the killing, the wounding, the mourning. Simultaneously they denounced warfare while they ardently supported that one war.

There was a paradox there, I felt, so there must be some plot to show that paradox, some characters to exemplify it.

I began to make notes: For all the cries of horror about war, there's a secret excitement in wartime that people will miss when the armistice comes—jobs for everybody, higher pay, hot news every time you look at a paper or turn the radio dial, nobody ever bored . . .

We'll never outlaw war, my notes said, if we keep on lying to ourselves about hating it. We do not hate it; we love it, but it's a harmful love, an illicit love, a whore who leaves us ashamed, guilty, maybe diseased with inflamed nationalism, superiority, hatred, prejudice, bigotry.

Could I write this in wartime? It could be a pretty shocking book, even insulting to anybody with a son or husband or lover killed or wounded or missing in action, but for the millions of others, war *is* a high point of otherwise drab lives, a *happy* time.

For its sardonic twist, title might be *Happy Days*.

It was exciting for me to get hold of even that much of an idea for a book. My log says, "Discussion with Sammy about 'nation *happy* during war.'"

Sammy? Why not Eric? Of course it was Eric to whom I would have turned first, but about three months before, the initial *E* had dropped out of the pages of my datebook. Not that we had quarreled, not that we had parted, but that Eric had dropped out of himself into an alcoholic world where the real Eric was lost for months to come.

He had collapsed one night at my house, falling to the floor unconscious, "passed out" in the pejorative phrase, remaining immovable and unreachable despite everything I could do to rouse him.

Frightened, not knowing his doctor's name, I called my own doctor, and Katherine Butler came up at once, examined him, summoned an ambulance and sent him to a hospital. But before the night was out, Eric betook himself out of the hospital and disappeared. For three days and nights, he was lost to me, to his office, to everybody else. At last he turned himself in to a special treatment center on the West Side, which he later called "a drunk tank" or a "drying-out tank."

I didn't see him for several months. He was gone from his usual life, gone from mine. It may have been then, during that dark and silent separation, that I realized I had outgrown, or had begun to outgrow, "neurotic love" in favor of a more mature variety.

For though I loved Eric, it was not with that compulsiveness that had been so basic a part of my attachment to Tom, then to Thayer, then to Ralph. I was unhappy about Eric, I kept imagining what he must be going through, and I wondered whether he would ever again be part of my life. But I found that I could keep on with that life, found that sadness and loss remained sadness and loss, not turning into collapse and destruction.

And so it was Sammy Tatem, more formally Graham Tatem, and not Eric, who was the first to hear my idea. I had met him eight years before in Bermuda, when I'd gone on the first vacation trip I had dared to take alone after my divorce, and for any suffering female, he was a perfect companion, intelligent, attractive and great fun. He was born in Bermuda, and despite being an Oxford man, via a Rhodes scholarship, was defensive about "being a colonial," but whenever I went to Bermuda, he was there, and whenever he came to New York, he sought me out.

I always talk out possible plots or ideas with good friends, those willing to listen, some of them even "eager to be in at the beginning," as they put it. I never did believe the warning, "If you talk it, you'll never write it," though I'd heard that Hemingway and other writers held this adage to be God's truth.

But I knew that others regarded it as rubbish. Eugene O'Neill, I'd been told, was once on his way to his barber's, when an idea for a play struck him. During the haircut, he told it to the barber—it took him about three minutes. A few days later, he ran into an actor he liked and told it to him—this time it took about ten minutes. Finally he told it to his wife Carlotta, and kept on talking for half an hour. That's when he knew he "had hold of something solid."

As I told Sammy, I also felt it was something solid, and I went back to making notes. I might tell my story in terms of two characters, one a soldier home from the war, out of uniform and back at his old job, feeling himself a nobody again, bored, let down, and the other a man who never was in uniform, a lawyer perhaps, with the American Civil Liberties Union, who was fighting another kind of war, that he thinks of as "the long war," for civil rights in America, against prejudice and injustice. He would never feel any postwar letdown, he would always know that elation from fighting in a cause larger than himself.

By now I began to do an outline of *Happy Days*. It was three pages long, single-spaced, typed on both sides of each sheet, in defiance of proper publishing procedure, for rationing had by then extended to paper and tinfoil and paper clips, hairpins, bobby pins, anything made of metal, as well as cloth, linen, cotton, anything that might be used for weapons, bandages, uniforms. Even our Christmas tree ornaments were no longer sparkling balls dusted with sequins and glitter, but muted plastic, hung on the tree not with wire but with string.

But just as I was making a clean copy of the outline to send to Dick, I was torn from all work by the horrifying news I heard on the radio. Clare Luce's only child, Ann, had been killed in an automobile accident. She was nineteen, a student at Stanford, and after having lunch with her mother at San Francisco, was driving back in an open convertible to Palo Alto with a college friend.

Since Clare had become Congresswoman Luce a year before, we were not only parted physically, but more than ever politically. She had made world headlines with her maiden speech in Congress, when she attacked Vice-President Wallace with what most of the nation's editorials, even in Republican papers, castigated as "a cheap wisecrack," or even worse.

"Much of what Mr. Wallace calls his global thinking," she had said, in her crispest voice, "is, no matter how you slice it, still globaloney."

I had winced when I read it in the papers, and when I heard it gleefully reported on the air. It reminded me of her nastiness about Dorothy Thompson and menopause, and yet this terrible news about Ann wiped the professional record clean and left only the human.

And there was a coincidence of timing that, for me, made it even more dreadful. From her office in Washington, but on her own notepaper, Clare had written me about *The Trespassers*, just as it came out, full of praise and predictions for my future, and ending with a handwritten postscript. "If your muse brings you to Washington, come to see me—I have a room. There is plenty of material for your pen here. *The* novel about Washington has never been done—and needs doing, like no other theme."

I had answered her, and at Christmas she had sent a card and small toys for Mike and Chris. Just two days before this frightful news of the accident, I had sent off a letter of thanks, full of happy chitchat about my two kids. If she were to read that letter *now* . . .

I tried to reach one of her many secretaries, to head it off if it were still in a pile of mail, to get it destroyed or at least kept away from her for a decent interval. I tried her office in Washington, her apartment in New York, her house in the country. I failed everywhere.

I wrote her as best I could. Letters of condolence are possible only when they are at heart a formality; when you really feel what the person you are writing is going through, they are a torment to write. Soon enough I got her reply, on plain black-bordered notepaper, that made me weep for her, and wonder again how any mother or father could endure the loss of a child.

Laura dear,
    Thank you for your letter. It helped in some intangible

way. (What is there of importance to the heart or mind which is not intangible?)

My lovely and gay darling child is gone from me in *this* world. I shall never be truly happy again . . .

Even these many years later, I cannot bring myself to go on with all of it, for it went into a kind of religious mood, with talk about being with Ann again in some other world. And then it ended with words about my own children.

Take care. My best to the boys. Are they still blowing bubbles over your shoulder? Or are they men now? I wish you and them all best, dear Laura.

Her letter shook me to the roots, and a pity and unexpected love rose in me. But as always, even after the shock of sudden death, the steady stream of living and working was finally resumed, and I finished copying the three tightly typed pages of my outline about nation-happy-during-war, and sent it off to Dick Simon.

This first idea of mine for my second book, he liked a lot, told me to go ahead. But that wasn't so easy, after all. I kept searching for an actual story line that would bring these two men together in a natural way, not in any slick formula plot. That proved obdurate; it wouldn't go; there was something unworkable, I began to feel, in having two intertwined themes, one about happy-during-war, and the other about the long war for civil rights. Yet I wouldn't abandon either.

Then one day I came on something that surged right across these two threads of mine, pulling them all out of shape. It was a first-page story in the National Affairs section of Time for the week of February 14, 1944.

It told of Congressman John Rankin, the Mississippi Democrat, addressing the House of Representatives on some bill, and referring to Walter Winchell as "the little kike I was telling you about."

"This was a new low in demagoguery," Time said, "but in the entire House, no one rose to protest." Far from it. At the end of Rankin's long speech, "The House rose and gave him prolonged applause."

I tore out that page from Time and put it on my desk. I kept going back to it, rereading it. I still have that very page, pasted into my press portfolio of *Gentleman's Agreement*, though I didn't know then that there would ever be any book by that name. Reading that page again today, I feel again something of the shock I felt then, not only at Rankin but at the House itself, where no one rose in protest.

And I remember that then and there, on that long-ago February day, I knew that my theme about a nation happy during war wasn't good enough. Of course my civil liberties lawyer would, during the novel, come across that page in Time, and of course that would help develop my plot.

But I had an uneasy feeling, just the same, that this would be too tangential a use of my own feelings. Maybe my shock and disgust ought to be the core of a novel, all by itself.

I had to think.

I did think. For the time being I stopped making further notes on my outline and let my mind drift and search. But once again worry about what I was earning became more insistent.

I'd been assured that authors of even moderate bestsellers could make a handsome side income on the lecture circuit, and not long after pub day I'd made my first appearance on a platform, though no "honorarium," as they called it, was involved. I did it partly because S. & S. urged me to, and partly to test myself out.

It had been a disaster. Together with William Shirer, Frederick Lewis Allen, and Elizabeth Janeway, whose first novel had also just appeared, I was driven up to a literary luncheon in White Plains. I made a ten-minute speech, which was duly applauded by the audience and praised by my co-speakers, but I knew perfectly well that compared to the other three, I'd been a dud, scared, rigid, and too obviously reading from the pages held in my shaky hand.

A second try, also without pay, was equally a disaster, though the audience was composed of experts in the refugee field, who looked on *The Trespassers* as written directly to their needs, and were thus ready to take me to their collective heart.

Even knowing that, I'd put in about three weeks writing out

the speech, cramming in new data about quotas and affidavits, and through all the cramming and writing I felt nearly ill with stage fright.

This time I was to be all alone on that platform, standing at that lectern, addressing a hundred people below me. If only I could be seated, the way I used to be in those big meetings with all the top people at Time, when I never felt a qualm, when I spoke as easily and cogently as any of them.

Maybe this second try wasn't actually a disaster, but it told me that I would never be a natural-born lecturer. All I could remember, for days afterward, was how I felt up there, in the new dress I had bought especially for the occasion, a green silk, with a knee-length fringe from waist to hemline, like a delicate hula skirt, a dress that betrayed me to my public, for its fringe kept up a slight swinging motion as if blown by a wind.

Every time I heard from my new lecture bureau about a possible lecture, the quaking came upon me, a shyness, a knowledge that lecturing was not for me, unless I spent years getting easy at it.

My father had lived for that hour on the platform, had always come home exhilarated by it, eyes bright with excitement, too elated to go to sleep. Maybe some seed of distaste about lecturing had been sown in me in my earliest childhood.

Soon I was telling my friends, and the lecture bureau and S & S that I didn't want my two kids "to be forever seeing mommy with an orchid on her shoulder and a suitcase in her hand, dashing out to a limousine and the airport."

I must have known that a few sour grapes were behind that noble statement, but I was back to my own solid ground: if I needed money I would have to write something to earn it.

Recently I'd had the new thrill of having a story *ordered* in advance from a synopsis shown to a magazine. And another new thrill when one of the script editors of United Artists out in Hollywood brought me an offer to try an original screenplay for William Bendix. On speculation, of course, with me taking all the risks and United Artists none, but never had I been approached by Hollywood to write a scenario, and even at this insubstantial rate of exchange I decided to try it.

I must have dropped everything else, for my log says, "Finished Brush-Off, 20 p. One wk. exactly." I turned it in and began to wait with the proverbial bated breath and on the proverbial tenterhooks. How much would they pay? Might it set me free to go back to my book idea?

Perhaps as an antidote, I wrote a clearly noncommercial story, no more than a few pages in length, about a young couple planting a garden on the flat roof of a four-story tenement walk-up "that lay, like a cowering and beaten dog, at the feet of the grand buildings along the East River."

It was a story of youth and wartime and separation, ending a year later with the garden all abloom and beautiful, just as the young man is called up for military service abroad. I managed to tell it with great economy, and called it "The Gardeners." It remains the only story I ever wrote in a single day, and it sold for only $300, but it was later indexed with "Distinctive Short Stories" in *Best American Short Stories of 1944.*

Soon came word from United Artists. *Brush-Off* was absolutely wonderful, but "it wouldn't play." It was then that I determined to go out to Hollywood myself and find out what I could about writing originals for the movies. What *would* play? How long should it be? What did they actually pay if they accepted it? I had heard rumors of ten thousand for a one-page outline, of twenty thousand, fifty thousand for a full piece of work.

I told my plans to Curtis Brown, and noted their skeptical mood as they called their Hollywood colleagues, Berg and Allenberg. It meant I'd have to borrow money for fares and hotels and also enough to keep my household going at home while I was out there, but I had made up my mind and if I had to borrow as much as $2,000, why, I would borrow $2,000.

I had already used up all the Schermans' loan, and could not contemplate going to them again. I had even made a bank loan, using my small amount of Time stock as collateral, and couldn't go back to the bank. I might possibly have asked Simon & Schuster for an advance on *Happy Days*, but talk of a new contract and a new advance seemed premature.

I considered asking my sister Alice for a loan; despite all their contempt for the ways of capitalism, Milton was a steady investor in Wall Street and in tax-free municipals, and doing very well. Alice and I had been seeing a lot of each other in the past months—since the Nazis attacked Russia, we were, for once, on the same side! Every communiqué could be shared, every bad dispatch worried over together, every good one rejoiced over. We could again talk politics without dissension.

But going to Alice meant being indebted to Milton, and though he probably would have been very nice about it at Alice's behest, I myself found it an uninviting prospect.

But I knew a number of people with whom I could feel easy about approaching for a loan. Most of them were men.

When you are in your thirties or early forties and divorced, unless you are one of the world's unfortunate wallflowers, you always know a lot of men, many of whom are married and restless, many themselves divorced, and many who are still single. Back then it never occurred to me that some of the bachelors were homosexuals, but I did realize that if they had reached their late thirties or forties without marriage and children, they were in some way difficult or odd or neurotic. But the word neurotic never alarmed me. Wasn't *I* neurotic? Weren't most writers, painters, composers, the non-Babbitts of the world?

One of these never-married single men was Ira Jewell Williams, Jr., a rich Philadelphia lawyer, only son and heir of an even richer Philadelphia lawyer, and just what people meant by the cutting phrase, "a typical Philadelphia lawyer."

I'd known him for a long time, and during Eric's absence he at last became what used to be called "a suitor." He really did propose marriage, and repeatedly.

Poor Ira. There couldn't have been a more unlikely person for me to marry. He was so decorous, so proper; he couldn't take you out without sending up a corsage first; he could order Mike around like a Victorian father—"Stand up, a lady has entered the room!"—me being the lady; most of all he could actually believe that when he did persuade me to marry him, he would be so proud and happy to know I would help him with a scholarly book he was planning to write.

For a moment I didn't get his full meaning when he confided this deep hope. To read his manuscript, I thought, make suggestions, even help him edit it. But then I heard him say something about collaborating and I stopped short. "A full partnership," he went on, "a real collaboration."

"But I'd be doing a book of my own."

"You'd no longer need to write another word," he said resoundingly, as if he were making me a pledge. "You'd never have to earn another dollar by yourself."

He really meant it; I'd marry him and give up my own writing for good. Yes, he liked *The Trespassers*; it was a good book, but a wife would want to further her husband's work. It was normal, it was right. It wouldn't be behind the scenes, but right up front—we'd sign the book, *By Ira and Laura Williams.*

I know I never counted to ten; I know I exploded. But as usual, a few days later, I had achieved some curbstone analysis of Ira's problems, to lay the blame on his overbearing father who still blue-penciled all his legal briefs.

So I kept seeing him and when the Hollywood plan arose, it was Ira whom I asked for my loan of $2,000. He was utterly delighted, as if I were doing *him* a favor.

I left for the Coast at the end of February. It was nearly ten years since I'd taken the famous train, the Chief, to meet Thayer in Reno for the vacation I never suspected was to be our last, but this trip held nothing of nostalgia for me. I was eager, determined to find some good way to support my kids and myself without returning to promotion. I knew I would never become a permanent Hollywood writer; despite the Thirty Years' War between the Zametkin conscience and the Hobson budget, I never did crave swimming pools and elegant foreign cars.

For my first few days I stayed with my friends Carroll and John Whedon and their young children, Tom and Jill. John was making a small fortune as co-author of "The Great Gildersleeve," a smash comedy series on radio, but there was nothing pretentious about them or the way they lived. They had a small house and garden, sans pool or Japanese gardener, but with one lemon tree and one grapefruit tree. And before my welcome could wane, I moved to a hotel.

My days at once filled with interviews, lunches, dates for drinks. I met Bert Allenberg, my agent; I phoned Shirley Collier, divorced from the writer, John Collier, and an agent herself; I dined with Arthur Schwartz and his wife, Kaysie, close friends of the Simons. He was the composer of such popular songs as "Dancing in the Dark," "I Love Louisa," and was out there for a Warner Brothers picture.

And I made some new friends; through Shirley Collier, I met Craig Rice, a writer of popular mysteries, and other writers; one night at the front desk of my hotel, as I was asking for my mail, giving my name, a man beside me said, "Did you just have a book published?"

It was Charles Jackson, out there in connection with the movie being made of *The Lost Weekend.* Then and there we sat down in the lobby, and later on up in my room with the door left ostentatiously ajar, and talked books and publishing and agents and movies. I wondered what it must be like to have a novel that everybody and his Uncle Adolph was reading or had heard about.

And all the time, between dates and meetings and new friends, I kept thinking about that book I wanted to start, and how I would have to rethink it and change it. In my luggage, along with my outline of it, was that page I had torn out from Time. Why I had taken it with me across an entire continent, I had no idea. It was as if it had become part of me, and had to go wherever the rest of me went.

And then came that particular evening in March that I could later think of as the night I got my idea for *Gentleman's Agreement.*

I was alone. I had left the good easyness with the Whedons and moved to the luxury of the Beverly Wilshire. I'd had room service send up dinner and then had gone out alone to a movie. I remember a sense of desolation as I returned to my fancy hotel room, a longing *not* to be in the film capital to interview movie moguls about originals, but at home writing a book I cared about.

Maybe, I suddenly thought, I should forget all about a nation being happy during a war, and limit myself to "the long war" against bigotry and prejudice. Then Congress and "the little kike" could really be a pivot for the whole plot.

Carroll and John Whedon had been as appalled as I by the story in Time. If they were Jewish could they have been any more alarmed about what was happening in our own country, while we were so busily fighting the Nazis?

A country never knows what's happening to it.

The words sounded in my mind as if I had spoken them aloud. They stood there, rigid, like red bricks in a wall suddenly erected to immobilize me. How antisemitic *was* this country, this America, these United States? Not just among the outright bigots like Congressman Rankin, Senator Bilbo, the white supremacist and Father Coughlin on the radio with his following of millions for his nightly hate talks, but other people, people who'd never call anybody a kike, people who said they loathed prejudice?

Suppose I started with that question in my book? And maybe my hero should be something more usual than a civil liberties lawyer? I sent in my annual ten dollars to the ACLU but I didn't know enough about how they operated, what one of their lawyers could or would do. I didn't know enough about the law itself. What I did know was writing.

Suppose he was a newspaper man, a reporter, a novelist. Phil Somebody, a simple name, nothing fancy. Suppose he had been in the war, a prisoner of war, just returning at last. There had been newspaper stories recently of the first return of POWs on the S.S. *Gripsholme*, sailing out of Lisbon. He could be one of them.

As such he wouldn't have seen any American newspapers or magazines for two years, not even permitted to see the armed services' papers, *Stars and Stripes* or *Yank*. He's really been out of touch with America—and now on the ship, he finds that old copy of Time.

He's as shocked as I was, as the Whedons were, and determines to do something about it, write something about it. Like the Whedons, he's not Jewish. I'm not sure why it seemed so clear to me from the start that he be not Jewish, though I think it might be first cousin to my instinct, after Lindbergh's antisemitic speech at that rally, to address "Choice—for Gentiles" not to America's few million Jews, but to the vast majority who were not Jews.

But if he was not Jewish, the research he'd have to do for whatever he was going to write would have to include not only what he himself knew or felt about antisemitism, but also what people who really were Jewish knew or felt about it.

Hard research that, elusive but essential. How to do it?

That's when I remembered an old joke I had heard years before, a joke about Michael Arlen, the fashionable British author of *The Green Hat*, a best-selling novel of the twenties.

It will forever seem strange to me that anyone so extraneous to my life as Michael Arlen should ever have played any part in it as a writer. But so unpredictable are the ways of an author's mind, so unforeseeable its ability to collect material, like a municipal worker in a park with his steel point at the end of a long stick, stabbing up old leaves, dead flowers, bits of paper, gum wrappers, cigarette butts—so unpredictable that I suppose I should not even be surprised at this singular connection between me and Michael Arlen and *Gentleman's Agreement*.

I had unexpectedly met him the night before, when Shirley Collier asked me to Romanoff's to meet Arthur Freed and his wife for cocktails. Freed had just produced *Meet Me in St. Louis* for Metro-Goldwyn-Mayer, and would go on to produce a string of smash musical films like *Easter Parade*, *On the Town*, and many more. (My log says, "Send Kleenex to Freeds," and lists their home address. In wartime, even among the great of Beverly Hills, Kleenex was an unattainable luxury, but I could still get some sent out from New York.)

Meeting Mr. Arlen reminded me of one of the few "literary" arguments I'd ever had with my father. I was still living in Jamaica when *The Green Hat* came out, and was so smitten with it that I urged my parents to read it and see how great it was. They looked skeptical and I got off some younger-generation sarcasm about people who thought nobody but the Russians had ever written real literature.

To my surprise, my father took it and said he would read it. A week passed and he handed it back to me, nodding, but saying nothing.

"What did you think?" He didn't answer. "Did you read it?"

Again he nodded and said nothing. *The Reader's Encyclopedia* says of the book, ". . . its popularity was largely due to the way . . . it captured the licentious, disillusioned spirit of the time. With a self-sacrificing heroine and a husband who kills himself on his wedding night because he has syphilis, the novel is a sentimental account of sexual license among the wealthy."

"Did you like it?" I insisted into my father's silence.

Almost apologetically, he said, "I still prefer Dostoevsky."

That little exchange with my father later became a favorite anecdote of mine, a merry little joke at my expense. And now, two decades later sitting next to Mr. Arlen, I had to keep my anecdote to myself.

I didn't really take to him anyhow; there seemed something too British upper-class about the way he talked, and shreds of an ancient joke about him came back to me, but I couldn't get hold of it.

Michael Arlen was the pseudonym he wrote under; he was born Dikran Kuyumjian, and never made any secret of it, though only a few people in the publishing world and the press even knew about it, not his millions of readers. The joke was about that, but the shreds of it couldn't be grasped and I forgot it.

But the retrieval system in my mind must have gone on clicking away in search of it while I slept and during all the interviews I had the next day, for after that dinner alone and the movie alone, while I was feeling a bit disconsolate in my hotel room, wondering if I should call my kids, thinking of my POW on the *Gripsholme*, and the tough research he would have to do, suddenly the shreds of that lost joke became whole, and I was back with Mr. Arlen.

Somebody in London, supposedly, had once said to him, "You sound so British, Mr. Arlen. Is it true that you really are Armenian?"

"Would anybody *say* he was Armenian," came the instant reply, "if he wasn't Armenian?"

Would anybody say he was Jewish if he wasn't Jewish?

Even now, as I sit here on a snow-quieted winter afternoon nearly forty years later, a thin ghost of that moment's sudden charge runs along my nerves, and prickles my skin.

It was the thread I needed, the story line to run through the entire book, a thin, tenuous thread, but strong enough to let me hang a dozen episodes from it. Phil would just say he was Jewish and sit back and see what changed in his life.

And I would write it down. I went to my portable typewriter

that I'd lugged with me from home. In those days, the scratch paper I used for first draft was a bright yellow, almost orange, and I rolled in a sheet.

That very sheet is pasted in my pressbook. The first line, deleted by slash marks, is perfectly readable.

~~Longing plunged through him, as abrupt as anger!~~

"But, Christ, Tom, there's got to be some way of beating it."

"Keep off it, Phil. You'll ruin yourself on it. It's an old story anyway. You can't—how the hell do you think you can change it?"

"*This* isn't old." He slapped the page of the magazine. "And not one person to stand up and cry 'shame'! That's not old either. Not at home, it isn't old, Tom." He pointed to the final lines. "It says at the end, they applauded him."

Suddenly longing for home seized him, as abrupt and hot as rage. He left the stateroom and went outside to the March gale, tossing the small white *Gripsholme.*

I stopped writing and began to pace about the room. A springing sureness kept leaping through me. I had my next book.

So if I were given to tidy little answers to complex questions, I could have tossed out one neat declarative sentence to that eternal, "How did you get the idea for it?"

"Well, I suddenly remembered an old joke about Michael Arlen—"

But nothing could ever let me be so simplistic. Until this very day, there are very few people in this world to whom I have ever even told the story.

For to do so would have been to wipe out all my life before that accidental encounter at Romanoff's.

What of the little seven-year-old girl in Jamaica, hearing that neighbor yelling at my mother, "Jews, what's more, Russian Jews, ZAMETSKI"—?

What of the adolescent getting her first summer job as Laura Z. Keane, because "the manager was so nice, I couldn't tell him *Zametkin*"?

What of that college girl in Baby Greek asking Professor Jones, "Sir, if we're supposed to be able to pronounce names like Clytemnestra and Aeschylus and Iphigenia, don't you think you could say Zametkin? It's quite easy."

And what of the girl who heard about Professor Lane Cooper and his Phi Beta Kappa key, and the young wife at the smart dinner table, saying, "Some of my best friends are Jews too, including my mother and father," and the writer of that brief sketch in the New Yorker about the perfect butler named Cohen? What of that story about little Otto Rosenberg Barrett?

And what of all my recent convolutions about a civil liberties lawyer fighting "the long war" against prejudice and bigotry?

And the woman of forty-three who carried that page torn out of Time all the way from one coastline to the other, as if it had forever lodged itself in her life?

No, as long ago as that night of March 9, 1944, I knew that it takes more than any one brittle anecdote to make a book. In my log, also pasted into my pressbook, down at the bottom, in ink, it says, "Got a possible book idea!" and the exclamation point instead of the question mark tells me I was more sure of myself than usual.

Inevitably, I woke up the next morning filled with doubts. Nobody would believe it; it was a good idea but not a whole novel. I couldn't have one man just writing a book. I'd have to think about it some more.

In any case, my days were filled with interviews. I was already having daily meetings with movie producers, script writers, personnel people, old friends from New York who might know of somebody trying to write an original and arrange a date so I could ask a few pertinent questions.

I saw Arthur Schwartz at Warner Brothers, and Bill Dozier at Paramount, Bill Fadiman of Metro-Goldwyn-Mayer—once I had five separate interviews on the same day, two of them at MGM. "Job looks hopeful," says my log. By that time, I had begun to think, If I can't get anywhere about finding out about writing originals, I might even take a script-writing job for a while, and try to pick it up that way.

And at last, exactly one month after I'd left home, I was offered a job at MGM, a full-time job at $600 a week.

Everybody who has ever landed a writing job in Hollywood has at least one ludicrous story to tell about it, and that $600 gave me mine. Before telling me of it, Bert Allenberg swore me to secrecy about what I would be paid.

"We don't handle clients that low down on the scale," he said pointedly. "If it got around, it could hurt us."

Six hundred a week to learn the business—$30,000 a year—and they were ashamed! I solemnly promised, shoving words like *cheap, phony, vulgar* back down my throat. What I didn't shove down my throat was a big strong NO! at Bert's next piece of good news.

I was to have a seven-year contract, on a sliding scale. My first raise, after only ten weeks, would be to $750, then to $900. In my second year my salary would go to $1,100 a week; in the third, $1,500; in the fourth $1,750 and then $2,000 thereafter. I would have to work forty weeks each year.

"No, never," I said. "I'll never sign it." (Eighty thousand for forty weeks—my inflation expert tells me that today that would mean about $400,000 a year. With a three month vacation, yet.)

Bert looked at me, not believing me. "Laura, you have to have a contract."

"A seven-year contract? Never. I never said one word about a contract."

"You said you *would* consider a job—you can't let me down, now that I got this for you."

I was mute, shaking my head from side to side. By now he was letting himself sound fed up. "The contract is just so no other studio can hire you away from them, if it works out."

"You mean I could quit if I wanted to, and go home?"

"They can't sue you if you do quit." He was so sure nobody would ever up and leave. I was so sure I'd be the one to do just that. But $600 a week! I'd been living in hotels, eating out, forever hailing a cab—there was no Hertz rent-a-car in those days, nor Avis nor anybody. My borrowed money was not just dribbling away but avalanching away. I reached for a memo pad on his desk.

"It is temporary, remember, I'm telling you now." I underlined temporary, signed my full name and handed it back to

334

him. Then I agreed to the contract and left, half-elated, half-depressed.

Two mornings later, I entered the vast white elongated MGM building, which vaguely reminded me of my beloved Goldwyn Smith Hall up at Ithaca, the fine arts building. My producer, i.e., my boss, was one Leon Gordon. I was given a pleasant office and a novel to render into a treatment. I made no note in my log of its name or subject matter, and haven't the vaguest memory of what it was about.

But I know I set to with a will and after the third day turned in about ten pages to a secretary in the pool that was used by beginners and lowly people like me who had no secretaries of their own. In a couple of hours she returned them and gave me a startling piece of advice.

"Don't write so fast," she said. "This much copy they expect after a whole month, not after three days. They'll think it's not any good."

That night I went back to my orange sheets, this time in pencil.

> As abrupt as anger, the longing for home plunged through him.

The opening lines were the same, but after Rankin and Congress it changed.

> "The Jews'll survive," Bill said. "We're survivors, kid. Nice of you to want to fight for us."
> "I don't want to fight for the Jews," Phil said. "I'm not thinking of the Jews. I'm thinking of America. Go on, laugh."
> There was no laugh.

This time I didn't stop writing until I had filled three whole pages. Like Eugene O'Neill, I found it taking longer, going further.

And of course every time I thought about it in the days to come, or wrote anything down, it kept changing. Day by day, driving to the studio, going to the beach, taking a bath, I would find new bits and pieces coming at me, bright leaves drifting from some unknown tree.

I would want a love affair in the novel, a love affair where ideas counted as much as attraction, so Phil couldn't be married. But I also wanted children in this story, with scenes about a kid who feels left out because he's Jewish, so I'd make Phil a widower, with a child or two. I'd do this, I'd do that—,

Only at the MGM studio, facing my unfinished treatment, did my mind clear itself completely of Phil and my novel. Each day's work, written and then rewritten as my work always had to be, ended up by giving me a good feeling that it was going well. In my infrequent meetings with Mr. Gordon, after I had sent in another section of the script, I could tell that he was pleased; he would make a suggestion here and there, ask me to try a slight switching of scenes, but he was ready with encouraging words and even with open praise.

And then, after four weeks, as April was drawing to a close, they dropped that particular project, and despite my seven-year contract, and without one day's warning, I was fired.

SEVENTEEN

MY INSOMNIA POINT, I soon discovered, was minus $11,000. Up to the time I was fired by MGM, I had never had nightmares because of money troubles, but in every life-explosion, there has to be a flash point, and minus $11,000 proved to be mine.

I wasn't there quite yet, but I knew I soon would be, and when I was, I began to wake with a start, a twist of anxiety close to fear inside me; I began to have dreams of destruction, my apartment in disarray, furniture wrecked, pillows torn, curtains ripped.

Being fired had no part in the insomnia—*that* just made me mad. I was bewildered by the suddenness of it, I felt insulted, but mostly I was sore. No producer at MGM was going to send me back home like the proverbial little starlet who didn't get herself discovered at Schwab's drugstore on Sunset Boulevard.

I phoned Bert Allenberg and told him I would stay right there, and would he find me another job? With *no* contract this time, not for seven years or any years. And while I waited, I would write an original all on my own.

I wrote the headmaster of Collegiate School for Boys, where Mike went, asking if he might leave a bit early and return a bit late next fall. I began to search for some small house near the beach where the kids and Rosie and I could live all summer. I even began to hunt for a used car, to escape the incessant taxis, and to meet our needs once we were living away from Beverly Hills.

There was a good deal of fantasy in all this, for California's housing shortage was at crisis level, decent used cars were snapped up, and railroad or airplane tickets were, by some unwritten system of rationing, restricted to the powerful and the military.

But movies were considered "essential to the war effort," on behalf of the men at the front or at camps everywhere, and there was a close friend of Shirley Collier's in New York who could get you anything—tickets for sold-out shows, your regular brand of cigarettes instead of wartime imitations called "Wings" or "Victory," even a drawing room for three on the Chief. He was not a black marketeer, but head of the large press that printed books for S & S and other publishers. So I asked Shirley to get his help—she and I had become good friends.

Could I do an original by myself? Had I already learned a sufficient amount about what Hollywood minds wanted? For the first time in years, I thought of that play I had written before I was married, *The Muttering Wind*, which might have been produced fifteen years ago by the Theater Arts Club in London, if I hadn't cabled that stupid request that they hold their offer open while I wrote a new and better ending.

Now I made myself think of my play in movie terms: a husband and wife in an agonizing experiment to restore to normal life the wife's brain-damaged first husband.

Phrased this way in studio lingo, it sent a sharp embarrassment through me. Written as a serious play, about two intelligent people flouting so-called morality, it had been something more than a glib little triangle.

But now I would do it as a movie and let it become what it would become. There it was, lying abandoned in my desk at home, right at hand as a possible plot, when I needed a possible plot in a hurry. What's more, a new title sprang to mind, *Three-some*, a movie title if ever there was one.

I called Rose in New York, told her just where to find it, asked her to mail it special delivery and told her of my new

338

plans. Then I asked Mike and Chris how they'd like to come on out to California and live on a beach for the whole summer.

I really was committed. As I hung up I thought of money. Even with the rest of my loan from Ira, and what I had saved from my four MGM paychecks, minus commission, I would be in an impossible bind in the jobless weeks ahead. The first and last month's rent for that house on the beach, the down payment on the used car, the railroad fares from New York, all our living expenses until I was on salary again—

I would have to make another loan. Another $2,000?

Should I telephone Ira, or write to him? I never doubted that he would lend it to me as eagerly as he had done the first time.

I reached for a pad and pencil and added up figures: the old $5,000 from the Schermans, plus whatever interest by now, the old $550 to Dr. Damon for Chris and Harkness, the older $1,000 to Bergdorf Goodman, the first $2,000 from Ira and now $2,000 more.

Eleven thousand in debt! That was my first night of acute insomnia, and it taught me something that was to stand me in good stead forever after. If I *had* to go into debt, okay, I had to, but I'd better always stay below that $11,000 mark.

Ira's check arrived, and so did the special delivery of my old play. But two assignments marked RUSH also did, from the Writers War Board in New York. By now any requests from the Writers War Board were virtually command performances, not to be evaded or delayed by pleas of looking for a job or trying to write an original.

Not that I wanted to evade or delay. Off on the coast, away from all the people I knew best, I had begun to feel an uneasy need to justify myself for not working more directly in the war effort. Actually, a year before, I had even made several tries at getting some sort of factory job in a war industry, once enlisting Allen Grover's help at arranging a job interview, and once really being interviewed at the Curtiss–Wright Airplane Division in Passaic, New Jersey. But alas, they could see I was not exactly a Rosie-the-Riveter type, and I had to retreat to doing "written war work."

Now the first of my two assignments was a difficult seven-page piece called "Double–Talk Politics," to become a feature article in liberal newspapers. My log gives me only the title and I can't remember its contents.

The second was shorter, and closer to me, for it was on my old familiar territory of helping refugees escape Europe.

It seems inconceivable now that as late as May 1944, the world at large still had only a limited conception of how far Hitler's "final solution" had gone or would go. The word holocaust had not even come into general use; everybody knew there were Nazi concentration camps, with brutal conditions, inhumane suffering, torture, but the full truth of the ovens and gas chambers of Auschwitz and Treblinka still remained hidden.

And the realization that was to arise so sharply in the years ahead, the bitter questions about why Roosevelt and Churchill had been so remiss or reluctant about ordering bombings that could have wiped out those gas chambers and concentration camps—all that was still lying quiescent in the minds even of most experts.

But it was an expert group that my second assignment was to deal with. It was known as Eleanor Roosevelt's Emergency Rescue Committee, though it had been started by others, and though in the past it had been very effective at arranging exits from Germany, Italy and occupied France, particularly for scientists, artists, political figures, it had grown less active in the mounting pressures of war conditions.

It was my job to write a letter to the New Republic about this and about the new conflicts over visa policy in general. It was hard for me to do without access to all my documentary material piled up in my files back home in New York, but somehow I met my assignment and its RUSH deadline.

And then at long last I could begin writing that treatment of *The Muttering Wind*, now firmly yclept *Threesome*. Interviews at studios began again, at a slower pace, since I had already been to just about every studio there was, but in between the interviews I kept going on the treatment.

Some of my fantasy about the summer was being nibbled away by events; I found no car, I found no house, I met politeness at most interviews but no offers. In Hollywood, where you're only as good as your last picture, I wondered how good a prospect I could seem, now that I'd been fired. I began to think back to that day when I had been half-elated and half-depressed at getting my $600 a week job; now I would hear some more "maybe" or "possible" from Bert Allenberg and feel only depressed. Even *Threesome* proved mulish and balky—I couldn't make the transition from the serious tone of my play to one more befitting a movie.

Everything that could distract me from any solid work, or even solid thought about what I was so sure would be my second novel, kept piling up to hold me back from it, road block after road block, checkpoint after checkpoint. It was not a merry month of May for me.

And then, all in a tumble, everything good began to happen. Just a week before May ended, I did find a house, an ugly boxy shack right on the beach, between Santa Monica and Malibu, near the entrance to Topanga Canyon. Its small living room was stuffed with cheap furniture and marred by plush drapes of a faded purple; it had two tiny bedrooms, a bath and a crowded kitchen; it was odd-looking even from the outside, for it was perched up on a stiltlike foundation of white clapboarding, separated one plank from the other by two inches of air, for ventilation.

But it was available and sixty-five dollars a month. I grabbed it. Two days later Rosie and the boys started from New York. The very day they left I located a car I could afford, an old Mercury, and I grabbed that too. Then I went off to buy cowboy hats and cowboy boots for the kids.

Having Mike and Chris again gave me wholeness again. I had been sending them postcards and presents all along, telephoning about once a week but this separation had grown to be twelve weeks long. It was almost with joy that I heard Rosie's request, on the very morning of their arrival, for a seven-day leave to go up to San Francisco.

Not too long before I had left for the coast, she had married a young college instructor in elocution, I think, who had recently enlisted or been drafted. Now he was up in San Francisco at an army base, due to be shipped to the South Pacific any day. As

341

the boys and I saw her off at the railroad station that same afternoon, I was glad I had no studio job and didn't have to ask her to wait till I found a substitute.

Then followed seven days and nights that were unlike any other seven in my entire writing life. The kids woke up at six, and in that tiny house, my sleep was over too. I dressed Chris, got our breakfast, washed dishes, made beds, spent the entire day with them, on the sand, in the ocean, taking them along when I shopped for food, doing some laundry, playing their games, reading stories to them and getting them ready for bed.

Chris had been a handful as a baby; in a tantrum he would bang his head on the floor until a purple welt stood out on his forehead; now as a toddler, the tantrums were fewer but he was still the "no I won't" kid.

During the last hour or two of the day, I was beginning to fold, blessing the moment when their bedtime came at last and they fell into the healthy exhausted sleep of childhood.

For me, though, that was a healthy exhausted signal to start my day's work on *Threesome*. At last it had begun to be less mulish; at last the opening scenes seemed right. I began to have a wild larky certainty that it would sell, and sell quickly. Perhaps in my brief tenure at MGM I *had* learned a lot about how you write for studios.

In my log, June 6 says, "Rose is back." And down across the whole bottom of the page, "D day—woke Mike."

He was only seven and a half, but to him it seemed that we had been at war during his entire life. He was forever hearing war news on the radio, hearing me and my friends talk about it, reading newspaper headlines himself about battles and bombings and the incessant count of the wounded and dead.

The landings at Omaha Beach in Normandy took place during the morning hours, but California was eight hours behind France, and so, for us it was the middle of the night when the first word came. I was the only one awake, and suddenly on the radio they were announcing the news and playing "The Star-Spangled Banner," and like a fool, I wept, and wanted my small son to be in on that moment with me, perhaps to remember some fragment of it all his life.

Chris was only two and a half, and he slept on, but I woke

Rosie too, and she heard it with us, and after Mike went back to bed, she and I stayed on for the next hours of communiqués from London, New York, Washington. She was thinking of her husband off in the South Pacific hearing the news, and I thought of Tom Mount, also out there somewhere, and of Dr. Gosselin and everybody else I knew caught up in the war.

And, unbelievably, five days later, I had a cable from Tom himself, returning from the Pacific and reassigned, soon to arrive at Camp Miramar at San Diego and could I meet him there?

Tom and Andrée and I were still friends though we had been seeing less of each other in recent years. I had sent galleys of *The Trespassers* to Tom, and he had written me warmly about it, but life and circumstance had been pulling us apart, year by year. This sudden cabled request that I meet him on his return stirred some old unchanged love in me for this difficult Tom Mount, now nearing fifty, and on the appointed day I drove to San Diego.

He was now Major Mount, fit and slim and tanned, no gray in his still-thick hair, and I remember that every time he was saluted by one of the men or a fellow officer, and snapped a salute in return, I thought how being an officer suited him, filling in the ego-emptiness there must have been in all those years of writing westerns under pseudonyms, instead of what he had dreamed of when he was young.

I stayed overnight—by myself, in quarters set aside for visitors—and the next day we drove across the Mexican border to spend the day at Tijuana and Agua Caliente, not far from San Diego. It was as if we were both young again, without a responsibility or care in the world; we talked of the night-flying he had done out there in the Pacific, not combat flying, but for his own rest and recreation—the old mania for airplanes had never left him. We talked of the good and bad reviews I'd had for *The Trespassers* and why I was in Hollywood and of marriages and divorces. I sensed some strain in him about Andrée.

By the time we got back to Camp Miramar, late that afternoon, and dined and said good-bye, I felt as if I'd had my first vacation since coming to the coast. I drove home to the beach, eager to work again on *Threesome*. With Rose there, I could give full time to it, and soon I was sending most of it off to a typist—

a dime a page and a penny extra for each carbon. (There were no Xerox machines as yet!) I was feeling more confident with each completed scene. No one could say, "But it won't play."

And the very next day I had a job interview with Virginia Van Upp at Columbia Pictures. A woman producer? That was a rarity indeed then, but she had had some major successes, like *Cover Girl*, starring the young Rita Hayworth, and though I'd been told she was temperamental and demanding, I liked her.

A week later I was hired. This time Bert Allenberg could nearly hold his agently head up: I was to get $750 a week. With no contract.

I started the following Monday, but at night I kept on with the final scenes of *Threesome*.

And in the middle of July it sold for $10,000. My own studio bought it, and even assigned me to write the screenplay.

The news sent me into a spin of joy. I had saved about $2,000 from my various paychecks out there and I could pay off all my debts in one day! All $11,000 in one shot.

And that, crazily enough, is exactly what I did, leaving me with a balance of about $300. My log for August 13 tells it all:

Got check today
& paid all debts

Schermans	$5,400
Ira	4,000
Bergdorf	1,050
Dr. Damon	550
	$11,000

Used 9000 from *Threesome*
& 2000 from Col. salaries

I'm free again!!!

The covering letters I sent out with the four checks must have been a bit manic, I'm afraid, though I remember only the way I addressed Bergdorf Goodman. "Darling Bergdorf," I wrote, not caring what the credit manager might make of that.

What everybody else made of my surprise move and my

obvious euphoria gave me some further spins of joy—all but one reply. Harry Scherman wrote that he "felt like Sentimental Tommy," and that the next time I needed a loan, I could just send him a postcard saying so. Bernardine scolded me for being quixotic in not waiting to find out what my taxes would be on this windfall, but that it was worth it in spades. I had an almost loving reply from Dr. Damon, and a not quite institutionalized one from Bergdorf Goodman. Each letter lifted me even higher.

But not the one I got from Ira. Dear Ira was apparently irate, play on words or no. A tone of outrage sounded in every line. I could scarcely make out why. As I recall it, he was trying to tell me that he had meant to be of real help, and here I was, cutting that good feeling short, as if I begrudged it and couldn't wait to end it. It was as if he were demanding an apology for what I had done.

I really tried to understand what had upset him. We had never discussed when he could expect repayment, and certainly he hadn't expected it so soon, especially of his second loan. But I knew there were more cogent reasons, not to be spoken aloud. Feeling me depending on him, I guessed, must have propped up his old Victorian sense of the way things should be between a man and a woman, and now, in one rude stroke, I had yanked those comfortable props out from under.

Poor Ira.

But my free-of-debt elation went right on, and on the fifth night after sending off those four checks, I began a real page 1 of the book about Phil and antisemitism in America.

But by now I was haunted by one kind of doubt I had not had before, unlike any author's usual doubts about how to start a new piece of work, whether to plunge right in or set the background first, what to name the characters, what they looked like, all the usual uncertainties of beginning.

This new doubt was not about technique at all. Could I, in good conscience, while we were at war, accuse America of harboring antisemitism and largely ignoring it, as Germany for so long had done? Was I not bound to wait until the war was at last over?

But when would that be? Another six months? Another year? All the guesses, from the first cruel one, "out of the trenches by Christmas," had all proved false. Maybe two years, maybe more?

The moment this question of harm-in-wartime posed itself, a kind of paralysis struck me. I would write and stop, write and tear up. I can see now, with some embarrassment, that it was pretty neurotic to feel so overburdened by conscience, but at the time the burden seemed so real to me, it was almost palpable.

And in the middle of August I took a step I had never before taken on anything I wanted to write—and was never again to take, not even once again.

I decided to seek some advance opinions about this book I planned, not only Dick Simon's opinion, as if this were merely a publisher's problem, but also the opinion of some of my friends with far more political instinct than Dick had ever shown me.

I was not asking them to judge my plot or story, whether it was good or bad, but only the *timing* of such a book at such a time. I wrote a nine-page outline, not a scene-by-scene synopsis which I could never do, except for a movie treatment where everything is contrived and neatly fitted, but a sort of thematic statement of what my book might be. I also wrote what might become the first two pages of chapter 1, to orient their minds a bit to the general tone of the book, before they began the outline.

The first line of page 1 had become inevitable. "Abrupt as anger, depression plunged through him."

By now my Phil had changed once more. He was no POW on the *Gripsholme*. He was a fiction editor in a publishing house, and author of two light historical novels, neither of them any great success. He is determined that his next book would not be another historical novel, an escape into the past, about colonial America or Civil War America, but about America today. And then he gets his idea and tells it to a girl he has just met.

"I'll just say I'm Jewish—"

"Jewish? But you're *not*, are you?" Instantly she added, "It wouldn't make any difference, of course."

But something had come across her eyes. Phil saw it, the instant, the unnameable thing. God, it *would* make a difference.

Here, right now, with liberal Kathy, he had stumbled into his first experience in his new role.

First of all I wrote to Dick. I had told him once or twice about "the idea I got in March," had said it was not about nation-happy-at-war, but had never given him any clue about the nature of the new idea, though I had admitted that it was becoming obsessive.

> I have repeatedly tried to forget it—or keep it for my third novel—but in all these months nothing else I think up seems half as important. That's why I say it's obsessive.
>
> I will wait eagerly to know how you feel about this— and if you show it to anybody else, I'd be so grateful for their reactions. I'll send it to a couple of people myself, I think.
>
> And I want to say something right out right now. If you think I should write it, but don't feel you want to publish it... I'll understand and never let it be a personal matter. Only when you read the attached will you know why I even bother to put in this strange paragraph.

I wrote to Norman Cousins, the young editor of the Saturday Review. The year before he had invited four first-timers to write about what they had learned from writing their first novels— Betty Smith of *A Tree Grows in Brooklyn* was one of us four— and he and I had quickly become friends, in magazine matters, political matters and weekly poker games, of which he soon became a regular member.

> If you think I should not—I may go ahead anyway, (an obsession is an obsession) but it would help me...

Then I sent outline and letter to Dorothy Thompson up at Twin Farms, Vermont. Two years earlier she had married Maxim Kopf, a little-known painter, Austrian by birth, and though life and circumstance were pulling us apart, as with the Mounts and me, I was still invited to many a politics-filled party at the house Dorothy had bought in Turtle Bay, the lovely enclave on East Forty-eighth Street in the city.

This is the damndest request and I feel some trepidation about making it...because you are so busy always...but I am in a good deal of conflict...many people would tell me to lay off...are they right? Would you tell me openly what you feel about this?

With Harry and Bernardine Scherman, I let myself go a little more personally, feeling that I didn't have to be, with either of them, so precise about my motive in checking out only the *timing* of this book. With them I could also be more practical.

And now, before I lose my nerve....this obsessive idea for a novel that would never sell to the movies, never sell to any magazine, and most likely never sell to the public. I am sending this to you before I even know whether Dick will even want to publish it.

Maybe I ought to drop this cold, be practical, try to write a book I believe in, that *might* sell to the movies, so I wouldn't have to come back here periodically to earn money to write books on.

Oh, goddamn it, why did *I* have to dream this idea up, instead of some fine rich author?

The first reponse from anybody was a telegram by fast wire. It was from Norman Cousins.

SINCERELY THRILLED WONDERFUL IDEA
SHARE YOUR OBSESSION TO SEE IT DONE

That wire was a good omen, I was positive, of the letters I had to wait for. The summer was ending—it was nearly Labor Day; people would be going off for the long weekend, and might have to put off thinking about my outline, and surely, about replies.

But I was wrong. All the letters came in a bunch, all dated late August or September 1, before the end-of-summer week-end. Each of them began with some variation of the stout affirmation: Writers should write what they're impelled to write.

Dorothy Thompson's began with that and then went on for two and a half single-spaced pages.

348

So, with the above qualification, let me say that although the concept is daring and ingenious and suggestive, it does... trouble me.

My first objection to it—and it's tentative and uncertain—is a political one. I am not sure that the book would not do more harm than good. I have come to the conclusion... that anti-antisemitism campaigns are very dubious means to overcome intolerance. They are (or may be, so it seems to me,) advertising campaigns for antisemitism.

Antisemitism will never be halted in America because the majority of people like Jews. They don't. They like individual Jews, whom they exempt... from their antipathy toward the race as a whole...

It seems to me that the position of the Jew in a predominantly un-Jewish society produces mutual neuroses and uneasinesses...

In fact your novel, if it were not a political tract... would be fascinating, but—forgive me—it would take a Dostoevsky to write it. For it would be a peculiar psychological case and study, typical of neither Jew nor Christian.

She ended with another exhortation about writers writing whatever they wanted to write, and her letter fascinated me. My main emotion, as I recall it, was surprise at the vigor with which she had said that the majority of Americans would never like Jews, though they might exempt a favored one here and there. The pet Jew? I do definitely remember that I was disappointed that she had skipped over the whole question of the war, and its possible demands on citizens not to choose wartime as the perfect time to accuse our country of anything like anti-semitism.

A small antidote came in a brief letter from Norman, the follow-up to his telegram.

A fresh and vigorous new twist... drop whatever you are doing, in order to get on with it.

Two letters from the Schermans came in the next mail. They had talked out the whole thing several times, the outline, the opening pages, my obvious misgivings. It was a very penetrating approach, wrote Harry.

349

...for the reader, of "seeing" antisemitism in its personal, and therefore, social aspects. There couldn't be a better one, and I can see how the idea possesses you...

You've picked yourself an exceptionally difficult theme...my first thought was, "what an excellent long short story or short novel." I myself see it as the latter...

But don't get the impression that I underrate it. It's really a big conception.

And from Bernardine, very much the same. She also thought I should try it in some short form.

I am afraid the reader would get worn down by the reiteration of one point; it is bound to be one point, no matter how you disguise it in incident. You *should* do it though! It could be so dramatic and important.

Richard Sterba unequivocally urged me on. "I recognize very well the difficulties...but it is worth every effort...though it needs extreme tact and delicacy..."

And then came two letters from Simon & Schuster. The first was from Lee Wright, who was to be my new editor for my next book, despite the fact that she was primarily an editor of mystery stories and crime novels. We had become good friends, frequent bridge players, though she and her husband, Jack Bassett, knew fifty times more about bridge than I did. She had gone all out for *The Trespassers*, and I had come to realize that though Dick was an inspired publisher and promoter of books, his basic interest was not in the long-drawn-out and delicate task of editing them through all the months of their life in manuscript form. Lee's letter included some points about writing in general: "I don't think any woman writer should attempt to make a man her central character." But generalities aside, her whole reply was on a rueful note of pained honesty.

I don't think you have the necessary objectivity to handle this thing. You are writing about a man who pretends to be a Jew in order to find out what they go through. But you who are writing this book are a Jew. How can you put yourself in his place?

There are generations of philosophic submission in your blood and bones. You were born with an instinctive acceptance of a special place in the world. He would be hurt in a very different way than a Jew would be hurt, because he would be both the victim and the persecutor.

Philosophic submission? I don't remember in what terms I balked at that concept on my first reading of the letter, but balk I most certainly did, before I even went on to the next paragraph. My agnostic father and mother—was it from them that I inherited this submission in my blood and bones? That special place in the world—had I ever been docile enough to fit into it? I read on:

I am afraid of this for you. You will put your heart and guts into it, and you won't get what you want. You will be accused of artificiality and special pleading, and you may do more harm than good. It is a great theme, but I think it has to be written by your hero, a liberal Christian man.

Dick's letter was not as long, nor as rueful. He said that he could see why the idea had held me for so long, said that a lot of people felt they ought to be doing something about anti-semitism, and that they felt helpless.

The problem is not to do something...but to do something effective. I think that if you write this book...readers will not believe that a gentile would pose as a Jew.

This is the premise of the book...if it is not accepted, the good intentions you have...will come to naught. It will be neither good propaganda nor a successful novel...

I think that this book, if you proceed with it, will turn into a rather heartbreaking experience for you no matter who publishes it.

No matter who publishes it. Was he telling me it might well be that he himself would not? I ordered myself, I remember, not to give in to my old failing of being over-sensitive, too easily hurt, too quickly anxious. After all, I myself had elected to seek opinions *in advance*, and now that I was getting something less than unanimity, I'd damn well better not cave in.

I doubt very much whether letters like Dorothy Thompson's and Lee Wright's and Dick Simon's could be written today. The world has come a long distance from the dark ages of 1944, when good people like them could think in so fearful an idiom.

Nor can I think without dismay of myself back there, paying such careful heed to what they wrote, pondering long and hard over each letter. But ponder I did, before I felt ready to answer anybody.

And one letter came to me not from somebody far away, to whom I had written, but from Carroll Whedon, whom I saw three times a week, and with whom I had talked everything out. For some reason she suddenly felt impelled to put in writing what she had been saying from the start, and even a brief bit of it now shows me why we remained lifelong friends.

> I think the book better be written—and the sooner the better—not to highlight the plight of the Jew...but...the even more appalling plight of the non-Jew...
>
> It is we who are driving many American Jews back into a spiritual ghetto...[with] this spineless acceptance of ugliness, this shrug-it-off attitude that says..."AWFUL, but after all, old girl, it's always been with us."

My first letter, after all the pondering, went to Dorothy Thompson.

> Let me jump ahead...and say I've decided only not to decide for a while...perhaps one fine day I'll find that my unconscious mind...has made the final decision. Then I'll either do it, reject it forever, or put it off for my third novel. But until I myself am clearer about the possible harm (not whether it would "do any good" which seems less important to me) I feel I must wait for greater clarity.
>
> ...But I do wonder whether the fear of "advertising anti-semitism" isn't responsible for a concurring silence about it....
>
> ...To answer your more personal objection, the artistic one...that only a Dostoevsky could do it *full* justice. Novelists would never write novels at all if they had to be sure they could do what a genius could do....

> ...I think you'd be damn interested to know that of the
> six or eight people I talked to or wrote to about this, the
> *general* reaction is to go ahead from Christians, and not go
> ahead from Jews.

In all my answers I repeated some of the phrases I had used
to Dorothy, the way you do when you are on vacation, sending
postcards to people who won't be seeing each other. But apart
from the repetition, each of my answers went directly to the
particular points raised by each person, and to each I gave a
rapid summary of what the others had said. To Norman Cousins, I wrote briefly—I had already thanked him for his wire and
note.

> I wish I had the right to send you copies of their let-
> ters...but I do not feel that I can make a sort of public
> forum of what they feel or say...
>
> I am not very happy to be writing this...I wish I could
> say, I'm going ahead and the hell with so-and-so's opinion.
> But I chose that so-and-so as a person who also hates anti-
> semitism...and if that so-and-so feels...this is bound to
> have bad repercussions...I surely must at least stop and
> think some more.
>
> One thing I am dead sure of. The people who think that
> *no* book should be written on antisemitism are dead wrong.
> I do not care what their arguments for silence are—they
> must be wrong. To keep silent is to connive...Maybe this
> book isn't the right one....

One point puzzled me about all the letters I had received, but
I kept silent about it in my replies, lest I seem to be harping on
it. Nobody had paid the slightest attention to the matter of
timing, *that we were at war*, and conceivably might still be when
my book was published. In a way I was glad they had all let
the point slide by, for it clearly said, Forget the war.

My answer to Dick said that I had decided only to "stall it
for a while." Then I told him to whom I had sent the outline.

> You see, Dick dear, in the weeks before I sent you the
> synopsis, I had a feeling you would be upset...to a greater

or lesser extent...I wanted other people's reactions too, but I felt that if I waited to send the synopsis out to others until *after* I had heard from you, it might look as if I were putting S and S's reaction on trial.

...I am enclosing copies of everybody's answers. I think they will fascinate you...God knows, they did me. I am withholding comment on all of them for now...

Anyway, Dick, a moratorium for a while.

But nothing thus far, nothing prepared me for what I was forever after to dub Dick's "heartbreak letter." It didn't come until late September, after I admitted to him that I couldn't stick by that moratorium.

I have even been writing a bit on it, weekends and evenings when I'm not too bushed. Because one of the issues in *my* mind now is...can I get enough storyline, emotional interest, etc. into it, to save it from being a lecture or a tract?...Only when I've written three or four chapters...only then will I need to meet the issue of whether to go ahead or abandon...I don't think you need to meet any issue until then either.

That must have sent alarm signals to Dick. I had reached a decision—I was going ahead. After three or four chapters I would never abandon it, and he knew it.

By return mail I received his reply, the longest letter he ever wrote me during his whole life. It ran four pages, first giving me a rapid summary, sometimes good-natured and sometimes acidulous, of what he had felt about all the letters I had sent him from my friends, and then getting down to the point he had to make.

I do know this about the outline for your novel...that Lee and I as well as Arthur Schwartz all think it would give you some form of heartbreak.

Heartbreak possibilities:

1. (Prelude) A letter like this.

2. If it is sent to Essandess, and Essandess tells you they like it, but really don't, and publish it anyway.

3. Essandess tells you they don't like it and don't publish it.

4. Another publisher tells you he likes it and publishes it. Then if the book doesn't go you will wonder whether he really liked it, or just wanted an author who was (a) extraordinarily personable and (b) had a sale of 25,000 copies on her first book.

5. No publisher tells you he likes it and it isn't published at all.

I admit there is a chance that Essandess might like it and publish it and that it might be a success, or, that if Essandess doesn't do it, some other publisher will. But I do think the cards are stacked terribly against this project.

That letter jolted me down to my bones. I think there must be a specific brand of misery reserved for authors when their publishers warn them off some cherished theme, for playwrights when critics walk out after the first act, for all creative people who feel the freeze of indifference or dislike.

I still can remember what that letter did to me, can remember my desperate wish that I could call Dr. Gosselin and arrange for a refresher course in analysis.

To borrow a phrase that had already proved itself my very own: As abrupt as anger, depression plunged through me.

---CHAPTER---

EIGHTEEN

NEARLY A MONTH WENT by before I could decide how
to answer Dick, and by that time it was the middle of October,
and good old life and circumstance had taken charge so thoroughly that I didn't even feel guilty about my silence.

It was time for Mike to go back to school—the extension
granted by his headmaster would soon run out. But I couldn't
leave California and go home too; I was still working on the
screenplay of *Threesome*, and my producer estimated that we
would need another month.

Having worked with him since August, I knew it would take
more than that. How many times he could ask me to rewrite a
scene, how often he could suggest that it might "play better" if
it preceded three other scenes! He seemed not to know what
every writer knows, that once you start changing sequences of
dialogue and action, you not only have to rewrite the scene
itself, but all the scenes leading up to it, and the scenes coming
after it.

Gloomily I tacked on another full month to his estimate, and
thought, My God, December! It will be December before I can
go back to New York.

The kids and Rosie would have to go without me. Again I
used pull to get railroad tickets, this time through my agents,
who could only manage one upper berth and one lower for the
three of them. We began packing for their trip, closing up the

house, with me preparing for separation from my family and life once more in a hotel.

At which point young Chris developed a ferocious boil on his bottom, and yelled with pain. This was two nights before they were to leave. He ran a fever, a high one, and Rosie and I took turns all night with hot compresses and dosing him with children's aspirin.

He got worse, and in the morning I drove him to our pediatrician, laying him down on his side next to me on the front seat, propping him with soft cushions.

The doctor knew as well as I that canceling Pullman tickets during that wartime shortage might mean a delay of weeks. I explained about Mike and school; I explained about myself and the studio; I asked if there was any conceivable danger in travel for Chris while he had this boil.

That doctor not only knew about Pullman tickets, but also about unfinished screenplays and he couldn't have been more positive in his instructions. It would be days before that boil could break or be lanced, no matter where Chris was, right here with me, or back home in New York. There was no danger added by travel; he would prescribe the right painkiller for a two-and-a-half-year-old, and that would act as a sedative too. If I trusted my nurse Rosie—

They left. I had made Rosie promise to wire me from their first stop, Albuquerque, and of course she did. And did again from every station where the train made a stop to take on fuel or water. Which led to one of those family jokes which, years later, became occasions for ribald laughter from Mike and Chris and me, every time some association of ideas led one of us to talk about Rose and that painful cross-country trip.

Rosie, it seemed, felt that there was something vulgar in the word boil, printed on the tape of a telegram. Her first wire avoided it.

CHRISTOPHER'S THING VERY RED
AND HARD BUT SLEEPS AFTER DOSE

The next telegram came a day later; apparently she had found time to get to the Western Union operator at some station during a stop for refueling.

CHRISTOPHER'S THING GETTING
BIGGER AND PURPLE RED BUT DON'T WORRY

The last wire came from Chicago, where they were changing to the Twentieth Century Limited, one night away from New York.

CHRISTOPHER'S THING GETTING
BIGGER AND PURPLE RED BUT DON'T WORRY

There was no ribald laughter from me when those telegrams arrived, nothing but gratitude for Rose's care about letting me know that my little boy was all right despite the pain and fever and crying. It must have been a dreadful trip for all of them, and when I knew they were at last at home, and telephoned to hear that Rose had taken a taxi from the station right to our own baby doctor, Benjamin Spock, I blessed her all over again. The THING was lanced by Dr. Spock and soon all pain would drain away for good.

Just before they left, before poor little Chris got his boil, I finally managed to answer Dick's letter. It was to be the last letter between us on this subject, and I put away my carbon of it in a special folder, together with the whole series of letters and answers. Two years later, when I started my pressbook of *Gentleman's Agreement*, I pasted in a large manila envelope, marked *Pro's and Con's about the Synopsis*, and there they have remained ever since.

The main part of my answer to Dick also dealt with heartbreak.

> When I try to think what the hell I gave up the security of business to become an author for, I think the possible heartbreak is just something I have to ignore....
>
> I think maybe I should go back to promotion and security for my boys if I am going to give up a book merely because it might bring *me* heartbreak, because I can't see...the use of enduring the chancey insecurity of being an author unless you write stuff that you yourself find a deep satisfying rightness in.
>
> Maybe this is not that book. Maybe I'll fail in finding ways to keep it a novel and a love story and a human story. Maybe it will smell "tract" to high heaven. If it does, then

I'll give it up because there's no satisfaction in writing a lousy tracty book. But I just won't know, unless I try about six chapters...

Maybe six other authors are right this minute finishing novels on the same subject—maybe not one will do much by itself, but perhaps all those authors could become a kind of force for ending the conspiracy of uncomfortable and scared silence which defaults to the rantings of the bigots, who don't practice that conspiracy of silence at all.

I didn't mean to get into all of this. A moratorium and a pox.

I dropped that letter down the slot—and dropped my last doubt with it.

The day the kids left I had moved to the Beverly Hills Hotel. It was nowhere near as luxurious a place then as it is now, but after five months in that sand-gritted boxy shack, I felt posh and pampered. I was restless at living alone again in a hotel, and glad to be so much nearer the friends I had made since my arrival last March.

One of these, Joseph Than, called Pepo, I had met through Shirley Collier. He sensed that I was by now bored with the studio and suggested that while I was at the Beverly Hills Hotel, we collaborate on an original he'd worked out in detail but didn't feel comfortable about writing in English.

He was a tall, distinguished Viennese, three years younger than I, and very much interested in everything political, perhaps a little more radical than I. We used to quarrel about the news, but, as I could always do except with my sister Alice, I managed to stay calm and judicious with him, as he could with me, no matter how much we disagreed.

And he was no amateur in films, trying to latch on to some writer with a studio job. He had been a writer-producer with major film companies in Germany, Austria and France, and was now at Warner Brothers, one of several people working on *Night and Day*, starring Cary Grant.

He was a widower, in love with a girl named Marina, whom he was to marry, so whatever notions I might have had about falling in love with him were dead-ended. But it had been a long time since I had been able to count on male companionship, and I'm sure that one reason I agreed to the idea of our collaborating on that original was the promise of spending many evenings working with him, instead of facing a vapid hotel room too often.

More than that, his own story of his pre-California life fascinated and horrified me. He was reticent about it until we had known each other for a much longer time, so I knew only the barest outlines at the beginning, but as it unfolded, it held me deeply.

His first wife had been a ballerina, also Viennese, not Jewish, though he was. They were living and working in Paris when the news came of *Anschluss*, but she had just heard that her mother was seriously ill, and determined to fly to Vienna to see her, despite Hitler's troops marching into Austria.

But when she reached her parents' house, she stood motionless on the doorstep. A sign had been affixed to the front door. *Juden Eintritt Verboten*. It was a private house. Nobody but her parents lived there. Nobody else could have put up that sign. Her own husband would be forbidden entry—

She never entered the house. A frenzy seized her to be back in Paris with Pepo. She telephoned him to tell him what her parents had done, and of her need to be with him at once. She paid a fortune to somebody at the airport, a bribe to get him to hand over his ticket for the Czech plane about to leave.

The airplane never reached Paris. It crashed, with no survivors.

Pepo barely managed it. When war came, he joined the French army; when France fell, he was interned by the Germans. Somehow he escaped to Spain and at long last, his health nearly wrecked, he had made it to America.

I don't remember much about the original we began to do together, except that his plot was full of action, slightly melodramatic and pretty sure to sell. I supplied the title, *Half a Sin*, another natural, we thought, for a movie title. It came from my girlish days at school, when I used to copy out bits of Wordsworth, Shelley, Keats, Browning, Milton into a special notebook for quotes.

This was from Tennyson's "In Memoriam." "I sometimes hold it half a sin/ To put in words the grief I feel." My log shows that we spent several evenings discussing it and plotting it out scene for scene, and that I began actual writing on it at 1 A.M. on November 18. Two days later I was at page 20. The following week, at the studio, I started what I announced to my producer was the final, final, final revision of *Threesome*. December 2 says, "My first expensive dress since 1940, $135. Hat, $40."

December 3 has one word, "Home." Mike would be eight years old in five days. I had missed his fifth birthday, but being in my hideout had caused that. No studio was going to make me miss another. My producer knew that. He accepted the final revision.

Nine long months had elapsed since I had made that sudden decision to go out to Hollywood and learn how to write originals that would earn enough to support us while I wrote my next book. The learning part must have succeeded somewhat, but the money part had failed.

True, I had earned $31,000 from my studio salaries and *Threesome*, but commissions and taxes had cut this to $23,500. Our living and travel expenses for the year had totaled $11,000, and I had paid off that $11,000 of debts.

Q.E.D. I was going back to New York woefully minus the financial freedom to devote myself full-time to my next book. I could have stayed on and on at the studio, Bert Allenberg assured me, and he was seconded by Virginia Van Upp. But not for a single minute was I ever tempted to become a permanent resident of the movie colony on the West Coast.

So there I was, going home with about the same amount of money I had had when I left, with no job, no promotion assignments, no contract or advance from my publisher.

But I did have a conviction that somehow I would manage. It was no Micawberish optimism that something would turn up, but my own certainty that I myself would turn it up by writing stories and novelettes again, and my own confidence that, God save the mark, I could go right back to Hollywood whenever I really had to, and land on a fat payroll once more.

It was the middle of February before I could get to solid, continuing work on *Gentleman's Agreement*, still without any title, even a working title.

There were my friends to see again, dinners to give them, or invitations to accept, the Schermans, the Whartons, the Masseys, who were again in New York, and the Simons—Dick and I said not a word about heartbreak letters.

Eric Hodgins I did not see. Before I'd left for the Coast the previous year, we had talked through a five-hour afternoon; my log says, "E. again, 2–7 P.M." but leaves me a mite uncertain about that reunion, except that I said something like, "So you too have found a way to hurt me." That must have been the day he told me he had gone gack to his wife, albeit very briefly, and that they were going to have a baby.

I couldn't have been mean enough to begrudge him the joy of having a baby—that could never have been why I said that he had at last found a way to hurt me. But before Eric's alcoholic disappearance he had begun to talk about his developing belief that we "would share our future"; once, when we were down at the Simons' house for an evening, he had spoken of that shared future with Andrea and Dick.

His son by his first wife was about twelve, and with a son off at school, a man could indeed hold a developing belief about some profound change in his life. But a new child by his second wife told me flatly that that developing belief would develop no more. Perhaps I had begun to share that belief.

And my own developing freedom from neurotic love that I had so lauded myself for not so long before suddenly did a pretty bad collapse. It was as if being hurt drew me to a more intense level of response and need, as if knowing that there would never be anything permanent between me and Eric, I suddenly found myself longing for permanence and nothing less.

Depression can be so irrational to the good mind that sees it for the dismal nonsense it sometimes is; yet the tenacity of it in somebody like me is as real as recurring bouts of a chronic ailment. And there's no handy little anodyne either.

Now, though I did not see Eric, I heard from some of my old friends at Time, that he had joined Alcoholics Anonymous, had even faced Harry Luce one morning to announce, "Harry, I am an alcoholic," which made me admire him. I was happy to hear about his joining A.A., and believed he would stick to it, and change a lot because of it. Those old friends also told me he had an infant daughter and, like many proud papas, was already her slave.

I did see Ira. He had, by now, managed to forgive my transgressions about promptness, and our relationship, such as it was, resumed. I hesitate to say outright that it was an affair, because it was so well-mannered, so decorous, so lacking in spontaneity. I remember thinking once, irreverently enough, that we were like a twenty-year-married missionary and his good pious wife. But Ira had at last given up any notion that in time I would marry him, and now seemed happy to take me to dinner, the theater or a nightclub, and to make a fourth at bridge with Lee and Jack Bassett. And I rejoined our weekly poker sessions.

Apart from that renewed social life, the Writers War Board claimed me almost as soon as I reached home, and regular meetings and assignments began once more. But "writing for the war effort" no longer seemed enough. That old itch to do some more tangible kind of war work bothered me more than ever. The notion about working in an airplane or munitions factory was gone, but the sense that there ought to be some place for me, away from my typewriter and away from a meeting—that only deepened.

So right after New Year's Day, I enlisted in the A.W.V.S., the American Women's Volunteer Services, known as the Motor Transport Corps to most people, to drive staff cars one full day each week for the army and the air corps, and trucks for the navy.

I was in uniform!

At headquarters they suggested that I apply for officer status, but any sort of executive job was not what I was after, so I signed on as a private. I had to take three separate driving tests, though I'd had my driver's license for over twenty years, and I was fingerprinted three separate times. As with the driving tests each of the services seemed to feel that only their own was valid.

I also had to buy my own uniform, a crisp, military-looking

suit, cap and shoes, at the reduced cost of $87, and memorize the set of regulations the Motor Transport Corps commanded its drivers to follow.

One of their safety rules was that any time you were on a long trip, you were to pull over to the shoulder of the road every hour on the hour, get out of your car, and walk around it four times, rain or snow or impatient passengers notwithstanding. Only then could you get behind that wheel and drive on. A printed card facing the passenger seat stated this regulation in formal terms and large letters, so no irritated lieutenant, major or bigger brass could take it on himself to speed you on. The one exception allowed was when there was a train or plane to make by a hair.

I reported every Friday morning at 8:30 and drove for nine hours, occasionally longer if my final destination was some airport or army base. The staff cars were khaki-colored Chevrolets or Fords, and passengers were usually a pair of officers of the lower ranks, but every once in a while it would be a general with no loftier car at his disposal.

That was for the army and air force. But for the navy, we drove trucks, light or medium-size, usually to transport thirty or forty sailors to the Brooklyn Navy Yard or to some Hudson River pier where they were to ship out.

There was a sense of big adventure for me, driving those trucks, for naval regulations specificied that any woman driving a truck had to have an armed escort sitting right up there in the cab of the truck at her side.

Obviously the United States Naval Command was not about to send off one woman alone, with thirty or forty gobs in a high state of excitement at going off to sea, most of them with many drinks under their tunics. One for the road, so to speak.

For me, that armed guard was never called into action. The only time the sailors made life hard was once when I drove them to a pier packed high with crates marked EXPLOSIVES. A lot of them waited around to watch me back up and pull forward, and back up again, as I maneuvered in inadequate space to turn my truck around. Each time I inched closer and closer to that wall of crates, the sailors would shout and jeer.

"Go on, Baby, blow it all up—BANG!"

"Lotsa room, lady—VAROOM."

They made small-boy sounds of dynamite exploding, yelled advice, not all of it in goody-goody language. But as I at last completed my turn and drove off, they cheered me.

Those nine-hour Fridays taught me what taxi drivers go through in city traffic, bridge traffic, at the terminals and airports. I learned what it was to drive all day in blizzards and torrential rains when your windshield wipers are inadequate or broken or missing. Twice I drove with my head stuck out the window of my truck, for hours on end, my windshield piled with snow and crusted with ice, just to be able to see. My armed escort took pity on me, and offered to take the wheel, but of course I refused, politely I hope, but with my new-found esprit de motor corps.

pages 16,17,18,19
The Break-through?
at last??
Chap I ended
Started Chapter II !!!!!
about 6 wks. of starts & stops &
discarding & "hold for later." Jeez.

That is my log for March 29, 1945. I must have thrown away a good 100 pages of false starts before I could reach page 15. For six weeks, I had been writing and rewriting that opening chapter, searching out the basic elements that would seem right to me—and keep on seeming right after all the doubts arose and fell.

Again my Phil had undergone a change, but this time it was the final one. It was not a cosmetic change but an interior one. Just as I had once rejected my civil liberties lawyer, just as my POW on the *Gripsholme* had been lost overboard, so now I had blackballed my author of two historical novels.

In the writing, I had come to see that this Phil who was determined to write about modern-day America and its sin of antisemitism would inevitably sound like a do-gooder, what Thayer used to call "a Christer," a touch too noble.

I had to get around this super-goodness, and after eighty-eight tries I finally saw that Phil must never be the originator of the idea of "doing something about it." Instead he would be handed the assignment to do a series of pieces, by somebody who was his superior, his boss, the editor in chief, say, of a big national magazine where Phil was a star feature-writer.

And Phil must, at first, resist the assignment with all his heart, on the ground that it will be a dud, full of committees and statistics that nobody will read. Smith's Weekly is a cross between Time and the New Republic, and up to now, Phil has done only free-lance pieces for it, and very successfully. Now he has just become a staff writer, moving his family to New York from California because of this full-time connection, and, quite naturally, he wants his first major project to be a sure-fire thing, not the dead wood this series is bound to be.

And it was on that note of Phil's reluctance that my novel at last began. Phil would go half mad before he found "an angle" that might spark some life and originality into his pieces; he would become exhausted, touchy, often depressed—just as I had been.

It felt right to me; I could cope with this opening situation. I could believe in this Phil and perhaps readers would believe in him too.

By the middle of April I sent the first thirty-five pages to Lee Wright, and a delighted note in my log quotes her. "Good, promising; main thing is the reader is engaged in the problem." She made no mention of her warnings in last summer's letter; nor did I. I can't remember that either of us ever did again.

Now my "writing forward" took a leap. By the end of the month, I was at page 54; I edited and rewrote and sent it not only to Lee but to Dick.

But my leap had to be short-lived. *Half a Sin* had been turned down by Columbia, and in due course by several other studios. I had had no income of any sort since my last studio paycheck last December. I had to go into debt again or sell my Time stock. But I already had a bank loan against that, and besides, I didn't want to sell it—it was my only bulwark against crisis, except for my friends.

And I couldn't see myself going to the Schermans again, nor to Ira. I didn't feel the same about owing money to a bank, where it was covered by my own collateral, and off I went to my bank and increased my loan quite handsomely.

For this $2,500 had to serve not only for living expenses, but for something else that I had to do. I didn't like this something else; I had seen it coming: I had tried to put it off. But now, barely five months after leaving Hollywood, I had to turn around and get back to a movie salary once more.

I wrote to Bert. He called Virginia Van Upp, and sure enough, I could have my old job back, as she had indicated before I left. And at the same $750 a week.

But this time I would not go out by myself. This time the kids and Rosie and I would all go out together, and come home together in the fall. I asked Bert if somebody in his office could find something on a beach for us to live in, I didn't care how lowly, even last year's shack.

The something they did manage to find turned out to be a luxury place at Malibu, the movie colony, owned by one of the major studios, where they could put up visiting film celebrities. I could have it for five months, for a mere $2,350, more than twice the rent of my apartment on Park Avenue. Again I had no choice but to grab it, though I did have one piece of luck. The first agent I had ever had, Helen Everitt, wanted to sublease my place in New York while I was away. I let her have it just for the bare rent, furnishings free.

Three days after I mailed the deposit that bound me to go to Hollywood again, my log shows that I worked on my novel until 4:30 and had to rush to meet Lee and Jack at the St. Regis at five. When I entered the lobby, I sensed that something definitely was wrong. It didn't look like an ordinary hotel lobby; people seemed to be standing in clusters, even the pages and elevator operators seemed to be talking, not in their usual rush. Across the lobby, I spotted Lee and Jack; they hadn't seen me, and as I waved to them, I saw that Lee was weeping.

"Don't you know?" she asked as I hurried over. "Haven't you heard the news?"

"What news?"

"Roosevelt is dead."

We never had dinner. We went back to my house and turned to the radio and listened, and talked, and listened again. Calamity

367

had struck—we three felt it was nothing less. What would this do to the nation, what would it do to the war? It was coming to a close; the Russians were advancing on Berlin, the Marines had raised the flag at Iwo Jima, Roosevelt had met Churchill and Stalin at Yalta—would this death change anything? Could Truman take over?

We stayed up for hours, talking, needing to be together, waiting for details. From all over the world came the radio reports of people weeping, governments aghast, of prayers being said by G.I.s and generals.

It was a Thursday night. The next morning I reported as usual to the Motor Transport Corps and drove all day.

It was early May when we boarded the Twentieth Century Limited, headed west, and it was on the train radio on our third day out, that we heard the great news of V. E. day. The war in Europe was over.

So it was on a high note that we arrived in Hollywood. How different from last year, when I was alone, with no job, no house, knowing not a soul but the Whedons! This time I even had two cars ready for me to use, both Studebakers, loaned to me for the summer by Dorothy Massey.

Best of all, this time I was firmly into my next book, not still searching; this gave me a sense of "feeling placed" for the next year or so. And this time, too, I was determined to earn not only my salary, but enough extra so that there would be no *third* return to Hollywood. A story idea had popped into my head, and in my spare time out here, I'd write that too. I had the title before I had the plot, *Lady Lucky*, and before May was over, everything was off to a good start, both on *Lady Lucky* and at Columbia Pictures.

One day in June I left the studio early. Because of gasoline rationing, we could work at home several days a week, driving in only for story conferences or working sessions on new scenes. This was June 19, my birthday. I was forty-five.

I remember the day perfectly. It was a clear hot afternoon, and I remember the hot leather smell in my car as I waited for the traffic signal at Hollywood and Vine. I have no idea of what was occupying my mind at this moment I can recall so clearly.

But suddenly I was thinking, Forty-five—that's middle age. Well, I'm going to have the best damn middle age anybody ever had.

There was no birthday party that night—I hadn't reminded anybody that it was my birthday. Mike and Chris had presents for me, shining shells and pebbles they had collected on the beach. We all had ice cream and cake, and as they went off to bed, I sat down at my typewriter.

Lady Lucky was to find some long odds stacked against it. I was never known as a patient Griselda, but my log tells me that back then, when it came to something I wrote, I had the determination of the damned, or the lunatic. Following the trail of entries in my log of just that one effort, tracking them down, one after another, reminds me now of Hansel and Gretel's trail of bread crumbs as they made their way through the forest. Only my crumbs were never eaten by the birds.

The first crumb appears on May 31. "Began Lady Lucky—novelette? story? original?" June 5 says, "Finished Lady Lucky...20 p. original." June 12: "Added 8 p. to Lady Lucky, 28 p." A week later: "6 p. Lady Lucky—34 pages." Two days later: "Gave Lady Lucky to V. Van Upp."

It was a romantic concoction whose outer scaffolding was the adage, "Lucky at cards, unlucky at love." The inner structure was a mix of a winning streak at Reno casinos, a losing streak at love and marriage, and a twisting around for a happy ending.

At the studio I was doing a treatment for *With This Ring*, so my saga of *Lady Lucky* is interrupted by some notes about that, about rewrites, new starts and finally turning it in. A day later came a new assignment, "Lenore Coffey original." I have no memory of what either one was about or even how they went over with Miss Van Upp.

But *Lady Lucky* she turned down. I couldn't have been too crushed, because far weightier news came just then from New York. Despite Dick's doubts, Simon & Schuster was drawing up a contract for my book, with an advance "payable on the demand of the author." My fifty-odd pages had been read by all the major people, and this was the result.

This time I limited the amount of the advance myself, to

$2,500, to avoid a repeat of my experience with *The Trespassers*, where everything the book earned was gone before it even appeared.

Lee and Jack came out to stay with me, and I gave them my one big party of the summer. Later Ira was a house guest too, and for all my busy life, I got in a lot of tennis with my friends, and occasionally with movie greats like the David Selznicks and Lenore and Joseph Cotten, Betty and King Vidor. I no longer felt like a stranger in paradise.

Early in August my log says, "Began complete rewrite of Lady Lucky." Across the lower half of the page, I printed in large capital letters:

ATOMIC BOMB—HIEROSHIMA

That's how I spelled it. I remember the moment I knew of it—Rosie running up the beach toward me, calling, "Did you hear about the bomb?"

"What bomb?"

"They bombed a place in Japan with a new kind of bomb, an atomic bomb."

She looked bewildered; she didn't know why it was so important, but the tone of the radio announcer told her that it was. I didn't know exactly why it was important, either, but I did know that something gigantic had happened.

Back in 1937, eight years ago, while I was still at Time magazine, there had been a couple of big science stories that had the tone of being monumental in importance. The first was a medical story, of the discovery of sulfanilamide, a miracle drug that would revolutionize medicine. The second was about the first successful atom-smasher, called a cyclotron, and even I, nonscientist that I was, knew from the length of the story, and from its solemn tone, and from the newspaper reports that followed for days—even I knew that it was a tremendous triumph for physicists.

I had read predictions of inestimable changes to come in the second half of the twentieth century, if ever this smashing of atoms could be put to practical use, that a new age would begin, in the inconceivable crescendo of growth and discovery that ran from the iron age, through the dark ages, into the modern age and now into the atomic age.

Now as Rosie said atomic bomb, I knew that a new era of warfare had begun. It would be days or weeks before I, or anybody, saw the first pictures of that billowing mushroom cloud, but even then I knew that a new killer had been let loose over a living city and I shivered in a new kind of dread.

But soon I returned to my rewriting of *Lady Lucky*. This time it grew to forty-five pages, and when it was done Bert Allenberg sent it forth to all remaining major studios. Any sensible person would have been sick of it by then, but who ever said I was sensible?

This second summer taught me something I was glad to know. I would need no special nobility of soul to stay away from the big money of Hollywood. I had no particular scorn for people who wrote for the movies, had none of those qualms people like Dorothy Parker, Scott Fitzgerald, William Faulkner and others seemed to suffer, never thought in terms of prostituting one's self.

What I did feel, and I think this is honest not only in retrospect, but for that very summer, was a kind of placid boredom in what I was paid to do. With the exception of the time the year before, when I was doing the screenplay of *Threesome*, which I myself had invented, all the rest of my work out there was to adapt what other people had invented, *their* books, *their* stories, *their* originals. And those projects seemed to me so empty of realness, so empty of the pump of real blood or the flinch of real pain, that I myself, as a craftsman working on them, felt no real pump of energy.

I had another bout of depression to handle as the summer was drawing to a close, a throwback to the private pain I should have by then exorcised for good. In the *Times* I read that Ralph Ingersoll had just married, and like helpless lowlands before a flooding river, my world was suddenly inundated with memories of the years when I had loved him, leaving me not only swamped by the past but overwhelmed with guilt at being ignoble enough to be jealous. He was forty-five and married, and I was forty-five and was not.

I used to say to Dr. Gosselin that I would probably never

marry again; he would calmly reply that I would marry again if I wished to marry again; I would insist that I was not the person to fall in love, the getting-married kind of love, every few years. I had now been divorced for ten years, an entire decade. It didn't help much to remember Dr. Gosselin's unperturbed assertions.

In any case, in September I was given one final assignment at the studio, called *My Empty Heart* and, as with the others, I made no copies and can't remember what it was about. I don't mean that I did sloppy work on it, but that what was really absorbing me was my longing to get back to New York. I think that by then even Mike and Chris were in a fever of wanting to go back home again, and as for me, I felt that if the studio tried to delay me, as it had the year before, I would flatly refuse.

It would be nice to report that the moment I was through with Hollywood, I put all commercialism behind me and went straight back to my unfinished book. But a parade of new rejections of *Lady Lucky* began, and the repeated nays stuck in my throat; it was beyond me just to say, Well, you can't win them all, and drop it for good.

And just one day after we got back, Dorothy Massey asked me to write some promotional material for a radio deal Raymond was undertaking. After accepting an entire summer's loan of their two cars, I could scarcely refuse, though I did object to any pay. She offered $200 a week for the six weeks it would take. This was deductible, she insisted, it was business, it was the only way she'd let me do it, and I was the only one she knew who could do it.

Sure, I said then, relieved to have a good excuse to doodle around a while at something I knew would be pleasant and easy. I needed time to adjust to my real life in New York. After any extended trip, even by train, I always felt what we today would call jet lag, with real effort needed to become reoriented to the familiar routines of home. It went beyond reopening the house, ordering newspaper delivery again, calling the laundry, arranging for milk delivery, stocking up with food—lots of that could be done for me by Rose and my maid, as soon as I hired a new one.

But I wouldn't let Rose be the one to take Mike and Chris

for checkups with doctor and dentist; it was always I who took them shopping at De Pinna for their suits and shirts and shoes and overcoats, and naturally it was I who paid required visits to school or headmaster or teacher—soon to be on behalf of Chris as well as Mike, for he was about to be launched into the groves of academe at Collegiate's nursery school.

And of course it was I who met any crisis that arose for either of the boys. There was one for Mike very soon after he had gone back to school. He was nearly nine now, and not a crisis-prone child, but this afternoon he came home in a state, dropped his bookbag at my feet, and flung himself at me in a torrent of tears and incomprehensible words about a test. He was always a good student—had he failed a test? He rarely cried; he was one of those children with an amiable disposition, no tantrums, rarely any problems. I was astonished. I sat down on the sofa and he threw his arms around my waist, almost butting his head into my stomach.

"I cheated," he cried, "I cheated, I cheated, I cheated."

At last I could make out what he was saying. I remember patting his shoulder, hugging him, ruffling his hair, telling him lots of schoolkids cheated once in a while, trying to get him to tell me just what had happened.

The boy next to him, it seemed, had shoved his test paper in math right to the edge of his desk, and Mike had peeked at the answers and put them right down on his own paper. Nobody had seen him; he hadn't been caught; only the boy next to him knew about it, and they were friends, but the minute he handed in his exam—

His sobbing began again. So it wasn't fear of punishment that had cracked him up, but the enormity of his crime. Well, I sat there, saying kindly maternal nothings to him, but I ached for his misery. Too well did I know what guilt and anxiety and tension could do to you; if my three years of analysis had done nothing else, it had taught me all about those vicious little monsters.

It was then that I got my idea. "Listen, Mike," I said to the back of his head. "I'll make a deal with you."

He looked up, still gulping back his sobs. "What kind of deal?"

"It's about getting *A*'s and *B*'s at school."

"*A*'s and *B*'s?" He didn't try to hide his confusion.

"If you get a *B*," I said slowly, "on an exam or a term grade, I'll give you fifty cents more than your allowance."

"And if I get an *A*?"

"Oh then, I won't give you anything."

He looked at me with astonishment. "Only for a *B*?"

"That's right. Every time you get a *B*."

I never had to explain further. I could feel his hunched up little shoulders go loose, I could see something like comprehension in the way he looked at me. Slowly the long gaspy breaths of childish sobbing fell away, and then he collected his book bag from the floor and went off to his room.

We never spoke of it again. For a while he would show me *B*'s and I would hand over fifty cents, but then he seemed to forget the deal.

I don't think he ever cheated at school again.

My jet lag about work lasted a luxurious ten days and then I tackled *Lady Lucky* once more. But my log for that day records a vital change. "Rewrite of L.L. for magazines. Now *Lucky Streak*."

Patient Griselda or gritted teeth or whatever, this new title meant more than a name change. Now inside the scaffolding, I built a labyrinth of new subplots and new action; it would be not only about a woman's love and divorce and remarriage, but about her need not only to help her husband's work, but to do some work on her own. I was ready to let it run to whatever length it needed; I was going to forget "what would play" and write what would *write*.

And on a kind of dare to myself, I called Dale Eunson, Cosmoplitan's fiction editor, who had given me the first order-in-advance I'd ever had, and told him I had a novelette, partly written, that he might like. Over lunch I told him about it; he asked for a synopsis, and I let that run, also, to whatever length it chose to run to. In a week I wrote, "Finished *Lucky Streak* syn. 26 p." That was longer than a normal short story.

And then, ten days later, comes a gleeful notation, a large scrawl of words and figures. "Cosmo ordered-in-advance—*Lucky*

Streak for $5,000! First part, 15,000 words; 2nd, 10,000 words. AT LAST."

It was a first for me. I had never written a two-part novelette. Nor had any magazine ever paid me $5,000. That was half what the movies had paid for *Threesome*.

I set to with a new burst of confidence. The next day I was at page 11. Progress! I was rewriting from the start. And then came a string of almost daily entries, until I could write, "Finished *Lucky Streak*. . . 106 pages, 32,000 words—in 5½ weeks from the day it was ordered."

Five and a half weeks sounds speedy, but it was December 2, over five months since that night in Malibu when I started it. A whole year would have elapsed before it appeared in the pages of Cosmopolitan. It was scheduled for the April and May issues next spring.

But then I would really see it in print. *Threesome* I had never seen on film. I had heard that it was still being doctored by other screenwriters, whom I never even talked to by phone, much less met for any exchange of ideas about it; they were assigned to change it so that it would meet "front office specifications." I remember saying, "It's been changed and cut so much, they'll probably end up calling it *Twosome*."

To this day I do not know whether it ever did hit the screen. I never asked. My life as a writer was soon to reach so marked a turning point, that it seemed to swivel away from everything I ever wrote in the past.

For just four days after I turned in *Lucky Streak*, I went back to my true beloved, those long-abandoned pages of what was to be *Gentleman's Agreement*. And as I said once before, I began again to write forward in a kind of demented rush.

By Christmas my fifty-four pages had doubled, and my sense of being placed had doubled as well.

NINETEEN

I WAS NEVER WHAT we today would call a workaholic. Even when I was in a rush of writing, I could always quit the desk and read a just-arrived magazine cover-to-cover without any guilt, or play with the kids for a while, or waste an hour on a stiff crossword puzzle, or two hours on the weekly double-crostic in the Saturday Review.

A couple of years before, Carroll Whedon had introduced crostics to me, and for a long time I was not very good at their dashes and boxes. Once, in a baffled snit, I asked her if they gave her as much trouble as they did me.

"I'm so good at them," she replied airily, "that it frightens me." We both laughed, but that may have aroused my competitive spirit, and I became an addict and began to insist on solving them without the use of reference books. Marc Connelly, Peg Pulitzer and a few other crostic laureates also disdained reference books, and like them, when I at last climbed to their eminent heights, I began to feel superior to crossword puzzle fans. By that time, Carroll had gone beyond crostics to the fiendishness of British crosswords, a breed far more complex than their American counterparts, and now it was Carroll who felt superior to double crostic fans like me.

My biggest addiction, though, was music, and I had no will-power whatever about resisting a newly acquired recording of Beethoven, Bach or Mozart. Long-playing records, the thin unbreakable 33s that held an entire symphony on one disc, had not yet come into being in my life; all my records still were the thick, heavy 78's, with six or eight records needed to play one symphony, so several of my bookshelves were given over to big husky albums.

For days, after buying some new album, I could leave my manuscript in the middle of a sentence, and spend an hour listening to my new possession. I could never keep on working if music was being played, could never treat it as background, as some writers can. I listen to music note for note, the way I read a book word for word, so music meant a full stop at my desk.

And I was no early riser, either; working at night so often, stopping at midnight, and too wound up to go right to sleep, I would read for an hour or two each night, and rarely stop before two, so of course I could not be one of those writers like Trollope, whom I marveled at, when I read that he would rise at five and finish his writing by breakfast time.

Even when I did get up each morning, I couldn't manage to start briskly at my desk. First I had to clear the decks, run my household, order drugs or flowers, arrange things for my kids with the parents of their friends, answer mail, pay bills, phone editors or agents or friends. Once I had left Time magazine, I never wanted a full-time secretary; I was my own secretary.

By nature I was a night owl, not a lark, and it never bothered me that I didn't begin writing until late afternoon. My friends often called me "organized" or "disciplined" and thereby showed that they knew mighty little about my thousand departures from my typewriter for tempting bouts of double crostics or reading or music.

But when I once was firmly launched on a piece of work, it is true that I wrote every day, maybe only a little, but *something*. Back then that meant even Saturday and Sunday, if no more than half a page; now I usually avoid my typewriter over weekends, unless I am in the inflamed final stages, approaching the end. Then to avoid my manuscript for a whole weekend would be like avoiding one lobe of my brain.

And so I began the new year of 1946 with a thin but solid

sheaf of manuscript before me, writing steadily day after day, not with that fluency I had had with my first novel, when I didn't know enough about writing a book to be discontented with what I set down, innocent of the flaws and faults that were later to make me squirm.

Now I would write and rewrite even after I thought some section was final, no doubt risking that loss of spontaneity that so often curses the too-belabored scene. But for all that willingness to return to a page or a stretch of dialogue a dozen times before I let it go, I did make progress.

Toward the end of January I was at page 186, with the first eight chapters done, a little past the halfway point of the book. I sent it all to Lee Wright and to Edith Haggard at Curtis Brown, who had been handling my magazine fiction for some time.

Edith read the whole thing overnight, called me in the morning with the enthusiasm any author loves to hear, and said she was sending it by messenger to Dale Eunson at Cosmo.

By this time I had several working titles, *Partial Eclipse*, *Seedbed*, *Make the Tree Good*, and *Make the Tree Corrupt*. Improbable as it now seems to me, it was the last one I liked best. It came from the Bible, and I had come upon it obliquely. A nonfiction best seller of the time was *Generation of Vipers*, an acidly witty attack on Momism by Philip Wylie, and I'd read that the title came from the Gospel According to Saint Matthew. So I looked up Matthew to find it, and then read on and on, and found several phrases about trees and fruit, all of which stirred me.

"Either make the tree good, and his fruit good," went one, "or else make the tree corrupt, and his fruit corrupt: for the tree is known by its fruit."

In good old collegiate style, I copied it all out on a page of my log, in solid blue ink. "Title?" I wrote below it. "Make the Tree Corrupt."

I'm no longer sure why I was so enamored of the phrase, though it must have meshed in with my belief that if parents are bigoted their children will be, and if they are free of it, their children will be decent too. My Phil had a kid of seven.

In any event that was the title borne by my eight chapters, as my manuscript went forth into the world of publishing.

Just two days later, two notes appear on one page of my log.

"Lee—2:30 to 5:30. Has reservations about book—some minor changes."

The other note is shorter. "Dale nuts about it!"

Cosmopolitan, in the middle forties, was nothing like the sex-saturated Cosmo of today. It ran a great deal of fiction by Somerset Maugham, Louis Bromfield, Edna Ferber, Paul Gallico, Pearl Buck, and articles by Francis Cardinal Spellman, Lloyd C. Douglas, educators, people in politics and the like.

Two weeks went by before I heard anything more from Dale Eunson. He had asked for a synopsis of the rest of the story, and I wrote a five-page one, "in vaguest terms." I also used those two weeks to make certain changes Lee had suggested, and to do a sharp job of cutting—some six thousand words went, and I felt fine when she said the cuts made a big improvement.

And then came February 20, and another page scrawled over from top to bottom in my log.

> Cosmopolitan bought book—
> 186 pages and synopsis
> of remainder—
> $20,000 !!
> Deadline—July 15

Much later Dale was to remind me of something I had forgotten. When he had ordered *Lucky Streak* before it was completed, he had set forth one condition: that he was to have first look at the novel I was writing.

"You won't want it," I had told him. "It's about antisemitism."

"Well, maybe I won't. But I want to see it."

I had promised that he would have first look, and now here he was buying it. Fiction editor though he was, he couldn't make a decision on anything as controversial as that all by himself; he took it up with the editor in chief, and then even with the executive vice-president of the company, Richard E. Berlin, who never was consulted on fiction.

"It's your baby," Dale was told. "If it goes bad, it's on your head."

It would run as a four-part serial, in whatever four issues preceded publication day. Nobody at Simon & Schuster or anywhere else could know when pub day would be, but the moment that was scheduled, Cosmo would be able to schedule installment number one. The final installment had to be on the newsstands the month the book itself appeared.

The contract with Cosmo contained all the usual things, with one addition. I would provide them with a different title.

With one of my sudden decisions, I left for Bermuda almost at once, "to rest a bit and then finish."

Rosie had just returned from a month's vacation, joining her husband who would soon be demobilized, and was coming back only for a half-time job. Through the Students' Employment Office at Columbia University, I had temporarily taken on a college man as an after-school sports companion, taking the kids to the park, biking, skating, playing ball. It was good for them, having a young man around. They liked him.

Apart from seeking a small vacation for myself, I had another motive in going to Bermuda—I wanted to find a house to rent for the whole summer.

No more California, no more Hollywood, no more three-day trips by train! You could fly to Bermuda in one day. No longer did you fly down by amphibian "clipper ships" that landed in the water the way you used to do in the middle thirties; since January of this very year, you went by what seemed huge four-engine Constellations, seating a hundred people, and you landed at a proper airport, originally a naval base during the war.

Sammy Tatem still lived there, still not married, though I think he had some important involvement going with somebody he had met. She wasn't there just then, however, and we proceeded to have lazy hours at the beach as of yore when he wasn't working, evenings of dancing, tours by bicycle. There was nothing motorized on the island back then, except for ambulances and fire engines and a few official vehicles for top government people; you went everywhere by bicycle, unless you were in evening dress, when you shifted to a horse-drawn carriage, but to me biking in Bermuda rated as a sport, not only as a means of transportation.

I did find a house, Lancashire Lodge, in Warwick, with plenty of room for us, and a separate cottage for guests. It was not one of the stately homes of England, but an attractive place, with pleasant furniture, shelves of Dickens, Hardy, Galsworthy, H. G. Wells, and every window looking out not only at typically English gardens but at the clear blues and greens of the water. The house was set close to the shore, on the bay side, not the ocean, and its ample grounds went down into an elongated spit of land, stabbing into the water, where there was a dock for the boat we didn't have. The kids would love that dock and the cleared bit of ground around it that served as a sandless beach.

I rented it for $300 a month, for June, July and August, and was shocked to be told that one could get a good maid for a pound a week—less than five dollars. When I said I could never pay such low wages, I was immediately rebuked by good Bermudians: "You Americans come down here, and spoil all our own chances to get good maid service at the proper wages."

I returned home with this economic challenge unresolved, ready for a long, uninterrupted, worry-free spell of work. Every page in my log began to show longer hours, more editing, more rewriting. And more manuscript.

But the one thing that can break through my writing-every-day-no-matter-what did happen less than a month after I got home. Chris came down with scarlet fever.

I don't care how sensible a mother you were back then, how free of hypochondriacal imaginings for yourself and your children. When illness struck, you filled with dread when the pediatrician said words like scarlet fever, almost as profound a dread as when he said polio.

There was no Salk vaccine as yet, there was no wonder drug for scarlet fever. You treated your child the way you would have treated him in the nineteenth century or earlier, with cool compresses, cool quick baths, some aspirin, and, if you were a believer, constant prayer. All I could so was to think endlessly, Please let him be all right, please let him, please. Rosie and I spelled each other near his bed through the days and nights.

Mike went into immediate quarantine, first going to live with the Bassetts, and then over to Rose's sister, Dotty, in Brooklyn,

I not only notified Collegiate School the moment I knew, but also telephoned the parents of every one of Chris's friends and schoolmates who might have been exposed to him during the incubating period, and to all the parents of Mike's schoolmates and friends as well.

My log stayed empty of any entry about work until the danger was over. Then I resumed my own fever of writing, and by the end of April, I was actually able to note in my log, "About 5 chapters to come." I must have meant "to go."

And soon I had a title everybody liked, *Horn of Plenty*. It came from a scene I had just written, where Phil is at last handing over to his secretary the first batch of his articles for her to type. He has rolled up his manuscript into a thick white column, held in by stout rubber bands, and as he starts to force the elastic bands downwards, the sheets furl out into a cornucopia, wide at the top, narrowing to the bottom.

"Horn of plenty," he thinks. "Full of all the good things, hate and indifference and hypocrisy. And maybe some hope too."

Lee Wright liked it, and so did everybody she tried it on at the office. Dale did too, and said they had signed up a famous commercial artist to do the illustrations. *Make the Tree Corrupt* at last lost its hold on me. I stopped visualizing a tree on the jacket design that would appear on my book, and transferred to visions of the graceful outward curves of a cornucopia.

And then Rosie gave me her news, news that made me jump up and kiss her, and news that shook me, all at the same time. She was going to have a baby, early in December. She had suspected it soon after her vacation with her husband, but now she was sure. She wouldn't be going to Bermuda with us. Or be with us in the fall.

Bermuda wasn't what mattered—it was losing Rosie for good. She had been part of my life and my children's lives for nearly ten years. From the start I had felt it a blessing to have come upon this good sweet human being in the midst of my own joy at adopting my eight-week-old Mike. It would be like losing a close friend to say good-bye to her for the last time. She felt that too, she said, and there would be no last time.

Soon it was the middle of May, with only one chapter to go. I had the audacity to make an entry that said, "May finish before

382

Bermuda." That would mean weeks ahead of my Cosmo deadline; there was no delivery date for Simon & Schuster.

I still kept up some semblance of social life through all this, with a few evening dates each week, for the theater, for dinner, for poker, with Ira and the Masseys and all my friends. I had become a member of the Authors League, and never missed a meeting.

But finish it I did. I, who had taken more than a year to get to page 15, had written the whole second half of my novel in ten weeks.

Of late I had been sending finished chapters to Lee and to Dale as they came back from the typist. Now I gave them the last two, reminding them that I still had to proofread the whole manuscript, so that minor changes might yet occur.

Then I threw myself into preparations for our June 1 departure, doing my proofreading at night, amid trunks, suitcases and toys. My second application to the Students' Employment Agency at Columbia had included not only the offer of good wages, but the news of an entire summer in Bermuda. There was no paucity of applications, and I interviewed quantities of freshmen, sophomores, juniors and seniors. An amiable, freckled redhead named Bill Callahan was my choice—and the kids' choice as well. Bill moved in with us the next day.

And then late one night, at two in the morning, still looking for typos and missing commas and misspellings in my manuscript, eager to wind up even the proofing before we left New York, reading page after familiar page, I suddenly saw the real title for my book. Two words flew up at me—words I had written weeks before, in one of the critical scenes of the entire novel, a bad quarrel between Phil and Kathy, because she has refrained from offering to rent an empty house she owns in the country to Phil's best friend, Captain Dave Goldman, just back from the front and in great need of a place to live.

"It just would be so uncomfortable for Dave, *knowing* he'd moved into one of those damn neighborhoods that won't take Jews."

"Kathy!"

"I loathe it, but that's the way it is up there. New Canaan's worse—nobody can sell or rent to a Jew there. But even Darien—well, it's a sort of gentleman's agreement when you buy—"

"Gentleman—oh, my God, you don't *really*, you *can't* actually—you won't buck it, Kathy? Just going to give in, play along, let their idiotic rules stand?"

I must have written and rewritten that scene my usual ten times; I must have read it twenty times in preparing the x-ed out and penciled-in pages so they'd be legible to the typist.

But until that moment, I had never *seen* those two words for what they were.

I stared at them; I remember doing it. I read the whole scene. I flipped pages over to the way end of the book, where I knew I had used the phrase once more. Yes, there it was; I read it in a different context, and it reinforced my certainty.

I looked at the telephone. By now it was two-thirty in the morning—I couldn't call Lee to tell her. I tried to sleep. An elated excitement swept me from sleeping to waking, what I call "happy insomnia."

I made myself wait until half-past eight and then I did call her. She was still asleep. She had been up reading until three, I later learned, so all my thoughtful restraint the night before had fixed it so I would tear her awake in the morning.

"It's the title, Lee," I said.

"No more changes," she said sleepily. "*Horn of Plenty* is—"

"*Gentleman's Agreement*," I said slowly. "Lee, listen, it's *Gentleman's Agreement*."

Her voice changed. She was wide awake in that instant. "*Gentleman's Agreement*—oh, it's so *right*."

The same thing happened later on, when I called Dale Eunson at his office.

"Dale, I have a better title—"

"We've already gone with *Horn of Plenty*—the illustrator has it. When the book comes out—titles often get changed in book form—"

"*Gentleman's Agreement*, Dale. It's when they quarrel—"

His voice changed too. "*Gentleman's*—I remember. Of course! We'll use it too."

Life in Bermuda was beneficence itself for all of us, for the first month or so at least.

I hired a horse and carriage, with a driver who liked children, for the long trips across the island to the ocean side, and nearly every morning saw the kids and Bill and me over there; we would have gone by bikes, like everybody else, except that Chris, at four and a half, was too young.

Tricycles were still his speed, and he raced around on the macadam road outside our place—with no automobiles on the island, he was safe, though Bill usually kept an eye on him from afar. In the water he could dog-paddle with surprising speed, and before the summer was out, he took it into his head one day to jump right off our dock into twenty feet of water, and dog-paddle himself back to shore, vastly satisfied with himself, eating up the applause we gave him.

Mike was not only a strong swimmer but a whiz at aqua-planing. I remember my tremors the first few times, as I watched him racing along on what looked like a wide single ski, being towed by a motorboat. Across the bay he looked about ten inches high, skimming the water at a speed of thirty knots.

He was old enough to be allowed to go off by himself on his bike, and when he got his weekly allowance of a shilling, he would go the miles around to Hamilton to buy a comic book. But one comic a week couldn't provide enough reading matter, and he took to browsing through the old books our landlords had left on their shelves, most of them looking like schoolbooks.

One afternoon he came in from the lawn, carrying what looked like a thick textbook, its cover faded and old, the printing on its spine erased by time.

"Do you say Puh–GOTT-y?" he asked me.

"Puh–GOTT-y? You mean Peggotty? What are you reading, Mike?"

"*David Cooperfield*," he said blandly.

He was nine and a half. A small geyser leaped up in me. So often, nowadays, when I hear parents bemoaning their children's lack of interest in books, when I read about educators talking learnedly about the deplorable decline in reading skills in the schools, I go surprisingly conservative for an instant and wonder how many hours a day those assorted youngsters spend in front of television sets.

Now, suddenly remembering Mike and *David Cooperfield*—I never corrected his pronunciation, never said it correctly until he caught on himself—remembering now, I think I've always believed that only those parents who read more than they watch TV will have kids who read more than they watch TV. And being an omnivorous reader myself, I sometimes wonder if the nonreaders have any idea of what they are missing. And of what they're training their children to miss.

What I soon was missing down there in beneficent Bermuda was writing on my book. I was so happy that it was finished, and yet I began to feel a little lost without its constant presence in my life. The Bassetts and Ira were coming down as my house guests for a while in July, and I looked forward to all the good talk and bridge and companionship, but I was restless, and at certain times even a little depressed.

And as June was drawing to a close, I decided to read my manuscript from beginning to end, without a pencil in my hand, trying to behave not like its author, but like an ordinary reader, starting in not knowing what was to come. By that time more than a month had passed since I had finished the writing, and I felt that I'd put enough distance between that final spurt of work and now to give me some perspective on it as a whole.

When I finished, I half-wished I had never thought of this without-a-pencil episode. I felt vaguely let down, a little uncertain. I told myself it was because I had read it nine thousand times, that it simply *had* to lose its freshness after so much time spent on it, but that uneasy sense persisted. I added a scene here and there, and rewrote a little, duly sending off any changes to Dale and to Lee, but the unease persisted.

While the Bassetts and Ira were there, I must have talked with Lee a good deal about this sense that something was wrong, but I can't really remember. The visit was troubled much of the time, anyway, because of Ira's drinking. He always was what's called a "social drinker," even a heavy drinker, but not an alcoholic. Once, at a New Year's Eve party at the Whartons', he had embarrassed me and everybody else by racing around after a maid in her black uniform and lace cap and apron, determined to bestow a New Year's Eve kiss. Carly looked at me, Dorothy Massey looked at me, both signaling commiseration. I had hauled him off in the middle of "Auld Lang Syne."

But here in Bermuda, for some reason, he was being heavier about his drinking than ever before. The kids began to ask me about it; I hated having them see him so drunk, weaving about, slurring his speech, being slightly ridiculous.

I began thinking of Eric Hodgins and his drinking, wondering whether he was still a member of A.A., a practicing member, and hoped fervently that he was. Lee had just told me that Simon & Schuster was publishing a book of his next winter, a short novel, his first, though he had written three books about scientific matters. (After all, he had an engineering degree from M.I.T.) This novel was being expanded from a piece about building a house that he'd done in Fortune in the spring; I'd read it and enjoyed it immensely. Now Lee's news about him made me realize that with Eric, I had never needed to worry about his drinking in front of the boys. Why was Ira so different?

It was Jack Bassett who took charge of the problem at last, emptying every bottle of scotch, gin, rum, rye and brandy down the drain of the kitchen sink—and doing it in Ira's presence.

There was a bit of a furor. I think that wretched visit was what finally ended it for me with Ira. I did see him again in New York, but only rarely, and finally not at all. Long afterward I heard he had finally married; his wife was about my age, also Jewish, a well-known and highly successful fashion designer for Bergdorf Goodman's made-to-order clothes. I wished them well and never saw them. But he continued his hard drinking until his death years later.

It was in August, when I was alone again, that I finally woke up to what was wrong about my book. Something *was* wrong, not with me, but with it.

And wrong right at the start, right in the opening scene. Phil has just been given his assignment; it depresses him; he resists it, sure nobody will want to read it.

But what *was* the assignment? I didn't say, not for the first page of the book, not for the second, not for several, maybe ten or more.

The word antisemitism was missing from all those early pages. Why? Why was I delaying page after page? Was I, like my Phil, afraid that nobody would want to read anything about antisemitism?

The discovery that I somehow had fought away from the word *antisemitism* dismayed me in some deep hollow pit. I hadn't done so purposely, of course I hadn't. I had wanted only to get the reader interested in Phil, his character, his widowhood, his loneliness—wanted to set the stage before revealing what his assignment was about.

But I had avoided that word that was so central to the entire book. Deny it as I would, that was the cold reality of it. Thank God I had waked up at last.

Then and there, I began to rewrite page 1. Now, in the first exchange between Phil and the editor, he asks, "Would anybody want to read five articles about antisemitism?"

Instantly I felt better; there it was, right up front. All my recent unease and disquiet disappeared; my good old unconscious had risen up to tell me what was wrong, and I had listened.

As always, changes in one scene meant changes in ensuing scenes, so it was not only parts of chapter 1 that I rewrote, but also parts of chapter 2. I had telephoned both Dale and Lee, telling them what I was doing and why, and they both denied the need for it. The first installment for Cosmo was already in galleys, Dale said, right on his desk, and Lee reminded me that the book was already accepted, was being copyedited, ready to go to the printers. It was like a repeat performance of their resistance when I said I had a title I liked better than *Horn of Plenty*.

And when they received my two revised chapters, the same kind of thing happened: Dale scrapped his galleys, and Lee changed the manuscript.

It had taken me two weeks to complete my changes, and my log for August 19 is exultant: "Chap II off by air—and mss. *really* finished."

Now there was nothing to do but wait for the magazine to come out and then to wait for pub day.

* * *

We flew back to New York the day before Labor Day and a couple of evenings later, I drove up to Stamford to see Dick and Andrea Simon.

Occasionally I had wondered whether Dick, now that he had finished my book, still clung to his heartbreak theory. Lee Wright had long since given up her misgivings, but she had never ventured a word about what Dick now felt.

I also wondered whether he remembered that he himself had given me the idea for a small scene in it. He and Bennett Cerf played golf at a country club in Westchester where all the members were Jewish. Once, when Leon Shimkin, one of Dick's own partners at S & S had applied for membership, he had been turned down.

"Leon just wasn't the right type," Dick had said.

Bennett didn't look Jewish, nor did Dick; their wives weren't Jewish. But Leon Shimkin did look Jewish—I never met his wife—and if I had told Dick that turning Shimkin down because he "wasn't the right type" was code for blackballing him because "he looks so Jewish"—if I'd told Dick that *that* was anti-semitism, he wouldn't have believed me. But I had written a little scene that made it clear. Also at a Jewish country club.

Now after we had exchanged all the news about the summers we had just had, we got around to *Gentleman's Agreement*, and I spoke of the golf club scene. "Do you remember telling me about it?" I asked. "You were my source."

He took it in good part, and was generally very pleasant about the book itself. There was only one place, he said, where, if he were my editor, he would ask me to make some changes.

"That part about a flick here, and a flick there," he said. "And that line, 'That's how they did it.'"

I knew exactly what part he meant. A Dr. Craigie, not yet knowing Phil was Jewish, had made a snide remark about Jewish doctors, and a Bill Johnson of the *Times*, already knowing it, had casually said, "Of course you'd be for Roosevelt."

Phil had thought to himself, A flick here, a flick there—that's how they did it. No yellow armband, no marked bench in the park, no Gestapo . . . but day by day, the little thump of insult . . . the delicate assault on the stuff of a man's identity. That's how they did it.

389

"I think you ought to say," Dick said, "'That's how the un-conscious antisemites did it. Not just 'That's how they did it.'"

"Dick, you're asking me to scuttle my whole point, the basic point of the whole book. I'm not going to *label* them 'uncon-scious antisemites'—I want to show them in action, let them speak their words, let them behave their behavior. All those nice people who'd tell you they hate prejudice. The book is *about* nice people."

We talked about it for quite a while; it was futile. I could not make him see why I felt as I felt. At last I said, meaning it, "Dick dear, even this late, you can decide not to publish it, you know you can. If you'd rather not—"

But he said he wouldn't dream of not publishing it, and we changed to matter-of-fact things. Pub day would be late in Feb-ruary, he told me, to start their spring season for 1947. It was lovely to have an approximate date to look forward to.

I not only had post-summer reunions with the Simons, but with all my friends, old and new, even with Pepo Than, now married to Marina and in New York. But there was one reunion that was totally unexpected.

My log for September 12 has one simple notation: "Larry Kubie, Bob Kubie, 7:30." For the life of me I cannot remember why I was seeing him and his son, but see them I did. And a week later, there is another note: "Larry—7," and then through October, many more. And beyond October.

It had been eight years since I had sought his help as a pro-spective patient, only to be turned away after three visits and sent to Dr. Gosselin. In that time I had occasionally heard or read about Dr. Kubie in newspapers or magazines; when Moss Hart's hit musical, *Lady in the Dark,* had opened a few years before, starring Gertrude Lawrence and making a sudden star out of Danny Kaye, many reviews said that the analyst in the show was patterned after Moss Hart's own analyst, Lawrence S. Kubie.

I had also run into him a few times at other people's houses, and every time I spoke to him, I was still very much aware that he was that lordly creature, A Psychoanalyst.

Now, for a while, as I began to see him and go out with him,

I had a sort of regression, back to the status of awed patient. I couldn't shake the self-conscious feeling that anything I said or did might have for him some concealed meaning that he would interpret analytically. Perhaps that made it all the more attractive a situation.

It had been a long time since I had had any involvement filled with intensity, with meaning. I know I felt constrained and also free; I told him things I told almost nobody, like the birth of Christopher. I let him take home the manuscript of *Gentleman's Agreement*, and his reaction to it seemed like an okay from on high.

When I finally asked Larry what had caused him to send me away from his office all those years ago, when he must have known it would seem like another bitter rejection by a man I trusted, the truth came out at last.

After his marriage and divorce, he had had a major love affair, complete with unhappy ending. His first sight of me reminded him of that woman, voice, inflections, looks, everything. Those three visits told him he could never be objective about me, that there would even be the possibility of too much emotion.

Any analyst feeling an attraction toward a patient was obliged, of course, for the protection of the patient, to send her elsewhere. Medical ethics, analytic practice, professional conscience all dictated that outcome.

Ethical, yes, and I admired him for it. I admired him for many things, his dedication to the belief that in the future, analysis had to develop new techniques so that it could be accomplished more quickly, less expensively, his frequent papers in psychoanalytic journals, his work with the New York Psychoanalytic Society and Institute—he even got me to write some promotion for the opening of their new building on East Eighty-second Street.

If ever there was a workaholic, Larry Kubie was one. Once when I stayed overnight at his house, I awoke at four in the morning—to find him dictating a medical article into the Dictaphone he kept right at his bedside.

I also was to learn, as time elapsed, that some analysts could be as mixed-up and impossible in their private lives as the rest of us mortals. But I was in no mood then to try to analyze Larry Kubie. All through the weeks of autumn, remembering the ever-mounting hopes I had had for my first novel, it was seeing him that helped me handle my fast-building anxiety about what would be the actual fate of my second.

TWENTY

THE NOVEMBER ISSUE OF Cosmopolitan ran a red streamer across its cover, "The novel all America will discuss." Their large newspaper ads called it "The best serious novel of 1946."

Almost as soon as it hit the newsstands, my life shifted into some mysterious higher gear. Letters began to pour into Cosmo; Dale told me they ran "a hundred to one in favor." There was hate mail too, name-calling, shrill, lunatic. "Jew-lover, nigger-lover, Commie pinko liberal."

All the letters were sent on to me, after whatever replies the magazine chose to make. I began the task of answering them, one by one, except the obscene ones. I was very soon swamped in eight-hour days of answering letters. Here at least I could make use of help; I, who could never dictate one word of a short story or a novel, did revert easily to my old office ability to dictate letters and memoranda to a skillful secretary.

The galleys from Simon & Schuster came not long afterward, and then the finished books. Dick had ordered a first printing of 17,500 copies, fewer than the first edition of *The Trespassers* by 2,500 copies.

It hurt. For all the absence of any further talk from him about heartbreak, this was speech enough. He had less faith in this book, and fewer hopes for it, than he had had in my first.

Then came further bad news. It had been turned down by both the Book of the Month Club and by the Literary Guild. There was no grapevine gossip about why the Literary Guild had passed it by, but the unofficial explanation of the BOMC rejection, privately made to Dick, was that since they had selected Sinclair Lewis's *Kingsblood Royal* just the month before, a novel about a young blue-eyed white man who discovers he is part Negro, they couldn't choose another novel so soon about any other kind of prejudice.

I don't remember whether Dick believed that, nor whether I did. What I do remember, and will never forget, is a pun made by Simon & Schuster's top salesman, Bob, I think, Seaman. "The real reason that book didn't make it," he said, "is that Dick Simon didn't back it hard enough. He's a sick man—and all his illnesses are psychosem*itic*."

One other bit of shoptalk struck me as a bad omen. Before sending me my ten free copies of *Gentleman's Agreement*, my presentation copies, Dick himself called me, to prepare me for delay.

"I'm rejecting the whole edition," he said. "It's printed on the kind of cheap paper we had to use when paper was rationed during the war; the pages have a gray, pulpy look. They'll have to run off a new printing on quality paper."

When I finally received my copies, I marked one, *First Copy*, and put it on my shelf, next to my first novel and *A Dog of His Own*. The two westerns by Peter Field were elsewhere, relegated to a closet where I kept files and research books.

So here were two books and a story for children, all three my own work. I loved the look of the new novel; they had used the Cosmo illustration for the jacket, in full color, a distraught young man straddling a chair amidst a whirl of crumpled-up paper, loose sheets, filled ashtrays, forgotten pencils.

I inscribed the other nine copies, and ordered about twenty more at my own expense. With an author's 40 percent discount off the $2.75 price, this did not constitute a great extravagance. In those days, when the butcher or grocer or doorman said, "You won't forget to give me a signed copy of that book of yours, will you?" I always said, "Of course I won't," and duly handed one over. Nowadays, I'm apt to retort briskly, "You won't forget to give me a free sirloin steak, will you?" Or some apt equivalent.

One problem arose about inscribing all those books—should I send one to my sister Alice? Three years before, when I sent her *The Trespassers*, we must have been in the center of another dreadful falling-out, despite our temporary truce on political matters when Hitler had invaded Russia. I had inscribed it, "For Al, because blood is thicker than—" and signed it, "Love, Laura." She had not even acknowledged receipt of it.

I think I must have sent her a copy of *Gentleman's Agreement*, or I would remember *not* sending it. I would have found that non-sending hard to do. I do know that the following year, when we were seeing each other again, she was quite wonderful about it—though even her enthusiasm was to lead us, indirectly, into trouble later on.

By that stage of my life, I was already beginning to have some bitter thoughts about the terrible schisms that could develop in families where there were passionate differences about politics. Occasionally I would find myself speculating about what families must have gone through, a century ago, about abolition and slavery. I would sometimes have a fantasy about writing a novel, not about two brothers facing each other on a battlefield, each ready to kill the other in the Civil War, but about two sisters torn apart by their convictions about Stalin and Russia.

That fantasy remained fantasy. Even in later years, when the rifts between us had widened into chasms, I never got as far as writing one paragraph of any outline of that particular book.

Late in November, there was "studio interest" in *Gentleman's Agreement*, and Bert Allenberg began submitting it to all the major ones. As I recall it, I paid little attention to this report; perhaps I was remembering all the protracted and diverse "studio interest" in *The Trespassers*, or the actual submission of *Lady Lucky* and *Half a Sin*.

But a week before Christmas I had a long-distance call from Hollywood. It wasn't Bert himself, but a young woman in his office, Meta Reis, later Meta Rosenberg, who was destined in time to become well-known as an independent producer.

"There's a lot of interest in *Gentleman's Agreement*," she reported. "Bert wants to know what price you think we ought to ask for it."

As I write these words now, I feel again the stunned disbelief that hit me as I heard her calm question. What price? For a movie that millions of people might see?

"Any price," I blurted out. "I don't know what price."

"Give me some idea. Bert wants—"

"I just don't know—*any* price—"

"For instance?"

"Oh, anything—five thousand dollars."

I don't think she laughed at me; I don't remember too much about that telephone call, except my own breathless answers.

But the next day they called me again. Three studios had shown firm interest, Twentieth-Century Fox, Selznick and Enterprise. They were sending out telegrams to them and to all other studios, setting 6:01 on December 23 as the deadline for any bids, four days hence, the Monday before Christmas.

But the very next day's log shows that they didn't wait for the official deadline.

Gentleman's Agreement
bought by 20th Century Fox
$75,000 flat, with
top of $125,000, depending
on sales!!

From Bert himself I heard the story of the preempted deadline. Darryl F. Zanuck had gone to Sun Valley for a four-day weekend, and had taken the bound galleys with him. He had read them overnight and then phoned his office. "Protect me on *Gentleman's Agreement*."

In movie parlance, Bert said, that meant, "Buy it now; don't let anybody outbid me. Accept their terms." Bert never bothered to tell me what he said to the other studios about the supposed date for possible bids, nor did I know enough then to ask.

He did say he was agreeing to a three-year split they offered on the main sum, and explained the escalator clause: for each book sold after the first 50,000 copies, I would receive a royalty of twenty-five cents. Thus, my income from the movie would be stretched over three years and not be taxed away from under me.

I spent the next day, a Saturday, with the Simons and the Whartons. I called the Schermans and the Bassetts and all my friends, anybody who had had anything whatever to do with the book, with the letters pro and con, with me during the writing of it. I didn't sleep much that weekend—happy insomnia was mine once more.

On Monday I began phoning all toy stores that carried Lionel electric trains; everybody was sold out in the Christmas rush except Macy's. I went there and bought the kids their first real electric trains, complete with yards and yards of track, straight and curved, an engine that could puff smoke, whistle at curves, cars that could couple and uncouple, even a freight car that could dump coal at a station by remote control.

Macy's offered to send them by special messenger, because all that steel weighed a ton, but I wouldn't risk some mishap or delay that close to Christmas, and staggered off to a taxi with the whole lot. It cost a lordly ninety-one dollars.

Mike and Chris, on Christmas morning, at last realized that something pretty marvelous had happened to mommy and her book.

Just about then I heard that something marvelous had also happened to Eric and his book. The Book of the Month Club had taken *Mr. Blandings Builds His Dream House*, and it had sold to the movies too. How strange, this juxtaposition of events in our two lives, both of us with books coming out almost together, both of us with our first movies.

I wondered whether Eric was thinking the same thing. I felt, somehow, that it would be wiser for me not to read his book the moment it came out; I knew it would be even better than his short piece in Fortune, which had started him on it, and I was sure I would like the longer version as much as I had its short one. It would be out the next week.

But I decided to stay away from it for a while, possibly with the notion that reading it in full book form might awaken memories tied into longings. Memories tied into longings had always spelled depression for me, and this was not the preferred time to slide into any old-time pit.

I read all his reviews, all of them good, and I made myself a small promise: After my own book is out, after everything is normal again, I'll read his and maybe even write him congratulations and best wishes. Then I found myself wondering whether Eric would read my book the moment it came out, or whether he would need, for whatever reasons, to put it off for a while too.

On the morning before New Year's Eve, the New York *Tribune* ran a brief story about Twentieth Century-Fox buying *Gentleman's Agreement*, ending, "The picture will be Darryl F. Zanuck's only personal production for 1947, and will have an all-star cast."

The first days of the new year seemed to have some note about the plans for the movie in every issue of every paper.

Moss Hart will do his first writing for the screen by adapting...

*   *   *

Zanuck announced that Elia Kazan was scheduled to direct...

*   *   *

Gregory Peck will have the leading role of Philip Green in...

*   *   *

First and second printings totaling 42,000 copies have been ordered... with paper for a third printing of 15,000 on order...

All these tidbits are from small clippings pasted into my press-book, which I had already begun to keep up to date. But the next piece of news rated another full page in my log.

Gentleman's Agreement
taken by Dollar Book Club
for August! Guarantee
minimum of 550,000 copies!
Guarantee minimum of
$32,000!
8¢ royalty on each
copy thereafter.

The Dollar Book Club was a sister to Doubleday's Literary Guild. Paperback editions were virtually nonexistent as yet; what was published in paperback sold for twenty-five cents a copy and was a pretty lowly creature in the eyes of all critics and even most readers. The Dollar Book Club put out real hardcover books.

By now prepublication publicity from Simon & Schuster was starting, and they were being as lavish and bold as they had been three years before, with my first book. Their opening trade ad was a double-spread in Publisher's Weekly, with terrific quotes from Charles Jackson, Norman Cousins, Margaret Halsey and others. A special box told of their plans for promoting the book—$7,500 for advertising, to start with.

Also it officially named publication day at last: February 27, 1947.

Eleven o'clock on the eve of pub day again found me at the all-night newsstand at Madison Avenue and Fifty-ninth Street. Again I had gone alone, to see what I had to see, with no witnesses to watch me.

But this time there was no slaughterhouse, no bleeding on the sidewalk, nothing but delight. Again it was a publisher's and author's dream, of reviews in both major papers right on publication day, and this time both were unrestrainedly in favor.

In the *Herald Tribune*, Lewis Gannett started with that quoted line of Kathy's, "New Canaan's even stricter about Jews than Darien," and went on through a terse summary of the whole plot, ending with a long final paragraph that sent my blood racing, as I stood there on the sidewalk reading by streetlight.

There are no Ku-Kluxers in Mrs. Hobson's story—just a lot of nice people, who...in varying degrees, by their "gentleman's code," feed the fires of Kluxism. Mrs. Hobson is subtle but not gentle...Her book...achieves a terrific emotional tension. It is, of course...a novel with a purpose. The test of such a novel is its success. This story gets under your skin. It makes you think furiously about your own code, your own silence. It probes. It hurts.

In the New York *Times*, Charles Poore's opening lines were to be quoted again and again, in ads for my book, in publicity releases, in Darryl F. Zanuck's expansive promotion for his motion picture.

Gentleman's Agreement...is bound to be one of the most discussed novels of the year. In fact, it is already one of the most discussed novels of the year.

It then went on to tell his readers why he was so sure, and I cannot pretend that I took it all with becoming modesty. I raced home in another cab, rereading by the dim overhead bulb the driver grudgingly kept turned on for me, called Lee and read her every word of each review. She took notes and called Dick. Dick called me, and asked me to read both notices to him. It didn't bore me a bit to comply, word for word.

How—or if—I slept that night I do not know. I do know that five minutes past nine in the morning, when most publishers and editors are still having their second cup of coffee at home before starting for their first appointments at ten, Lee called me. She was already at the office.

"You'd better get yourself down here as fast as you can," she said. "You'll never see anything like this for the rest of your life."

I was there twenty minutes later. Even in the reception room, I heard the commotion, telephone bells ringing incessantly, voices repeating number of copies ordered, addresses of bookstores, names of jobbers to try, promises of special speed on delivery dates. Messenger boys kept arriving from bookstores in the city,

Western Union was delivering another telegram every few minutes.

In the office shared by Lee and Jack Bassett, they were both at their phones, also scribbling orders, to be sent along later to the right department; in Dick's office, he was actually taking orders himself, and his secretary as well—everybody in the place filling in for the beleaguered sales department.

I was almost ignored, except for shouts of congratulations—never before had I been so delighted at being overlooked and neglected.

There did come one minute when Dick rushed over and kissed me resoundingly. "That first cheap-looking printing," he said, "the one I rejected—remember?" He didn't wait for me to nod. "Well, it's still in the warehouse—all seventeen thousand copies, and I've ordered them sent back again—cheap or not, they'll help us out of this jam we're in!"

And there also came a few minutes later on, when Lee and Jack and I could stop and hug each other between their phone calls. It was then that an extraordinary little event occurred, which I couldn't possibly catch on to or evaluate at the time.

Leon Shimkin, the financial wizard of the firm, came in, also full of cheer and big predictions. He had a sheet of official-looking paper in his hand, like a royalty statement.

"There's one thing, though," he said, after his congratulations, "I've been looking it up this morning"—he pointed at the paper in his hand—"and what with further returns, there still is $972 unearned on your account for *The Trespassers*."

I glanced down at the sheet he was holding. I hadn't seen many royalty statements in my life as yet—you only get two a year, six months apart—but this certainly was one.

"And it's customary," Mr. Shimkin went on, "to make up that deficit—" The phones were jangling again but I heard every word.

"Oh, sure," I said instantly. "Do it, square it away from all *this*—" I waved largely at the litter of notes and figures on Lee's desk and Jack's. They were busy with the phones again; I don't think this quick little exchange between Shimkin and me even registered with them. With a nod to me, he left.

I've told this story as a publishing anecdote again and again, amazed at my own gullibility. And I would guess that my naive verbal assent rendered it all perfectly legal!

It was only long afterward that I discovered that it wasn't customary at all to make up a deficit on one book from its more fortunate successor. Most people I've told my anecdote to think it a bit of cute chicanery. Or worse.

But at the time I never even told my agents about it. It was all lost in the wonderful turbulence of that day, and of the months ahead.

What was not lost, what I have never forgotten, was the rest of that morning. By noon, the orders and reorders had totaled ten thousand copies.

It was the first official day in the life of *Gentleman's Agreement*.

AFTERWORD
—and FOREWORD

WHEN I BEGAN THIS autobiography, I envisioned a single volume, starting with the day I was born and ending with yesterday.

But doing research on your own life is an experience unlike any I have ever known. As I unearthed those long-forgotten adolescent diaries of mine, and then took down from a high neglected shelf that college scrapbook, and went on to the date-books of my first youth and the work logs that came afterward, I found that a sentence here, a jotted note there, the title of a story, the timetable of my working hours, the numbers of pages, even those stylish little *D*'s and *Don't D*'s of my evenings—each of these could bring to life again some long-buried moment or event, and make it pulse again with the red beat of life.

At times I fretted about the length of my manuscript, considering what episode to leave out, but each time I did omit for the sake of shortening, my story felt truncated and somehow maneuvered, instead of what I had promised myself it would be—set down as it really was.

And so, my old instinct to "let it run," abetted by my publisher's urging that I do just that, took me on an ever-widening voyage of discovery, an ever-deepening search not only into my own materials, my own emotions and necessities, but into the times I lived in, the controversies, the political dilemmas, the changes in concepts, in mores, in hopes and fears about my own life, and about the world's life.

The twentieth century, after all, was *my* century too. Thus, I found myself writing not only about my past but *the* past, as I perceived it, and when I speak now of one particular day being the first official day in the life of *Gentleman's Agreement*, I do so knowing well that, for a book or for a human being, no single day is anything but an arc in that eternal circle that makes a life.

This, then, is not the end of my story, but only a pause in the telling of it, with this brief postscript doubling as a preface for the rest of it still to come.

—New York, May 15, 1983

INDEX

409